# Singing in Style

# Singing in Style

## A Guide to Vocal Performance Practices

**Martha Elliott**

Yale University Press

New Haven and London

Set in Adobe Garamond and Stone Sans types by The Composing Room of
Michigan, Inc.
Printed in the United States of America.

Library of Congress Cataloging-in-Publication Data

Elliott, Martha.
    Singing in style : a guide to vocal performance practices / Martha Elliott.
        p.    cm.
    Includes bibliographical references and index.
    ISBN 0-300-10932-6 (cloth : alk. paper)
    1. Singing—Interpretation (Phrasing, dynamics, etc.)    2. Performance practice
(Music)    3. Vocal music—History and criticism.    I. Title.
    MT892.E45 2006
783′.043′09—dc22

2005009701

A catalogue record for this book is available from the British Library.

The paper in this book meets the guidelines for permanence and durability
of the Committee on Production Guidelines for Book Longevity of the
Council on Library Resources.

10 9 8 7 6 5 4 3 2

*To Michael and Emily*

# Contents

# Acknowledgments

This book came into being when I was searching for a publisher for my Princeton University senior thesis on the three versions of Beethoven's opera *Fidelio*. Friend, colleague, and Beethoven scholar Scott Burnham introduced me to Harry Haskell, then music editor at Yale University Press. Harry was not interested in publishing my thesis, but he did think I was the right person to work on a project he had in mind about vocal performance practice. I was excited and eager and had no idea what I was getting myself into or how much I would have to learn about research, writing, and the technical aspects of assembling a book like this. I also had no idea how fascinating and rewarding the work would be. Throughout the long process of developing and writing this book, Harry has been an unfailing source of wise counsel and generous support, and I am deeply grateful to him for both the opportunity and the help he has given me.

I am also grateful to everyone in the Mendel Music Library at Princeton University, especially Paula Matthews, Daniel Boomhower, and Dan Gallagher, for all their ongoing advice in matters large and small. Other members of the Princeton University Music Department offered help on many fronts, and I am most thankful to Scott Burnham for moral support; to Mary Roberts for technical help; to Peter Westergaard, Steve Mackey, and Simon Morrison for research contributions; and particularly to Wendy Heller, who reviewed the manuscript with a fine-tooth comb from the perspectives of both a musicologist and a singer. She also introduced me to her friend Michael Burden, an invaluable source of information. Caryl Emerson, chairman of Princeton's Department of Slavic Languages and Literatures, also offered generous help, including the tape of Maria Olenina d'Alheim's master classes and the translating services of Ivan Eubanks, for which I am deeply appreciative. I must also offer thanks to the many musical colleagues who either read the manuscript and offered suggestions or shared their own performance stories; these colleagues included Drew Minter, Phyllis Bryn-Julson, Paul Sperry, Benita Valente, Mary Nessinger, David Ronis, Matthew Lau, Cheryl Bensman, Peggy Kampmeier, and Sarah Freiberg. Sarah Freiberg (my cousin) also merits special appreciation for reading a first draft and providing invaluable writing suggestions. Tremendous thanks go to Bob Wagner for his beautiful music examples. Lauren Shapiro and her editorial team at Yale University Press have been a joy to work with and were especially generous in helping me navigate my first publishing effort.

To my friends and relatives, who have heard me talking about this project as it has developed, I offer gratitude for your patience and support, especially to Terry Desser, Mildred Freiberg, Barbara Westergaard, Anne Gray, Mary Jean Link, and Candus Hedburg. Unbounded thanks also go to my many students, who over the years have provided a fascinating laboratory in which to experiment with historical approaches to vocal technique and style. Of course I couldn't have completed this book without the support of my family, parents, and beloved daughter, Emily. To my husband, Michael, who talked through every idea, read every sentence, and patiently waited when I got lost in my computer; who is my love, my friend, my teacher, and my favorite performing companion: I can't thank you enough.

# Introduction

This book introduces the issues of historical performance practice as they relate to singers and vocal repertoire. It also investigates the elements that contribute to the style in which an individual work of music, from a specific period and by a particular composer, should be sung. Most important, it explores the working relationships between singers and composers from the seventeenth century to the present and traces how their collaboration shaped changing trends in style. The early music movement and the accompanying explosion of interest in historically informed performances have produced a tremendous amount of information on performance practice. Most of it is geared toward instrumentalists, though a great deal of information exists about singing and vocal repertoire. This book presents the pertinent scholarly information about vocal performance practice from the early Baroque through the twentieth century so that singers can make informed stylistic choices about such topics as ornamentation, articulation, use of vibrato, working with period instruments, and language issues, to name just a few common concerns.

Each chapter deals with a specific historical period and introduces some background information about the singers and composers, the vocal repertoire, and the stylistic conventions of that period. Specific repertoire examples will be discussed as well, showing how to use the music itself as a context for making stylistic choices. Information on performance practice is not just a list of rules. Too many frustrating contradictions and unanswerable questions remain within all the specific instructions and directions in the historical treatises and their modern interpretations. Often the music itself, when understood within a general stylistic context, can help us make appropriate choices about tempo, phrasing, articulation, and ornamentation.

Since I don't include exhaustive treatments of these issues, source lists for further study are arranged by topic at the end of the book in the "For Further Reading" section. References include major primary sources such as treatises, letters and memoirs of composers and performers, and commentary from other writers and critics of the time. Secondary sources include historical and analytical writings and books and articles on performance practice. You can read this book in sequence from beginning to end or look up a particular topic such as improvisation in the Classical era or tempo and rhythm in German lieder. If you do read the chapters in order, you will be able to follow evolving trends relating to notation, ornamentation, articulation, legato, rubato, tempo, vibrato, portamento, language, and national character, as well as who dictated the fashions: the singers or the composers. A short conclusion at the end of each chapter summarizes the important issues introduced for that period.

This book concentrates primarily on songs, sacred music, and chamber music rather than on opera. Opera necessitates dealing with issues of vocal type and casting preferences that are outside the scope of this book. It is important, however, for singers to take into account their own vocal type, as well as the natural strengths and weaknesses of their instrument, when choosing repertoire. In considering the specific works and their historic contexts in the following chapters, singers should evaluate whether their voices are appropriate for an early seventeenth-century lute song, an eighteenth-century French cantata for haute-contre, or Schoenberg's *Pierrot lunaire.* They must decide whether they can learn and incorporate the necessary techniques for a given genre or style into their vocal production. Ideally, a singer would be infinitely flexible and able to reinvent his or her voice to suit any situation, but that is an unrealistic expectation. I hope that the information in this book will help singers make sensible choices about repertoire that is appropriate for their individual instruments and their natural abilities.

I want to add a cautionary word about reading the primary sources. Throughout the history of music, the discussion of singers and singing seems to have inspired heightened passions and heated debate among both performers and admirers. But the language we must use to talk about singing—in a voice lesson, at a rehearsal, or in a concert review—is subjective and imprecise at best. Even new developments in scientific technology for vocal pedagogy may only complicate the problem of communicating with language about something that has to do with subtle internal sensations. By the same token, the response a singer can inspire in a listener is equally ephemeral and must be described with language that is metaphoric and poetic. When considering a historic text, which has been translated into modern English from another language from another century, we must sift through a vast number of general elements relating to the culture and the historic context in order to grasp the sense of the meaning before we can even attempt to contemplate how it relates specifically to singing. In other words, it is hard enough to communicate about singers and singing within our own language and cultural references. The historic documents, even when interpreted sensitively by modern scholars, can only give us a shadowy impression of what singers in the past sounded like, or how they sang.

The information in this book is not meant to transform modern singers into authentic recreations of historic personalities, nor is it meant exclusively for the "early music singer." Rather it is meant to provide tools for the wide variety of situations in which singers may find themselves. The repertoire included in historically informed performances now reaches toward the early twentieth century. In recent years both taste in singers and ideas about appropriate voices for certain repertoires have changed dramatically as well. Even given a specific area of the repertoire, the choices in performance approach are many: Handel's *Messiah* or the Bach Passions, for example, can be presented with a full modern orchestra, large chorus, and "opera singers" as soloists or, on the other extreme, with period instruments and a smaller complement of singers who are "early music specialists," or with any kind of combination of elements in between. Even within the early music world, the quest for authenticity, which was a primary goal ten or twenty years ago, has lost some of its intensity today. Both musicologists and performers are deciding that it is not possible, nor in many cases desirable, to re-create the exact conditions of a first performance. This then leaves performers with a wealth of historical information to choose from in order to create modern performances that are vivid, energized, interesting, and compelling for today's audiences.

Really, the only way to experience truly "authentic" music making is to collaborate with a composer on the premiere of a new work. The last chapter of the book explores how performance issues are put into stylistic practice today. Even in our world of computer-based musical scores with specialized notation and elaborate performance instructions, decisions about an infinite array of nuances involving phrasing, dynamics, diction, and articulation cannot possibly be fully indicated in a score. In a new work, even decisions about style that could be notated may be made between the composer and performer in a rehearsal or in a conversation on the phone but not make it into the final version of the score. The singer who performs the premiere or records the work may add personal, idiosyncratic nuances that then define its style for the future. The composer may make a suggestion to a performer that clarifies or is even contrary to the markings in a published score, or he or she may disapprove of the personal interpretations a singer adds and prefer the way a different singer handles the music in another performance situation.

All these interactions between composer and performer will be seen repeatedly as we consider the issues of historical performance practice. When you actually experience these types of interactions in the twenty-first century, then it is easy to appreciate the same kinds of issues when you read about them taking place in an earlier century. By working on new music you will not only contribute to the growth of musical culture in the present and produce musical documents that musicologists will scrutinize in the future, but you will also gain a new understanding of the process of creating a music and a style of the past, while working toward the timeless goal of realizing the composer's intentions.

# Chapter 1 The Early Baroque

This chapter presents an overview of seventeenth-century vocal music and practice in Italy, England, and France. (Germany will be discussed in chapter 2.) In addition to considering issues of compositional development over the course of the hundred years in question, it will also review differences in national style. It will explore the imprecise nature of Baroque notation, the changing relationship of text and music, pitch in different geographical areas, instrumental accompaniment, and the development of figured bass. Difficult questions without easy answers must also be considered: What did the singers sound like? What was their approach to technique? What kind of ornamentation did they use and where, and how did that ornamentation change over the course of the century?

Much general advice is given in the many treatises from this period, but these comments were directed at students, teachers, and professional musicians who were already familiar with the prevailing conventions and styles of the times. Specific situations were not often discussed, and decisions about tempo, articulation, and ornamentation were usually left up to the individual performer, who was expected to know how to apply the general instructions. Today we must do the best we can to make sense of this information. Yet even then, Bénigne de Bacilly, whose treatise *Remarques curieuses sur l'art de bien chanter* (1668) was one of the first and most important discussions of French vocal style, understood the difficult position of the student singer:

> We are saying, therefore, that there is a general vocal method which can be learned. But the specifics (which are the application of this method to a particular air; to *this* word and to *that* syllable) are matters of such subtlety that often good taste is the only guiding rule. For this reason, it is necessary (among other virtues) to refer yourself to the judgment of a wise person in these matters. Also, it is just as often necessary to refer to the thousand different nuances of the vocal art, and also to those singers who have had more experience. In this way, the student will learn from those who have performed longer . . . since it is obvious that singing is not always learned through a knowledge of its rules.[1]

Even though we cannot imitate the singers of the seventeenth century, we can learn from the varying approaches of the singers of our time who have specialized in this repertoire and developed their own understandings of the instructions from the past. The more time you spend working on specific musical examples, the more familiar you will become with a particular corner of the repertoire, and you will find that the music itself holds many answers to questions of performance practice and style.

**Baroque Notation**

By our modern standards, Baroque notation may seem quite imprecise. In the seventeenth century, composers and performers did not expect notation to be self-sufficient or to convey every detail in a work. Composers did not believe they had to notate the music exactly as it should sound or even to include all the information the performers needed, such as tempo, dynamics, instrumentation, or consistent rhythms and ornaments. Often composers collaborated closely with performers or participated in performances themselves. If a composer were involved in the rehearsal process, he could tell the performers exactly what he wanted. If not, performers felt knowledgeable enough about the stylistic conventions of the time to make their own choices about tempo, dynamics, instrumentation, and other variables. All performers, including singers, were also expected to know harmony and counterpoint in order to add embellishments and alter the rhythms in appropriate places. If a singer were also a composer, as many were, including Giulio Caccini, Barbara Strozzi, Michel

Lambert, and Henry Lawes, they didn't need to write these things into the score. Thankfully, some scores with added ornamentation do survive, and thus we can derive some ideas about the embellishments then used. Yet specifically notated ornament indications vary widely from country to country, composer to composer, and even within a single work. This factor will be discussed more fully in the subsequent sections on ornamentation.

An early Baroque score offers only the bare bones of the music, needing the experience and judgment of the performers, combined with their inspiration and spontaneity, to bring it to life. The same is true of a jazz standard, which invites performers to add improvisation, rhythmic alteration, and melodic embellishment in a variety of tempos and moods. It was only in the late nineteenth and early twentieth centuries that composers began to insist their music be performed exactly as it was written. Consequently, they began to include more precise performance instructions in the score. As a result of this relatively recent practice, we are accustomed to treating any score with reverence in order to serve the wishes of the composer. Most Baroque scores, however, don't begin to include all the performance information we need, or to fully indicate what the composer wanted or expected. We must take the responsibility for making numerous musical decisions and adding our own personal touches.

### Scores and Editions

The first thing to do when learning a piece of Baroque music is to evaluate the score being used. A good place to start is to find a facsimile of an early print or manuscript. More facsimile editions are being published now, and it is also possible to gain access to original manuscripts in university libraries, special collections, or on microfilm. When you look at an unedited score, however, you must be prepared to do a good deal of mental editing for yourself.

For example, example 1.1 shows a 1623 print of Arianna's Lament from Claudio Monteverdi's *L'Arianna* (1608), the only surviving excerpt from this opera. When looking at this score, you must read the vocal part in soprano clef (middle C on the bottom line), move the text to fit the syllables with the correct notes, take into account the old-style print for the letter "s," and occasionally realign the bass notes with the vocal line. Since there is no key signature, you must decide how to interpret the accidentals that are provided, taking into account harmonic and melodic considerations. You must also not become distracted or misled by various ink splotches. You may notice, however, as you compare this to the familiar version in G. Schirmer's *Twenty-four Italian Songs and Arias,* first published in 1894, that the aria is in D minor instead of F minor

Example 1.1. Monteverdi: "Lasciatemi morire" from *L'Arianna* (1608), from a 1623 manuscript printed in Venice, reproduced in *26 Italian Songs and Arias,* ed. John Glenn Paton, Alfred, 1991.

in the medium-high edition or C minor in the medium-low edition, bar lines appear in different places, and the music varies in a number of crucial spots. In the opening measure, the bass line stays on an A against the B-flat in the vocal line to create an anguished dissonance, which has been softened by the change of harmony in the Schirmer version. During the second "lasciatemi" (m. 2), the vocal line rises a whole step instead of two half steps, as in the Schirmer score. There are also differences in rhythms and text underlay at "in così dura sorte, in così gran martire" (mm. 6–7). There are even wrong pitches in the seventeenth-century print for the penultimate "morire" (m. 8). If you look at the last "lasciatemi" you can also see a confusing notation of both a flat and a sharp sign, which might explain the chromatic vocal line found in the Schirmer score.

Working from old manuscripts and prints takes some getting used to, and you need to be familiar with sixteenth- or seventeenth-century time signatures, as well as different clefs. Virtually all vocal music from the seventeenth and early eighteenth centuries is notated using C clefs (including soprano, alto, tenor, and bass), which either indicate which voice part should sing or contrive to avoid ledger lines by arranging the music all on the staff. Some scores are less problematic to read than others, and with experience it becomes easier to work with older notational practices. Since much seventeenth-century vocal music does not exist in modern editions, an ability to read earlier musical notation will give you access to a much broader repertoire. These skills are not difficult to acquire and can be invaluable tools for finding the true spirit of the music. Robert Donington presents a helpful discussion in his *Baroque Music: Style and Performance.*[2]

In the nineteenth century, editors who prepared collections of early Baroque vocal music tried to make the scores easier to read. They also corrected inconsistencies and made decisions about tempo, dynamics, phrasing, ornamentation, instrumentation, and accompaniment. As a result, these scores can contain too much information that, if followed strictly, will produce a distinctly nineteenth-century interpretation. It then becomes the performer's task to sort through the notes and markings and decide what is editorial and can be left out versus what is part of the original score and necessary to keep. A good compromise is to find a modern edition with clear and legible notation accompanied by scholarly commentary and a minimum of added editorial markings. We are fortunate that many more such editions of seventeenth-century repertoire are becoming available.

### Thoroughbass

Most solo vocal music of the early Baroque consists of the vocal line with a bass line accompaniment. Early seventeenth-century songs were often transcriptions of choral works, with the counterpoint of the other vocal parts condensed into an accompaniment part for lute or other instrument. John Dowland wrote lute songs that used a form of notation called tablature to indicate fingerings to facilitate the contrapuntal accompaniment texture. As the seventeenth century progressed, however, the contrapuntal nature of the accompaniment was simplified into a single bass line from which chords were to be constructed. This accompaniment, known as thoroughbass or basso continuo, gave support to the vocal part while allowing the singer greater flexibility. (For more information, see "Chapter 1: Accompaniment Instruments and Figured Bass" in "For Further Reading.") Occasionally a number or a sharp or flat would be written below or above a bass note to indicate the harmonies. This practice was basically a shorthand method for telling the instrumentalist what notes to play. In the preface to his *Le nuove musiche* (1602), Giulio Caccini gave detailed instructions regarding how to execute his "new music": "I have been accustomed, in all the pieces that have come from my pen, to indicate with numbers over the bass part the thirds and sixths—major when there is a sharp, minor when a flat—and likewise when sevenths and other dissonances are to be made in the inner voices as an accompaniment."[3] Later in the century more "figures" were added to the bass line as the music became harmonically more complex, hence the term "figured bass."

Thus it was not only the singer who was expected to improvise ornaments and embellishments. The accompanist had to invent and compose a complete part from the bass line and whatever figures may have been indicated. Composers had conflicting attitudes about whether to include figures or not. In his *Concerti ecclesiastici* (1610) Giovanni Piccioni commented that "I have not chosen to put any sort of accidentals, such as sharps, flats, and figures, over the notes as many do, because to such organists as are not expert, they are a source of confusion rather than otherwise, while to those who know, and to competent men, such accidentals are not necessary, since they play them correctly by ear and by art."[4]

The skills required to "play correctly by ear and by art" include a thorough knowledge of harmony and voice leading, as well as a familiarity with the appropriate style of embellishment and ornamentation. One of the most plentiful areas of information on performance practice is the literature on lute playing and thoroughbass realization. The general approach to reading basso continuo is not that different from reading guitar chord charts printed in scores of Broadway or pop songs: these are printed above the vocal line or below the bass line of the piano part. "G7," for example, specifies the bass note and the chord that goes with it. The player decides how to get from one chord to another and what rhythm and embellishments to add. Performers of Baroque music must similarly learn how to navigate harmonic progressions. This can be fairly simple in the early 1600s, but it becomes more complex for later music.

While it is certainly not unusual for modern folk or pop singers to accompany themselves on a keyboard or guitar, singers today who are interested in early music may not have the ambition to learn how to accompany themselves on the lute. (It is crucial, however, for singers to be thoroughly familiar with the bass line of Baroque music and to understand how it interacts with their vocal line.) One alternative is to find a colleague who has experience reading from a figured bass. The other possibility is to find a modern edition of the music with a good realized accompaniment. This may be harder than it sounds, as Howard Mayer Brown explains in his *New Grove Dictionary of Music and Musicians* (1980) article on editing: "If the editor provides a stylistically appropriate realization it may seem idiosyncratic and subjective and inappropriate for certain performance situations. If he leaves it plain it may be insufficient for less experienced performers. If he provides a fully fleshed out harmonic accompaniment it is cumbersome and distracting for experienced performers. If he provides the bare minimum to indicate the harmony he is called unimaginative and insensitive to style."[5] The problems facing modern performers with regard to realizing a thoroughbass are thus not that different from those that faced composers and performers of the seventeenth century. Ultimately, the realization of a figured-bass accompaniment should suit the particular performers and performance situation.

**Accompaniment Instruments**

Another element of choice is the instrument that provides the thoroughbass accompaniment. Sometimes a composer would specify a particular instrument in the score. More often the instrumentation, even in larger ensembles, was not indicated. Certain instruments were more popular and fashionable at different times. The success of John Dowland's *The First Booke of Songs and Ayres,* published in 1597, inspired many more English publications of similar lute-song books through the 1620s. In France the nobility considered lute playing a required social skill, and it remained the preferred solo and accompaniment instrument well into the 1640s. Many song publications, however, suggested a choice of instrumentation, as in Dowland's 1603 *The Third and Last Booke of Songs or Aires. Newly Composed to Sing to the Lute, Orpharion or Viols.* For the amateur player with less experience at providing a complex chordal accompaniment, it may have been easier to play the bass line alone, though it was possible to play some chords on the viol. The decision of what instrument to use in a given situation could also have been based on what players and instruments were available. Roger North, a contemporary of Purcell's who wrote a great deal about the music of his time, describes accompanying his brother's singing: "and it being necessary to the sound of a voice, whatever it is, to have an instrument to accompany, and I being well habituated to the viol and the fingering, I used to touch the principall notes as well as I could, and by degrees to putt in cords, and at last to full harmony, as the instrument would afford."[6]

As thoroughbass began to replace tablature during the early decades of the century, performers had a wider variety of bass instruments to choose from, either plucked or bowed. The most widely preferred instrument for song accompaniment was the theorbo, also known as a chitarrone, which was a large lute with an extension to its pegbox, or a second head, to accommodate more low bass strings. Caccini recommended singing with a theorbo in *Le nuove musiche*. The single instrument, especially when played by the singer, allowed an intimate and flexible accompaniment for spontaneous ornamentation and an expressive rendering of the text.

In sacred music the organ was used. The character and capabilities of different organs existing in the seventeenth century varied widely from region to region and even from church to church. In the opera house, combinations of instruments were often used to provide a richer, more varied, and dramatic texture. In his *L'Orfeo* (1607) Monteverdi called for three theorbos, harps, two harpsichords, organ, and regal, a small portable reed organ. At the Paris Opéra, Lully used a *grand choeur* for the large instrumental sections and a *petit choeur* including bass viols, theorbos, and a clavichord to accompany the solo airs. The harpsichord became more popular for vocal music later in the century, and singers often used it to accompany themselves. Roger North, however, warns beginners not to sing with harpsichords or other loud instruments "for they by imitation will carry off a tincture of the instrument."[7] The practice of combining a sustaining instrument (viol, cello, bassoon, and the like) to double the bass line with a chordal instrument (lute, theorbo, harpsichord, organ) to provide the harmony is more commonly seen in later Baroque music. Its presence in music of the seventeenth century depends upon the particular repertoire and performance situation.

The modern performer has numerous accompaniment alternatives when singing early Baroque secular songs: collaboration with an experienced lutenist or viol player, or finding transcriptions of lute songs for modern guitar. Other options include working with a harpsichordist who knows how to play from a thoroughbass, or finding a suitable realized accompaniment. For sacred works an organ is certainly appropriate, though you must decide whether to work with a reproduction of a Baroque instrument or a modern organ and then make the necessary choices about suitable registration. To sing with a modern piano is, of course, an option, but one that creates a very different sound and texture from what the composer expected to hear.

## Pitch

The flexible and inconsistent nature of pitch in the early Baroque is an extremely complex issue that has an enormous impact on singers. To transpose a work even a half step in either direction can make a tremendous difference in the technical and expressive qualities of a voice. Yet the difficulties in determining at exactly what pitch certain music was performed has caused considerable debate among musicologists, leaving the modern performer with still more choices to make.

In the early seventeenth century, organs in different churches and towns were tuned to different pitches depending on their individual construction and pipe configuration. Sometimes the length of the pipes was affected by the relative wealth of a church: shorter pipes cost less money and produced a higher sound. The temperature inside a church and its organ pipes would also affect the pitch, which could vary as much as a whole tone depending on the weather. Tuning or repairing an organ could also affect its pitch upward, and over time some organs became so high that they had to have new low pipes added to readjust their pitch downward. Organs in different countries varied in pitch as much as a fourth. As the vocal ranges of singers were more predictable than the length of the organ pipes, complicated systems of transposition were needed to accommodate choirs or solo voices who sounded better in lower keys. Lutes were constructed in all different sizes, with no standard pitch for a given instrument. Wind and brass instruments which survive from the period provide still more clues as to the widely varying pitch standards in different areas. The problems which arose when instruments tuned at different pitch levels had to play together necessitated complex transpositions and extra crooks for wind and brass instruments. Singers had to adjust to the tuning of accompanying instruments, but were also encouraged to choose songs and transpositions which would show off their voice comfortably, without strain in the low or high range.

The standard modern pitch of $a' = 440$ cycles per second was established in 1939 at an international conference in London, but the tradition of using $a' = 415$ as a standard for Baroque instruments came into practice much more recently, mostly as a convenient solution to the complex problems involved in establishing historical pitch levels. For the modern singer, the decision to sing certain repertoire at a lower pitch level may allow one to achieve a different sound quality or to execute certain ornaments more easily. The particular problems associated with the French repertoire for *haute-contre* (high tenor) or the English repertoire for countertenor, for example, may be seen in a different light with regard to the pitch levels at which this music was originally sung. By the same token, pitch levels for low voices must also be evaluated. We are accustomed to singing in a much higher range than most seventeenth-century music demands, so the actual height of the notes at modern pitch is not necessarily a problem. But the technical ramifications of singing in a lower pitch range and the physical sensations affecting diction, breath support, and general muscular tension or relaxation can contribute significantly to the overall sound and style a singer can create.

### Vibrato

The use of vibrato in the early Baroque is another controversial issue that has particular importance for modern singers. Writers of the time had conflicting opinions and terminology regarding the use of what we would call vocal vibrato:

> The *tremolo*, that is, the trembling voice, is the true gate to enter the passages and to become proficient in the *gorgia*. . . . The *tremolo* should be short and beautiful, for if it is long and forceful, it tires and bores. (Zacconi, 1596)[8]

> A singer must have a pleasantly vibrating voice (not, however, as some are trained to do in schools, but with particular moderation) . . . he must be able to maintain a steady long tone. (Praetorius, 1619)[9]

> *Fermo* or the maintenance of a steady voice, is required on all notes, except where a *trillo* or *ardire* is applied. It is regarded as a refinement mainly because the *tremulo* is a defect. . . . Elderly singers feature the *tremulo*, but not as an artifice. Rather it creeps in by itself, as they no longer are able to hold their voices steady. (Bernhard, 1649)[10]

> The quality of a singer's *cadence* is a gift of nature, and yet it can be acquired or at least corrected and perfected through good training and good exercise. Therefore, there are many people who have an acceptable voice without having a *cadence* at all. Others have it, but it is too slow for certain places where the *tremblement* ought to be compact and compressed; others have *cadences* that are too fast or sometimes too coarse, a quality which is commonly called *chevrotante*. (Bacilly, 1668)[11] [Caswell translates *cadence* as "vibrato," and *chevrotante* as "wobbly, tremulous, bleating."]

The greatest elegance of the finest voices is the prolation of a clear plain sound. And I may add, that in voice or instrument it is the most difficult part to perform. (Roger North, ca. 1695)[12]

Let him learn to hold out the notes without a shrillness . . . or trembling . . . the trouble in holding it out, he will get a habit, and not be able to fix it, and will become subject to a fluttering in the manner of all those that sing in a very bad taste. (Tosi, 1723)[13]

Most writers and singers today agree that vibrato is a natural part of healthy singing. The controversy surrounding its use in Baroque music is usually a question of degree. It is clear from the above quotes that some vibrato was used with cautious moderation, probably more as an ornament than as an ongoing presence. The natural vibrato heard in singers was sometimes admired and imitated by instrumentalists: organs included a trembling "vox humana" stop, and string players were instructed to sweeten a note with a certain trembling caused by the movement of the fingers on the strings. Women were often described as having vibrato more often than men, and young singers probably had less vibrato than the more mature ones. Yet vibrato should not be confused or interfere with the specific vocal ornaments described by the terms *tremolo, trillo, trill,* and *tremblement.* Unfortunately the use of these terms by seventeenth-century writers is inconsistent, causing much disagreement among modern writers and interpreters. It is important to distinguish between a note that is affected by an intensity fluctuation, caused by a slight change in air pressure resulting in a narrow vibrato, and a note whose actual pitch is altered by a specific ornament. (This distinction is discussed in more detail in the sections on ornamentation.) Most of the writers cited above specifically warned against pitch fluctuation, especially on long notes. If vibrato was present in the seventeenth century, it was probably small and shimmering and did not alter the pitch of a note to a discernible degree.

In John Dowland's "I saw my Lady weepe" (ex. 1.2), the opening phrase demands several long-held notes, which should be maintained, according to the advice in the quotes above, with a steady tone. In reviewing the harmony of the song, we see a number of dissonances between the voice part and the accompaniment: the repeated As in the tenor part of the accompaniment against the B in the voice part in m. 3; the G-sharp and B in the bass and alto parts of the accompaniment against the C in the voice in m. 4; the A in the bass against the B in the voice in m. 5, and later in that measure the B in the alto part of the accompaniment against the A in the voice; and finally the 4–3 suspension in

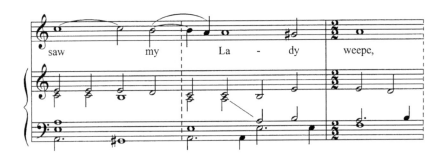

Example 1.2. Dowland: "I saw my Lady weepe," mm. 1–8, from *The Second Booke of Songs or Ayres* (1600), reproduced in *An Anthology of Elizabethan Lute Songs, Madrigals, and Rounds,* ed. Noah Greenberg, W. H. Auden, and Chester Kallman, Norton, 1955.

m. 6. Here is a situation where a tone with little or no vibrato can be used as an expressive device to highlight the delicate anguish of the song by tuning against the dissonances. Varying the type of vibrato can intensify the emotion of the music and text.

Vocal vibrato is caused by air pressure flowing through the vocal tract. The size and speed of the vibrato are determined by the quality of air pressure as it relates to the degree of tension in the vocal apparatus. In the twentieth century, singers had to learn to sing louder in order to fill larger concert halls and opera houses, carrying over larger orchestras and producing more penetrating high notes. This more forceful, consistent flow of air pressure and more muscular, athletic approach to tone production have led to the modern "operatic" vibrato, which can alter the pitch of a note anywhere from a half step to a major third and can go both above and below the principal tone of the note. In the case of the Dowland example, a sung tone with a fairly wide and continuous vibrato would not be able to inflect the different levels of dissonance against the harmony. In more florid music of the period, a consistent vibrato of more than a quarter tone might blur the delicate distinctions between trills, *trillos,* and rapid *passaggi.* Yet regulating vibrato for early music is not just a question of "straightening" the tone. The modern singer should think about adjusting the pressure of the airflow that supports the tone, thereby reducing the pressure in the throat, rather than merely removing the vibrato by tightening the throat.

In the seventeenth century, performance spaces differed greatly from what we are used to for public music today. While music was composed to fill large churches and grand palace halls, singers in the seventeenth century often performed in small, intimate settings with instruments that made soft and gentle sounds. As discussed above, the range and pitch level of most of the music were quite moderate, and singers could use a more relaxed and flexible flow of air to support and sustain their tone. They were often cautioned against shouting or forcing their voices beyond their natural limits. Even the great churches, where voices were praised for their ability to fill large spaces with sound, would not require the kind of volume or effort expected of opera singers today. A sweet, soft, and beautiful sound was prized:

> For singing does not arise out of bellowing . . . for no song is embellished by roaring and screaming; . . . the higher a voice rises the quieter and lovelier should the note be sung. (Finck, 1556)[14]

> One sings in one way in churches and public chapels and in another way in private rooms. In [the former] one sings in a full voice, but with discretion, nevertheless . . . and in private rooms one sings with a lower and gentler voice, without any shouting. (Zarlino, 1558)[15]

> I heard a beautiful voice, powerful and sustained, and when he sings on the stage he will make himself heard in every corner very well and without strain. (Monteverdi, 1610)[16]

> Let him take care, however, that the higher the notes, the more it is necessary to touch them with softness, to avoid screaming. (Tosi, 1723)[17]

Monteverdi's sense of "powerful and sustained" was quite different from that of a modern singer who knows what demands the music of Verdi, Puccini, or Wagner place on the voice. Monteverdi's singers would not have been able to conceive of the limits to which we have stretched our vocal abilities. Yet modern singers who are steeped in nineteenth-century repertoire and accustomed to the twentieth-century development of continuous vibrato cannot help but bring that perspective with them when they approach earlier music. While current taste in singers for early music seems to have shifted from the straight, white sound favored ten or twenty years ago to voices with more natural vibrato, vibrato must be used in a manner appropriate for seventeenth-century music. Singers must take into consideration the harmony of the music, the articulation of ornaments, and the ideal of gentle and unforced tone production.

### Words and Music

Vocal music of the sixteenth century was primarily polyphonic. Its many vocal lines intertwining in complex counterpoint often made the text difficult to understand, and in many cases the rhythmic setting of the words was far less important than the voice leading of the polyphony. Singers also added dazzling ornamental *passaggi* to the already complex texture, obscuring the words even further. By the end of the sixteenth century a reaction against this practice brought about the development of solo song in Italy, with England, France, and other parts of Europe following close behind. The new monody had a simple accompaniment and a solo vocal line whose main objectives were to make the words intelligible and to convey the sense or "affect" of the text. In addition to delighting the ear with sweet, soft sounds, a singer's primary goal was to communicate the passions of the text and to move the affections of the listener:

> Music is naught but speech, with rhythm and tone coming after . . . since they could not move the mind without the words being understood. (Caccini, 1602)[18]

> Let every singer conform his voice to the words, that as much as he can he make the *Concent* sad when the words are sad; and merry when they are merry. (Dowland, 1609)[19]

> It would also be necessary to have a single guiding precept; that is, that they should tend to speak in singing and not, like this one, sing in speaking. (Monteverdi, 1616)[20]

One of the great perfections of song consists of good pronunciation of the words, and rendering them so distinctly that the auditors do not lose a single syllable. (Mersenne, 1636)[21]

This drastic reaction against the overly florid singing style of the late Renaissance led composers and theorists at the beginning of the seventeenth century to issue grave warnings to singers lest their embellishments interfere with the communication of the words and the drama. As the new style of declamatory song became more established, however, increased ornamentation returned, and vocal display regained prominence. By the end of the century the importance of musical and vocal issues had once again overshadowed the significance of the text.

### Historical Pronunciation

In re-creating historically informed performances, historical pronunciation is not often included, yet there are a number of sources available for the interested reader. (See "Chapter 1: Historical Pronunciation" in "For Further Reading.") The difference, for example, between today's "BBC" English and Restoration pronunciation is significant, enough perhaps to make a Restoration text unintelligible to modern English-speaking audiences. Depending on the situation, some modern performers choose intelligibility over authenticity, yet many levels of compromise can be achieved. While Italian pronunciation (not including the many dialects) is much the same today as it was four hundred years ago, issues related to seventeenth-century French pronunciation can be incorporated into modern diction and will be discussed further below.[22]

### ITALY

Italy was the home of the Florentine Camerata, whose study and investigation of the ideals of ancient Greek theater inspired the birth of the "new music" or *stile recitativo* of the seventeenth century. The Italian *seconda prattica,* as the new style was also called, led the way for the development of solo song throughout the rest of Europe. Traveling Italian musicians and foreigners who studied in Italy spread the word and the style, which was widely emulated and imitated. Italy also had the most singable of all languages and thus a predisposition for *bel canto.* Rodolfo Celletti, in *A History of Bel Canto,* points out that the term itself was unknown in the seventeenth and eighteenth centuries. He suggests that the original goal of bel canto was to create a beautiful fantasy world, with fairy-tale operatic settings, unusual vocal timbres from high-voiced castrati, and delicate, virtuosic vocal display as a sort of antithesis to the commonplace vulgarities of daily life. Today we associate bel canto with beautiful singing in general and particularly with the famous Italian schools of vocal training that began in the early Baroque. But the conservatories of Naples and other Italian cities were not the only places where singers were trained. Many learned from family members who passed on the traditions from generation to generation. Singers could be associated with a church or a court, or could merely sing at private gatherings or for their own enjoyment. Most Italian Baroque singers were complete musicians, skilled on an instrument as well as in composition and theory.

### Voice Types and Registers

High voices were the most favored in the early Baroque. While women singers achieved great fame in opera and concert, castrati became popular in churches where women were forbidden, and by the end of the seventeenth century they dominated the stage. Tenors were also favored; Giulio Caccini was himself a renowned tenor, and Monteverdi composed prominent tenor roles in his operas. Much of the advice in many of the early treatises is aimed at high voices: Caccini for tenors, and Pier Francesco Tosi, a castrato at the height of his singing career in the late 1600s, for sopranos. While the bass voice was never as popular, there is evidence of virtuosic low male singers as well as some castrati with lower alto or mezzo ranges.

The use of different vocal registers and the importance of properly combining or blending them are discussed at length in many sources. Earlier vocal music had a modest range of not much more than an octave. By the end of the seventeenth century, however, music that now spanned almost two octaves required singers to expand their ranges and manage the use of different registers. The chest voice (*voce di petto*) was referred to as the "natural voice," while the head voice (*voce di testa*) was called the "feigned voice" or "falsetto." Although male falsettists were common in church choirs, even in the age of the castrati, the use of falsetto in male voices inspired many differing reactions. Caccini preferred the singer to "sing with a full, natural voice, avoiding falsetto," so as not to have a noticeable break in the sound of the voice or a tense forced quality in the high range.[23] Tosi was in his seventies when he wrote his *Observations on the Florid Song* in 1723. He formed his opinions based on the singing style of the late 1600s and recommended uniting the two registers "that they may not be distinguished." Tosi goes on to remark that "Among the Women, one hears sometimes a soprano entirely *di petto,* but among the male sex it would be a great rarity."[24] Modern singers who are used to blending the different registers of their voice into one smooth-sounding whole might not think this particular issue is especially relevant to them. What we must consider, however, are the warnings against screaming and the preference for gentle, soft higher notes. Women might feel free to add a little chest voice to very low notes, and both men and women might want to blend a little more head voice into the higher notes. The specific range of a particular work and the pitch at which you choose to sing it would also affect decisions about this issue.

### Ornamentation

Ornamentation in the seventeenth century falls into two general categories: graces and diminutions. Graces are the smaller ornaments that don't significantly alter the contours of the melody but rather adorn it with trills, *trillos, gruppi, esclamazioni,* and *messe di voce.* Diminutions or divisions, on the other hand, divide larger note values into smaller portions by filling them in with more rapid notes, often necessitating the recomposition of the melody. Because a white whole note or half note would thus be transformed into a series of black eighth, sixteenth, or even thirty-second notes, this was also called "coloring" the notes, or *coloratura.*[25] In the sixteenth century, performing improvised diminutions was as much a display of contrapuntal composing ability as of vocal technique and agility, and many of the treatises of the period suggested patterns for certain situations. In the seventeenth century, the new importance of the words caused restrictions to be placed on where and how a singer could improvise ornaments, so as not to disturb the communication of the text. The ornaments were also intended to enhance the text and add heightened expressivity to a singer's performance.

#### *DISPOSITIONE* AND DIVISIONS

The ability of a singer to execute diminutions with clear accuracy and dazzling speed was often called *dispositione di voce.* Many seventeenth-century writers described articulating the notes with the throat, or *gorgia,* and while this notion may sound dangerous and unhealthy to modern singers, it is a special technique that allows great speed and clarity. It is not the same thing as diaphragmatic articulation, and it is difficult to achieve with a heavy tone or large vibrato. Tosi suggests that it is easier "to make one sing soft than loud," even though divisions must be sung both *piano* and *forte.*[26] Both Zacconi and Monteverdi stress the importance of combining chest and throat for a good *dispositione.* Modern scholars interpret Monteverdi's recommendations to mean a legato flow of breath with a well-articulated throat. If the breath is not smooth, then the throat sounds harsh; if the throat is too smooth, then the notes are not articulated enough.[27]

Singers were criticized if their *passaggi* were too detached with aspirated "h's," which sounded like laughing, a howling wolf, or "a little animal bleating because it has lost its mother."[28] They were also warned not to use their tongues or lips to help with the vigorous articulation of the notes. It was understood that some singers had a more natural *dispositione*, while others had to work harder to achieve the desired agility and clarity by patient practicing: singing divisions slowly at first and then gradually increasing the speed. Some singers whose voices were not naturally flexible were told to avoid divisions entirely if they could not do them well. It was important to keep an evenness of time and motion (Tosi), or "tempo and measure" (Zacconi), and it was also important to add *passaggi* at appropriate times and places, and not too often. "The diminutions would become tiresome when the ear is saturated with them," cautioned Giovanni Camillo Maffei,[29] while Zacconi observed that "that singer will always be praised who, with a few ornaments makes them at the right moment."[30] This "right moment" was often at a cadence. In his *Compendium musices* of 1552, Adrian Petit Coclico offered a number of suggestions for ornamenting cadential sequences (see ex. 1.3).[31]

Many writers prescribed diminutions only on long syllables, only on certain vowels (preferably "a" or "o"), only on the penultimate syllable of a cadence, or only where it would add appropriate intensity to the meaning of the text. Well-known countertenor Drew Minter has offered some suggestions for cadential ornaments, illustrated in example 1.4.[32]

THE TRILL

Of the smaller type of graces, or *accenti,* the trill was considered the most important. In his *Le nuove musiche,* Caccini describes a trill on one note: in order to rearticulate the pitch the singer must "re-strike each note with the throat."[33] This device was also known as a *trillo* and sometimes referred to as a tremolo (which could easily be confused with vibrato, depending upon the context), and it was used by Monteverdi and other composers of the early seventeenth century.

Students were instructed to practice slowly and to gradually increase speed until their trills were fast and cleanly articulated. Scholars disagree about whether the gradually increasing note values shown by Caccini in example 1.5 indicate how to perform the figure or merely how to practice it.[34] It is generally

Example 1.3. Coclico: cadential ornaments from *Compendium musices* (1552), reproduced in Carol MacClintock, *Readings in the History of Music in Performance,* Indiana University Press, 1979, pp. 32–33.

Example 1.4. Italian cadential ornaments by Drew Minter: final measures of "Disprezzata regina" from act 1 of Monteverdi's *L'incoronazione di Poppea.*

Trill, or plain shake

Gruppo, or double relish

Example 1.5. Caccini: from *Le nuove musiche* (1602), reproduced in *Source Readings in Music History: The Baroque Era,* ed. Oliver Strunk, Norton, 1950, p. 24.

understood today that the ornament is not strictly measured but flexible and expressive. It can include a change in speed, either increasing or decreasing, depending on the specific musical and dramatic situation. Julianne Baird, in a November 2002 master class at Princeton University, advised students to consider two different types of ornaments on one note depending on the dramatic context: fast, using the throat, for a lighter, happier situation; and slower, using the diaphragm, for a more anguished or sobbing effect.

The figure in which two pitches alternate either a whole or a half step was originally called a *gruppo*. Later in the century, as the *trillo* fell out of use, this figure became known as the shake or trill. It, too, was articulated in the throat so that the two pitches could be clearly heard. Both the *trillo* and the *gruppo* could be used wherever a grace was needed, at the discretion of the singer. Most often this would be at cadences, as long as it was not used so frequently that every phrase became tiresomely similar. It is thus important for singers of Baroque music to be able to make clear distinctions between notes that vibrate with vibrato and those that are rearticulated either on one pitch (as a *trillo*) or on two pitches (as a *gruppo*).

### *L'INTONAZIONE* OR INTONATION

Seventeenth-century singers were always expected to sing with true and clear intonation. Tosi recommends adjusting one's intonation with such subtlety when singing with stringed instruments that a D-sharp would not be confused with E-flat and sound out of tune.[35] "Tuning the voice" had another meaning as well: Caccini describes starting a phrase on the note a third or a fourth below the written note, depending on the harmony, touching it very lightly and then sliding gently to the intended note. He does not recommend this grace for beginners, nor does he recommend lingering on the approach note.[36] Giovanni

Bovicelli called this ornament *cercar della nota* (searching for the note), and he instructed singers that "to lend grace to the voice . . . you begin a third or fourth below [the given note] depending on the harmony of the other parts . . . [and] the longer you hold the first note, the shorter the second, the more grace will the voice gain."[37]

### ESCLAMAZIONE AND MESSA DI VOCE

An alternative to *cercar della nota* for starting a phrase on a long note is to begin softly and then increase the volume in an *esclamazione,* which Caccini thought was "the proper way to put forth the voice with grace."[38] Another possibility is to "begin singing with a decrescendo, then on to an *esclamazione,* which is the most basic means of moving the affect [and] is really nothing but a certain strengthening of the relaxed voice."[39] A *messa di voce,* or "increasing and abating of the voice" as Caccini calls it (crescendo and decrescendo as we know it), could also be used as an expressive device on a long note.

### SPREZZATURA OR RUBATO

Caccini explains that, in order to successfully convey the passions of the text in his "new music," a singer must have a certain "noble neglect of the song" or *sprezzatura,* which we would understand as rubato. To achieve the "speaking in singing" effect of the *stile recitativo,* the singer is allowed both to bend the notated rhythms to fit the natural rhythm of the words and to shape the tempo to fit the text's mood. Tosi describes this practice as "stealing the time" and recommends it for use with a single instrument in music of a pathetic or tender nature. He instructs that the bass must continue in an exact time, while the voice can delay or anticipate for the sake of expression. In lively or joyful works, however, the tempo must be kept even and steady, particularly to show off *passaggi* and *dispositione.*

The *stile recitativo* of Monteverdi's *Due lettere amorose,* for example, demands a flexibility in rhythm and tempo in order to communicate the variety of moods and emotions in the text while avoiding monotony. In example 1.6, I might decide to sing the first phrase in m. 1 a little more slowly and thoughtfully, then increase speed during m. 2 and aim for a strong arrival on the first half note of "viva" in the middle of m. 3. I could also choose to start a little faster and then linger and elongate "tenebre mi viva" to highlight the shadowy darkness suggested by the text. I would treat all the repeated notes in m. 6 with a lot of flexibility, giving more emphasis and length to the strong syllables on "cotanto," "martire," and "sconsolato" while moving more quickly and lightly

Example 1.6. Monteverdi: "E pur destina," mm. 1–6, from *Due lettere amorose* (Venice, 1623), facsimile edition, Fondazione Centro Studi Rinascimento Musicale, 1973.

over the less important syllables. A wide range of deliveries are possible, depending on how you choose to interpret the text and convey the drama.

Monteverdi also composed highly ornamented vocal music. In the 1609 score for the opera *L'Orfeo,* the aria "Possente spirito" shows two vocal lines, one plain and one highly ornamented. Perhaps the singer was allowed to choose whether he wanted to leave the aria as written, improvise his own ornaments, or use Monteverdi's. In the motet "Laudate Dominum," Monteverdi writes out *trillos* and diminutions for some of the cadential phrases (ex. 1.7). Exactly how much additional ornamentation singers used is something we can only guess at, but we can explore composers' preferences by examining scores with their own added ornamentation.

In both *Le nuove musiche* of 1602 and *Nuove musiche e nuova maniera di scriverle* of 1614, Caccini indicates that in order to avoid the tasteless excesses practiced by some singers he has written out most of what should be sung in the score. He includes *trillos, gruppos,* some *cercar delle note,* and diminutions. He instructs singers to add *esclamazioni, messe di voce, sprezzature,* and some decoration of final cadences, and provides examples of each in his preface (ex. 1.8).

One of the most famous songs to come from Caccini's collections is "Amarilli, mia bella" which was known all over Europe and continued to be popular

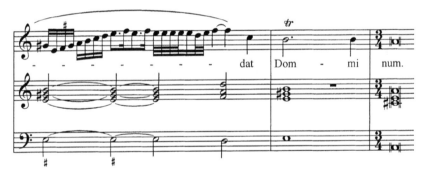

Example 1.7. Monteverdi: "Laudate Dominum," mm. 68–75, from *Tutte le opere*, vol. 15, 1940.

well into the nineteenth century, when it was included in a collection of *Arie antiche* published by Ricordi in 1885. That version, which is significantly altered in the Romantic style, is the one printed in G. Schirmer's *Twenty-four Italian Songs and Arias*. If you examine the original score printed in Hitchcock's A-R edition (see note 3) and consider using a gentle, soft tone, adding rubato, incorporating some *esclamazioni* or *messe di voce* on the long notes, perhaps a *trillo* or *gruppo* at a cadence, and understand the diminutions in the final mea-

Example 1.8. Caccini: from *Le nuove musiche* (1602), reproduced in *Source Readings in Music History: The Baroque Era,* ed. Oliver Strunk, Norton, 1950, pp. 26–27.

Example 1.8. Continued

Example 1.8. Continued

sures as a notated cadential flourish, you may gain a new appreciation of the song in the context of seventeenth-century Italian style. To learn how to prepare your own cadential ornaments, start by becoming familiar with the examples given in this section and then experiment with your own variations. As you find more examples in other repertoire from the period, you will begin to understand what kinds of contours and rhythms are typical for early seventeenth-century Italian music.

RECITATIVE AND ARIA

By the middle of the century, the ornate *stile recitativo* had become less fashionable. In operas, oratorios, and cantatas, Italian composers began to make a clear distinction between two basic modes of expression: recitative and aria. Recitative involved setting the text in a way that imitates the rhythm, inflection, and syntax of the words. Recitatives may be *secco* or dry with only continuo accompaniment and should be speechlike. Accompanied or *accompagnato* recitatives, in which the orchestra participates, were often used for particularly dramatic moments. An arioso is a lyrical version of a recitative; the words are still a decisive factor, but there will often be a more ornate and expressive melody. In an aria musical considerations take precedence. Italian arias in the middle of the seventeenth century were usually quite brief, but as the century went on they became longer and more elaborate, with more extensive instrumental accompaniments. By the third quarter of the century, the majority of arias were written in *da capo* form (literally "from the head"): an ABA form in which the repeat of the A section was usually ornamented. G. Schirmer's *Twenty-four Italian Songs and Arias* includes a number of examples of seventeenth-century arias by Alessandro Scarlatti, Giacomo Carissimi, Alessandro Stradella, and others, but there are hundreds of others from operas and cantatas that are just as rewarding to sing and fascinating to study.

ENGLAND

If the music of Italy was influenced by the singable language and passionate emotions of its people, the music of England was in turn shaped by its strong theatrical tradition, magnificent poetry, and rhetorical approach to language. The early seventeenth century was still the time of Shakespeare, when the text of a lute song was often of higher quality than the music. Decisions about inflecting the grammar of a text were just as important if not more so than vocal display or ornamentation. Few treatises about singing in England survive, but much historical information exists about English oration, gesture, and acting; Robert Toft's *Tune Thy Musicke to Thy Hart,* in particular, offers much in-depth discussion and extensive references.[40] Musical performances in England saw many changes throughout the seventeenth century: from the country houses of great families to the court entertainments of James IV, to the period of civil war when all theaters were closed and church music was discontinued, to the Restoration of the 1660s, which brought an even greater flourishing of theatrical diversions. The end of the century was dominated by Henry Purcell, who was responsible for many significant contributions and innovations in vocal music—both sacred and secular, solo and choral, orchestral and theatrical.

English music was influenced by both Italian and French traditions. Italian monody was available in England as early as 1610. Caccini's "Amarilli" of 1601 was included in Robert Dowland's *A Musical Banquet* of 1610 as well as in six other sources, some in highly ornamented versions. By the 1620s the polyphony of John Dowland's lute songs seemed old-fashioned in comparison with the newer declamatory songs based on the Italian *stile recitativo.* Figured bass came into use in the 1630s, and Playford included a translation of Caccini's *Le nuove musiche* preface (entitled "A Brief Discourse of the Italian Manner of Singing") in his 1653 edition of *An Introduction to the Skill of Music.* Playford's *Introduction* was reprinted many times through to the end of the century, indicating the prominence it held in vocal approach and instruction. The influence of French dance was also felt during the Restoration period as the popularity of triple-time dances found their way into vocal music. The rhythmic and harmonic organization of these dance forms provided a musical rather than textual foundation for English song settings. Purcell defined the height of English rhetorical style by combining both Italian and French influences in his vocal music. He set longer, more complex texts by juxtaposing contrasting sections of ornamented recitative with lively duple- and triple-meter dances.

## Voice Types and Ranges

Before the Restoration, women were not a part of professional performances in England. They certainly could have sung for friends or family as part of informal or amateur gatherings, but the treble parts sung in churches and theaters were performed by boys, as were the female spoken roles in plays. Women were allowed to perform professionally after the theaters reopened in 1660, and Purcell had a number of extremely capable women (and girls as young as twelve or thirteen) singing for him. Earlier in the century, however, there would not have been the kind of trained virtuoso female performers known in Italy. The men and boys, on the other hand, would have been exceptionally well trained, as Purcell was himself from the age of seven in the choir of the Chapel Royal. Choral parts were typically indicated as treble, countertenor, tenor, and bass, and it is possible that in some situations the soloists' parts would have been designated similarly. Yet this was not always the case, and determining the ranges and possible voice types for specific English choral and solo vocal music of this period is a complicated business. For a thorough discussion of this issue, see the chapters by Timothy Morris and by Olive Baldwin and Thelma Wilson in *Performing the Music of Henry Purcell.*[41]

The particular question of what kind of male voice sang the countertenor parts has caused much speculation and controversy among musicologists and performers. Taking the lower pitch of the day into account, many of the "alto" or countertenor parts would have been too low for what we call a countertenor today. Extending down to G or even E below middle C would require some use of chest voice for the lowest notes.[42] Some scholars suggest that Purcell wrote for two different types of countertenors with lower and higher ranges, while other authorities have settled on the idea that the seventeenth-century English countertenors were high light tenors singing with their natural voices rather than falsettists. Yet Peter Giles, in his detailed and informative *The History and Technique of the Counter-Tenor,* argues that this voice type did use head voice or falsetto, either consistently throughout the entire range or blended into the high notes, depending on the music and the particular voice.

Lower pitch also influenced other voice parts. Tenor parts could have been sung by what we today would call baritones, and the bass voice, which enjoyed much more popularity than in Italy or France (particularly in the music of Purcell), would have sung the bass parts. In an article about Purcell's sopranos, Olive Baldwin and Thelma Wilson recommended that sopranos today sing the songs of Purcell at a lower pitch level in order to achieve "clarity and ease."[43]

Other circumstances may have shaped vocal assignments. Songs for the theater were often written for a particular performer, but songs were frequently lifted from one context and freely adapted for another play or performer, a typical and important Baroque tradition. Sometimes the singers in a play also acted and the actors sang, and it is worth noting that while some theater singers were also trained members of the court or chapel choir, many were not and would have had more modest vocal ability. It is interesting to imagine how our theater singers of today—Broadway performers or actors who sing, as opposed to singers who act—might approach Purcell's theater music.

## Ornamentation

English ornaments, like the Italian ones, are divided into two basic categories: small graces and more elaborate divisions. A number of English sources show ornamentation tables, including Playford's *Introduction,* Thomas Mace's *Musick's Monument* (1676), and Christopher Simpson's *The Division-Viol* (1665). In *The Performance of English Song,* Edward Huws Jones suggests that because there was such close interaction between singer and lutenist or viol player, and therefore some imitation of ornamentation was bound to have taken place, it is helpful to consult these instrumental ornamentation tables when considering vocal graces.[44] (Jones also includes a detailed discussion of accompaniment instruments and thoroughbass.) We are also fortunate to be able to study a number of manuscripts of highly embellished songs from the first decades of the seventeenth century. These provide a glimpse into the use of graces and divisions in early English song. (These manuscripts are discussed in detail in Jones, and some are printed clearly in Toft, pp. 94–100.)

GRACES

Sifting through the conflicting names of graces can be confusing and frustrating, yet it is more important to be familiar with the musical gestures and how to use them than with what they are called. Many important graces taken from Caccini are reprinted in Playford (ex. 1.9). English sources rename the Italian graces with such colorful names as "beat," "backfall," "elevation," "cadent," and "springer." These can also be turned into varieties of "shaked graces." Caccini's *trillo* is called a "trill or plain shake," while the *gruppo* is referred to as a "gruppo or double relish." But remember, don't be intimidated by the names or the ornament tables; get to know the gestures so you can apply them.

Sometimes graces were written out in the music, and sometimes they were indicated with signs. The signs, which appeared in manuscripts only occasionally, were inconsistently used and could be misleading as to the relative importance of the figure. The graces must be lighter and more delicate than the principal notes of the melody, yet inflected to highlight the harmony and the text. Roger North wrote about the difficulty of notating graces: "It is the hardest task that can be to pen the manner of artificiall Gracing an upper part. It hath bin attempted, and in print, but with woeful effect. . . . The spirit of that art is incommunicable by writing, therefore it is almost Inexcusable to attempt it."[45]

An anecdote involving Purcell, who was known for writing out much of his

Sources:   Manchester. Public Library, Watson Collection, ms 832 Vu 51[ca 1660]
Simpson, Christopher. The Division-Viol. London 1665
Playford, John. An Introduction to the Skill of Musick. London 1674
Mace, Thomas. Musick's Monument. London 1676

Example 1.9. Graces from later seventeenth-century English sources, reproduced by permission of the author from Robert Toft, *Tune Thy Musicke to Thy Hart: The Art of Eloquent Singing in England, 1597–1622,* University of Toronto Press, 1993, p. 102.

desired ornamentation, is described in the memoirs of an actor, Colly Cibber: in discussing the performance of Jemmy Bowen, a young singer who often worked with him, Purcell is quoted as having said, "O let him alone, he will grace it more naturally than you or I can teach him."[46] This remark is difficult to interpret. Drew Minter suggests that Jemmy Bowen's fellow singers may have complained that he wasn't adding enough extra ornamentation, and Purcell defended the boy's simpler approach. Baldwin and Wilson caution that "more naturally" does not necessarily mean more simply. Michael Burden believes that Bowen most likely did add extra graces, and that Purcell's comment "meant that he would naturally (i.e., with more innate musicality) ornament the piece. I don't think it implies anything about the ornamentation one way or the other."[47]

For modern singers who want to grapple with this difficult situation, it is best to recognize what type of a figure can be considered a grace, so that even if it is written into the music it can be performed as an ornament. The same kinds of figures can then be added to other passages that seem in need of further decoration. This is particularly helpful in Purcell, who, as Roger North said, "hath given us patterns of all the graces musick can have."[48]

In the opening phrase of "The Fatal Hour" (ex. 1.10a) Purcell has incorporated variations on the elevation, backfall, double backfall, and shaked backfall into his composed melody. Example 1.10b shows a skeleton melody onto which the ornaments have been layered. If you compare Purcell's melody with Toft's list of graces, you can see which gestures and pitches are ornamental and which are part of the more fundamental structure. With these distinctions in mind, I would probably give more importance to the first G in m. 1, move lightly through the sixteenth notes that follow, and make a strong arrival on the first F in m. 2. Similarly, the first F in m. 2, which is really an appoggiatura to the E, would be stronger than the sixteenth notes and resolution that follow. Considering the melody in terms of the graces it contains will certainly influence how much weight or importance you choose to give to each sixteenth note and how you shape the phrase overall.

DIVISIONS

Divisions were not often written into published song books, except in a few songs of the *Ayres* (1609) of Alfonse Ferrabosco. These brief examples and the divisions seen in manuscript scores indicate that a florid Italian style of embellishment was occasionally used in early English song. The florid passages in mm. 5, 10, and 15, of example 1.11, for instance, are not notated in a precise

Example 1.10. Purcell: a) "The fatal hour," mm. 1–7, from *The Works of Henry Purcell,* vol. 25, Novello; b) "The fatal hour," mm. 1–5, skeleton melody.

Example 1.11. Ferrabosco: "Why stayes the bridegroome," manuscript source with ornaments, reproduced by permission of the author from Robert Toft, *Tune Thy Musicke to Thy Hart: The Art of Eloquent Singing in England, 1597–1622*, University of Toronto Press, 1993, p. 97.

Example 1.12. Purcell: "Fly swift, ye hours," mm. 1–6, from *The Works of Henry Purcell,* vol. 25, Novello.

mathematical relationship to the original rhythm. This seems to indicate a flexible tempo and the use of rubato in order to accommodate all the notes, practices in keeping with the declamatory style popular in the early decades of the century. This manuscript shows examples of longer divisions as well as smaller graces in the first measure alone. In Purcell's music, divisions are precisely written out and governed by the flow of the musical form, as illustrated in "Fly Swift, Ye Hours" (ex. 1.12).

Both Toft and Jones have concluded that the historical evidence indicates a wide variety of valid approaches to performing seventeenth-century English song. Some sources show elaborate ornamentation, while others suggest more modest added graces or even none at all. A book of music owned by one Elizabeth Seger in 1692 contains a number of Purcell songs with extensive added embellishments. Baldwin and Wilson suggest that these could either be examples of the bad taste of an amateur singer or her teacher, or inducements to singers to start out with too much ornamentation, which is easier to correct than too little.[49] Decisions regarding pitch and instrumentation in the earlier repertoire can also be made based on the performance circumstances and personal preferences and abilities of the performers. Jones offers a fascinating comparison of several manuscript versions of John Wilson's song "Take, O take those lips away."[50] The contrast between the ways in which professional and amateur singers of the seventeenth century might have performed this song can show modern singers some of the many options open to them.

## FRANCE

Grace and beauty are two of the most important defining characteristics of French Baroque music, which strove to bring to life the French language and the dance. Louis XIV, a dance enthusiast, set a tone for the entertainments at his court, which provided ample opportunities for dancing by the courtiers and the king himself. The vocal music, performed as part of the *ballet de court* (court ballet), was often meant to accompany dance as well. In his *French Baroque Music*, James Anthony notes that there was no Monteverdi in early seventeenth-century France to develop the dramatic possibilities of these lavish entertainments, *ballets mélodramatiques*, into operatic forms. It was not until Jean-Baptiste Lully served the king as court composer and master of the *musique de la chambre* in the 1650s and '60s that vocal music in a theatrical context began to reach its full potential. The French theater also had a strong influence on the developing vocal music, and composers took special pains to preserve the intrinsic rhythms and stresses of the French language. Theatrical declamation at that time was highly stylized and quite different from modern spoken French. Bénigne de Bacilly devotes the entire third section of his *Remarques* to a discussion of word stress, vowel length, and the distinction between long and short syllables. He also compares the French and Italian languages and concludes that "the Italian language permits more freedom than the French, whose strictness (which is perhaps excessive) tends to hold composers in check." The flexibility of musical treatment in Italian vocal music is particularly due to the elision of syllables and to word repetition, which were not allowed in French.[51]

As Italian singers came to perform in France, the distinct separation and even rivalry of the two styles were noticed and discussed by numerous writers:

As to the Italians, in their recitatives they observe many things of which ours are deprived . . . the passions and affections of the soul and spirit, as for example anger, furor, disdain, rage, the frailties of the heart, and many other passions with a violence so strange that one would almost say that they are touched by the same emotions they are representing in the song; whereas our French are content to tickle the ear, and have a perpetual sweetness in their songs. (Mersenne, 1636)[52]

Moreover, in vocal settings of Latin and Italian, all kinds of words are utilized without resulting in outcry from the ranks of the critics. Lightning, Thunder, Stars, Purgatory, Hell . . . and also a large number of expressions which might seem quite odd in French. . . . The very use of such expressions would be considered barbarous in French airs, which can accept only sweet, flowing terms and familiar expressions; for an air to be of good quality it is not enough that the music be beautiful: it is also necessary that the words be beautiful, . . . and above all that they are not shocking or repulsive. (Bacilly, 1668)[53]

Anthony has compiled a list of nouns and adjectives from numerous French sources describing the differences between French music, which was considered the embodiment of *le bon goût* (good taste), and Italian, which was viewed as *la corruption du goût.* The Italian list includes *bizarre, brilliant, colère, extravagance, rage, violence,* and *vivacité.* The French list includes *beauté, calme, charme, délicate, douceur, élégante, grâce, noble, tendresse, touchant.* Modern performers approaching this repertoire should keep in mind how the French saw themselves and their music during this period.

### Voice Types and Ranges

Just as the French were not comfortable with the excessive emotional expressivity of Italian music, they were also uneasy with the castrato voice and the sexual ambiguity, so popular in Italian opera and culture of the time, that it personified. With the exception of imported Italian music performed in Paris, castrati were rarely used in France. Some women sang at court, and groups of "pages," or boys, were also kept to sing the *dessu* parts for the *musique de la chapelle* and the *musique de la chambre.* But the favored voice for the leading roles was the *haute-contre,* the specific nature of which has provoked considerable debate. Most authorities understand this voice, thought to be similar to the English countertenor, to be a high natural tenor with a range from d to b'. Given the probable low pitch standard in France, it is possible that falsetto was not used, or perhaps it was only used for the very highest notes or for a special sweet and touching effect. Bacilly defends tenors against the abuse and inappropriate remarks commonly piled on them for using falsetto, because "it is soon realized that the vocal art owes everything to this high falsetto voice, because of the fact that it can render certain *ports de voix,* intervals, and other vocal decorations in a fashion entirely different from that of the normal tenor voice."[54]

In choral music the *haute-contre* sang the alto part in an arrangement that was similar to that of the English choir. Voice parts were designated as *dessus* (sopranos: women, boys, falsettists, or castrati), *haute-contres* (altos: men), *tailles* (tenors), *basses-tailles* (baritones), and *basses-contres* (basses).[55] The lower tenor voice was neglected in this period, and the solo bass voice was reserved for special circumstances according to Bacilly: "The Bass voice is suitable for almost nothing but the emotion of anger, which appears rarely in French airs. As a result, this voice range must be content with partsinging and . . . singing the bass part rather than the melody."[56] Low male voices were also conveniently used to sing operatic demons or villains.

Since most of the significant music making was at the court of Versailles, it followed that most of the performers, both musicians and dancers, were members of the court. The musicians were most likely professional, but professional dancers, particularly women, were not used until well into the middle of the century. Solo singers were known as *acteurs* and *actrices pour les rolles.* Though the system of training could not compare to that in Italy, and some singers went to Italy to study, Bacilly, who was a respected voice teacher himself, devotes considerable space in his *Remarques* to a discussion of choosing a suitable instructor. From his comments, it is apparent that many masters professed to teach singing, but not all possessed the qualifications he thought they should. Whereas some of the writing about singers and singing from the seventeenth century is difficult for us to relate to, much of Bacilly's discussion—particularly of types of voices—is extremely clear and remarkably valid for singers today. He cautions big voices not to try to reduce their total volume and thereby compromise vocal quality; rather they must "relax and never force the voice so that it will have the vocal quality it ought to have."[57] From his discussion of voices it is obvious that though smaller, higher, sweeter voices were preferred, there were as many different-sounding singers then as there are today.

### Dance Forms

One of the important keys to tempo and phrasing in French Baroque music is a familiarity with the particular dances which served as the basis of the musical forms. Dances from the period include familiar names such as gavotte, minuet, sarabande, and gigue, as well as lesser-known forms including the loure, bourreé, canarie, passacaille, chaconne, and passepied. Each has its own distinct character, meter, and tempo, which are described in depth by Anthony.[58]

These dances were central to the large dramatic and operatic productions. At the same time, many of the smaller vocal forms such as the *air de cour* and motet were also based on dances, which were an inseparable part of French music. If you have a chance to take a Baroque dance class you can learn firsthand how these dances feel in the body. If you have a sense of how to dance to a certain piece of music, it will tell you a lot about how you ought to sing it.

### Notes inégales

Another particular characteristic of French Baroque music is *inégalité,* a tradition of performing music in a rhythmically uneven fashion even though it may have been written evenly. As our modern jazz players know, in certain situations a series of eighth notes might need to "swing" instead of being played with metronomic evenness. The rules for *inégalité* are complicated, but basically the performer alters the rhythm of the written notes to make them anywhere from slightly to very unequal. This can range from turning a pair of eighth notes into a softly lilting triplet all the way to double dotting. It is usually applied to notes in stepwise motion rather than skips; it is used on the fastest-moving predominant note value in the work (often eighth notes, but sometimes sixteenths or quarter notes); and it should add an appropriate gracefulness to the music and avoid choppy or jerky motion. In his article on *notes inégales* in the *New Grove* dictionary, David Fuller suggests that the degree of inequality should be determined by the character of the situation, the expressive needs of the work, and the taste of the performer.[59] For vocal music, Bacilly cautions that "given two notes of equal length, one of them is interpreted as being dotted while the other is not. However, the student will also notice that this indication is never indicated in the printed notation and for good reason. If this interpretation were written out in dotted rhythms, the probable result would be that the singer would perform them in the jerky or jumping style typical of the old 'Gigue.' This style of vocal interpretation is no longer acceptable; therefore, it is necessary to interpret this dotted rhythm as delicately and subtly as possible so that it doesn't seem overdone."[60]

Sometimes composers indicate that they do not want inequality by writing "notes equal" or "tempo equal" in the score. Staccato markings, or instructions for *marqué, détaché,* or *mouvement décidé,* also indicate that inequality is not desired. It is required, however, when the score indicates *note puntate, notes inégales, pointé,* or *couler. Piqué,* which is also used to describe a ballet step, can mean either sharply dotted, or staccato and not dotted. Many questions and choices thus face the performer, and, not surprisingly, the issue is filled with controversy. Much has been written about the general question of rhythmic alteration in Baroque music if you wish to investigate it further. (See "Chapter 1: General, and French" in "For Further Reading.")

## Ornamentation

Most of the following discussions of ornamentation and diction are taken from Bacilly. His lengthy and detailed presentation in the *Remarques* has been translated into accessible English by Austin Caswell and is highly worth reading.

### DISPOSITION

Like the Italians, the French described the ability of a voice to move with speed and agility, and to execute subtle trills and appoggiaturas with delicate finesse, as *disposition.* The articulation is described as coming from the throat, and a lighter tone and steady breath are recommended for ease of movement. Yet Bacilly recognizes that some voices will have a natural ability to execute one kind of agility while other voices will be naturally good at another kind of movement. Patient practice, in the morning, was considered the best way to improve *disposition.*[61]

### AGRÉMENTS

*Agréments,* the small delicate ornaments that the English called graces, were used in the French *air de cour.* These solo songs, usually accompanied by a single stringed instrument, were composed of two verses. The first was a simple melody, and the second was more ornately composed. While certain *agréments* were needed in the first verse, it was the second verse, commonly called the *double,* which the singer was expected to embellish with more elaborate ornaments. Bacilly says it is permissible to vary the tempo of a song in order to add ornaments that bring greater refinement and charm to the performance, even if it is a dance piece: "It is completely unfair to criticize this style of performing by saying that the airs aren't danceable, as thousands of ignoramuses have done. If this were to be the intention of the performing singer, then his function would be no more than that of a viol."[62]

On the nature of notating ornaments, Bacilly expresses an opinion similar to that of Roger North's: "The majority of these ornaments are never printed in the music, either because they cannot accurately be reduced to print because of a lack of appropriate musical symbols, or because it may be thought that a superabundance of markings might hinder and obscure the clarity of an air and thus result in musical confusion."[63] He also notes that the following *agréments* are almost always used to ornament long syllables, not short.

### PORT DE VOIX

This is not to be confused with *portare la voce* or portamento, whose seventeenth-century Italian meaning, "to carry the voice," is slightly different from what we understand it to mean today. The *port de voix* (ex. 1.13) is similar to an appoggiatura from a half or whole step below, comparable to Playford's beat, and can be used at cadences and half cadences. In the French context the

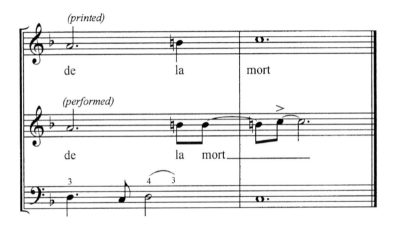

Example 1.13. Bacilly: *port de voix*, from *Remarques curieuses sur l'art de bien chanter* (1668), ed. and trans. Austin B. Caswell, Institute of Mediæval Music, 1968, pp. 66–67.

rhythm is altered slightly so as to delay the arrival on the upper note, which is then repeated gently in a *coup de gosier,* or slight glottal rearticulation. In a *demi-port de voix* the long upper note is not rearticulated. *Port de voix* can also be applied to rising thirds and fourths at cadences, but it is slightly more complicated to determine when those are appropriate.

*TREMBLEMENT*

This term can be understood to be comparable to the Italian tremolo, which, as previously mentioned, had several different meanings. Caswell has chosen to translate it as "vibrato" in some situations. The trembling quality is also sometimes referred to as *flexion de voix,* which adds brilliance to singing and could also be understood as vibrato. The other meaning of the term *tremblement,* sometimes called *cadence,* is a cadential ornament like a shake or trill that starts on the note above the written pitch and can be used in a descending melody (ex. 1.14). It is like a mirror image of the *port de voix* and can be used as an alternative to that ornament. Bacilly states that the *tremblement* is "one of the vocal art's most important decorations," which must be performed quickly, delicately, and in the throat. The preparatory note before it is the *appuy,* and the note leading gently from the *tremblement* to the final note is called the *liaison.*

Two other terms closely associated with *tremblement,* which may also indicate some kind of ornamental vibrato, are *étouffé* and *doublement du gosier.* The *doublement du gosier* is described as a repetition of one note in the throat, similar to the *trillo.* It is called *animer* when used on the viol. The *étouffé* is described as follows: "after having sung the *appuy,* . . . the voice starts to *trembler* but actually only seems to as if only wanting to *repeat* the note on which it would ordinarily make a complete *cadence.*"[64]

*ACCENT* OR ASPIRATION

The *accent* is a tone touched very lightly with the throat, as if an appoggiatura, leading either up or down, were phrased off to a gentle staccato. Sometimes called a *plainte,* it is used where the meaning of the text warrants it. Depending on the situation, a long note can be shortened using an *accent,* but Bacilly warns not to use it too often on an air's final notes, where a gentle surge and ebb, comparable to a *messa di voce,* would be more graceful.

DIVISIONS

While all the above *agréments* could be added to the first verse of an *air de cour* or similar vocal piece, more extended and complex diminutions (which were

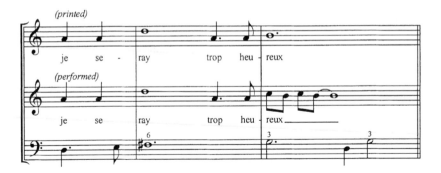

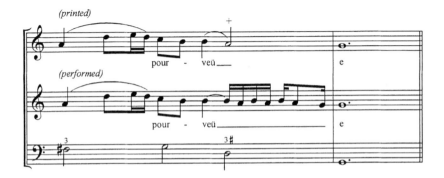

Example 1.14. Bacilly: *tremblements,* from *Remarques curieuses sur l'art de bien chanter* (1668), ed. and trans. Austin B. Caswell, Institute of Mediæval Music, 1968, pp. 69, 84.

roundly criticized and derided by some) were allowed in the *double,* or second, more ornate verse. The challenge was to add notes and readjust the new text of the second verse to the melody of the first verse without disturbing any of the requirements for long and short syllables. As was the case throughout the Baroque, some singers wanted to show off vocally while their critics wanted to preserve the intelligibility of the text. Bacilly generously encourages diminutions, but within the bounds of good taste and respect for the language. (See H. C. Wolf's edition of *Original Vocal Improvisations* for ornamented versions of airs by Bacilly.)[65] Lully is said to have disapproved of improvised diminutions in general, and he severely limited ornamentation, particularly in recitatives.

## Diction

Bacilly stresses the importance of clear, precise diction, but he warns that it is not enough for the words to be easily understood as in familiar speech. In singing, as in public speaking or the theater, proper declamation gives more weight and gravity to the words by infusing them with appropriate force and energy. Enunciating all the necessary syllables, plural endings, and articles, emphasizing expressive consonants, and highlighting the difference between long and short syllables are all elements of declamation for singing. Yet these techniques must not be confused with expressive singing in general and must be used in combination with overall dramatic expression.

### VOWELS

Bacilly cautions seventeenth-century French singers against some of the same mistakes that modern singers make in singing in French. The mute "e" must be pronounced, in many situations where it would not be in spoken language in order to contribute to the rhythm and rhyme scheme of the poetry. He suggests a closed, dark vowel, such as "eu" and warns against an open sound of "a" or "eh." He advises singers to be careful when singing the nasal vowels "an," "en," and "on" not to let the "n" sound come in too soon, and he remarks that this is the only situation when singing through the nose is acceptable. He also cautions singers when considering the two possible pronunciations of "oi," which can sound like "ai" in some situations. Today we would understand *reconnois* to be an old-fashioned spelling of *reconnait*. In general Bacilly recommends using the written pronunciation to avoid fooling the ear with words that rhyme in spelling but not in sound, or words whose meaning is altered when adapted to the rhyme. Yet if words like *reconnois* and *fois* do rhyme, then you pronounce them as written.

### CONSONANTS

Certain consonants deserve special consideration and attention, particularly "r," "l," "n," "m," and "s." In most situations when these consonants are found between two vowels, they should be pronounced simply and lightly, even if they are doubled as in *belle*. When "r" and "l" are used preceding or following another consonant, they need more force and intensity, particularly when they precede, almost as if they were doubled. *Pardon* and *charmant* need more emphasis than *prendre* or *agréable,* but *cruelle* or *ingrate* can take more energy if the context and the meaning indicate it. The "l" in *malgré* can take more energy than the one in *plaisir,* but you must be careful not to insert a shadow vowel between the consonants, resulting in *malegré.* This caution holds for other consonant combinations as well. Bacilly advises that "n" must be more gentle than the vigorous "r," and singers must be careful not to add an extra "n" before the initial consonant of a word, a mistake modern students make as well.

Consonants before a vowel can be elongated or suspended, a technique Bacilly calls *gronder* (growling). The most important consonant to suspend is "m" as in *mourir* or *moment,* in which the first "m" is elongated but the second one is not because it is between two vowels. Other consonants can be treated this way as well, including "n," "f," "j," "v," and "s," as in *non, enfin, jamais, volage,* and *sévère.* Final consonants follow complex rules regarding plurals, persons, and verb forms, as well as liaison and separation made for phrasing and breathing. All these devices are used according to the context and sense of the poetry and are governed overall by *le bon goût.*

SYLLABLE LENGTH

Bacilly's discussion of long and short syllables makes up the entire third part of his *Remarques* and was one of his primary reasons for writing the treatise. He emphasizes the need to identify the long syllables so the singer will know where to add ornaments and how to adjust the melody of an *air de cour* for the second verse of text. Within a series of long syllables, it is further necessary to establish a hierarchy of slightly longer and shorter ones. For the modern student of French language and music, some of these distinctions are obvious, while other circumstances present difficulties and questions. Bacilly considers many problematic situations in great detail. For the present discussion I will try to summarize some of his rules without venturing into the vast areas of exceptions.

Syllables that are usually long:

penultimate syllables of feminine words: *imaginable, cruelle*
monosyllables ending in "s," "z," and "x": *aux, bas, prez*
monosyllables with "n" following a vowel: *mon, rend*
syllables within words with "n" following a vowel: *danger, défendre*

Syllables that are usually short:

penultimate syllables of masculine words: *secret, espoir*
monosyllables: *de, te, me, que*

Elisions and other surrounding syllables can change the relative length of an otherwise long syllable. The final syllable of a song or air is usually considered long regardless of its length in another context, particularly the mute "e." The context and dramatic meaning of the poem also contributes to the relative importance of long and short syllables. Phrasing, inequality, and ornamentation are all affected by the rhythmic contours of the text, resulting in small, delicate phrases, *détaché* articulation, and graceful embellishments.

Here are some of the main issues introduced in this chapter: A score of early Baroque music is not a complete representation of the composer's wishes or a record of the first performance. When you approach a seventeenth-century work, you will need to make choices about a variety of issues that may include instrumentation, realization of a figured-bass accompaniment, tempo, character, articulation, and ornamentation. We have seen that the text is always an important guide in these matters. You will also need to make informed choices about the kind of edition you use. Look for modern scholarly editions and check the accompanying commentary. Also become familiar with reading the increasing number of reproductions or facsimile editions of composers' manuscripts and the early prints that are available from publishers and in libraries. They can give you access to a wealth of wonderful seventeenth-century repertoire otherwise unavailable.

By considering the period's writings about vocal production and technique as well as the instruments and performing spaces, you can develop a sense of the sound ideal for voices in the seventeenth century. It appears that in some respects it was quite different from what we expect to hear from classically trained singers today. The language used then to describe agility and vibrato is extremely confusing and foreign to us. Yet the writings give the general impression that singers were instructed to sing with less breath pressure and muscular force than we use today, resulting in a gentle and flexible tone that allowed the voice to move with increased speed and a small, hardly noticeable vibrato. Singers today should not try to remove the vibrato from their voices or sing with a straight tone or tight throats for early Baroque repertoire. Rather they should experiment with their flow of breath to achieve a softer, gentler tone.

Trends in ornamentation varied dramatically both from nationality to nationality and over the course of the century. We have seen, and will continue to see throughout this book, how fashions in ornamentation have ranged from modest tastefulness to unimaginable virtuosity. From the seventeenth century to the present we will see an ongoing negotiation between singers and composers about who is responsible for what kinds of ornamental additions. Singers today must first become familiar with the specific kinds of ornamental patterns used in music of different times and places in the early Baroque. The only way to do this is to study and practice many examples from specific works and primary sources. Then you can try to create your own variations on those patterns within the bounds of the specific style you are performing.

# Chapter 2 The Late Baroque

This chapter examines music from the first half of the eighteenth century, including works by J. S. Bach, Handel, and Rameau. It discusses the development of vocal music and singing styles in Germany, France, and England and considers how they were affected by the overwhelming popularity of Italian opera and the fame of Italian singers. It reviews how the relationship between words and music continued to develop, and it discusses different national approaches toward ornamentation. Issues presented in chapter 1, such as scores and notation, figured bass, early instruments, vibrato, pitch, rhythmic alteration, dance forms, and the relationship between composer and performer, are reconsidered from an eighteenth-century perspective. This chapter also addresses the larger issue of articulation in Baroque music and its relationship to harmony, dissonance, rhythm, tempo, and text.

Many of the best-known eighteenth-century treatises providing useful information about style and performance practice are German: C. P. E. Bach's on keyboard playing, Leopold Mozart's on violin playing, and Johann Joachim Quantz's on flute playing. Though written during the transition between the late Baroque and early Classical periods, they reflect the practices of the previous generation. Most helpful for singers is the 1757 *Anleitung zur Singkunst:* a translation with commentary by J. S. Bach's student Johann Friedrich Agricola of Tosi's 1723 treatise. Julianne Baird, the well-known soprano and translator of Agricola, maintains that vocal music was considered more important than instrumental music during the early to middle eighteenth century, and thus Agricola's *Anleitung* was possibly more popular in its time than the manuals by Quantz and C. P. E. Bach.[1] The Italian approach of Tosi, upon which Agricola is based, exerted a major influence on singing style. Also important were French treatises by Jean-Baptiste Bérard and Michel Pignolet de Montéclair, which helped to define and set apart the French style of declamation and ornamentation. (See "Chapter 2: Primary Sources" in "For Further Reading" for all these treatises.)

As the antagonism between the Italian and French styles raged on among musicians and critics, Italian singing and French dance continued to have widespread influence on music all over Europe. By the second half of the century, German composers such as Telemann had combined the best features of the rival camps with their own typically German style. By knowing something about each of the three major national schools of composition and performance practice—Italian, German, and French—a singer can evaluate which elements of each are present in a particular work and choose appropriate stylistic approaches.

### Scores and Notation

As discussed in chapter 1, Baroque composers expected that their performers would be familiar with basic principles of style and performance practice. Information that we now expect to find in a score, such as instrumentation, tempo, or exact rhythms, was often omitted or indicated in a way that we find problematic. As in the seventeenth century, singers and instrumentalists were expected to add appropriate ornamentation, both small and quite elaborate, which was not written in the score. Nikolaus Harnoncourt suggests that a Baroque score is actually more a record of the composition itself than a set of instructions for performance.[2] If the composer was part of the performance, as was often the case, questions of notation or interpretation could easily be answered in rehearsal. Different courts or churches throughout Europe had varying numbers of musicians in their service, depending on their budget or the taste of their patron. Instrumentation, transposition, ornamentation, and even tempo could depend on the available performers or on the acoustics of the room. Music was often recomposed or adapted for different performers or performance situations. Revising a work could also generate renewed enthusiasm and prevent pirated performances. The score was just a starting place; composers and performers made generous use of the variable resources available to them.

### Modern Editions

In the second half of the nineteenth century, historians and editors started producing historical editions of Baroque music. While this effort resulted in much fine work, these editors tried to fix the "mistakes" and correct the "inconsistencies" found in eighteenth-century scores. Their editorial adjustments often led to interpretations from a nineteenth-century perspective. More recent editions of Baroque music try to present scores closer to their original "bare-bones" form, while still providing suggestions for solving some of the more problematic issues. These critical or Urtext editions often include extensive commentary about sources and editorial procedures. Paul Steinitz, in his *Performing Bach's Vocal Music,* warns that "dynamics, phrasing and tempo marks given in nearly all vocal scores, other than those from Bärenreiter and Curwen, should be viewed with the utmost suspicion and checked against Urtext full scores and musical common sense."[3] While this opinion is a bit extreme, it is advisable to be cautious in evaluating Baroque scores, particularly vocal scores.

On the other hand, using collections of Handel arias transposed into keys other than the original is not necessarily inconsistent with eighteenth-century practice. Arias were frequently transplanted from one situation to another, from opera to opera or theater to chamber, as well as being transposed or recomposed to suit a particular singer. French cantatas were often designated for soprano or tenor, depending on who was available. It is always interesting to learn of a work's originally intended voice type, but it is equally appropriate to sing Baroque arias out of context or in transposition.

Another important issue regarding modern piano-vocal scores of Baroque works is the piano reduction of the continuo and obbligato lines. The majority of vocal works from the early eighteenth century are for voice and continuo alone or for continuo with one or more obbligato instruments. Because musical textures became more complex in the eighteenth century, it is more important for performers to be able to see the different lines of counterpoint and how they interact with one another. It is also necessary to distinguish the composed instrumental lines from improvised continuo filler. A piano reduction that combines all the different components into one homogenized texture may be easier to play at a choral rehearsal, but it is not helpful for studying the work and making decisions about rhythmic alteration, ornamentation, and articulation. When evaluating the score of a Baroque work, check the date of publication and read the preface (if there is one). Consider the editorial markings, the realization of the continuo part, the arrangement of the instrumental lines, and any accompanying scholarly commentary. Decide whether the edition has made too many restrictive decisions for you or has left some room for flexibility.

### Tempo

Many treatises advise considering the music itself and its mood or "affect" in order to determine a proper tempo:

> The pace of a composition, which is usually indicated by several well-known Italian expressions, is based on its general content as well as on the fastest notes and passages contained in it. Due consideration to these factors will prevent an allegro from being rushed and an adagio from being dragged. (C. P. E. Bach, 1753)[4]

> One must deduce [the tempo] from the piece itself. . . . Every melodious piece has at least one phrase from which one can recognize quite surely what sort of speed the piece demands. (Leopold Mozart, 1756)[5]

For singers, the text is the best place to look to determine a work's dramatic "affect" and mood. The rhythm of the diction plus the emotional quality of the words and music provide invaluable clues to an appropriate tempo. These elements, combined with a review of the faster note values or more intricate passages, should yield a good notion of how the piece needs to move. In the eighteenth century, words given as tempo indications were often more descriptive of a mood than a specific speed: *allegro*—cheerful; *allegretto*—rather gaily but gracious; *andante*—walking comfortably; *adagio*—at ease; *grave*—serious. Meter indications also suggested a certain kind of movement based on the number of strong beats per measure: 3/4, which was felt as three beats, had a very different character than 3/8, which was felt in one. Other factors contributing to tempo choice included a singer's personal temperament, the way his or her particular voice moved, the acoustics of the room, and the needs of the instrumentalists. In general, Baroque tempos can be faster than what we may be used to. (For more about choosing Baroque tempos, see Donington, *Style and Performance*, 11–19, and Cyr, *Performing Baroque Music*, 29–47; both sources are listed in "Chapter 1: General" in "For Further Reading.")

If a vocal work is based on a dance form, the traditional movement of that dance also implies an appropriate tempo. Meredith Little and Natalie Jenne, in their book *Dance and the Music of J. S. Bach,* suggest that the "Et exsultavit" movement of the Magnificat is a minuet (ex. 2.1a). The character of this classic French dance in 3/8 has been described as noble, with an elegant simplicity. The recommended speed of the dance ranges from very lively to moderate, with one strong beat per measure and the phrase starting on the downbeat. This seems appropriate for the "Et exsultavit," which has no tempo indication

Example 2.1. J. S. Bach: a) "Et exsultavit," mm. 1–14, from Magnificat, NBA II/iii/67; b) "Quia fecit," mm. 1–6, from Magnificat, NBA II/iii/96.

but does have strong syllables on each downbeat in a 3/8 meter. The thirty-second-note figures scattered throughout the bass line, first violin, and vocal lines function as written-out ornaments and can help determine the upper limits of a brisk tempo. Little and Jenne also suggest that the "Quia fecit" aria for bass is a gavotte (ex. 2.1b). This popular dance was characterized by two large beats per measure, with the phrase starting on the upbeat. The character was usually described as graceful, and it could be either joyful or serious in a variety of tempos within the moderate range. Bach's aria has no tempo indication, and it is important to bring out the gavotte phrasing and rhythm—"quia" leading to "*fec*it," "mihi" leading to "*ma*gna," and so on—in a moderate tempo.

## Articulation

In *Music as Speech*, Harnoncourt explains that Baroque music has a discernible grammar. It is made up of small pieces, or figures, that fit together like words to form phrases, sentences, paragraphs, and larger forms. The seventeenth-century idea of constructing music based on the rules of rhetorical speech and oration reached new levels of complexity in eighteenth-century music. Many writers of the time distinguish between musical figures that should be grouped together and those that should be separated. Most instrumental treatises discuss specific bowing or tonguing techniques to produce a wide variety of detached and slurred articulations. Often the goal was to create the impression that the instrument was playing syllables and words of different relative lengths and importance. Emphasizing the contrast between stressed and unstressed notes, which were sometimes referred to as "good notes" and "bad notes," is one of the fundamental principles of Baroque articulation. Highlighting the difference between heavy and light also applies to measures and whole phrases, building a complex hierarchy of tension and release, dissonance and resolution.[6] As Quantz wrote, "Musical ideas that belong together must not be separated; on the other hand, you must separate those ideas in which one musical thought ends and a new idea begins. . . . You must know how to make a distinction in execution between the *principal* notes, ordinarily called *accented* or in the Italian manner, *good* notes, and those that *pass*, which some foreigners call *bad* notes. Where it is possible, the principal notes always must be emphasized more than the passing."[7]

Singers have an easier time making decisions about articulation because we have a text with built-in syllabic stresses and grammar. We also have consonants, which serve to separate the vowels in each syllable. Baroque composers used the parameters of syllable stress and length, metric placement, and harmony and dissonance to create different levels of emphasis and relaxation throughout a work. As Bacilly discussed at length in 1668, using the varying lengths of vowels and consonants can help to clarify the difference between long and short syllables in French. Fifty to one hundred years later in the late Baroque period, this technique still helped to highlight the stressed and unstressed notes and to bring out interesting contours of the melody line. The idiosyncrasies of the German and Italian languages lend themselves to this approach as well. German has many percussive consonant clusters and guttural sounds that produce a different kind of articulation from the fluid, legato flow of Italian. Each language possesses its own particular rhythms and contours that contribute to the distinct national flavor and character of the music. The metric placement of syllables and words also contributes to the contrast between stressed and unstressed notes. Most of the time, stressed syllables and important words fall on strong beats of the measure, reinforcing the expected metric hierarchy of "good" and "bad" notes. When a strong syllable falls on a weak beat, the resulting rhythmic clash can add more interest and texture to the musical fabric.

The harmonic movement of the music also affects the heightened importance of some notes over others. Dissonance was considered more expressive than consonance. Performers were expected to add dissonant appoggiaturas to increase expressive tension and to highlight the contrast between heavy and light. "Above all," Agricola wrote, "it is the dissonances which make the harmony more interesting. According to the rules of good taste, dissonant notes, in general, are produced more loudly than consonant notes."[8]

In example 2.2, the first few measures of J. S. Bach's "Wenn kömmst du, mein Heil?" duet provide an opportunity to see how these tools can be used. In the opening phrase the soprano starts on a weak beat of m. 8 with the relatively short and unimportant syllable "wenn." "Kömmst," more important because it is the verb, falls on a strong downbeat and has an active and energetic ornament attached to it. The "k" has a percussive attack that, when combined with the more emphasized and ornamented downbeat and the weaker "wenn" syllable, should produce the desired contrast and slightly separated articulation that are characteristic of early eighteenth-century style. "Kömmst" itself is not a long syllable. In getting from "kömmst" to "du," you must sing through a slightly noisy consonant cluster of "-mmst d-". If you take a little time off the "ö" vowel and linger briefly on the "mm" before moving on to the shorter and weaker "du," you will create a graceful valley after the peak of the downbeat. This approach will also highlight the weaker rhythmic placement of "du mein" as you

Example 2.2. J. S. Bach: "Wenn kömmst du, mein Heil?" a) mm. 1–3; b) mm. 8–10, from BWV 140, NBA I/xxvii/151.

prepare for the next strong arrival on "Heil." "Heil" is an important word in the text; it is a long, smooth syllable and is further emphasized by a dissonant appoggiatura on a strong beat.

Late Baroque musicians preferred a slightly separated articulation even in long melismas on one syllable. Agricola instructs students to "imagine that the vowel sound of the division is gently repeated with each note . . . just as with a stringed instrument, [where] a short bow stroke belongs to each note of the division." If divisions are slurred, "the singer must guard against allowing the notes to become unclear." He also suggests that the first note in a group of three or four fast notes should receive a slight emphasis to maintain clarity and a steady tempo.[9] Deciding which notes to stress in melismas depends on the pattern and sequence of the melody and its relationship to the harmony. Dividing a long passage of fast notes into smaller pieces makes the melisma easier to sing and highlights the music's stressed and unstressed contours. Rather than applying a modern conception of a smooth, consistent flow of tone throughout, we can bring clarity to the texture by using expressive diction and varied articulation. By looking for the natural rhythmic variety of the language, as well as the intricate contours of melody and harmony, we can find the tools of stylistic articulation in the music itself.

### Rhythmic Alteration

By the early eighteenth century, rhythmic alteration was not only limited to employing *inégalité* in French music. Dotted figures, which we today understand to have specific proportion and duration, were interpreted with much more flexibility. A dotted eighth and sixteenth note, for example, could be performed with different degrees of length and crispness, ranging from a gentle triplet to a "double dot" (this is not necessarily a precise mathematical relationship) depending on the character of the situation. Standard and idiosyncratic conventions in notation led to frequent inconsistencies in rhythms and articulation marks. Some of these differences could have been intentional on the part of composers, but some could also have been due to sloppy penmanship and scribal errors. While triplets, dotted figures, and even eighth-note figures often appear to be interspersed interchangeably throughout a work, it may be necessary in one situation to change an even figure to agree with a dotted one, or a dotted figure to agree with a triplet. When different rhythms appear simultaneously, they pose particular problems that need to be solved on a case-by-case basis. Again, depending on the character of the music, dotted figures would most likely be softened to accompany simultaneous triplets, since it was unusual to have a two-against-three rhythm in Baroque music.

In the air from Montéclair's cantata *Ariane et Bachus* shown in example 2.3a, the flute plays a melody notated with dots. When the voice enters in m. 15 with the same melody, it is notated with equal eighth notes. Later, in m. 27 (ex. 2.3b), when the flute and voice play the melody together in thirds, it is notated with dots in both parts. Still later the voice sings an even eighth-note figure over a dotted countermelody in the bass. The performers must decide how to reconcile these rhythmic inconsistencies. Given that the tempo marking is *Lent* and the text is sad and mournful, you would probably not want to emphasize the crisp, bright aspect of the dotted figures. Considering that the music is French, you could also decide to use *inégalité* to soften both the dotted and nondotted figures into some degree of gentle, lilting triplets. In another work you may decide that the different rhythms are deliberately composed into the motivic landscape and therefore need to be highlighted to provide variety and excitement. It should not be taken for granted, as we do today, however, that the literal rhythms shown in the score were exactly what the composer wanted.

The inconsistent use of slur marks in Bach scores have left performers and scholars perplexed for generations. John Butt, in his detailed study of Bach's articulation marks, refuses to believe that the incongruities are due to careless and hasty penmanship in the heat of composition or reflect indifference to a haphazard performance.[10] Harnoncourt feels that the differences in articulation markings found in many Baroque scores add to the complex texture of distinct layers typical of Baroque music.[11] Still, some of these discrepancies could merely be mistakes or oversights. In vocal repertoire, slur markings usually indicate syllabification and word underlay, which may in turn inform the articulation of an instrumental line. For singers, the text offers the best guide for making decisions about phrasing and rhythmic alteration. The dramatic and emotional quality of a work will tell you how gentle or energetic to make its dotted figures. The internal rhythm of long and short syllables of words can also help suggest how to phrase notes together or ways to reconcile inconsistent rhythms.

## Legato

While the primary approach to early Baroque articulation was separated and detached, the use of legato gained favor throughout the eighteenth century. Singers were the model for both. Just as instrumentalists were encouraged to

Example 2.3. Montéclair: *Ariane et Bachus,* a) mm. 11–19; b) mm. 27–31, from *Cantatas: Book 3* (1728), modern edition *Cantatas for One and Two Voices,* A-R Editions, 1978, pp. 33–34.

create diction and grammar with their articulation, they were also advised to emulate the *cantabile* style of singing:

> Each instrumentalist must strive to execute that which is *cantabile* as a good singer executes it. The singer, on the other hand, must try in lively pieces to achieve the fire of good instrumentalists. (Quantz, 1752)[12]

> The human voice glides quite easily from one note to another; and a sensible singer will never make a break unless some special kind of expression, or the divisions or rests of the phrase demand one. . . . Indeed it is good practice to sing instrumental melodies in order to reach an understanding of their correct performance. (C. P. E. Bach, 1753)[13]

Agricola tells the voice teacher "he should take care that the notes emitted by the student are well connected to one another and thus legato."[14] Bérard mentions a kind of legato singing in which syllables are connected by a linking sound that is sung softer than the words themselves.[15] Butt proposes that the emphasis on legato singing grew as the eighteenth century progressed, but he cautions us not to apply a modern understanding of continuous legato to an eighteenth-century context.[16] Leopold Mozart compares an ideal adagio bow stroke to the gentle crescendo and decrescendo that singers use on long, sustained notes.[17] The soft swelling and diminishing of the *messa di voce* was still a commonly used gesture for both instrumentalists and singers. The *strascino* (drag) and the portamento or *portare la voce* (carrying the voice) are explained by Agricola as gestures in which the notes are bound together into a smooth flow. But the very fact that writers explained how to execute these special gestures suggests that they were not used as a matter of course. They were to be distinct events, interspersed with the more detached kinds of articulations as the music and the text demanded.

### Vibrato and Breath

Vibrato in the early eighteenth century was still considered an ornament, to be used selectively in appropriate situations. However, it was written about in a significantly more positive light than in the previous century:

> The *flaté* is a type of vibrato which the voice makes by means of several small, gentle exhalations without raising or lowering the pitch. [This is done] on a note of long duration or on a note of repose. . . . If the *flaté* were used on all important notes, it would become unbearable in that it would render the melody tremulous and too monotonous." (Montéclair, 1736)[18]

The Tremolo [vibrato] is an ornamentation which arises from Nature herself and which can be used charmingly on a long note, not only by good instrumentalists but also by clever singers. . . . it would be an error if every note were played with the tremolo. (Leopold Mozart, 1756)[19]

The vibrato on one note—is also an ornament that in singing is especially effective on long sustained notes, particularly when applied toward the end of such notes . . . but not all throats are capable of this type of execution. (Agricola, 1757)[20]

The use of vibrato can be thought of as part of a varied palette of articulations. Stressed dissonances surely need little or no vibrato, but long notes can benefit from a tasteful amount, depending on the harmony. Modern singers, who are accustomed to using a steady flow of breath and tone, should try to find flexibility in their use of breath, rather than tightness in the throat, in order to negotiate different types of vibrato, ornaments, and articulation. Bérard includes a lengthy discussion of breath and different kinds of exhalations to go with different "affects" or moods: "For good expirations, the interior air must be made to leave with more or less force, with more or less volume, according to the character of the song. There is no doubt that the art of good inspiration and expiration will multiply the powers of a singer, and will give him great facility in executing the ornaments well."[21] Specific ornaments will be discussed below in the sections on national styles.

## Pitch

The pitch situation was still quite complicated in the eighteenth century. The works of Bach, written for various local organs and ensembles, are a maze of complex transpositions for organ, trumpets, woodwinds, and strings, depending on where each work was composed and performed. Since the organ in Leipzig was tuned particularly high, the continuo parts composed for those performances were usually written a major second lower than the rest of the instrumental parts. In order to be performed in Leipzig, works written in Weimar had to go through another layer of transposition and adaptation in order to be suitable for the instruments. The largest concern, however, was for the range and comfort of Bach's singers and particularly the male sopranos and altos, who could not sing comfortably if the ranges were too high.[22]

Agricola includes a lengthy discussion of such problems. He mentions the differences between the high tuning in Lombardy and Venice and the much lower pitch in Rome. He describes the difficulties of learning an aria in one key and then having to sing it higher or lower in another city. In addition to the stresses they put on the extremes of a singer's range, such adjustments caused great confusion in negotiating the transitions from the natural voice to the falsetto or the middle range to the head voice: "under such circumstances, the happiest singers are those in whom the unification of the natural voice and the falsetto does not cause much difficulty and who, in case of necessity, have a few extra notes in their high and low registers."[23] The same would be true today for a singer who had to sing performances of a Bach Passion or Handel's *Messiah* with a modern orchestra one day and a period instrument ensemble the next.

### Period Instruments

Singers can learn a great deal about articulation, sound, and nuance in Baroque music by working with period instruments (restored original instruments or new reproductions of old instruments). Players who are skilled and knowledgeable about Baroque style can demonstrate characteristic instrumental gestures such as crisp, detached articulation, *inégalité*, or the gentle rising and falling of bow pressure that Leopold Mozart likened to the *messa di voce*. The particular construction and playing techniques of early instruments produce an articulation model that we can imitate.

The sound of many of these instruments is softer, gentler, and more mellow than their modern counterparts. Due to the complexities of early tuning systems, many early instruments can create interesting variety in tone color and intonation, depending on what key they are playing in. Singers can emulate this variety of sound, which differs so markedly from the consistency of strength and range of modern instruments. Reproductions of early instruments are generally built to conform with the now standardized Baroque pitch of $a' = 415$ cycles per second. Singing a half step lower than the modern $a' = 440$ allows for more relaxed sound production and makes some of the subtle gestures of articulation easier to employ, particularly in the high range. Since the total volume of sound produced by a period orchestra or chamber group is much less than that of the comparable modern group, the total amount of effort for singing and projecting can be similarly less. It is possible, of course, to apply elements of Baroque style to performances with modern instruments, but certain compromises undoubtedly have to be made because of their higher pitch, greater volume, and more consistently brilliant tone.

### Recitative

Recitative in the early eighteenth century was written for three different types of performance venues: church, chamber, or theater. Each demanded its own stylistic approach. Tosi instructs that the singer should be allowed the most freedom in Italian church recitatives to shape the rhythm to the text and to add expressive ornaments. In theater recitatives, by contrast, the singer has little freedom to play with the rhythm and should add no ornaments. Chamber recitatives fall somewhere in between, being less serious than those for the church but somewhat closer to those for the theater. Agricola comments: "All three types of recitative share in common that which the author has specified above for the church recitative: that it is not sung in strict time. One must be guided more by the length and shortness of syllables in common speech than by the written value of the notes in the recitative."[24] He shows other additions to the written notation that the singer must make, such as passing appoggiaturas and trills, both within the body of the recitative and particularly at cadences. In example 2.4, for instance, the singer should fill in descending thirds with passing notes but keep the penultimate note on the upper portion when a cadence is approached by a fourth.

Much has been written, both in the eighteenth century and more recently, on the accompaniment of recitative. Particularly problematic issues include the timing of cadences and the length of bass notes. In the theater, cadences were often telescoped or truncated in order to keep the dramatic action moving. Tosi's term for these was *cadenze tronche*. If a fast dramatic pace was desired, the penultimate and final chords of the continuo were often played under the singer's penultimate or final note, as in the above examples. This was not necessarily the only choice in period practice. If the dramatic situation were more serious or contemplative, the cadence might come after the singer's last note. Again, the words provide the most important guide to making decisions about pacing and character of both the vocal line and the accompaniment.

Bass notes in recitatives were often written as long notes, either whole or half notes. Yet it was understood that they might not be held for their full notated value. Scholars today speculate that writing long note values may have been faster and easier than writing quarter notes and rests and would have shown the harmonic progression more clearly.[25] Figures written to go with the bass notes varied widely in type and frequency from composer to composer and even within a particular composer's work. In the cases of J. S. Bach or Handel, who often played their own continuo parts, the notation did not need to be precise or complete because the composer, who was also the performer, knew how long or short to play the bass notes and what figures to add.

In the Italian opera tradition *secco* (dry) recitatives moved along briskly and were usually accompanied by a harpsichord whose sound decayed quickly. In contrast, recitatives in the church music of Germany would move more slowly

Example 2.4. Agricola: appoggiaturas in recitatives from *Anleitung zur Singkunst* (1757), reproduced in Julianne Baird, *Introduction to the Art of Singing*, Cambridge University Press, 1995, pp. 174–75.

and be accompanied by the sustaining sound of the organ. Accompanied recitatives, in which strings or winds are composed into the texture, were treated more like arias or ariosos. They were performed with less rhythmic flexibility and more sustained sound. For the *secco* recitatives, which emulated the Italian style, German sources cautioned the continuo players against prolonging the annoying organ drone, which might drown out the vocalist's words. Instead, they encouraged both keyboard and cello/viol players to play shorter notes. In his *St. Matthew Passion* Bach wrote long note values in the score for the *secco* recitatives but wrote quarter notes and rests in the continuo parts. Many scholars and performers have concluded that it was conventional practice to play all *secco* recitatives with short bass notes. Yet Patrick Rogers, in his *Continuo Realizations in Handel's Vocal Music,* presents evidence to suggest that some recitative situations, particularly those involving harpsichord, demand something more sustained than the highly detached approach recommended for the organ. The existence of changing figures during rests or long sustained bass notes requires a flexible interpretation of the length of bass notes and the placement of chords. This illustrates that one bit of advice from a primary source cannot necessarily be applied to all situations. Singers should be aware of the complex issues involved and the kinds of choices that need to be made regarding Italian and German recitatives.

French composers had a completely different approach to setting text in recitatives. From Lully to Rameau, recitative was written out in a complicated sequence of changing meters intended to capture the poetic construction and heightened rhythmic execution of theatrical declamation. Singers and instrumentalists were expected to follow the flow of the written rhythm closely. Expressive diction and artfully placed ornaments, rather than rhythmic freedom, helped to convey the emotion of the text. In the example from Rameau's cantata *Le berger fidèle* (ex. 2.5), the singer and the accompanying instrumentalists must observe the notated rhythm more strictly than in German or Italian styles in order to stay together through the changing meters of fours, twos, and threes. Italians who criticized French music often complained that they couldn't tell where the recitatives ended and the arias began, because the contrast in pacing and flow between recitative and air was not as great as in Italian music.

## ITALIAN INFLUENCE

The most characteristic feature of the Italian style of singing in the late Baroque period was the virtuosic display of dazzling vocal showmanship. The famous

Example 2.5. Rameau: *Le berger fidèle*, recitative no. 5, from *Cantatas: Book 1* (1728), modern edition Deutscher Verlag, 1969.

Italian singers were sought all over Europe: the great castrati Farinelli, Pistoc-
chi, Bernacchi, Senesino, and Guadagni were known for their phenomenal
breath capacity and control. The renowned Italian women singers Faustina and
Cuzzoni created a sensation in London by competing for attention in Handel's
operas.[26] Singers tried to best each other and the accompanying instruments in
an attempt to gain the audience's favor and to steal their attention away from
eating, talking, and general distractions. By the time Tosi wrote his *Observations on the Florid Song* in 1723, he condemned what he considered to be the
horrid excesses in ornamentation that singers were inflicting on Italian music.
Yet contemporary reports indicate that ornamentation became even more elaborate as the century progressed. Charles Burney, a noted historian and critic of
the time, wrote a great deal about the performances of singers in the early eighteenth century. In his *General History of Music,* written in the latter half of the
century, he comments that Farinelli's ornamental display "which excited such
astonishment in 1734, would be hardly thought sufficiently brilliant in 1788 for
a third rate singer at the opera."[27]

It is difficult to know exactly what kind of ornamentation singers added or
what was fashionable at a given point in the century. From accounts of performances, instructions in treatises, and some surviving manuscripts with written-
out ornamentation and cadenzas, we can glean some ideas of how to re-create
the Italian virtuoso style.

## Ornamenting Arias

The *da capo* aria, whether in opera or cantata, became the place to show off
one's vocal and compositional skills. There were four principal ornamentation
types: appoggiaturas and trills; first-section aria variations and interpolated divisions; slow-section melody recomposition; and thrilling cadenzas.

### APPOGGIATURAS

As already mentioned, the use of certain musical gestures was common knowledge to musicians of the early eighteenth century. This was certainly the case
with appoggiaturas and trills, which were often not notated but rather expected
to be added by singers in appropriate places throughout arias and recitatives.
Tosi even mentions that Italian singers would laugh if a composer indicated an
appoggiatura that they would have naturally added on their own.[28] *Appoggiare*
in Italian means "to lean," and an appoggiatura is made by leaning on an auxiliary note. This usually adds dissonance to a strong beat, creating more contrast
between strong and weak or tension and release. (This type of ornament in the

seventeenth century was called a beat or backfall in England, and an *accent* or *port de voix* in France.) I have already mentioned cadential appoggiaturas in recitatives. Most of the writers of the major eighteenth-century treatises devote entire chapters to the proper use of appoggiaturas.[29] Their commentary is extensive and can be confusing and contradictory. Sometimes appoggiaturas are indicated by small notes written before the main note to be ornamented. Many times composers notated these ornaments in an instrumental part but not in the vocal line. In other scores appoggiaturas are composed directly within the melody. By studying the appoggiaturas that are indicated or written into the music, you can learn what kinds of situations demand or can support added appoggiaturas. Tosi himself was confident that the ear could tell you when an appoggiatura is needed and when it is not.

The well-known aria "Sebben, crudele" by Antonio Caldara provides many instances of both written and unwritten appoggiaturas (see ex. 2.6). As the aria appears in the Schirmer *Twenty-four Italian Songs and Arias* edition, it features an eighth-note accompaniment that was added for the 1885 Ricordi edition of *Arie antiche*. The original 1710 manuscript shows an accompaniment of half and quarter notes, which gives the E-minor aria more of a minuet-like feel and makes the appoggiaturas easier to see. In example 2.6a Caldara includes a written-out appoggiatura on the first beat of m. 8, the second syllable of "lan*guir*." In the second rising chromatic theme (ex. 2.6b), he writes 4–3 suspensions in mm. 28 and 30 that feel like appoggiaturas on the second syllables of both "cru*de*le" and "lan*guir*." In the answering descending phrase he writes dissonant suspensions in each measure on "sem*pre fe-de*le" and "*ti vo*glio." All these effects (marked with arrows in the example) act like appoggiaturas, adding tension to a strong beat by creating a stressed dissonance that is then resolved into a relaxed consonance.

If you wanted to add more appoggiaturas as additional ornaments, in the opening phrase you could repeat the E of "cru-" as a dissonant upper neighbor note on the "de-" of the downbeat of the next measure. The "-le" on C, which passes from the D of the first beat to the B of the third beat, can also be thought of as a passing appoggiatura, though it doesn't receive as much emphasis because it falls on a weaker beat. (It is interesting to note that in the 1885 version of the aria included in the Schirmer anthology this "-le" syllable has been moved to the third beat, smoothing out the phrase and destroying the feeling of a passing appoggiatura.) Dissonant lower neighbor notes can also act as appoggiaturas. In the first statement of "Sempre fedele" you could add a dissonant lower neighbor note to the "fe*de*le" syllable by repeating the B of "*fe*dele" on the

Example 2.6. Caldara: "Sebben, crudele," a) mm. 5–8; b) mm. 27–34, modern transcription from 1710 manuscript in *26 Italian Songs and Arias,* ed. John Glenn Paton, 1991. Used with permission of the publisher. © Alfred Publishing Co. All rights reserved.

downbeat of the next measure. In this situation it would also be permissible to add an upper neighbor appoggiatura by jumping up a minor third to the half step above the "fe*de*le" syllable.

Usually appoggiaturas are stressed and sung or played on the beat. They can be performed louder than the neighboring consonant notes, except for passing appoggiaturas, which fill in thirds. These can be lighter in emphasis and come before the beat, as in "fede*le*" in the above example. Stressed appoggiaturas usually take half the value of the note they are decorating (or two-thirds the value in triple time), regardless of the value of the written small note if there is one. They can be shorter or longer than this, depending on the harmonic and rhythmic context, but the point is to prolong the expressive dissonance so the release into consonance is all the more welcome.

TRILLS

While the trill in the early eighteenth century was similar to its seventeenth-century ancestor, it was also used decoratively and structurally. It was expected at major cadence points and could also be used to decorate internal melodies and less important cadences. It could be combined with appoggiaturas and other types of preceding ornaments, as well as with various kinds of concluding figures. In its simplest and most common form it starts on the upper note, which is usually stressed, with a trill between that and the main note, resolving on the note below. A great deal of controversy concerns the upper-note start of trills. Some scholars and performers believe that all Baroque trills should start from above. Frederick Neumann, in his *Ornamentation in Baroque and Post-Baroque Music,* provides evidence that some situations demand a main-note start instead.[30] In any case, it is important to evaluate the surrounding melodic and harmonic circumstances, as well as other motivic details in the music, when making decisions about trills. Using the Caldara aria as an example again, you could add a trill to "lan*guir*" in mm. 7–8 by starting on the D above the written C on the downbeat, trilling on the C and D, and finally resolving to the B. You must decide, however, whether the trill is appropriate for the dramatic effect you want to create here. In the final phrase before the middle section (m. 33), an expected cadential trill should be added to the second beat of "*voglio*" by starting with a reemphasized G from the downbeat and then trilling on G and F-sharp.

DIVISIONS AND IMPROVISED VARIATIONS

Tosi recommends that the first part of a *da capo* aria needs only a few tasteful added decorations, perhaps appoggiaturas and trills, while the middle section can withstand slightly more. However, the restatement of the first section of the aria, or the *da capo* (from the head), requires the most creative invention on the part of the singer/composer. If the rhythms are slow, you can use the seventeenth-century technique of diminution, filling in parts of the melody with passing notes and smaller note values. If it is a fast aria, you can try varying the patterns and contours of the coloratura. Bear in mind that any alterations you make must be in keeping with the rules of voice leading and counterpoint. Just as important, the style of the ornaments must be from an eighteenth-century vocabulary. You must be careful not to use familiar coloratura patterns from vocal music by Mozart, Rossini, Donizetti, or other later composers when ornamenting Baroque arias. The more you are familiar with early eighteenth-century repertoire (both vocal and instrumental), the more appropriate patterns and figures you can choose from and copy when planning ornaments and cadenzas for a *da capo* aria. It is also invaluable to listen to the ornaments of experienced singers and to review the examples of ornamented manuscripts that survive from the period. Ultimately you want to highlight your own technical strengths and musical good taste.

Handel was a German-born composer whose formative training had been in Italy. Since he wrote Italian opera in England primarily for Italian singers, the Italian style influenced most of his vocal music. He worked closely with many famous singers and wrote music specifically designed to suit their particular strengths. He also often reworked music originally written for one singer to be more suitable for another singer. Example 2.7 shows an aria from his opera *Ottone* (1723) transcribed from a manuscript with added graces. Hellmuth Christian Wolff suggests that this manuscript was in a collection of transposed arias that were ornamented and performed in concerts by the castrato Guadagni. In contrast, Winton Dean concludes from the scholarly evidence that the ornaments were added to the transposed music by Handel himself for a performance of the opera in which a contralto had to substitute for the famous soprano Cuzzoni, who was ill. Whatever the circumstances, the added graces provide a fascinating example of ornamentation in a period style.[31]

CADENZAS

Agricola's German translation and extensive commentary on the treatise of Tosi offers us the most detailed instructions for improvising cadenzas in the Italian style. He describes three main cadence points in an aria that, in the seventeenth century, would have been decorated with a small trill. As time went on, further embellishment was added before the trill, which gradually began to cause a de-

Example 2.7. Handel: "Affanni del pensier" from *Ottone* (1723), mm. 7–17, transcription of ornaments in *G. F. Handel: Three Ornamented Arias,* ed. Winton Dean, © Oxford University Press, 1976. Used by permission. All rights reserved.

lay in the arrival of the final note. "Finally there was an attempt to adorn this delay with all kinds of improvised divisions, runs, drags, leaps—in short, all the possible figures that the voice is capable of executing."[32] These cadenzas, which Agricola supposes originated between 1710 and 1716, can be added at the final cadence at the end of an aria's first section and possibly also at a cadence within the aria if it seems appropriate. A cadenza can also be added at the final cadence of the middle section and certainly at the final cadence of the concluding section or at the repeat of the opening section. Tosi disapproved of an accompaniment's coming to a complete halt for a cadenza.[33] Julianne Baird supposes that cadenzas in the early part of the century were performed over a continuously moving bass line, at a slow tempo marked adagio or andante. Later, as cadenzas became more elaborate, the continuo players would have to wait longer for the singer to reach the final note.

Agricola instructs that improvised embellishments must maintain the affect or character of the work. If possible, thematic material or motives from the aria should be used, while also including some sort of surprise—perhaps notes from outside the range of the aria. The singer should show off his or her strengths, while also following the rules of good voice leading and composition. Usually the cadenza is sung on the syllable preceding the trill, though the word underlay can be adjusted somewhat to provide a comfortable vowel. Most important, it should be performed all in one breath, though singers in the eighteenth century devised ways to sneak breaths in order to prolong their moment of glory. Some singers performed truly improvised cadenzas, but there is evidence to suggest that they also wrote them out and practiced them ahead of time. This was probably more necessary for double cadenzas involving two singers or a singer and an instrumentalist. Both Agricola and Quantz recommend planning ahead for double cadenzas to avoid mistakes in counterpoint or a collision in performance.[34]

### Handel's *Messiah*

One of the best-known works of Baroque vocal music, Handel's *Messiah* has been performed virtually every year since its first performance in Dublin in April 1742.[35] In Handel's lifetime, each performance used somewhat different performing forces according to the location and the personnel available. Consequently, Handel made abundant changes to the score, rearranging and rewriting many passages and redistributing the arias to different singers. Each singer, of course, brought personal strengths and idiosyncrasies to the music's interpretation and ornamentation. It is difficult to determine what changes

were made for purely practical reasons and what revisions were for compositional considerations or Handel's own changing preferences. It is certain that
there is no definitive version that is absolutely "authentic" or "correct." By the
end of Handel's lifetime, a slightly more standard version had evolved, incorporating changes the composer made in 1750 for the famous Italian castrato
Guadagni, who performed some of the arias formerly sung by English female
altos. In 1767 a full score was published, further standardizing the work and
making it available to the general public. By the end of eighteenth century, increasingly larger performing forces were used, taking the work farther away
from its modest beginnings and on toward the nineteenth-century tradition of
grandiosity.

Today a wide variety of styles in *Messiah* performances cover a broad spectrum of possibilities from small period-instrument orchestra with early music
singers to full modern symphony orchestra, large chorus, and opera-singing
soloists. As in Handel's day, different approaches to interpretation and ornamentation abound. A recent *New York Times* review of a Christmas season of
*Messiah* presentations bemoaned the misunderstood and misused excesses in
ornamentation, both instrumental and vocal, in all but a few of the performances.[36] The *Times* critic's complaints of lack of good taste sound curiously
reminiscent of some seventeenth and early eighteenth-century writers, including Tosi. Whatever performance situation you may find yourself in, particularly for *Messiah* or other Handel oratorios, you will undoubtedly have to
compromise to get along with your musical colleagues, including singers, instrumentalists, and conductor. The more information you have about different
stylistic approaches, the more choices you can make in trying to achieve the
goal of singing with good taste.

### GERMANY

Music in Germany had been under the influence of the Italian style even in the
seventeenth century, when Christoph Bernhard followed in the footsteps of his
teacher Heinrich Schütz and went to Italy to bring back singers for the Dresden
chapel. He also brought back the principles of *seconda prattica* in his treatise of
1650, *On the Art of Singing; or Manier*.[37] In the eighteenth century Italian
singers were still sought to adorn the operas and chapels of courts and noble
households in Germany, just as French dancing masters were employed to
teach the German aristocracy the most fashionable French court dances. While
Italian singing and French dancing exerted strong influences on music in Ger-

many, two other elements helped to give German Baroque music its own distinct style. One was the importance of Lutheran doctrine in church music and education, as exemplified in the music of J. S. Bach. The other was the involvement of Frederick the Great, king of Prussia, in the musical life of the court of Berlin.

Frederick, who ascended to the throne in 1740, was an enthusiastic amateur performer and composer. He studied flute with Quantz and performed with C. P. E. Bach at the keyboard. Both musicians, along with Agricola, were also in his employ. Frederick enjoyed involving himself with every aspect of musical life and production at his court, yet his energetic participation in musical matters led to strict rules and limitations governing composition and improvised ornamentation. Some of these restrictions were specifically designed to prevent tasteless excesses by Italian singers. Others may have been a result of Frederick's generally conservative musical taste. The king ordered all ornaments in *da capo* arias to be written into the music by the composer, including all appoggiaturas and trills. He is said to have forbidden any improvised ornamentation, yet he probably studied this very technique with Quantz. (One of Frederick's own composed cadenzas and ornaments for an aria by Johann Hasse can be found in the Wolff collection of vocal improvisations.[38]) Agricola's interpretation of Tosi's Italian style, particularly his discussion of ornamentation, reflects the more restrictive approach characteristic of the Berlin School.

## Ornamentation

APPOGGIATURAS OR *VORSCHLAGS*

The critical question regarding appoggiaturas has to do with the placement of the ornamental note in relation to both the main note and the beat. Varying solutions can be seen in different examples of German music from throughout the late Baroque period. Agricola, as well as Quantz, C. P. E. Bach, and Leopold Mozart, translated appoggiatura as *Vorschlag*. This was not to indicate that the ornament should come before the beat, but rather that the decoration should come before the main note. Agricola lists four reasons to add appoggiaturas: "1) better to connect the melody, 2) to fill in the movement of the melody when it seems somewhat empty, 3) to enrich the harmony, 4) to impart to the melody more liveliness and brilliance."[39] He also instructs that appoggiaturas should be slurred to their main notes, and that when the main note precedes a rest, the appoggiatura may take the entire value of the note, which then resolves on the rest. An appoggiatura should not be added after a long pause, on the first note of a work, or in a situation where parallel fifths or octaves would result. A short appoggiatura that comes before the beat could be used in a passage where passing notes fill in descending thirds. Agricola cautions singers and composers not to use appoggiaturas to change the mood of a work: serious into brilliant or lively into melancholy. The appoggiaturas must also not be used so consistently as to become monotonous or too busy.[40]

Other ornaments which come before the main note include the *Schleifer* (slide) and the *Anschlag* (compound or double appoggiatura). In both cases the main note is preceded by two or sometimes more ornamental notes. In the slide the auxiliary notes come from below or sometimes above. In the compound appoggiatura the main note is surrounded by decorative notes from above and below. Agricola, as well as Quantz, C. P. E. Bach, and others, indicate that these ornaments should be performed on the beat.

The alto aria "Erbarme dich" from Bach's *St. Matthew Passion* (ex. 2.8) illustrates a situation where this is not always the case. In this aria the slide ornament is notated in a variety of different ways and poses some interesting problems of execution. It first appears as an ornament sign before the first downbeat of the solo violin melody (see ex. 2.8a). (Neither the slide sign nor the appoggiatura before the second beat appear in Bach's autograph score; they were added to the original violin part by Bach's chief copyist, presumably under his supervision.)[41] In the first beat of the second full measure (not shown), a slide-type figure is written out in the violin line leading the melody up to the second beat, clearly coming before the beat, not on it. When the voice enters with the same violin melody, no ornaments are indicated in the first measure, yet the written-out slide before the beat occurs in mm. 16, 17, and other places where the voice sings the comparable thematic figure from m. 2 of the violin melody (see ex. 2.8b). In m. 20, however, a sign for a slide appears in the voice part before the second beat, while in the instrumental line the violin plays a downward written-out slide rhythm that starts *on* the second beat (see ex. 2.8c). This juxtaposition may suggest that, at this particular moment, the slide in the voice part should come on the beat as well in order to make a parallel rhythm with the violin.

In the soprano aria "Zerfliesse, mein Herze" from Bach's *St. John Passion,* the slide is used as a thematic figure throughout the aria, but it is always written out in both the voice and instrumental parts and always comes on the beat (see ex. 2.9). In the duet "Wenn kömmst du, mein Heil?" from Bach cantata 140 (see ex. 2.2), the slide figure is notated as an ornament sign in both the violin part

Example 2.8. J. S. Bach: "Erbarme dich," a) m. 1; b) mm. 16–17; c) mm. 19–20, from *St. Matthew Passion*, NBA II/5/179, 180, 181.

and the two voice parts whenever it appears. It could be performed on the beat throughout, yet Neumann points out that in m. 33 of the duet (as well as in several places in "Erbarme dich") an on-the-beat rendition of the ornament would result in parallel motion to an octave with the bass line, voice-leading mistakes "which were not likely to have been intended."[42] John Butt counters this opin-

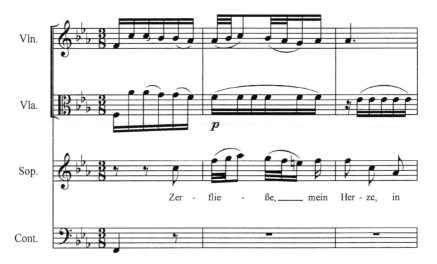

Example 2.9. J. S. Bach: "Zerfliesse, mein Herze," mm. 16–18, from *St. John Passion,* NBA II/4/143.

ion by suggesting that the ear would not catch such a voice-leading mistake as part of an ornament. He and other scholars therefore argue that ornaments should not be subject to such strictness in the laws of harmony.[43] Once again, no single rule from a treatise can be applied to all situations. Each question must be answered using the surrounding material as a guide.

TRILLS

Many writers describe what they consider to be a well-executed trill, but Agricola is one of the few to give practical advice on how to achieve it. He recommends practicing both a whole-step and a half-step trill (because some singers find one easier than the other) and alternating the notes slowly at first as if they were slurred and dotted, the lower note longer, the upper note slightly shorter (ex. 2.10a). This approach helps ensure that the main note is sung louder than the auxiliary note. The singer can then gradually increase the speed and diminish the dotted quality, all the while making sure to keep the intonation of the two pitches clear and true. Eventually the singer should begin the trill on the upper auxiliary note and possibly attach an ending or termination (ex. 2.10b). The termination is usually performed at the same speed as the rest of the trill without being newly articulated or detached. If the music is slow or serious, however, the termination may be held slightly longer—particularly when following a cadenza (ex. 2.10c). Depending on the syllabification and the charac-

ter of the orchestral entrance after a cadenza, no termination may be necessary.[44]

The speed and duration of a trill also depend on the situation. A slower, sad
aria could withstand a slower, longer trill. Slow trills were generally frowned
upon by Italians and Germans, who thought them to be typically French (even
though the French thought their own trills should be fast and light). Quantz
complained that an excessively rapid trill sounded like a flutter, and he preferred a trill of moderate speed.[45] Agricola describes a short or half trill for fast,

Example 2.10. Agricola: trills from *Anleitung zur Singkunst,* reproduced in Julianne Baird,
*Introduction to the Art of Singing,* Cambridge University Press, 1995, a) p. 129; b) p. 129; c)
p. 142; d) p. 134; e) p. 134; f) p. 132.

lively pieces (ex. 2.10d). He also describes a mordent, which is more typically a keyboard ornament. Similar to a half trill, it starts on the main note and alternates with the note below (ex. 2.10e). Other vocal trills that were primarily keyboard ornaments included prefixes either from above or below (ex. 2.10f). Ideally, a singer of late Baroque music should be able to master many different kinds of trills—major, minor, short, long, rising, and descending, with prefixes and suffixes—and know how to use them tastefully and effectively in the appropriate situations.

### J. S. Bach and His Singers

Johann Sebastian Bach wrote more ornaments into the fabric of his music than many of his contemporaries. He was even criticized for writing notes normally left to the performer's discretion. As previously mentioned, his ornaments could be notated in different ways according to the situation and were used both as decorative and structural musical elements. In general, the complexity of Bach's music leaves little room for improvised divisions or cadenzas. Simple appoggiaturas or trills can be added to some passages. In arias instrumental parts can guide decisions on small ornaments to complement thematic gestures in obbligato lines. However, the text is most important in determining ornaments and articulation.

The main purpose of Bach's vocal music was to serve the Lutheran Church and its doctrine. In eighteenth-century Germany music held a much more prominent role in educational and religious life than it does today. It was a powerful tool for transmitting the word of God to the community. Communicating the text and conveying the proper "affect" had been important goals in vocal music in the seventeenth century. In the context of Lutheranism, what mattered more than tickling the ear and moving the passions was enhancing the message of the sermon and saving souls. Thus it is crucial to consider the text in shaping the tempo, character, dynamics, articulation, and ornamentation.

When making decisions about performing Bach's music, we may not re-create the exact conditions under which his music was originally performed. Knowing something about those conditions, however, can further our appreciation and understanding of the music. While Bach was cantor in Leipzig, from 1723 until his death, he provided music for the Thomaskirche and taught the boys at the adjoining Thomasschule. Responsible for the music at several other churches in Leipzig as well, Bach used the schoolboys as singers and instrumentalists for various services throughout the week. It is thought that at that time boys' voices changed much later than they do today, perhaps as late as sixteen or seventeen, resulting in stronger, more experienced trebles and altos. It is also possible that some of Bach's altos continued to sing in falsetto after their voices had changed. Tenors and basses may have been older students at the school or recent graduates, though little information on the identities of individual singers exists.

The number of Bach's singers has proved to be a fascinating and controversial question. Probably only his best pupils sang his music at the Thomaskirche. The more inexperienced ones performed less demanding music in the other church services. A famous and much-discussed document known as the *Entwurff* reveals that Bach barely had enough musicians to cover all the services, especially taking into account absences due to illness or singers doubling on instruments. On August 23, 1730, he requested that the town council pay for twelve or preferably sixteen singers in each choir instead of the usual eight. Joshua Rifkin has suggested that since Leipzig was not a wealthy town it probably could not afford as many musicians as Bach wanted. Rifkin hypothesizes that most of Bach's choral works were performed with only one solo singer per part.[46] Scholars before Rifkin knew that Bach's cantatas were usually written for both "concertists," who sang all the choral and solo music, and "ripienists," supplemental singers who filled out the larger choral sections. Since Rifkin's revelatory articles and recording of the B-Minor Mass in the early 1980s, no one has unearthed sufficient evidence to prove him wrong, yet scholars today believe the question is still open for debate. Today's concert promoters and audiences have not embraced the "one voice on a part" performance tradition, and the convention of using chorus (small or large) and soloists (from within the chorus or not) remains preferable. As with Handel's *Messiah*, when performing Bach's choral works you may find yourself in a variety of performance situations. The most comprehensive discussion of all the relevant issues is Andrew Parrott's *The Essential Bach Choir.*[47]

## FRANCE

It is from Quantz, through his opinionated criticisms of both Italian and French music and singing, that we get an interesting glimpse into some of the elements that make up the early eighteenth-century French style. In the final chapter of his *Versuch,* Quantz compares the three prominent national styles. He proclaims that German mid-eighteenth-century music combines the best elements of all the nationalities in a forward-looking, mixed or universal style.

On his way to that conclusion, he reveals several useful details about the rival camps:

> The French manner of singing is not designed, like the Italian, to train great virtuosos. It does not at all exhaust the capacities of the human voice. French arias have a spoken rather than a singing quality. They require facility of the tongue, for pronouncing the words, more than dexterity of the throat. That which should be added in the way of graces is prescribed by the composer, hence the performers do not have to understand harmony. They make hardly any use of passage-work, since they maintain that their language does not allow it. As a result of the lack of good singers, their arias are mostly written so that anyone who wants to may sing them; this affords satisfaction to the amateurs of music who do not know much, but offers good singers no particular advantage. The only distinctive quality of their singers is their acting ability, in which they are superior to other people.[48]

Quantz explains that the French thought Italians placed too much importance on passage work and vocal display at the expense of dramatic expression and text. Quantz agrees with this opinion in some cases. The French also found Italian arias endlessly repetitive and too full of vulgar bravura. Yet within the context of the secular cantata, the Italian style had an important influence on French music and singing.

### Secular Cantatas

After the death of Louis XIV the court was no longer the center of musical life in France. In the salons of Paris, the poetic form of the cantata became popular and found musical expression in the Italian-inspired *cantate française.* These secular cantatas were composed both for small informal gatherings and for larger events in fashionable society. They were performed by both amateurs and professionals. Like their Italian counterparts, French cantatas were written for one or more solo singers and continuo, with or without obbligato instruments. They usually consisted of three recitatives and three airs, portrayed some mythological or allegorical story, and included flowery poetry, amorous entanglements, and a concluding moral. They became wildly popular in Paris in the period between Lully and Rameau. Most composers of the time, including André Campra, Nicolas Bernier, Louis-Nicolas Clérambault, Montéclair, and Rameau were drawn to the form. In his book *The Eighteenth-Century French Cantata,* David Tunley presents a thorough introduction to this wealth of repertoire, which he says "provides a fascinating study in musical style."[49] He also includes a list of facsimile scores and performing editions in appendix Aii of the book.

Most cantatas were scored for a single voice, usually soprano or tenor, using a C clef on the first line (soprano clef) or sometimes our more familiar G clef. Some cantatas were scored for lower voices in alto and bass clefs, but transposition was commonplace. Instrumentation could be dictated but could also remain flexible, depending on the musicians available. The most common instruments used were violin and/or flute, harpsichord, bass viol, and/or cello.

### Ornamentation

As Quantz mentioned, improvised diminution was less common in the eighteenth century. Some appoggiaturas were written into scores, but most vocal ornaments were indicated with a simple "+" or "t." The performer could determine the specific ornament based on the dramatic context and the nature of the syllable. In his 1755 *L'art du chant,* Jean-Baptiste Bérard, a leading Parisian opera tenor and respected voice teacher, presents common diction mistakes and shows the proper pronunciation of both vowels and consonants.[50] His recommendations are remarkably similar to those of Bacilly's *Remarques* a century earlier. Bérard complains of the lack of ornamental notation and asks singers to look within the character of the word to avoid choosing the wrong ornament for a particular passage. His discussion of specific ornaments is worth reading but somewhat frustrating, owing particularly to the lack of notated musical examples.

Other useful sources for information on French ornaments include Michel Corrette's *Le parfait maître a chanter* (1758) and Montéclair's *Principes de musique* (1736). Tunley has compiled a table of vocal ornaments with musical examples from Corrette on pages 205–8 of his *The Eighteenth-Century French Cantata.* A-R Editions' volume of Montéclair's *Cantatas for One and Two Voices* includes a translation of the vocal ornamentation section from his *Principes* in an appendix.

There are some discrepancies in the use and translation of certain terms when describing French vocal ornaments. As mentioned in chapter 1, Austin Caswell translated Bacilly's use of *cadence* to mean "vibrato." Sidney Murray translates Bérard's use of *cadence* to mean "trill," while Tunley specifies *cadence* as "final trill." In James Anthony and Diran Akmajian's translation, Montéclair clarifies the term by distinguishing between *cadence,* which is "an ending or conclusion of the melody which is to music what a period is to prose," and *tremblement,* which is an instrumental term for "trill." "There are *cadences* or conclusions of melodies without *tremblements*," Montéclair writes, "just as there are *tremblements* without *cadences.*"[51] Trills can be long or short, with or without a preparation or prefix. They can flow right into the continuing melody or prepare the final note of a phrase with an anticipation. They can be "well beaten" and clearly articulated or give a subtler shimmer to the line, depending on the sense of the text. Montéclair also distinguished between *balancement* (tremolo) and *flaté* (vibrato). Other subtler inflections and shadings of a note included the *son filé* (spun sound), perhaps without any vibrato, and the *son enflé et diminué,* comparable to a *messa di voce.* Once again, as with seventeenth-century ornaments, it is more important for singers to know how and where to use a particular ornamental gesture to shape a phrase or add expression to a word than it is to know what it is called by whom. Example 2.11 illustrates some of the most basic ornaments from Montéclair, Bérard, and Corrette. Examples a–e are sometimes notated with small notes; these ornaments can also be added in appropriate places where not indicated. Examples f–j are usually written in scores as a "t" or "+."

In Montéclair's cantata *Ariane et Bachus* (see ex. 2.3), a variety of ornaments are indicated by small notes and "+." The appoggiatura on the downbeat of m. 16 should be stressed and on the beat to add tension and anguish to the word "cru*el*." The small note on the downbeat of m. 17 functions as the appoggiatura to a prepared trill on the syllable "Mino*tau*re." It should also come on the beat. The small note attached to the second beat of m. 17 should come slightly before the beat, forming a conclusion to the trill that leads into the unaccented silent syllable "Minotau*re*." This is a common rhythmic gesture, particularly for setting a final mute "e," similar to the passing appoggiatura in Italian and German music. The trill on the downbeat of m. 18 is also prepared by a written appoggiatura. In this case both the appoggiatura and the trill may be shorter and faster than those of the previous downbeat, owing to the shorter syllable and the need for dramatic emphasis on the word "in*grat*." In contrast, the trill on the downbeat of the following measure could be longer and slower, prepared by a dissonant B-natural appoggiatura, to create the appropriate "affect" for Ariane's sadness ("douleurs"). One might even add a passing note, by itself or with a trill, between the C and A-sharp in m. 18 before the half cadence at "douleurs." In fact, when the opening phrase is restated with the flute in m. 30, the arrangement of ornaments is altered to include this figure.

Example 2.5, from Rameau's *Le berger fidèle,* shows how various ornaments can function in a recitative. In the first measure, the trill on "ber*ger*" can start on the C of the preceding syllable and be quite short so as not to disturb the flow of the line to the half cadence on the second measure's downbeat. Here, though no ornament is indicated, you could approach the D on "pré*sen*te" with

Example 2.11. French ornaments from Montéclair (in *Cantatas for One and Two Voices,* A-R Editions, 1978); Corrette (in David Tunley, *The Eighteenth-Century French Cantata,* Clarendon Press, 1997); and Bérard (in *L'art du chant,* Pro Musica Press, 1969).

a *port de voix,* either by itself or with a mordent. (In his annotated examples of repertoire at the end of *L'art du chant,* Bérard adds many such small graces to both airs and recitatives.) In m. 3, if the trill on "fu*nes*te" starts on the G of the preceding note, it would give dramatic color to the word. At the full cadence in m. 4, a *coulé* can be added on the beat. The expressive dissonance need not be hurried here, because of the fermata. Likewise, in mm. 7 and 8 on "rare" and "beau," prepared trills can highlight the words and fill the elongated note values. Or you might prefer to save the trill for "beau" and instead color "rare" with a subtler inflection. As Quantz pointed out, the French style has a more spoken than sung quality. Each of these ornamental gestures is a distinct event that, when combined, will result in a collection of small, detached phrases. As you become more familiar with French music from this period, you will recognize similar situations in which to use standard ornamental gestures.

One of the important points presented in this chapter is the issue of tempo. In Baroque music the tempo is often based on a combination of the meter, the note values, and the tempo term. Popular court dances also influenced the tempo and character of certain works based on those dances. Remember to take all these elements into account when choosing tempos for Baroque music.

This chapter continued to reflect issues introduced in chapter 1, including choosing scores wisely and working with figured bass. Whenever possible, try to find an Urtext or critical edition score that shows all the lines of counterpoint, rather than a piano reduction. Work with early instruments if you can, and take advantage of their distinctive qualities of sound and articulation. Singing at the lower pitch used in the eighteenth century will also allow you to use subtler shadings of tone color, vibrato, and articulation.

Articulation is another significant element in late Baroque music. Remember that the music is made up of small pieces joined together like words in a sentence. These small musical pieces can be combined to form phrases, clauses, sentences, and paragraphs. Make sure to highlight the differences between the stressed and unstressed, the heavy and light, and the dissonant and consonant notes and phrases. Use the words to emphasize these contrasts. Remember that a legato or cantabile approach was used at times but that the favored articulation was separate and detached. Take advantage of the rhythmic differences in the Italian, German, and French languages to give the music from each country its own particular style of articulation.

Each of those countries took a different approach to ornamentation. You must know both how to execute particular ornaments written into the music as well as how and where to compose or improvise additional ornaments and ca-denzas, if appropriate. As with seventeenth-century ornaments, the best way to become familiar with the eighteenth-century variety is to research and study as many examples of ornamentation from this period as possible, and from each nationality. Once you are comfortable using what you have found, you can ex-periment with creating your own ornaments in the same style. Remember that arias from operas and cantatas were often transplanted, transposed, and recom-posed to suit the needs of the particular singer who was singing them at a given time. Feel free to take advantage of this practice.

# Chapter 3  The Classical Era

This chapter considers the vocal style of the Classical era, including the music of Haydn, Mozart, and Beethoven. The term "Classical" was not coined until after 1830 and was not used by the composers of the late eighteenth and early nineteenth centuries. Both performers and composers of the time continued many of the traditions of the late Baroque, while adapting their musical style to fit new social and artistic circumstances. Charles Rosen's landmark book *The Classical Style* indicates 1750 as a boundary marking the end of the high Baroque and 1775 as an important transition point for Classical music.[1] Sandra Rosenblum's *Performance Practices in Classic Piano Music* documents late Baroque practices in use from 1690 to the 1740s, early Classical practices starting from the 1730s and reaching into the 1770s, and "mature" Classical style in place from the 1770s to the early 1820s.[2] This chapter examines how many important ideas from the Baroque period continued to exert strong influence on vocal and instrumental music during this period of transition.

Performers and composers used and respected the mid-eighteenth-century treatises by Quantz, C. P. E. Bach, and Leopold Mozart, until well into the nineteenth century. Treatises from later in the eighteenth century by Daniel Gottlob Türk, Domenico Corri, Johann Adam Hiller, and Giambattista Mancini contributed new thoughts on familiar topics (see "Chapter 3: Primary Sources" in "For Further Reading"). The rhetorical principles of music as speech, inflecting the difference between good notes and bad notes or strong and weak syllables, were still important ideas, as were using rubato and communicating the "affect" or emotional tone of a work. Dance forms, with their characteristic rhythms and tempos, continued to play a significant part in music of all kinds. Performers also continued to participate in the compositional process by adding ornamentation. As in the past, the ornaments, whether small graces or more elaborate improvisations, still depended on the situation and the individual tastes of composer and performer.

Yet many things were changing, including the kinds of performance venues and the people who were performing. During the period leading up to the French and American Revolutions, the court patronage system was gradually replaced by the rise of a new middle class. Professional performances moved out of the private domain of the aristocracy and into a more public realm that sometimes demanded larger performance spaces. This in turn led to the need for louder instruments and a more projected performing style for both instrumentalists and singers. At the same time more amateurs wanted to make music in their homes, and the growth of the music publishing industry made it possible for more people to acquire performance materials. All these elements contributed to the development of a new compositional style and a new interaction between composers and performers to suit the changing circumstances. This chapter will revisit issues of scores and notation, instruments, tempo, articulation, legato, vibrato, recitative, and ornamentation, as well as examine how the developments of the Classical era contributed to changes in performance practice.

### Scores and Editions

In the Classical era, composers started to notate their scores more carefully and completely. As in the Baroque period, if the composer were performing himself or leading a performance, usually from the keyboard or violin, it was possible to omit certain details from the score. Issues of tempo, articulation, and ornamentation could be worked out in rehearsal or determined spontaneously in performance. Today it is impossible to pinpoint definitive versions of most eighteenth-century works owing to the flexible nature of performance situations, and the changes made by and for particular musicians. Yet as notational practices became more sophisticated, composers tried to include more specific performance instructions in their scores to assure a proper rendition. This effort was not always successful, however, as we learn from Wolfgang Amadeus Mozart's letter of January 14, 1775, regarding *La finta giardiniera*: "Next Friday my opera is being performed again and it is most essential that I should be present. Otherwise my work would be quite unrecognizable."[3]

As the music printing industry grew, published scores became more common than manuscripts and were used by both professionals and amateurs. For the growing new market of amateur musicians, composers prepared easy-to-play and easy-to-acquire scores. The numerous folk-song arrangements for voice and piano trio composed by Beethoven were conceived for performance by amateurs. George Thomson, the Scottish publisher who organized the project, implored Beethoven to write the parts in an easy and familiar style so that society ladies could play them. He even requested that some of the accompaniments be rewritten because they were too difficult.[4] According to A. Peter Brown, the first edition of Haydn's already popular *The Creation* was prepared as a souvenir or collector's item and was never used by Haydn in performance. Brown suggests that this published score, printed on special paper and supervised and signed by Haydn, was not necessarily an accurate record of the performance tradition but was designed instead to appeal to the concertgoer or amateur musician for home use or as a keepsake.[5]

Sometimes first editions followed the composer's manuscript closely. Often, though, there were discrepancies such as last-minute alterations by the composer or copying and engraving mistakes. Some publishers in London began issuing collections of popular arias with "realized" accompaniments and the ornamentation, printed in small noteheads, used by famous artists. For some works of Beethoven, no autograph manuscript or corrected copy exists. The first edition, published either in his lifetime or shortly after his death, is the closest to the original source available.

By the second half of the nineteenth century, Breitkopf & Härtel had published the complete works of Mozart and Beethoven. A complete set of Haydn's works followed in the first decades of the twentieth century. As mentioned in chapter 2, the editors of these scores "fixed" inconsistent articulation and ornamentation markings, and they added phrasing marks to create the sense of long line and style consistent with nineteenth-century performance traditions. Many of today's modern editions of Classical works are still based on these nineteenth-century editions. As with similar scores of Baroque music, these nineteenth-century texts should be viewed with a degree of suspicion and compared, when possible, with the more recent critical Urtext editions of Haydn, Mozart, and Beethoven.

The following examples illustrate some of these discrepancies. In the old Mozart complete works (*W. A. Mozarts Werke,* edited by Ludwig von Köchel and others), the song "Dans un bois solitaire," K. 308, has no tempo indication at the beginning but does have an *Adagio* marked at m. 54 for the words "il me blesse au coeur." This is reproduced in the Peters and Dover editions, with an editorial *Allegro* added at the beginning of the song. In the new Mozart edition published by Bärenreiter, *Neue Mozart Ausgabe* (NMA), the opening of the song is marked *Adagio,* with no *Adagio* at m. 54. Changing the opening tempo makes a big difference in the pacing of this song. Similarly, the Peters and Schirmer piano-vocal scores of Haydn's "Nelson" Mass, based on the old Breitkopf & Härtel Haydn complete works (*J. Haydns Werke,* edited by Eusebius Mandyczewski and others), show various articulation marks that were added to the vocal line. These include long and short slurs and staccatos that do not appear in the new Haydn critical edition published by Henle. The Peters and Schirmer scores have also realized some of the ornaments in ways that conflict with Henle's Urtext edition. Finally, a Peters piano-vocal reduction of Mozart's *Sechs Notturni* for two sopranos, bass, and three clarinets is full of crescendos, diminuendos, and **mp** and **mf** markings, which Mozart rarely used. These dynamics are nowhere to be seen in the original sources, according to the NMA.

This does not mean that we should not add dynamic shading, articulation, and phrasing to Mozart and Haydn. We should, but we must be aware of what was originally indicated by the composer and what is an editor's suggestion. The autograph manuscript is the best source for determining the composer's intentions. Early editions can also offer valuable information, but a reliable Urtext edition with the latest critical scholarship will show what today's editors believe to be the most accurate presentation of the score.

## Classical Instruments

### KEYBOARDS

The development of the fortepiano had a profound effect on the kinds of articulation that were central to Classical style. According to Sandra Rosenblum, the fortepiano began to appear in public venues by the 1760s; previously it had been used only for private gatherings. During the 1770s the harpsichord remained the instrument of choice in most situations, but the piano began to be heard in some orchestral and opera performances. By the 1780s, even though the harpsichord was still used, particularly for continuo parts, the piano had become the dominant keyboard instrument. Its more substantial sound and its ability to vary dynamics and articulation inspired composers to write music that took advantage of these innovations. Of course the fortepianos of the late eighteenth century probably more closely resembled the harpsichords of that time than today's concert grand pianos.

While undergoing changes and improvements throughout the period, the early instruments varied from country to country. The technical differences between the early pianos of the English and Viennese schools influenced both the style in which they were played and the kind of music composed for them. English pianos were generally larger and heavier than their Viennese counterparts. Their hammer action produced a more powerful blow to the strings, and the damping mechanism enabled the sound to ring a bit. English instruments also sported larger hammers, wider keys, thicker strings, heavier cases, and more notes on the keyboard. These features produced a louder, fuller, more sustained sound compared with the lighter, clearer, quickly decaying sound of the Viennese pianos, known for their *sprechend* (speechlike) style. Mozart was arguably one of the greatest keyboard virtuosos of his day. His playing of the Viennese fortepiano is described by his contemporaries as brilliant, full of character and grace. Yet Beethoven, a renowned pianist himself, played both Viennese pianos and a Broadwood piano from London and reportedly described Mozart's playing as choppy, with no legato.[6] This anecdote reveals that the variety of the pianos available in the Classical era had an important impact on the taste and style of the time, particularly regarding articulation and legato.

STRINGS

The development of a new violin bow by François Tourte in the 1780s had a comparable impact on string playing. The new bow was heavier, with more hair in a flatter, wider configuration. It was more balanced and could withstand greater tension, allowing the player increased volume and brilliance. It was now possible to sustain a longer line and approach a more legato style of playing. Yet Classical string playing was still closer to the light, articulated style of the Baroque than to our modern conception of a projected, sustained sound. Baroque, transitional, and Tourte bows were all used in the late eighteenth century, and it wasn't until the second decade of the nineteenth century that the full potential of the Tourte bow began to be realized.

Both Jaap Schröder and Robin Stowell believe that some of the relaxed clarity and elasticity of the Baroque string sound was sacrificed with the use of the

Tourte bow. The key to achieving a Classical style is to combine well-articulated gestures, dynamic variety, and a clear, relaxed sound that is "intense but not tense."[7] This seems to be good advice for singers as well: When performing Classical works with modern instruments, you may need to make compromises regarding tone color, volume, and intensity to match the more powerful and sustained instrumental sound. When singing with a fortepiano or with Classical strings, you can use a lighter, more relaxed tone, as well as a less sustained, more articulated sense of phrasing.

## Articulation and Legato

The eighteenth century witnessed a gradual progression along a continuum from detached articulation toward a more legato style. In the Classical era, the Baroque ideal of crisp, detached articulation, which highlighted the differences between heavy and light and made the music speak as if it had text, was still important. In elaborating on Alfred Brendel's remark that a phrase in a Mozart piano sonata was like a vocal line, fortepianist Malcolm Bilson has commented that "in Mozart's time a vocal line meant clear inflection between strong and weak syllables, strong and weak beats, stressed versus unstressed. This is spelled out clearly by Mozart's careful slurring and articulation marks."[8] Dominico Corri's vocal treatise of 1810 reveals an approach to Classical singing based on his studies with Nicola Porpora, the famous teacher of Farinelli and Bernacchi. While Corri acknowledges that the character and inflection of the words is of utmost importance, the advice he gives for singing solfeggio without words offers valuable clues for vocal articulation:

> To give them meaning requires the rise and fall of the voice, which as I have before explained, is, in Songs regulated by the sense of the words; Solfeggio not having the assistance of the words, the following rules may be of use . . .
>
> 1st.  On every note of any duration, use the Messa di Voce.
> 2d.  Every note ought to have, as it were a different degree of light and shade according to its position.
> 3d.  When the passages are, of gradual notes, Slur and join them with nicety; When leaping passages, give a well articulated accent.
> 4th.  On the last note of a passage, always die the Voice, and at each note of the final phrase, end thus $<\,>$ this swell must be done as gently as possible, only as much to accent the sound, and immediately die it away.[9]

As the eighteenth century drew to a close, preference shifted away from detached articulation toward a smoother, more legato flow. This new ideal was inspired by cantabile singing and manifested in the English pianos and Tourte bow. In his *Klavierschule* of 1789, Daniel Gottlob Türk quotes C. P. E. Bach and disagrees with his instruction from 1753 that notes that are neither slurred nor detached should be held for half their notated value. Türk recommends that for notes played in the "usual manner," the finger should be lifted from the key only a little earlier than required by the value of the note. He also suggests using a variety of articulations according to the tempo and meter. Faster, brighter compositions demand a lighter, shorter touch, whereas serious, solemn, or pathetic music demands a heavier, more sustained execution.[10] By the end of the century a number of new keyboard treatises, including one by Muzio Clementi in 1801, recommended legato articulation: "When the composer leaves the Legato and Staccato to the performer's taste; the best rule is, to adhere chiefly to the Legato; reserving the Staccato to give spirit occasionally to certain passages."[11] In the 1804 fourth edition of Leopold Mozart's *Violinschule,* the earlier assumption that non legato was the "usual" manner of playing was revised in favor of a slurred, sustained sound for cantabile passages, "even more imperative in an Adagio than in an Allegro."[12] Neal Zaslaw observes that "this evolution from a more detached style of playing to a more legato one means that in music from the beginning of the period the slurs are the most important marks of articulation whereas in music from the end of the period the dots and strokes indicating detached playing have acquired that role."[13]

We must remember, however, that the "cantabile" legato ideal for music of the late eighteenth century is nowhere near the long, continuous lines associated with music from the late nineteenth or early twentieth centuries. Corri reminds singers to shape phrases by using crescendo and decrescendo (ex. 3.1), similar to the *messa di voce* used on one note. In vocal music, the text and dramatic context set the tone for articulation, and so it usually has fewer articulation markings than instrumental music. But just as eighteenth-century instrumentalists used good singing as a guide for their style, modern singers can also use Classical instrumental style as a guide for their approach to Classical singing.

### Tempo and Rhythm

DANCE FORMS

The traditional court dances of the seventeenth and early eighteenth centuries, though no longer fashionable for dancing, remained well known to composers and musicians in the Classical era. Each dance form had a physical association

# THIRD REQUISITE.

A Phrase in Music is like a sentence in Language, with this difference, that one word will not form a sentence, but one Note can form a Phrase in Music.

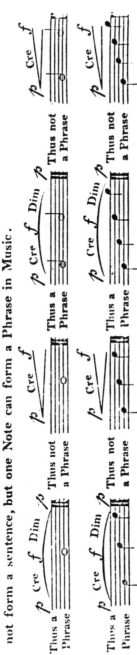

Example 3.1. Corri: from *The Singer's Preceptor* (1810), reproduced in *The Porpora Tradition*, ed. Edward Foreman, Pro Musica Press, 1968, p. 65.

with a character and tempo that carried over into new musical contexts. In the Baroque period each dance had been linked to a particular "affect" that colored the entire piece. In Classical music the expression of dramatic gesture became more flexible within a single composition. Now a composer could express more than one mood or character by juxtaposing contrasting "affects" within one piece, and a particular dance type could be used to express a variety of emotions.[14] For example, a minuet could be slow, creating a noble and stately atmosphere, or faster, with a lighter, more graceful feeling. The sarabande, which had been slow and haughty in the Baroque, was now somewhat faster, almost closer to a slow minuet, yet still serious and grand. The gigue was a fast country dance in 6/8 with a rustic, peasant feeling. (Mozart's *Don Giovanni* offers many examples of dances that form the basis of much of the vocal music.)

METER AND TEMPO TERMS

The central place of dance in musical life made eighteenth-century musicians familiar with the connection between meter and tempo. Specific meters had particular associations with a kind of movement related to a dance. A tempo term in combination with a time signature could also create many different possible degrees of relative speed. *Allegretto* 4/4 is a very different situation from *allegretto* 2/4, which is different from *allegretto alla breve* or 2/2. Similarly, an *andante* in 3/4 would move quite differently from an *andante* in 3/8.[15] According to theorists of the time, the larger the note value described by the denominator of the time signature, the heavier and slower the movement should be; conversely, the lightness and liveliness of the tempo would increase as the bottom number increased. Thus 3/8 would be more lively than 3/4, and 2/2 would move with more weight than 4/4.[16] Beethoven wrestled with the relationship between note values, meter, and tempo as he recomposed his song "Klage," WoO 113. In the second version of the song (ex. 3.2c and d) he added descriptive tempo terms, changed the meter of the *minore* section, and offered these observations:

> That which now follows will be sung still more slowly, *adagio* or, at the most, *andante quasi adagio. Andante* in 2/4 time must be taken faster than the tempo of the song here. As it appears, the latter cannot remain in 2/4 time for the music is too slow for it. It appears best to set them both in C time.
>
> The first [part], in E major, must remain in 2/4 time, otherwise it would be sung too slowly.
>
> In the past, longer note values were always taken more slowly than shorter ones; for example, quarters slower than eighths.

Example 3.2. Beethoven: "Klage," first version WoO 113, a) mm. 1–4; b) mm. 15–17; second version WoO 113, c) mm. 1–4; d) mm. 14–17, *Beethoven Werke* XII/i/180, 182.

The smaller note values determine the tempo; for example sixteenths and thirty-seconds in 2/4 time make the tempo very slow.

Perhaps the contrary is also true.[17]

Tempo terms discussed in treatises by Quantz, C. P. E. Bach, Leopold Mozart, and Türk and in Jean-Jacques Rousseau's 1768 *Dictionnaire de musique* fall into the following basic order from slow to fast:

*largo*—slow
*adagio*—moderately slow
*andante*—going; an easy walking pace between slow and fast
*allegro*—quick, or moderately fast
*presto*—fast[18]

Qualifying adjectives or diminutives can further refine the shade of the tempo. For example, *larghetto* (a little slow) is less slow than *largo*; *più allegro* or *molto allegro* is faster than *allegro*; and *allegretto* (a little fast) falls between *andante* and *allegro*. The qualification of *andante* created much confusion in the late eighteenth century. Some thought *più* or *molto andante* meant "more going" and therefore faster, while others understood it to mean slower. *Andantino* was the most confusing of all, sometimes falling between *larghetto* and *andante* and other times indicating a tempo faster than *andante*. In a letter to Thomson regarding the folk-song arrangements, Beethoven asked for clarification regarding the uncertain nature of *andantino*: "If among the airs that you may send me to be arranged in the future there are Andantinos, please tell me whether Andantino is to be understood as meaning faster or slower than Andante, for this term, like so many in music, is of so indefinite a significance that Andantino sometimes approaches an Allegro and sometimes, on the other hand, is played like Adagio."[19]

Classical tempos must thus be chosen with great subtlety, yet they have a crucial impact on the flow and character of the music. To find the right tempo for a Classical song or aria you must evaluate the general mood of the text and music as well as the intricacy of the ornamentation. You should also take into consideration the rate of harmonic movement, which proceeded more slowly than in Baroque music owing to the increased importance of the four-measure phrase.[20] Keep in mind that early instruments, with their lighter, clearer sound, can sometimes navigate faster tempos than modern instruments.

TEMPO FLEXIBILITY AND RUBATO

"Playing in time" was extremely important to Classical composers. Theorists demanded it in treatises, and Mozart complained bitterly when his students or colleagues did not keep strict time. Yet Mozart himself played with rubato in slower, more lyrical movements, and he described his method in a famous letter to his father on October 24, 1777: "Everyone is amazed that I can always keep strict time. What these people cannot grasp is that in tempo rubato, in an Adagio, the left hand should go on playing in strict time. With them the left hand always follows suit."[21]

Both Türk and Corri explain similar approaches to tempo rubato:

> There is something taken away (stolen) from the duration of a note and for this, another note is given that much more. . . . from this it can be seen that . . . the tempo, or even more, the meter as a whole is not displaced . . . for the bass voice goes its way according to the meter (without displacement), and only the notes of the melody are moved out of place. (Türk)[22]

> It is a detraction of part of the time from one note, and restoring it by increasing the length of another, so that, whilst a singer is, in some measure, singing ad libitum, the orchestra which accompanies him keeps the time firmly and regularly. (Corri)[23]

The notion of "stolen time" goes back to Tosi, who described vocal rubato for pathetic airs in just this way (see chapter 1). Classical instrumentalists continued to be encouraged to listen to distinguished singers as a model for the use of flexible rubato in slow or "cantabile" music. The adagio style allowed for the inclusion of more extemporaneous ornamentation and a flexible tempo for expressive purposes. Allegro arias left less room for added ornaments and hence maintained a stricter tempo. Contemporary accounts describe Beethoven's playing as both rhythmically flexible and strictly in time. He chose to vary his handling of the rhythm and tempo depending on the character of the music. Certainly the notion of flexible tempo for Classical music is not as exaggerated as what we would apply to late Romantic music, but it should be employed to some extent, perhaps more than we might think.

THE METRONOME

Before the metronome came into use around 1812, eighteenth-century musicians may have based certain tempos on the speed of walking or on the ticking of a grandfather clock. Corri recommends that his vocalises and exercises be practiced at an andante pace that can be determined by the pulse of a watch.[24]

In their book *Interpreting Mozart on the Keyboard,* Paul and Eva Badura-Skoda mention another pendulum-based measuring device called the Rhein Zoll, which was used in 1793 by an acquaintance of Mozart's to gauge the tempo for Pamina's aria "Ach, ich fühl's." Converted into a metronome marking, the tempo measured by this device would have been eighth note = 138–48.[25] Given that the aria is indicated as *Andante* 6/8, the combination of tempo term (*Andante* meaning between slow and fast) and meter (6/8 suggesting a more lively movement than 6/4) suggests that it should not move as slowly as it is often sung today. If the tempo measurement from 1793 is at all accurate, it suggests an even faster tempo than might be imagined.

It is well known that Beethoven loved the metronome: "So far as I am concerned I have long thought of giving up the nonsensical designations of Allegro, Andante, Adagio, Presto; Mälzel's metronome gives us the best opportunity to do this."[26] While the metronome markings he assigned to his works leave clear evidence as to his desired tempos, many of which are on the fast side, some can be puzzling and difficult to make work in performance.[27] Johann Nepomuk Hummel, Mozart's student, and Carl Czerny, Beethoven's student, added metronome markings to various works of Haydn, Mozart, and Beethoven, based on their supposed knowledge of the composers' preferred tempos.[28] Both Antonio Salieri, who played continuo for Haydn, and Sigismund Neukomm, one of Haydn's pupils, wrote down metronome markings for the tempos they believed Haydn used when he conducted *The Creation.*[29] It is extremely difficult to evaluate how accurate these early markings are. Even today, composers often misjudge their own music when assigning metronome marks. While most vocal music from the Classical period did not receive metronome markings, it is still worth considering the implications of early metronome markings. The generally fast tempos assigned to instrumental music may well reflect the prevailing eighteenth-century tempo preferences.

RHYTHMIC ALTERATION

As composers included more carefully notated performance instructions in their scores, they became more precise in notating rhythms that had been problematic in Baroque scores, particularly "mixed meters" such as two eighth notes against three or dotted notes against triplets. As the eighteenth century drew to a close, these rhythmic situations were understood to be more literal and less in need of fixing or "alteration." In example 3.3 from Beethoven's "Adelaide," the eighth notes in mm. 7–8 should contrast with the triplets in the accompani-

Example 3.3. Beethoven: "Adelaide," op. 46, mm. 5–10, *Beethoven Werke* XII/i/25.

ment. In m. 9 Beethoven indicates the triplet rhythm in the vocal part that should coordinate with the triplets in the piano part.

At the same time there are instances in the music of both Mozart and Haydn where it is desirable to make rhythmic alterations, particularly concerning overdotting or double dotting (described in chapter 2). Corri mentions that different styles of music, from cantabile to bravura, take slightly different interpretations of dotted figures. In music in the French style, which can be seen in both Haydn and Mozart, overdotting is particularly welcome. For "national airs" of Scottish, Irish, and Welsh character, Corri recommends overdotting and the use of the "Scotch snap" rhythmic figure, in which a dotted note is preceded rather than followed by its complementary shorter note.[30]

### Voice Types and Ranges

The Classical period saw the gradual decline of the castrato voice and the increased use of female sopranos and mezzo-sopranos in opera and concert music. Both Haydn and Mozart wrote music for castrati, but by Beethoven's time castrati were much less popular. Women still did not sing in church (with the exception of nuns in convents), and therefore castrati, adult male falsettists, and boys continued to supply churches and concert choruses with treble voices. Sometimes, as for performances of Haydn's *The Creation,* which was usually produced in a theater and not in a church, female soloists joined the male chorus for the tutti sections.[31] The tenor voice became more popular and was featured in more substantial opera roles. Tenors still blended their chest voice into a falsetto for their high range. Some tenor parts from the period extend lower than would be comfortable for most tenors today and could be considered to fall in the baritone range. The baritone voice was not commonly distinguished as its own category yet, however, and so low tenors navigated these roles using their chest voice for the low range and head voice for the higher notes. The bass voice was featured in comic and buffo opera roles, as well as in concert and oratorio, although not as prominently as the higher voices.

Sopranos, on the other hand, were singing higher and higher, as Mozart described in a letter of March 24, 1770. He was visiting the house of a famous soprano in Parma, and he jotted down her after-dinner vocal feats, which soared to well above high C.[32] Yet Corri warns singers not to push the voice beyond its normal compass. It is possible to extend the range, he says, but it is like the stretching of a piece of leather: it must be done gently and carefully, or the material will break. He recommends transposing music to suit the natural range of the voice, sacrificing the low notes in favor of relaxed high notes.[33] Transposition was still a common practice, so voices with in-between ranges could sing comfortably.

### Mozart on Singers

Mozart complained bitterly when he heard arias that didn't suit their singers. He preferred to become familiar with a particular singer's voice and abilities before he composed, and to "fit the costume to his figure," as his father described.[34] The favorite singer of his early years, with whom he was also in love, was Aloysia Weber. He loved her cantabile singing, which, he wrote, "goes to the heart."[35] This expressive quality impressed him much more than all the runs, roulades, and general fireworks of famous divas singing bravura arias. In a letter of July 30, 1778, Mozart described to Aloysia how he wanted her to work on the concert aria "Ah, lo previdi" that he had sent her: "I advise you to watch the expression marks—to think carefully of the meaning and force of the words—to put yourself in all seriousness into Andromeda's situation and position!—and to imagine that you really are that very person."[36] Of course Mozart did compose his own fireworks for singers, particularly in *The Abduction from the Seraglio*: "I have sacrificed Constanze's aria a little to the flexible throat of Mlle. Cavalieri. . . . I have tried to express her feelings, as far as an Italian bravura aria will allow it."[37] From this and other letters it is clear that he preferred a genuine dramatic expression of simple and honest feelings to empty technical display or to overly sentimental, or false, cloying sweetness.[38]

### Vibrato and Portamento

Mozart describes his taste for vibrato in relation to a bass singer in a letter of June 12, 1778:

> Meisner, as you know, has the bad habit of making his voice tremble at times, turning a note that should be sustained into distinct crotchets, or even quavers—and this I never could endure in him. And really it is a detestable habit and one which is quite the contrary to nature. The human voice trembles naturally—but in its own way—and only to such a degree that the effect is beautiful. Such is the nature of the voice; and people imitate it not only on wind instruments, but on stringed instruments too and even on the klavier. But the moment the proper limit is overstepped, it is no longer beautiful—because it is contrary to nature.[39]

In writings from the Classical period we see more positive remarks concerning vocal vibrato. It was still, however, a much different phenomenon from today's wider, more continuous vibrato. It is difficult to determine from Mozart's remarks above whether he meant that natural "trembling" occurred all the time or only in special circumstances. String treatises recommend a finger vibrato combined with a swell to imitate a singer's *messa di voce* on a sustained sound. Flute players also used both finger vibrato and breath vibrato, mostly on long notes and in slow, tender music, modeled after good singers. So we know that some kind of small vibrato was occasionally used by singers and instrumentalists.

The term portamento received a number of different definitions and usages in Classical period treatises. Primarily a vocal ornament, portamento was also used sparingly by instrumentalists. While it is not what we associate with the late nineteenth-century gesture, Corri calls *portamento di voce* the "perfection of vocal music": "It consists in the swell and dying of the voice, the sliding and blending one note into another with delicacy and expression—and expression comprehends every charm which music can produce; the Portamento di voce may justly be compared to the highest degree of refinement in elegant pronunciation in speaking. Endeavor to attain this high qualification of the Portamento, and I must again repeat, deliver your words with energy and emphasis, articulate them distinctly."[40]

The fact that Corri mentions portamento in association with clear articulation of the text implies that it was used in the service of the words, rather than for vocal show and heightened general expressivity as we would understand it today. Charles Burney, in *The Present State of Music in France and Italy,* described the term as "conduct of the voice: the *portamento* is said to be good, when the voice is neither nasal nor guttural." In describing French singers whom he disliked, he said "the French voice never comes further than from the throat; there is no *voce di petto,* no true *portamento* or direction of the voice."[41] From these remarks it seems that the term in the eighteenth century had more to do with a general kind of placement of the voice, a connection of breath and tone that produced a pleasing flow and helped to make the text clear and inflected, rather than an audible slide from one note to another.

### Recitative

The rules for Classical recitative remain similar to those for recitative in Baroque music. The words are the most important element for determining the rhythm, tempo, and character of the music. According to Corri, recitative "resembles speaking in Musical notes—but mere description cannot fix the exact measure of that inflection of tone necessary to be used, which should be a medium of sound between speaking and singing. . . . No particular degree of Time is marked to Recitative, but is left to the Singer to prolong or shorten notes which he ought to do agreeable to the passion and accent of the words."[42] Mozart heard several melodramas performed in 1778 that delighted him: "there is no singing in it, only recitation, to which the music is like a sort of obbligato accompaniment to a recitative. . . . I think most operatic recitatives should be treated this way—and only sung occasionally, when the words *can be perfectly expressed by the music.*"[43]

Most theorists continued to instruct that recitatives for church, chamber, and theater be delivered differently. According to Corri, church recitatives require a slower, more serious delivery with few if any ornaments. Theater recitatives require a pace appropriate to the dramatic action and need no ornaments except an occasional mordent or short trill. Chamber or concert recitatives could include more ornaments, particularly at fermatas or on final cadences. Hiller (1780) distinguishes between recitatives that are *secco* (dry) and those that are *accompagnato,* or accompanied by instruments or composed in an arioso style. Accompagnato recitatives can be more sung than declaimed and can include more elaborate and expressive ornamentation. As for the accompaniment, according to an item in the Leipzig *Allgemeine Musikalische Zeitung* of 1810, the Baroque practice of shortening the bass notes was considered old-fashioned. From the newspaper's imaginary dialogue between representatives of the "old way" and the "new way," it is clear that "modern" Classical composers notated their works as they intended them to sound, and therefore the bass notes would be sustained for their full value.[44]

APPOGGIATURAS IN RECITATIVE

Singers were still expected to add appoggiaturas within the body of a recitative and at cadences even if they were not written in the score. Standard practice included filling in descending passing notes between thirds and repeating the penultimate note at cadences approached by a falling fourth (see ex. 2.4). In this situation Hiller also allowed jumping down a third to the upper neighbor note.

Much disagreement, however, exists among modern scholars regarding the general treatment of appoggiaturas in words with feminine endings (unstressed final syllables). Will Crutchfield offers evidence from the period to support the ideas that a "blunt ending" (two of the same pitches in a row) would always be undesirable and that any feminine ending, whether in a recitative or an aria, demands an appoggiatura.[45] Frederick Neumann, on the other hand, contends in his *Ornamentation and Improvisation in Mozart* that contemporary treatises indicate that additional appoggiaturas were optional, depending on the situation and the meaning of the words. He suggests that note repetition could convey insistence, determination, anger, or defiance, while an added appoggiatura in such a situation would soften or weaken the dramatic effect.[46] Appoggiaturas from below were much less common than those from above, though one could be used to create a yearning quality or a question. It is also possible to jump to an upper neighbor note to create a falling appoggiatura. For words with masculine endings (stressed final syllables), Neumann recommends an unornamented approach in most cases, and Hiller (1774) advises avoiding monotony by not adding too many appoggiaturas.

Overall, added appoggiaturas in recitatives can help shape the inflection of the text. In deciding where to use them, let the dramatic intent of the words be a guide. In the following lines from the recitative preceding Mozart's concert aria "Bella mia fiamma," K. 528 (ex. 3.4), I would choose not to fill in the third between "Ah" and "tutto" with a C-natural, even though it is possible. I would rather not use an appoggiatura to weaken the strong impact of "tutto," and I would save the passing note C for the word "mio" leading to "furor" because it adds more tension to the sense of "my fury." I would also not add an appoggiatura to the E-natural of "fu*ror*," because of the angry feeling of "fury"; in a different textual and dramatic context, I might want to soften the masculine ending with an F appoggiatura. In contrast, I would add an appoggiatura to the first syllable of "mio" in the next measure, either a G lower neighbor or a B-flat upper neighbor, to add a more anguished, sighing feeling to "my death." (The NMA edition suggests the B-flat.) In the next phrase, "Cerere" could take a C-natural upper neighbor on the first syllable, "Alfeo" could take an F in place of the first E-flat, the first syllable of "sposa" should take a D-natural to fill in the third from the E of "diletta" (the NMA suggests that one as well), and the raised fourth for the cadence is already written into the "addio." Singing all of these appoggiaturas consecutively might be too monotonous, as Hiller warns, so I would probably leave out either the one on "Cerere" or on "Alfeo."

## Ornamentation

As in the Baroque period, ornaments in Classical music fall into two basic categories: essential graces and added improvisation. Throughout the eighteenth century, singers wanted to show off their vocal talents by adding embellishments and cadenzas to the score. In many instances, composers expected and appreciated these personal contributions. Yet singers could just as easily go far beyond the bounds of what composers wanted. Contemporary evidence reveals accounts of both dazzling ornamental display and horrid excess. Treatises of the period advise using taste and good judgment and warn against abuse, yet surviving manuscripts with added ornamentation show virtuosity ranging from the modest to the unimaginable. Styles varied from region to region, with Italian music and singers using the most elaborate and rhythmically flexible ornaments. German works were more restrained and specific, and tended to include more ornamentation composed directly into the music. Christoph Willibald

Example 3.4. Mozart: "Bella mia fiamma," K. 528, mm. 33–37, NMA II/7/iv/40.

Gluck stirred up controversy in France with his harsh critique of operatic practices that put the vocal display of singers above the simple and honest flow of the drama. Singers today must find a way to reconcile these conflicting elements and decide how to incorporate the vocal traditions of the time with the composers' desires.

As in recitative, the choice or execution of a particular ornament should be innately connected to the dramatic sense of the text. In Classical vocal music, embellishments such as appoggiaturas, trills, and turns can be variously indicated with ornament signs, small notes, or regular-sized notes or added to an unadorned line at the discretion of the singer. Often an accompanying instrumental line can suggest either how to execute an indicated vocal ornament or how to add a complementary one. In certain situations it may be desirable to coordinate the two lines exactly. That is not always necessary, however, and it may even suit the dramatic context to have contrast. Piano reductions of orchestral scores often simplify instrumental rhythmic and ornamental notation, so when in doubt, consult a reliable full score.

APPOGGIATURAS IN CONCERTED PIECES

The appoggiatura, the most popular and important of the essential graces, can be indicated either with a small note of varying value or written into the music using a regular-sized note. This ornament was notated inconsistently even in the late eighteenth century. The execution of the appoggiatura can be handled in a number of ways as well. Unlike Baroque appoggiaturas, which are most often stressed and on the beat, Classical appoggiaturas can be variously short and on the beat, short but before the beat, or long and on the beat.

In the accompanying examples from "Adelaide," op. 46, appoggiaturas are notated in several different ways. In m. 13 (ex. 3.5a), Beethoven writes out a short appoggiatura using two regular eighth notes. In mm. 15 and 17, he writes out long appoggiaturas using two regular quarter notes. In m. 19 he writes a small eighth note next to a large quarter note; this could be performed either as two eighth notes to match the articulation of "zittert" in m. 13 or as two quarter notes to match the gestures in mm. 15, 17, and 21. The mid-eighteenth-century treatises comment that an appoggiatura before a rest can take the full value of the note and resolve on the rest, although the Badura-Skodas maintain that Mozart never applied this rule.[47] "Adelaide" also has other interesting elements to consider. The appoggiatura in m. 19 is the first one on a single-syllable word; it is also the first to be approached from below. This may be the reason Beethoven wrote it as a small note instead of with a regular note value. Mm. 105

Example 3.5. Beethoven: "Adelaide," op. 46, a) mm. 12–21; b) mm. 104–105, 145–146; c) mm. 59–61, *Beethoven Werke* XII/i/25–30.

and 146 (ex. 3.5b) show another inconsistency. In the earlier measure Beethoven writes out an appoggiatura as quarter notes. In the later measure the same music is written as a small quarter note before a half note. Here Beethoven indicates the desired execution of the ornament seen elsewhere in the piece. Clues

Example 3.6. Mozart: "Das Veilchen," K. 476, mm. 1–39, manuscript Zweig 56, used by permission of the British Library.

to appoggiatura lengths can also be found in the text. The small sixteenth notes in mm. 59 and 61 (ex. 3.5c) should reflect the "rustling evening breezes" of the words: thus they must be sung fast and light and before the beat as grace notes.

According to Neumann, Mozart varied his notation to indicate different lengths of appoggiaturas: a quarter-note appoggiatura should be a long note; an eighth note could be long or short; and a sixteenth or thirty-second note usually indicates a short note.[48] The Badura-Skodas prefer to distinguish between "stressed" and "unstressed" appoggiaturas in Mozart, rather than long and short, and they counsel that the accentuation of the appoggiatura is more important than its actual length.[49] The harmonic context can also have an important influence on whether the appoggiatura should be stressed or unstressed. If the appoggiatura adds expressive dissonance to a situation, it can be stressed. If the main note is itself a dissonant passing note or upper neighbor (as in ex. 3.5c from "Adelaide"), then the appoggiatura should not distract from the harmonic tension already present.

In the opening of Mozart's "Das Veilchen" (ex. 3.6), the autograph clearly shows eighth-note appoggiaturas. Since they each add a dissonant upper neighbor to their main note, I would sing all of them on the beat and gently stressed, but not too long. Here is a situation where the vocal part and the accompanying line do not have to coordinate exactly. Some modern scholars and editors have latched onto the rule that an appoggiatura before a dotted note gets two-thirds the value of the main note. They would suggest therefore that the appoggiaturas on "*Wiese*" and "*un*bekannt" should last longer than the others: an eighth note, with the resolution only taking a sixteenth. A rule is less important, however, than the specific musical context, and in this situation I would rather inflect the appoggiaturas to convey the dramatic sense of the text: a simple, innocent flower standing unobtrusively in a meadow.[50]

Appoggiaturas can also be added where they are not indicated. As previously mentioned, many blunt endings and masculine endings in concerted pieces can take added appoggiaturas. Appoggiaturas indicated in an accompanying instrumental line may also be added to an unadorned vocal line.

TRILLS AND TURNS

The notation of trills in Classical vocal music is more consistent than other ornaments; they are usually indicated simply as *tr*. That one sign, however, can indicate a number of different trills, all depending upon the situation: prepared or unprepared; long or short; slow or fast; and with a variety of concluding suffixes. The upper-note start, or the prepared trill, was accepted for most Baroque trills and continued to be popular well into the nineteenth century. However, many passages in Classical music demand an unprepared trill with a main-note start. As with appoggiaturas, the variables in the performance of a trill should be determined by the musical and dramatic context. In general, cadential trills, like those in example 3.7, can take an upper-note start.

A main-note start is preferable when the addition of an upper-note appoggiatura would confuse the harmony, melody, or rhythm. In example 3.8a from *The Creation*, the melody includes a passing-note figure, even without the trills. This figure stresses the upper note, creating a sighing quality. The addition of a gentle trill is meant to imitate the soft cooing of the doves. Starting the trill on the note above the upper note would weaken this effect by making the whole figure too busy.

In example 3.8b a main-note start would simplify a complex situation. Melodically, the trill note is already decorated with a lower neighbor. It is also approached from the opposite direction by an instrumental line, which then echoes the vocal line. A main-note start would thus assure the clarity of the melody and the counterpoint within the relatively fast-moving tempo of *Alle-*

Example 3.7. Mozart: a) *Exsultate, jubilate,* K. 165, mm. 62–65, NMA I/3/157;
b) "Domine" from Mass in C Minor, K. 427, mm. 26, 41, NMA I/1/v/46.

a)

b)

Example 3.8. a) Haydn: "On Mighty Pens" from *The Creation,* mm. 68–69, Novello, 1904; b) Mozart: "Domine" from Mass in C Minor, K. 427, mm. 14–15, NMA I/1/v/45.

*gro moderato.* Most modern scholars agree that trills approached melodically by stepwise motion can take a main-note start.[51] Frederick Neumann offers sensible advice: If the trill is taken away and the plain melody can use the addition of some kind of appoggiatura, then the trill can be started with the corresponding type of preparation. If not, then a main-note start is probably advisable.[52] This

Example 3.9. a) Mozart: "Laudamus te" from *Mass in C Minor*, K. 427, mm. 31–34, NMA I/1/v/35; b) Haydn: "With Verdure Clad" from *The Creation*, mm. 7–8, with possible turn executions; c) Haydn: "With Verdure Clad" from *The Creation*, m. 20, Novello, 1904.

test can also be used in deciding whether to use a suffix. Most long trills demand a concluding turn, but it can be omitted from a short trill if it would disturb the melodic flow.

Turns can be indicated with an ornament sign or written out with small notes, which is more common in vocal music. In example 3.9a Mozart adds sixteenth-note appoggiaturas in mm. 32 and 34 of "Laudamus te" from his Mass in C Minor. In the first measure the small notes transform the figure into a written-out turn. In the second measure they indicate a pattern of four equal sixteenth notes. Singers were allowed a certain amount of freedom in the rhythmic execution and placement of a turn to accommodate the needs of drama and diction (see ex. 3.9b). Singers were also allowed more expressive freedom with the placement of a *Schleifer* (slide), which could come on the beat, before the beat, or somewhere in between, depending on the needs of the text (see ex. 3.9c).

IMPROVISATION

Most performers of the late eighteenth century had a much more complete musical education than performers do today. Training in harmony, counterpoint, and composition gave performers the needed skills to prepare or improvise embellishments in a style complementary to the music. The adagio style left room for singers to add trills, turns, appoggiaturas, and diminutions, the smaller note values that fill in a simple melody line without necessarily changing its contour. The allegro or bravura style could also use added appoggiaturas, trills, and diminutions, but within a more active and exciting rhythmic context. Hiller (1780) distinguishes between pulling, dragging ornaments (*gezogene*) for the pathetic style and pushing, thrusting ornaments (*gestossenen*) for the allegro style. He and Mancini (1777) both recommend recomposing passagework in a bravura aria to suite the taste and ability of the singer. They describe what is written in the score as a mere sketch or outline, a point of departure for the imagination of the singer.[53] As the rondo form eclipsed the popularity of the *da capo* aria, the return of the principal melody became an important opportunity for singers to display their ornamental and compositional skills.

The following examples from an aria by Luigi Cherubini with prepared variations by the famous castrato Luigi Marchesi show the difference between adagio and allegro ornamentation, as well as the dazzling array of virtuosic possibilities within each style. Example 3.10 shows a brief excerpt of possible ornamentation for the opening adagio section; example 3.11 shows a number of variations on the first few measures of the rondo theme.[54] Marchesi was greatly admired in his day, even by Burney, who found him "elegant and refined," although he was occasionally criticized for excessive ornamentation in recitatives.

Fermatas also provided a showplace for cadenzas of varying lengths. Corri offers suggested generic cadenzas in every possible key, some with as many as fifty notes of scales, turns, and trills. These would be used at a final cadence or at a pause within an aria, perhaps before the reprise of the rondo theme (see ex. 3.12). Burney harshly condemned the excessive cadenzas of some Italian singers

Example 3.10. Marchesi: Cherubini variations on opening adagio measures, reproduced in Robert Haas, *Aufführungspraxis der Musik: Handbuch der Musikwissenschaft,* Akademische Verlagsgesellschaft Athenaion, 1931, p. 225.

Example 3.11. Marchesi: Cherubini variations on rondo theme, reproduced in Robert Haas, *Aufführungspraxis der Musik: Handbuch der Musikwissenschaft,* Akademische Verlagsgesellschaft Athenaion, 1931, p. 230.

he heard: "This fault is general throughout Rome and Naples, where such a long-winded licentiousness prevails in the cadences of every singer, as it is always tiresome, and often disgusting; even those of great performers need compression . . . A few select notes with a great deal of meaning and expression given to them, is the only expedient that can render a cadence desirable."[55]

NB. The following Cadenzes may be Shortened by omitting the Notes under this Signa ︴ If they are found too long or too difficult.

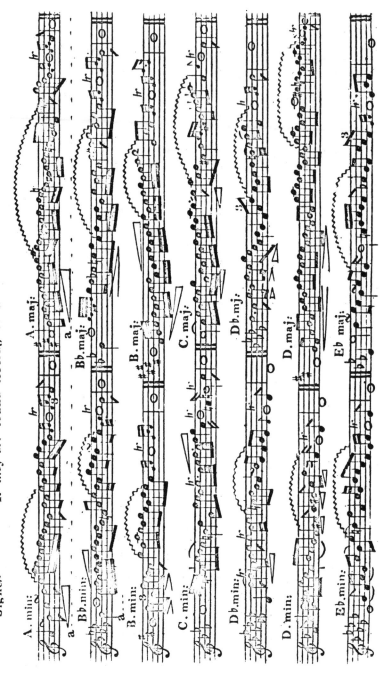

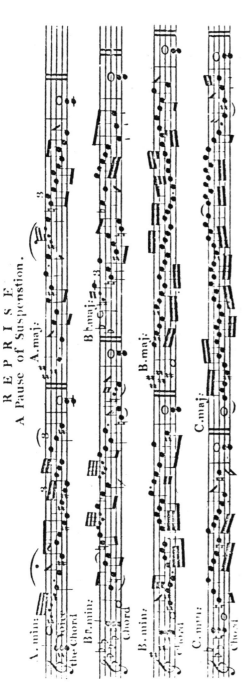

Example 3.12. Corri: cadenza suggestions from *The Singer's Preceptor* (1810), reproduced in *The Porpora Tradition*, ed. Edward Foreman, Pro Musica Press, 1968, pp. 75–76.

Other fascinating examples of period ornamentation can be seen in Will Crutchfield's article "Voices" in the Classical section of *Performance Practice: Music after 1600*. It includes ornamented music by Giuseppe Sarti, Nicola Antonio Zingarelli, Domenico Cimarosa, and Corri, as well as an extensive example of Mozart's suggested ornaments for J. C. Bach's aria "Cara la dolce fiamma." Mozart's ornamented versions of his own arias "Ah se a morir mi chiama," K. 293, from *Lucio Silla* and "Non sò d'onde viene," K. 294, written for Aloysia Weber, can be found in Neumann's *Ornamentation and Improvisation in Mozart*. While the J. C. Bach aria offers an invaluable example of the best kind of adagio ornamentation, it is interesting that Mozart's ornaments for his own music are much more simple and modest than what he added to the J. C. Bach aria. Haydn's ornamentation of his own music can be seen in the tenor aria "Quando mi dona un cenno" from the oratorio *Il ritorno di Tobia* in the Henle complete works critical edition.[56] Ornamentation in surviving manuscript sources for *The Creation* can be found in A. Peter Brown's *Performing Haydn's "The Creation."* Here it is again illuminating to note the differences between the extensive and elaborate Italian-style additions to the *Tobia* aria compared with the conservative ornamentation for *The Creation*.

Many modern scholars concur with some early nineteenth-century critics: examples of early Classical vocal music by second-echelon composers can be considered skeletons to be filled in by the imagination of the performers. However, the mature works of the greatest composers of the Classical era represent a more complete working out of the musical material and hence need much less in the way of ornamental additions. For the music of Haydn, Mozart, and Beethoven, significant disagreement exists among modern performers and scholars over how much and what kind of ornamentation and improvisation to employ.[57] Singers today must study the surviving examples of Classical ornamentation and also become familiar with the general patterns and gestures used throughout the Classical repertoire in order to choose those "few select notes" that Burney preferred.

Important issues revisited in this chapter include articulation, tempo, ornamentation, and the need to choose scores wisely. Many editions of Classical music based on nineteenth-century sources contain mistakes and discrepancies; they also may include too many editorial additions regarding dynamics, tempo, and articulation. Whenever possible, consult an Urtext edition to obtain the most recent scholarly commentary.

Articulation in Classical music was still under the influence of the early eighteenth century's crisp, detached approach. Legato was becoming more popular, but the prime performance objective should be to reveal the differences between light and shade, or stressed and unstressed syllables and musical gestures. If you can work with a Viennese fortepiano or Classical strings, their lighter, clearer texture will help you achieve the delicate contrasts so necessary for Classical music. When choosing tempos for Classical repertoire, keep in mind that the meter and the note values have an important influence on the flow of the music. Dance forms, the text and general character of the work, and various tempo terms and metronome markings should also factor in the choice of tempo. Using subtly flexible rubato is appropriate in slower music, but keep the bass line steady as you gently shape the melody line.

Classical music demands significant but well-chosen ornamentation. You must know how to execute small graces written into the music as well as how to add appoggiaturas, trills, and turns in recitatives and other appropriate places. You can also improvise diminutions and cadenzas. As with Baroque ornamentation, you should study as many examples from period sources as you can and then aim to prepare your own variations in the same style.

# Chapter 4 Italian Bel Canto

This chapter discusses the Italian vocal style of the early nineteenth century, including music by Rossini, Bellini, and Donizetti. This repertoire is commonly called bel canto, a term with a tangled web of meanings and associations. Literally, it means "beautiful singing," which is probably how it was used in seventeenth- and eighteenth-century vocal treatises. In the mid-nineteenth century the term took on a larger significance. The 1838 publication of a collection of songs by Nicola Vaccai entitled *Dodici ariette per camera per l'insegnamento del bel canto italiano* may have been the first time the term was seen in print in this particular usage.[1] Later in the nineteenth century, as part of the wave of nationalism that swept through Europe, "bel canto" was used to contrast the Italian vocal approach with the German declamatory style of the Wagnerians. Ferdinand Sieber's collection of eighteenth- and nineteenth-century songs entitled *Il bel canto* (Berlin, 1887) was offered as an antidote to "offensive shrieking of dramatic singing" in the German style.[2] In dictionaries after 1900 the term often describes the florid vocal style of the eighteenth-century Italian Baroque, epitomized in the art of the castrati. German musicologists of the early twentieth century extended the definition to include seventeenth-century Italian vocal repertoire and style as well.

Some writers and voice teachers insist that bel canto is a vocal technique; others believe it to be a conceptual approach characterized by smooth, flowing melodies. Still others say it describes a general approach to singing that culminated in the florid style of Rossini. In a conversation from 1858, Rossini himself expressed his requirements for a bel canto singer as having a naturally beautiful voice, blended registers and an even tone from the low to the high range, diligent training resulting in effortless delivery of highly florid music, and a command of style not taught but rather learned from listening to the best Italian singers. It is not clear from the context whether he was using the phrase in its literal or more general meaning, but he did regret that the tradition was already dying out by the middle of the nineteenth century.[3]

The early nineteenth century saw the continued growth of a middle-class audience hungry for diversions and entertainments of all kinds, including music. Public concerts increasingly required larger halls, which in turn required louder orchestras and soloists. The greater demand for performers resulted in the expansion of the conservatory system, which now provided more thorough and systematic instruction to both instrumentalists and singers. Choral societies flourished as more people, including women, were invited to sing in choruses not affiliated with churches or choir schools. The public eagerly followed the latest new symphonies, concertos, operas, and star performers, and wanted to be able to play their favorite melodies at home. Private concerts took place in fashionable households, including music making by amateurs and appearances by celebrities. Virtuoso musicians such as violinist Niccolò Paganini and pianist Franz Liszt also took to the road, performing across Europe.

As the opera industry grew, practices that had begun in the seventeenth century gained momentum and popularity. New Italian operas were repeated in different cities as word of their success spread and audiences demanded their own productions of the latest hits. More operas were thus being regularly performed by singers other than those for whom they were originally written. It had been common in the eighteenth century for singers and composers to make changes and substitutions in an opera production, and in the early nineteenth century composers continued to help fashion changes and adaptations for different singers and new productions. Increasingly, however, the composer, who typically was paid far less than the prima donna, was not involved in productions following the premiere or had little control over the whims of star singers.

This book focuses primarily on vocal repertoire outside the realm of opera. In the case of the early nineteenth-century bel canto period, however, the definitive technical and stylistic decisions regarding new works were made by opera singers, collaborating with composers. While the musical examples for this chapter are chosen mostly from the nonoperatic repertoire, we must consider the early nineteenth-century opera tradition to understand the singing style of the period.

### Scores and Editions

Because composers now had less to do with the performances of their works, they began to mark their scores more carefully, aiming to ensure a reasonable performance without their presence. Italian composers were a bit more casual about this need than their more exacting German neighbors. As opera productions took to the road, publishers became increasingly involved in the preservation of the composer's wishes by producing carefully printed sets of orchestra parts that were rented to local opera companies. The wide availability of piano-vocal scores, however, enabled the more unscrupulous to reorchestrate the music and produce operas while avoiding the rental fees for the published parts. Donizetti complained bitterly to his publisher Giulio Ricordi (founder of the foremost publishing house of Italian music) about these kinds of abuses. By 1840, copyright laws prevented such piracy, and the publishers kept track of which operas were being performed where and by what singers.

Publishers also issued much new music for home use by amateurs. Since the only way for most concertgoers and opera lovers to hear their favorite music again was to play it themselves on their pianos at home, publishers, with the help of composers, prepared editions of popular arias, sometimes with the ornaments of famous singers included. Arrangements of well-known orchestral pieces for piano, piano duet, or chamber ensemble were also popular. The bel canto composers also wrote songs and miniature versions of arias for performance in the home.

In general, first editions of songs or piano reductions of opera scores from this period are reasonably reliable expressions of the composers' wishes. Many modern piano-vocal scores of Bellini and Donizetti operas are essentially reprints of early- or mid-nineteenth-century publications. Facsimiles of various opera score manuscripts, with fascinating editorial commentary by Philip Gossett and others, are available in some libraries. Some scholarly work has been done on Donizetti, and a critical edition of Bellini's works is in preparation but not yet available. Ricordi's modern editions of Bellini's *Composizione da camera* (chamber songs) are usually based on their own previous or original editions, either as exact reprints or lightly edited. A semicritical edition of Bellini songs, edited by Francesco Cesari, was published in Milan in 2000. Ricordi is in the process of publishing new critical editions of Rossini's works, edited by Philip Gossett, Bruno Cagli, and Alberto Zedda. Many of the Rossini operas have been issued, and some piano-vocal reductions are now available; many include appendixes with extra variants or cadenzas; the volumes of songs have not yet been published.

Thus, for early nineteenth-century Italian bel canto repertoire you don't have to be as careful in choosing a score as for earlier repertoire. However, the more specific information you can find at the beginning of a score about its sources, the better.

## Articulation and Phrasing

In the early nineteenth century, legato style gained favor over the usual detached articulation of the eighteenth century, particularly in Italian vocal music. If composers wanted a detached articulation they now asked for it by marking the score with various accentuation marks. These could include dots, strokes, dashes, and accents for differing degrees of stress, separation, or staccato. Composers also used a wide variety of dynamic accents including *sfz, sfp, rf, sf, f,* or *ff* to highlight variations in articulation.[4] In vocal music the text continued to be the main inspiration for articulation, and by including various accentuation marks in their instrumental works, composers may have been encouraging instrumentalists to shape their lines as if they had words. As mentioned in previous chapters, many instrumental treatises advised players to listen to good singing for examples of expressive articulation. The violinist Charles de Bériot, husband of the famous singer Maria Malibran, discusses the importance of emulating good singing and expressive pronunciation in his 1858 *Méthode de violon*:

> We cannot repeat too often that the performer will not be perfect until he can reproduce the accents of song in their most delicate forms. . . . It is then of the highest importance for the singer to articulate clearly the words which he undertakes to interpret. . . . It is well understood that the degree of intensity of this pronunciation should be in harmony with the spirit of the piece. . . . These are the varied and diverse shades of expression which the violinist should render, giving to his bow a soft pronunciation for calm and serene music, and employing it with graduated force in passionate music. This accentuation gives to the instrument the prestige of words: we say that the violin speaks in the hands of the master.[5]

Vocal method books of the time, including, among many others, those of Gesualdo Lanza (1809), Domenico Corri (1810), Giacomo Gotifredo Ferrari (1818), and Isaac Nathan (1823) stress the importance of communicating the text by using appropriately placed breaths, phrasing, and expression to complement the dramatic meaning of the words.[6]

The most famous discussion of vocal technique and style from the period (and probably the most widely available in libraries today) is the younger Manuel García's *Traité complet de l'art du chant*. Written in 1841 and revised in 1847, 1854, and 1872, it was translated into English as *Hints on Singing* in 1894.[7] The García family had an extraordinary influence on opera and singing in the nineteenth century. García's father was the famous tenor Manuel del Popolo Vicente Rodríguez García, the first Almaviva in Rossini's *The Barber of Seville*. In addition to singing florid tenor roles, García the elder was also famous for his portrayal of Mozart's *Don Giovanni*, which he sang in transposition. As a composer, performer, and impresario, he brought his family of singers to New York in 1825, introducing Italian opera to American audiences by producing operas of his own as well as works by Rossini and others. The company included his wife as well as his son Manuel and his daughter Maria. Both of his daughters, Maria Malibran and Pauline Viardot, later became famous divas.

While Manuel the younger was not as successful onstage as his father or his sisters, he went on to become one of the most important voice teachers of his day. His treatise, though written years later, captures the approach and style he learned from his father in the first decades of the century. It is divided into two parts: the first deals with proper production of tone and vocalization of vowels, while the second begins with a detailed discussion of using phrasing and articulation to communicate the meaning of the text, which García says is of the greatest importance. He stresses the correct pronunciation of consonants and the appropriate stress of syllables with regard to grammatical position and spoken inflection. One of García's students, the noted English baritone Charles Santly, remarked that while it may seem easier to sing in Italian than in English, the proper pronunciation of the Italian language takes much care and attention. Santly stressed to his own students "the necessity for refinement, delicacy, and finish in the execution of all detail, whether of music or language; attention to these distinguishes the artist from the artisan."[8] García includes many examples of passages requiring noble, pathetic, impassioned, and buffo effects from operas by Rossini, Bellini, Meyerbeer, Mozart, and others, with detailed instructions on the rhythmic placement of consonants in order to achieve the desired dramatic results.[9]

Even more interesting is the discussion of phrasing and breathing that follows. García presents two kinds of breaths: full and half. A full breath would take enough time for a deep intake of air, while a half breath would be more like a short catch breath. He recommends changing the written rhythm of a phrase, if necessary, to fit in an appropriate place to breathe. A particularly fascinating example is his recommendation for Zerlina's aria "Batti, batti" from *Don Giovanni* (ex. 4.1). In the phrase "starò qui come agnellina," he suggests changing the rhythm of the dotted eighth and sixteenth notes in the measure of "qui come angnel-" to an eighth note followed by a sixteenth note and a sixteenth rest for "-lina" in the next measure, in order to catch a quick half breath before the next phrase. In some scores of this aria, particularly in aria collections, the rhythm is printed as dotted in the first measure followed by two even eighth notes in the second measure. In 1789 Mozart wrote two dotted rhythms, but what we see in some modern editions is García's suggested alteration from 1841. García's influence was so strong that his recommendations became part of the aria's performance tradition and made their way into published scores.

In the early nineteenth century, singers considered the score a flexible starting place, tailoring the music to fit their particular needs and abilities. For example, García suggests changing the underlay of syllables, if necessary, to facilitate breathing and phrasing or to correct a composer's poor text setting. He advises against breathing in the middle of a word unless absolutely necessary, and he recommends that any changes made to accommodate breathing be as unobtrusive as possible. As well as adding rests when the composer did not indicate them, García suggests places to sing through written rests in order to connect phrases for dramatic effect. He also discusses altering triplets or dotted figures to fit the character of an aria. For majestic or martial music, overdotting or double dotting may be called for, while for more gentle sentiments, softening a dotted figure into a triplet can add expression. For passages of coloratura García suggests emphasizing or accenting the first note in a group in order to shape the phrase and avoid monotony. He also recommends giving dissonant notes slightly more emphasis, and he shows how and where to use the breath to add expressive sighs and sobs (a device most modern singers avoid). Many annotated examples from Handel, Mozart, and early nineteenth-century opera punctuate his discussion. García's eighteenth-century musical examples offer a fascinating glimpse at a nineteenth-century perspective on Classical style, while his early nineteenth-century examples give a definitive view of singing style at the time. For singers working on early nineteenth-century Italian opera repertoire, I strongly recommend reading and studying the entire treatise.

Example 4.1. García: rhythmic alterations for Mozart's "Batti, batti" from *Don Giovanni* in *A Complete Treatise on the Art of Singing: Part Two,* Da Capo Press, 1975, p. 64.

### Tempo, Rhythmic Flexibility, and Rubato

Just as the flow of rhythm became more flexible in the early nineteenth century, so did the flow of tempo and the use of rubato. Since traditional court dances now held a much less prominent place in social life, they had less influence on the shape of music than in the Classical era. The combination of meter and prevailing rhythm, which used to give a strong indication of the appropriate tempo and character of a work, no longer had as important an impact. In addition, by the end of the eighteenth century a single work often contained a number of different thematic elements, each with its own character or mood and each demanding a slightly different tempo. Nineteenth-century composers started using more qualified and descriptive tempo terms such as *Allegro agitato, Larghetto espressivo,* and *Andante sostenuto,* along with terms such as andantino and cantabile to describe the tempo they wanted.

Unfortunately, these vague terms did not necessarily clarify the distinctions among subtly different tempos. Clive Brown notes that Rossini, in his Paris operas, used a variety of slow tempo terms without any specific hierarchy of slowness. Brown also notes that in many situations Rossini seems to have indicated a 4/4 or *alla breve* meter without any obvious reason. Sometimes a piece marked 4/4 feels decidedly "in 2," while another piece marked *alla breve* feels "in 4."[10] Without an accompanying metronome marking, it is sometimes difficult to determine precisely what a composer meant by a certain tempo marking. Even a surviving metronome marking, while supplying a reference point or starting place, can be misleading. The character and flow of the music must provide the clues, unless one is thoroughly familiar with a particular composer's tempo preferences.

In vocal music of this period, the text often provides answers to questions of tempo. In the early nineteenth century, the singer had more license to surge ahead if the text became excited or impassioned, or to hold the tempo back a bit if the dramatic situation became sad or tender. It was common for a crescendo to be accompanied by an accelerando, just as a diminuendo would accompany a rallentando. García remarked that "the works of Donizetti and Bellini contain a great number of passages which, without bearing the sign of the rallentando or accelerando, yet require their use."[11] Often singers might do exactly the opposite of what the notation suggests. Charles Rosen states in *The Romantic Generation* that "the sudden increase of speed at the end of the phrase would have been executed by Rossini singers with a slight expressive slowing down."[12] This kind of tempo flexibility required the accompanist or orchestra to adjust tempo along with the soloist, whether it be for an entire section or just a measure or two. Such coordination would be even easier to accomplish with a piano accompaniment in a chamber setting.

Of course the amount of rhythmic flexibility employed depended upon the context of the music and the choices made by a particular singer. Certainly the famous singers of the time had different strengths and abilities when it came to flexibility and agility. The renowned Giuditta Pasta, for whom Bellini and Donizetti both wrote important roles (including Amina, Norma, and Anna Bolena), was said to have excelled in unadorned cantabile singing. Contemporary accounts report that her voice was not as flexible or fast as those of some of her rivals. In contrast, Isabella Colbran, who eventually married Rossini and most probably influenced his vocal writing, is said to have had more difficulty sustaining a steady tone or singing in tune in slow, simple passages, yet she excelled at fast, brilliant fioritura.

Just as the amount of flexibility varied from singer to singer, it also varied from composer to composer. García states that the music of Haydn, Mozart, Cimarosa, and Rossini demands a complete exactness in the rhythmic movement; any changes one might make in the values of the notes should not interfere with the steady movement of the measure.[13] While Rossini's music may demand more precision and exactitude than the music of Bellini and Donizetti, there is no question that the flow of rhythm within measures and phrases was becoming more flexible for both solo instrumentalists and singers.

The other kind of rhythmic flexibility was tempo rubato. Here the voice or solo instrument goes out of phase with the accompaniment, which continues in a steady flow as the soloist steals or borrows time, only to return it later in the measure or phrase. This practice, introduced as *sprezzatura* in the seventeenth century, had been used throughout the eighteenth century. The agogic accent, which falls into the realm of rubato, was a particularly important expressive device throughout the nineteenth century. If a certain note merits special accentuation for textual or general expressive reasons, the soloist may stress and hold it slightly longer than notated. The stolen time for the agogic accent must be returned, however, and the general flow of the music left undisturbed. García offers many operatic examples in which the rhythm can be expressively altered using rubato and agogic accents. He encourages the use of rhythmic alteration and flexibility to suit a wide variety of situations, and he sternly admonishes against performances that are metronomic and stiff. Many nineteenth-century tutors encouraged singers to be expressive by varying the rhythm within the measure, the flow of phrases across several measures, and the tempos of larger sections within an entire song or aria.

A singer's taste and abilities determined the degree to which he or she employed these devices. As we will see with portamento, vibrato, and ornamentation, tutors recommended using caution and moderation with regard to tempo modification. The use of rubato by a sensitive musician should result in an almost imperceptible flexibility throughout a performance. Contemporary accounts, however, indicate that many singers and instrumentalists used flexible rhythm and tempo to a great degree, often beyond what some now would consider good taste.

### Voice Types

A singer in his youth, Rossini considered the castrato voice his ideal, both for its virtuosic and expressive capabilities. He wrote one role in an early opera, *Aureliano in Palmira* (1813), for the last castrato who appeared on the operatic stage, Giovanni Battista Velluti. The final operatic role written for Velluti was in Meyerbeer's *Il crociato in Egitto* (1824). By then the public had lost interest in the castrato voice, particularly in London, where Velluti was seen as a curiosity at best and a disgusting freak at worst.[14] Opera composers turned to the heroic contralto voice as the closest replacement for the primo uomo castrato. Some roles, including several for which Giuditta Pasta was famous, required the female lead to be in male dress, thus putting a woman in what would have been the castrato's part. Both Pasta and Malibran were said to sound male in their lower registers and female in their higher registers, thus appealing to Italian opera audiences' love of sexual ambiguity. Rossini used this low female voice type for comic heroines such as Rosina in *The Barber of Seville* and Angelina in *La Cenerentola*. Both Pasta and Malibran sang soprano roles as well.

The tenor voice gained full acceptance in the roles of the young hero or lover and was also used in character parts. Rossini's *Otello* includes three demanding tenor parts. Most tenors still blended into their head register above $g'$. Adolphe Nourrit, who premiered numerous roles written for him by Rossini, Meyerbeer, and others, sang the many high Cs in Rossini's *Guillaume Tell* in his head voice. He reigned at the Paris Opéra from 1826 to 1837, when his rival, Gilbert-Louis Duprez, made his debut as Arnold in *Guillaume Tell*. Duprez caused a sensation, assuring his success in Paris and his place in tenor history by singing the famous high Cs in full chest voice. This was too much for poor Nourrit, who withdrew from the stage and later committed suicide. Rossini, however, much preferred his singing to Duprez's. "That tone," Rossini said, referring to the chest-voice high C, "rarely falls agreeably upon the ear. Nourrit sang it in head voice, and that is how it should be sung. [Duprez's note sounds] like the squawk of a capon whose throat is being cut."[15]

The lowest male voices still largely played buffo characters or wise old teachers and fathers. Their parts tended to have more robust singing and fewer passages of ornate coloratura. Antonio Tamburini's vocal gifts, however, led Bellini and Donizetti to compose a new kind of baritone role, making use of a higher tessitura and longer, more legato lines. The baritone Giorgio Ronconi also inspired Donizetti to write roles that took advantage of his superior acting skills. The collaborative efforts of these singers and composers paved the way for the dramatic baritone roles later seen in Verdi's operas.

When writing a new opera, Bellini is said to have worried more about the contracted singers than the libretto. Despite the celebrity of Rossini, Bellini, Donizetti, and other successful composers, singers continued to transpose and substitute numbers to suite their taste and comfort. They also used an approach called *puntatura,* whereby they would keep the music in its original key but readjust certain pitches to fit their ranges. This could involve lowering extremely high notes or, more commonly, moving particularly low notes higher.

Yet starting in the 1840s, the young Verdi began to place ever more importance on the dramatic and musical flow of the entire opera, insisting on making all such changes himself rather than leaving them to the discretion of the singers.

### Technique

In *Bel Canto in Its Golden Age,* Philip Duey observes that the principles of good singing remained remarkably consistent throughout the many treatises from Caccini to García. Writers and teachers since the seventeenth century have stressed natural methods and the cultivation of natural abilities, and they have even reproduced some of the same phrases to describe desirable qualities in a singer.[16] From the early seventeenth century to the time of Rossini, the musical goals for singers were a sweet, pure tone, blended registers, command of the *messa di voce,* a facility for executing florid ornaments, and an ability to convey the emotions of a text.

Writers in the early nineteenth century tried to explain how to achieve these goals in more concrete terms. Isaac Nathan discusses the transition from the middle register to the high voice and distinguishes between the falsetto and "feigned" voice in the upper range. The falsetto, he reports, is produced by the aperture of the mouth "in the small cell or cavity above the arch of the mouth, called the internal nose." The feigned voice is formed "at the back part of the head and throat just above the glottis where the uvula is situated."[17] He warns against carrying the chest voice up too high. Instead the singer should strengthen the higher tones using a *messa di voce* in the feigned voice before joining it to the chest voice.

By contrast, writers described how Pasta could use different registers of her voice in different ranges. For example, she could carry her chest voice up to g″ above the staff but also use her head tones for pitches in her middle range.[18] García the elder taught Malibran how to develop this ability so that she could reportedly sing any note except those at the extremes of her vocal range in either chest, middle, or head register. She used this capacity to great dramatic effect.[19] Most writers from this period and earlier urged singers not to force their voices in either volume or compass. While Malibran was famous for her variety of tone colors and dramatic flair, she rarely chose to make a sound that was not beautiful.

After experiencing severe vocal trouble and leaving the stage, García the younger studied the anatomy of the vocal organ while working in an army hospital. He presented his findings to the French Academy of Sciences in 1840 as *Mémoire sur la voix humaine.* His continued interest in the physiology of the larynx led to his development of the laryngoscope in 1854. He incorporated his findings into the various versions of his *Traité complet de l'art du chant* and discussed the position of the larynx in relation to the *timbres clairs et sombres* (clear and dark tones), but he continued to place great importance on blending registers and the development of beautiful tone. He also presented over 200 annotated exercises on various scale patterns for the development of agility. García instructed that these scales and roulades should be performed legato in most cases, with each pitch "perfectly connected and distinct."[20] He expected his students to be able to execute each exercise on all five Italian vowels at the tempo of quarter note = 120: a daunting challenge indeed.

Another important vocal pedagogue of this time was Nicola Vaccai. Frustrated by his lack of fame as an opera composer, Vaccai enjoyed great success as a voice teacher to members of society. As an alternative to the endless hours of tedious scales required of professional singers and students, he composed short exercises with texts by Pietro Antonio Metastasio, the most important Italian librettist of the eighteenth century. Through this *Metodo pratico di canto italiano per camera* of 1833 (the *camera* indicating salon singing as opposed to opera singing), his amateur students learned all the fundamentals of technique and ornamentation while singing charming little songs.

Rossini, like many composers before him, wrote a series of vocalizzi and solfeggi for the more professionally minded student. His vocalises are exercises in agility to be sung on one vowel, usually "ah." The solfeggi are wordless melodies to be sung on the sol-fa or solfège syllables. Rossini believed that these exercises were critical for developing and maintaining flexibility and should be practiced every morning: first softly and slowly, the second time softly and faster, and finally full voice and very fast.[21] He composed a mere eighteen vocalises, which would probably take about thirty minutes to complete as he instructed. According to García, this kind of exercise should be followed by a period of rest; he cautioned his students not to practice for more than a half hour at a time. If singers today want to develop the vocal suppleness and flexibility necessary for this repertoire, thirty minutes each morning is a worthwhile investment.

## Vibrato

Vibrato in this period was still much more restrained than what we are used to today. The terminology used to describe it also remained confusing and difficult for us to interpret. A pure, steady tone was the ideal, and Nathan suggests that "any unsteadiness or tremor of voice is to be remedied by taking the note softer; a contrary course only serving to increase and confirm the defect."[22] This comment probably doesn't mean to sing with a tight, straight tone but rather with less of the muscular pressure that creates the kind of vibrato commonly heard today. In *A Complete Dictionary of Music* (1806) and the subsequent *A Musical Manual or Technical Directory* (1828) by Thomas Busby, vibrato is defined as "A term used in the Italian opera, to signify that at the note, or passage, to which it refers, the voice is to be thrown out, in a bold, heroic style."[23] This definition suggests that vibrato was used as a special effect only in certain dramatic circumstances. García calls this expressive device the tremolo and discusses its use under the large heading of "Passions and Sentiments," in which he also discusses the use of sobs, sighs, and laughs:

> The tremolo should be used only to portray the feelings which, in real life, move us profoundly; the anguish of seeing someone who is dear to us in imminent danger, the tears which certain movements of anger or of vengeance draw from us etc. Even in those circumstances, the use of it should be regulated with taste and moderation [*mesure*]; as soon as one exaggerates the expression or the length of it, it becomes tiresome and awkward. Outside of the special cases which we have just indicated, it is necessary to guard against altering in any way the security of the sound, for the repeated use of the tremolo makes the voice tremulous [*chevrotante*]. The artist who has contracted this intolerable fault becomes incapable of phrasing any kind of sustained song. It is thus that some beautiful voices have been lost to the art.[24]

This discussion is accompanied by many operatic examples in both declamatory passages and in combination with portamento in both recitatives and concerted numbers. García indicates use of the tremolo by a wavy line; this marking can occasionally be found in scores. At times Donizetti and others wrote *vibrato* as a special instruction. An accent mark could also indicate a slight vibrato more in keeping with Busby's definition. At an earlier point in his treatise, García discusses other expressive effects that he calls "echo notes" and "repeated notes." These involve a controlled regular pulsation of the voice on one pitch: "One will carefully avoid aspirating the different articulations of the same tone, or performing them by a trembling or quivering of the voice."[25] It is a delicate, hardly noticeable effect that can be used on long notes and is suitable only for high, light female voices. Whether the vibrato used is the natural trembling of the voice that Mozart described or a special gesture used for emotional and dramatic effect, it should be hardly noticeable and should not alter the pitch.

To gain an idea of the small, controlled vibrato fashionable in the late nineteenth century, we can listen to early twentieth-century recordings. Soprano

Adelina Patti, who had an unusually long performing career from the 1860s until 1914, must have carried with her some of the style she heard growing up in
the 1850s. Her recordings from 1905, and many by other turn-of-the-century
singers, offer invaluable examples of the use of vibrato, tempo flexibility, rubato, portamento, and ornamentation.[26]

### Portamento

Many early nineteenth-century writers distinguish between legato and portamento. Legato is the smooth connection of one note to another without inter-
rupting the sound, while portamento connects two distant notes by gliding
lightly and smoothly from one to the other. Different writers give varying instructions on whether the intermediary notes should be clearly heard or hardly
noticeable.[27] In his *Practical Method of Italian Singing*, Vaccai offers clear advice on two kinds of portamenti:

> By carrying the voice from one note to another, it is not meant that you should drag
> or drawl the voice through all the intermediate intervals, an abuse that is frequently
> committed—but it means, to *unite* perfectly, the one note with the other. When
> once the Pupil understands thoroughly how to unite the Syllables, as pointed out in
> the first Lesson, he will more easily learn the manner of carrying the voice as here in-
> tended: of this however, as before observed, nothing but the voice of an able Master
> can give a perfectly clear notion. There are two ways of carrying the voice. The first
> is, by *anticipating* as it were almost insensibly, with the *vowel* of the preceding Sylla-
> ble, the note you are about to take as shown in the first example [ex. 4.2a]. In Phrases
> requiring much grace and expression, it produces a very good effect; the abuse of it
> however, is to be carefully avoided, as it leads to Mannerism and Monotony.
>
> The other method, which is less in use, is by deferring, or *postponing* as it were al-
> most insensibly the note you are going to take, and pronouncing the Syllable that be-
> longs to it, with the note you are leaving [ex. 4.2b].[28]

García confirms that the first method, the "anticipation grace," had gained
favor in the nineteenth century and that the second method, the "leaping
grace," seen frequently in Corri's *A Select Collection of the Most Admired Songs,
Duetts, &c.* (1782), was more fashionable in the eighteenth century. García
writes about portamento using the French term *port de voix*, which no longer
retained its Baroque meaning of appoggiatura from below. In contrast to Vaccai, he recommends a more audible slide between pitches, both distant and
close together. He advises that the character of the words and music should determine the quality of the portamento: full and rapid for vigorous sentiments,
slower and more gentle for tender and gracious movements.[29] He also gives ex-

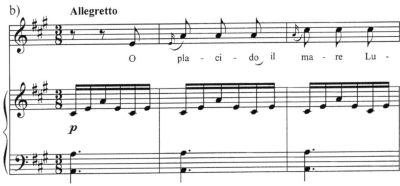

Example 4.2. Vaccai: *Practical Method of Italian Singing,* lesson XIII, "Portamento," a) anticipating, p. 30, b) postponing, p. 33. The modern Schirmer edition, based on the London 1834 edition, has remained in print since 1894.

amples where a singer can breathe between the note of the portamento that anticipates the main note, and the main note itself (exs. 4.3a and b).

Slurs marked in vocal music could indicate either that a vowel should continue for more than one pitch or that a legato articulation is required. Occasionally portamento was marked specifically in scores, but a slur mark could also indicate portamento, especially if the slur connects notes with two different syllables. In the Donizetti song excerpted in example 4.3c, the *portando* is indicated in the score (either by Donizetti or an editor). (In a similar passage from *La regata veneziana,* shown in example 4.3d, Rossini also marks *portando* in the score but has written the gesture out in regular-sized notes.) If you want to breathe before "Ti giuro amore," carry the C up to the F with a crescendo, sing the F on the "o" syllable of "desio," then breathe and reattack the F on "Ti" as a *subito piano.* The portamento here can also be performed the same way without a breath between "desio" and "Ti." The change in dynamic level and accompaniment texture at "Ti giuro amore" implies a new dramatic feeling for that section of text; perhaps some tempo flexibility or rubato could also be used here to good effect.

Contemporary accounts reveal terrible abuses of portamento, sometimes describing Italian singers sounding like meowing cats. These sorts of complaints only got worse as the nineteenth century progressed. Singing treatises had of course been discussing portamento in its various guises since the seventeenth century: Caccini's *strascino* and *cercar della nota* (see chapter 1) developed into Corri's portamento and García's *port de voix.* Early twentieth-century recordings clearly show the use of this technique, which took on the derogatory connotations of crooning and swooping later in the twentieth century. Both Ellen Harris and Will Crutchfield, in their "Portamento" articles in *The New Grove Dictionary of Music and Musicians* (1980) and *The New Grove Dictionary of Opera,* point out that singers specializing in early music have not incorporated this element of voice production into their style. Just as we may be reluctant to use García's sobs and sighs, singers today may feel uncomfortable adding portamento to the "pure" style of singing that became fashionable by the late twentieth century. Certainly combining portamento with today's fuller and more muscular vocal sound and continuous vibrato would produce a very different effect from that of most of the singers we hear in early twentieth-century recordings. Clive Brown has tried to notate the use of portamento heard in Patti's recordings.[30] Once the gesture is notated, however, it seems to indicate something less subtle than what we hear on the recordings. Vaccai's advice re-

Example 4.3. Examples of portamento. a) and b) García: *A Complete Treatise on the Art of Singing: Part Two*, Da Capo Press, 1975, p. 20, passages from Rossini's *La gazza ladra* and *Sigismondo*; c) Donizetti: "Eterno amore e fè" from *Collezione di canzonette* (undated), mm. 37–41, reprinted in *Composizioni da camera*, Ricordi, 1961; d) Rossini: "Anzoleta avanti la regata," mm. 16–18, from *La regata veneziana* (1835), Ricordi, 1967.

mains true: this is an art "which nothing but the voice of a skillful Master can communicate perfectly to the learner."[31]

## Ornamentation

Continuing the trend of the late eighteenth century, composers in the early nineteenth century wrote more ornamentation into their scores. Treatises of the time continued to advise the use of good taste and moderation, yet contemporary accounts describe performances so highly ornamented that they rendered the music unrecognizable. According to a famous anecdote, the great castrato Velluti was said to have added so much embellishment to *Aureliano in Palmira* that Rossini couldn't recognize his own melodies. Rossini supposedly vowed from that moment on to write all ornamentation into his scores to avoid having his music disfigured and upstaged by the vain display of singers.[32] In another tale involving a much older Rossini, the young Patti sang a particularly florid rendition of "Una voce poco fa" at one of his Saturday soirées. The composer then remarked, "Very nice, my dear, and who wrote the piece you have just performed?"[33] Despite these stories, scholars believe that Rossini and other early nineteenth-century Italian composers expected and encouraged singers to add their own ornamentation. As in earlier repertoire, singers were obliged to choose ornaments suited to an aria's text and dramatic context. The more exceptional artists were masterful at this, while less experienced or talented singers were criticized for using generic formulas that showcased their technical strengths at the expense of both words and music.

Composers were generally becoming more careful about notating the rhythms of small graces, yet these could also be added where not indicated. More elaborate embellishment could be used in cadenzas, or substituted for coloratura supplied by the composer. Some singers truly improvised on the spot. In 1829 Rossini contrived for the competing divas Henriette Sontag and Maria Malibran to appear at a private salon concert in Paris. After each sang some solo songs and arias, the composer and the guests persuaded the rivals, after much protesting, to sing a duet from his *Semiramide*. What followed was an impromptu battle of ornaments, but one that began a new friendship and a legendary collaboration.[34] Some singers kept notebooks in which they worked out possible variations and cadenzas in advance. Rossini composed several leading roles for the French singer Laure Cinti-Damoreau, who excelled in the Italian style. Her detailed notebooks, housed in the Lilly Library at Indiana University, are now available from Dover Publications.[35] During the period of Italian bel canto opera, singers and composers worked closely together on matters of ornamentation. In the end, however, whether the composers approved or not, it was the singers—particularly the famous stars—who controlled what happened in performance.

Composers in the early nineteenth century also wrote more appoggiaturas than their predecessors, with the precise values they wanted shown by regular-sized notes. This practice helped to clarify the often difficult decision about how long or short to make an ornamental note. Sometimes composers still wrote appoggiaturas as small notes, perhaps to communicate a desire for a slightly different type of stress or emphasis, or perhaps merely as an inconsistency. Many passages in songs and arias, and particularly in recitatives, of this period still need additional appoggiaturas for words with unstressed final syllables or to add heightened expression to a dissonant note. Some composers, notably Rossini and Donizetti, rarely indicated appoggiaturas, assuming that the singers would know where to put them. Bellini and Verdi were more conscientious about notating appoggiaturas where they wanted them.

Eighteenth-century rules governing the length of appoggiaturas still applied to music of this period. An appoggiatura (either printed or added) preceding same pitched notes would often take the entire value of its main note. For example, in the recitative shown in example 4.4a, the first A of "valle" should be sung as an added B-flat appoggiatura. The small notes in the following measures should take the entire value of the note they precede. In example 4.4b, the small note can be either a quarter to make the rhythm match the quarter/ eighth rhythm of the previous half cadence, or it can be an eighth if you don't like the clash that occurs between the G in the vocal line and the A in the right hand of the piano part. A little rubato would easily solve that problem, however.

If a small ornamental note adds expressive dissonance to its main note it is probably intended as an appoggiatura. In example 4.4c, for instance, the small note should receive more length and emphasis—an eighth note in this case— than its shorter cousin, the grace note.

By 1830 most small ornamental notes written with a slash across their tails were understood to be grace notes. (As we have seen in Bellini's "Quando incise" from 1829 [ex. 4.4a], in earlier music that was not always the case.) In contrast to the appoggiatura, the grace note (acciaccatura) is performed so lightly and quickly that it is almost impossible to tell whether it happens on or before the beat. This grace was introduced in the Classical era as a short appoggiatura

Example 4.4. Bellini: a) "Quando incise su quel marmo," mm. 8–12; b) "Vanne, o rosa fortunata," mm. 11–12; c) "Quando incise," mm. 37–39, from *Composizioni da camera* (1829, 1835), Ricordi, 1948.

Example 4.5. a) García: *Traité complet de l'art du chant: Part I* (1847, facs. Geneva, 1985), p. 67; b) Rossini: "L'orgia" (1835), mm. 17–21, reprinted in *Serate musicali,* Ricordi, 1997; c) Bellini: "La farfalletta," mm. 8–12, from *Composizioni da camera* (1829, 1835), Ricordi, 1948.

(see chapter 3) and became more popular in the nineteenth century. In lesson VIII of his *Practical Method,* Vaccai notates grace notes as small sixteenth notes and instructs that "the Acciaccatura differs from the Appoggiatura in as much as it does not interfere with the value or the accent of the note to which it is pre-fixed."[36] García notates the acciaccatura as a small eighth note and warns that it must not relax into triplets lest it lose its lively and resolute character (see ex. 4.5a). In the passage from a Rossini song in example 4.5b, the principal note G on the downbeat of m. 19 is already a dissonant passing tone between the A and the F, and so the small ornamental A must be performed as quickly and lightly as possible. In example 4.5c the ornamental note should also be performed rapidly on the syllables "ci" in m. 9 and "pre" in m. 11.

TRILLS AND TURNS

Just as the shorter, faster version of the appoggiatura gained favor in the early nineteenth century, so did the main-note start for trills. García repeats familiar advice: the trill should be clear and distinct, and students should practice it slowly at first, using a dotted rhythm and gradually increasing speed and evenness as the voice becomes more flexible. For an isolated trill he shows a special preparation from below, but for most situations he says no preparation or termination is needed.

Turns and mordents were becoming more popular, written into music by composers and added freely by singers. Composers continued to use different kinds of signs for accented and unaccented four- and five-note turns, which were easily confused. To help clarify which pattern they wanted, composers increasingly wrote out more turns using both small and regular-sized notes. Singers probably substituted the patterns they preferred, adding and interchanging the ornaments at their pleasure.

As with the trill, a main-note start for turns was becoming more popular, but other turn patterns were acceptable as well. In example 4.6a one can see that Bellini has written a turn sign in m. 26 and then a slightly different turn pattern in regular-sized notes in the following measure. Donizetti has written two different patterns of turns for the cadenza in example 4.6b. The speed of a turn is determined by the musical context: If the accompaniment stops, as in examples 4.6b and d, then the singer can take time to shape the turn. If the accompaniment continues as in example 4.6c, then the turn should be fast to keep pace with the flow of the music. In general, turns were performed more slowly as the nineteenth century progressed.

Other small graces called mordents, *gruppetti,* or compound appoggiaturas

Example 4.6. a) Bellini: "Quando incise su quel marmo," mm. 26–27, from *Composizioni da camera* (1829, 1835), Ricordi, 1948; b) Donizetti: "La ninna nanna" (1839), mm. 121–22, reprinted in *Composizioni da camera,* Ricordi, 1961; c) and d) Rossini: "Anzoleta avanti la regata," mm. 40–41, 44–45, from *La regata veneziana* (1835), Ricordi, 1967.

added several delicate ornamental notes to a main note. Vaccai explains that "the mordent is the ornament which offers the greatest variety, as well as the greatest difficulty in its execution, on account of the lightness and neatness which it requires. It consists of two, or three notes, and adds much to the grace of the Phrase, without taking anything away, or interfering at all with the intentions of the Composer."[37] In his examples (see ex. 4.7a), the ornamental notes all come before the beat and thus steal time from the preceding note.

These kinds of ornaments could be written into the music with small or regular-sized notes (see exs. 4.7b and c) or added at the discretion of the singer. The use of rubato and rhythmic flexibility in combination with these small graces gave singers some freedom in their execution. The exact pattern of a trill or turn or the rhythmic placement of a grace note or mordent was less important than the charm and expression the figure added to the melody.

### Cadenzas and Improvised Florid Embellishment

Manuel García recounts an incident from 1815 in which his father was asked to sight-read his part at the first rehearsal for a new opera: "When his first aria had been reached he sang it off with perfect phrasing and feeling, but exactly note for note as written. After he had finished, the composer said 'Thank you signor, very nice, but not at all what I wanted.' . . . The Elder García was skillful at improvising . . . he made a number of alterations and additions, introducing runs, trills, roulades and cadenzas. . . . The old composer shook him by the hand. 'Bravo! magnificent! That was my music as I wished it to be given.'"[38]

The art of improvising florid embellishments reached its peak with the Italian singers of the early nineteenth century. The best way to learn stylistically appropriate ornamental additions is to study surviving examples of ornamentation from the period. According to Will Crutchfield's article "Voices" in Brown and Sadie's *Performance Practice: Music after 1600,* hundreds of examples of added embellishment exist in manuscript form and in published scores from the period. These contain ornaments by famous singers, composers including Rossini and Donizetti, and various unattributable sources. Some of these sources are in European libraries or private collections. The easiest place to see some of these examples is in the *New Grove* (2001) articles on "Rossini" and "Improvisation: Nineteenth Century," and the *New Grove Dictionary of Opera* "Ornamentation" article. Crutchfield's article includes many examples of added cadenzas and flourishes, mostly from well-known opera arias. Robert Toft's *Heart to Heart: Expressive Singing in England, 1780–1830* includes orna-

Example 4.7. a) Vaccai: *Practical Method of Italian Singing,* lesson IX, pp. 20–21, mm. 21–27; b) Rossini: "La promessa" (1835), mm. 18–19, reprinted in *Serate musicali,* Ricordi, 1997; c) Bellini: "Sogno d'infanzia," mm. 46–47, from *Composizioni da camera* (1829, 1835), Ricordi, 1948.

mented examples of arias by lesser-known Italian composers, songs by English composers, and some examples from Handel and Mozart. These sources can provide a starting place for the more adventurous reader. Another invaluable source for ornamentation of this period is Austin Caswell's collection "Embellished Opera Arias," published by A-R Editions. It presents over twenty complete arias by Bellini, Rossini, and others, often including several alternatively ornamented versions of particular sections of the aria. Caswell's initial commentary presents detailed information on sources and specific ornaments. He also includes general information on the period, the music, and the singers. (See "Chapter 4: Performance Practice–Ornamentation" in "For Further Reading.")

Several basic trends can be discerned in the embellishments of this period. The first was embellishments which did not disturb the basic flow of the melody. García recommends varying a simple melody when it is repeated. In a letter to Rossini, the English soprano Clara Novello asked whether it was necessary or permissible to make variations in the *da capo* section of an aria. Rossini replied that "the repeat is made expressly that each singer may vary it, so as best to display his or her peculiar capacities."[39] This kind of embellishment could also be used in strophic songs. The variations could be slight, such as changing the rhythm or adding some of the small graces discussed above. Or they could include a bolder alteration of the melody, perhaps introducing a higher tessitura, a more florid line, or a more technically difficult pattern, all the while keeping the larger rhythm of the section steady. Caswell comments that in arias, particularly those by Bellini, singers would often leave a cantabile melody in the slow cavatina section plain and unadorned, varying only the fioritura to suit their own abilities. Many times the composer wrote customized coloratura for a particular singer performing a role or aria. The alternative embellishments Rossini wrote for Pasta in the aria "Non più mesta" from *La Cenerentola* take the vocal line higher than the original and also simplify some of the long runs.[40]

The final coda section of a fast cabaletta was a prime place to show off. García includes four pages of suggested variations on standard coda formulas at the ends of arias. Example 4.8 shows a brief glimpse of the vast possibilities he offers in his treatise; the lines of text are from the various arias used to make the variations. According to Crutchfield, the now common final cadential fermata is a late nineteenth-century invention. In Rossini's time the coda would continue into the final cadence with a burst of florid activity and no pause or ritardando.[41]

Example 4.8. García: coda variants from *Traité complet de l'art du chant: Part II* (1847, facs. Geneva, 1985), p. 72.

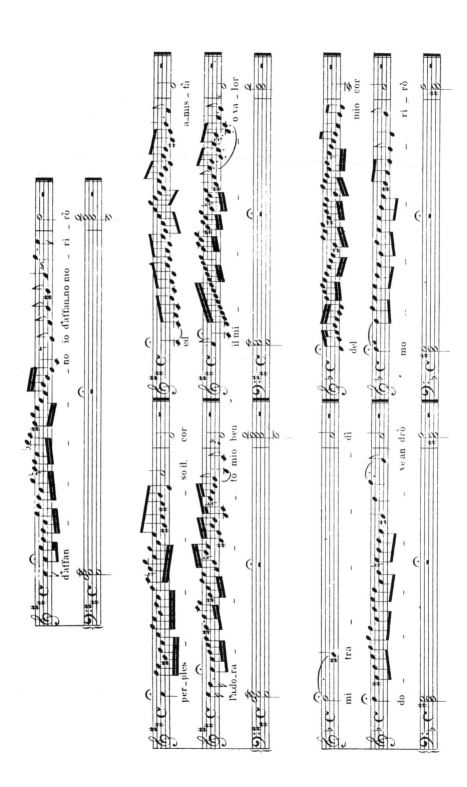

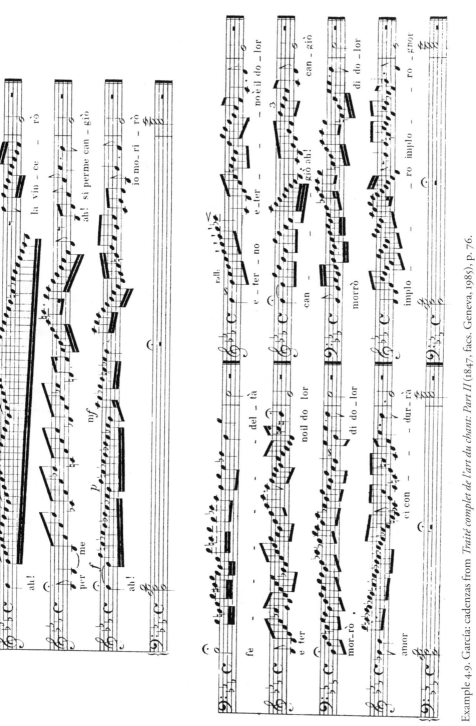

Example 4.9. García: cadenzas from *Traité complet de l'art du chant: Part II* (1847, facs. Geneva, 1985), p. 76.

The other basic kind of embellishment involved adding cadenzas. García includes six pages of suggested cadenza formulas to suit a variety of harmonic situations. Again, example 4.9 shows only a fragment of his offerings. Cadenzas from this period served the function they did in earlier music, namely to highlight the end of an aria or section (ex. 4.10a). They could also now appear at several interior moments of pause within an aria, perhaps denoting a change of thought or musical idea (ex.4.10b). Sometimes they were indicated with a fermata; sometimes the composer wrote out a specific cadenza, which the singer could change to suit his or her taste and abilities (see also ex. 4.6b). Other times the score would be marked merely *a piacere, col canto,* or *colla voce,* which allowed the singer the freedom to proceed "at their pleasure" by adding something simple or more elaborate depending on the dramatic context (ex. 4.11a). In a strophic song such as Rossini's "La partenza," perhaps the instruction *con molta grazia* inspired the singer to vary this cadential figure in every verse. In other situations, when the accompaniment becomes sparse or drops out altogether, the singer does not have to keep pace with a steady rhythmic flow and has more freedom to adorn or vary the melody (ex. 4.11b; see also ex. 4.6d). A cadenza need not be as long or elaborate as García's suggestions, especially in the more intimate songs.

Cinti-Damoreau, who taught at the Paris Conservatoire after retiring from the stage, encouraged her students not to perform her ornaments verbatim, but rather to use the varied formulas as the basis for their own inventions. This is still good advice today. As with the improvised embellishments of earlier periods, you must first become familiar with the particular formulas and patterns of this period and then use that vocabulary to create your own ornamentation.

The early nineteenth century was the culmination of the Italian bel canto approach to technique and ornamentation. This period's stylistic principles came from the opera house but were equally at home in the realm of chamber song. The gentle, relaxed production favored since the seventeenth century was still central to this style. Legato was more popular than it was in the eighteenth century, but the expressive and dramatic articulation of the text remained crucial. Vibrato was still small and shimmering, but now it was sometimes specifically notated as a special effect. Portamento was much more common, but it was not meant to be overused.

Florid ornamentation had reached its most elaborate state and could be used to vary the return of a *da capo* aria or rondo form, as well as to differentiate the verses of strophic songs. More modest variation could be added to slower sec-

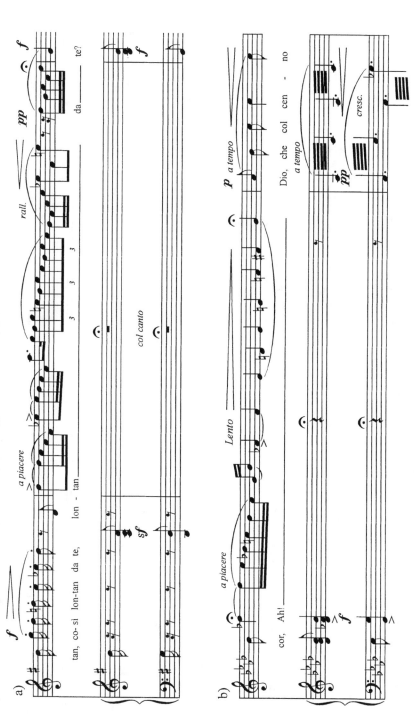

Example 4.10. a) Rossini: "La partenza" (1835), mm. 55–57, reprinted in *Serate musicali*, Ricordi, 1997; b) Donizetti: "Una lacrima" ("Preghiera") (1841), mm. 31–32, reprinted in *Composizioni da camera*, Ricordi, 1961.

Example 4.11. a) Rossini: "La partenza" (1835), mm. 20–22, reprinted in *Serate musicali*, Ricordi, 1997; b) Bellini: "Per pietà, bell'idol mio," mm. 32–35, from *Composizioni da camera* (1829, 1835). Ricordi, 1948.

tions of arias or songs, and small graces, including appoggiaturas, grace notes, trills, and turns, were added at the singer's discretion. Cadenzas small or large were often included at a variety of places throughout arias or songs. Today's singers wishing to learn how to compose or improvise their own ornamentation for Rossini, Bellini, Donizetti, and other bel canto composers should study as many examples from this repertoire as they can and be careful not to confuse these embellishments with the patterns from earlier periods.

New issues introduced in this chapter have to do with rhythm and tempo. The scores of the early nineteenth century started to include more descriptive tempo terms that don't necessarily help in selecting an appropriate speed. Tempo is also much more flexible in general for this repertoire, often changing frequently to accompany shifts in text and dynamics. Rubato should be used as well to shape the rhythm and enhance expression. García instructs singers to adjust the rhythm and tempo to suit breathing, phrasing, expression, and ornamentation. You can enjoy considerable freedom in your approach to rhythm and tempo for this repertoire, all in the service of dazzling ornamentation, beautiful singing, and heightened expressivity.

# Chapter 5  German Lieder

This chapter discusses the German lied and its development through the nineteenth century. It will consider songs by Schubert, Schumann, Mendelssohn, Brahms, Hugo Wolf, and Richard Strauss, as well as by Louis Spohr, Liszt, Wagner, and others. The lied was first viewed as a marginal form in such compositions as Mozart's "Das Veilchen" and "Abendempfindung" and Beethoven's "Adelaide" and his song cycle *An die ferne Geliebte.* In the hands of Schubert, the lied and the song cycle began to realize their greater potential. Many composers considered their lieder insignificant in comparison with their larger symphonic compositions. This smaller form, however, was able to convey many important themes of nineteenth-century Romanticism while appealing to a large audience, both in private and public.

The richness of the German poetic tradition in the hands of great masters such as Goethe, Heine, Rückert, and others helped shape the course of the Romantic movement. Poems and vast landscape paintings depicted the individual's place in the natural world and helped define the German national identity. The growing educated middle class in German-speaking countries showed a heightened interest in poetry and art, as well as an increased appetite for literature, science, and music. Journals of all sorts emerged to satisfy the public's need to discuss intellectual and philosophical issues. Many Romantics sought to synthesize numerous artistic elements into a unified whole, eventually epitomized by Wagner in his music dramas and his concept of the Gesamtkunstwerk. The lied was a perfect miniature form combining music and poetry, art and literature, natural landscapes and the interior life of the individual seeking a place in the world.

Composers wrote lieder for a variety of reasons. Most nineteenth-century lieder were inspired by particular people, circumstances, or emotions and of course by the wealth of magnificent poetry that begged to be set to music. Schubert set poems chosen or written by his close friends, and he intended his songs for performance in his inner social circle. He may also have foreshadowed his own death with his final great song cycle *Winterreise*. Schumann responded to the tempestuous circumstances leading to his joyous marriage to Clara Wieck with an outpouring of 138 songs within the single year of 1840. Brahms fancied a number of female singers with rich, low voices and wrote songs with their instruments in mind. He also had a close working relationship with baritone Julius Stockhausen, who was a performing colleague as well as the recipient of music composed for his voice. Composers also set poems to music as an expression of the ideals of the Romantic movement, and they discussed these philosophical concepts in journals. Schumann founded one of the first music journals, *Neue Zeitschrift für Musik,* which included theoretical writings as well as reviews and critiques of new songs. Wolf, who also spent time as a music critic, declared that his songs were written "for epicures, not amateurs."[1]

Yet it was the general amateur public that demanded a constant supply of newly published songs to be used for home entertainment. Many composers took advantage of the fact that a good deal of money could be made from the sale of songs. Carl Loewe, Robert Franz, Mendelssohn, Schumann, and Brahms all wrote songs, duets, and quartets geared to the abilities of amateur musicians. Private music making took place in virtually every educated home. Piano and voice teachers in the cities had no want for students from wealthy and middle-class families. The lied was a welcome guest at private gatherings both small and large, and many composers performed their songs in these less formal situations.

The lied figured in the development of public concerts as well. As the nineteenth century progressed, professional public concerts became more numerous and more varied in programming. Songs, solo instrumental selections, melodramas, and poetry readings gradually began to appear on the same concert programs with symphonies, concertos, and choral works. Even touring virtuosos such as Liszt and Clara Schumann appeared with assisting artists, both vocal and instrumental. Influential or charismatic performers such as Mendelssohn, Liszt, and Strauss had the power and freedom to promote their own lieder and those of their colleagues. Liszt, a particular favorite with the public, was an enthusiastic champion of many of his fellow composers. He introduced audiences to many Schubert songs through his dazzling piano fantasies on their themes. Brahms was not a virtuoso like Liszt or Clara Schumann, but as a pianist he often performed chamber music and lieder. In the 1850s and '60s his collaboration with Stockhausen in public performances of *Die schöne Müllerin, Winterreise,* and the cycles of Schumann brought this repertoire to a wider public. It also introduced the idea of the solo vocal recital. At first contemporary critics had "an apprehension of great monotony" compared with the familiar marathon smorgasbord concerts of the day.[2] The public enjoyed the more focused experience, however, and the concept took hold.

By the end of the century, homogenous concert programs featuring only orchestral selections, chamber music, or lieder had become common. Orchestrations of songs, or songs conceived for voice and orchestra, like those of Mahler, were in demand for orchestral concerts. Many lieder composers, in addition to performing as pianists, were also well-known conductors who could program their songs on their orchestral concerts. Mendelssohn, Spohr, Brahms, Liszt, Mahler, Strauss, and Wagner all conducted their own works. Over the course of the nineteenth century, the lied was thus transformed from a miniature form for private consumption to a large, expansive form for the public concert hall. Yet, whether performed by Schubert and his amateur musician friends at a private gathering in 1820 or by Strauss and his wife Pauline at an orchestral subscription concert in 1903, the lied demanded close communication between singer and accompanist and provided an intimate experience between performers and audience.

### Editions

A wide variety of German lieder editions are available today. Some are based on nineteenth-century publications, some on recent scholarship. Many composers meticulously prepared their lieder for public use, and the most reliable presentations of their original markings and performance instructions are editions published in their lifetimes. Songs also appeared in journals or monthly music magazines, carefully prepared for public appreciation. By the end of the nineteenth century, Breitkopf & Härtel had published complete editions of the works of Schubert, Schumann, Mendelssohn, and Brahms. These were most often based on scores published while the composers still lived. Most modern editions of these composers' works are either reprints of these sources or based on them. Bärenreiter has published a new scholarly Urtext edition of Schubert, the *Neue Schubert Ausgabe* (NSA), and new editions of Schumann, Mendelssohn, and Brahms are under way, although they do not yet include all the vocal music. For the most part, modern editions of German lieder that are based on nineteenth-century sources are reliable representations of the composers' original intentions.

Schubert was not aggressive about publishing his music. He often wrote out extra copies of songs to give to friends, making slight changes in each copy—hence the five versions of "Die Forelle."[3] He also revised songs for various reasons, including compositional choices and performance adjustments (the eighth-note accompaniment of "Erlkönig" was easier for him to play than the triplets), resulting in multiple versions of many songs. In 1821 several of his friends had "Erlkönig" published at their own expense, and it became hugely popular. This opened the door for more songs to be published and performed at fashionable society soirees. Yet while 187 of his 600 songs were published in his lifetime, most of his music remained unknown until other leading composers championed it after his death. Brahms was involved in editing Schubert's instrumental music for the Breitkopf & Härtel *F. Schuberts Werke* edition, and Eusebius Mandyczewski oversaw the lieder. (The modern Dover volumes of songs reproduce this work, and most other readily available editions are based on it.)

Max Friedlaender, an oratorio and lieder baritone who had studied voice with García and Stockhausen, undertook an important second career as a musicologist. In 1887 he wrote his dissertation on Schubert and thereafter devoted all his attention to scholarly work on German folk songs and lieder. His editions of Schubert songs, published by Peters, are based on nineteenth-century sources.

Bärenreiter's NSA versions of Schubert's songs, edited by Walter Dürr in the 1970s, include many variants based on manuscript sources not included in the older complete-works edition. Dürr's scholarly commentary, in German, offers fascinating details about each song.

Clara Schumann edited the first complete compilation of Robert's works after his death, and most editions of the songs are based on it. Although Mendelssohn did not consider his songs a high creative priority and composed them mostly for amateurs, he carefully prepared his song manuscripts for publication. Most modern editions of Mendelssohn's lieder are reprints. While Brahms's inspiration to write songs was more personal, he, too, carefully supervised their publication. Wolf took particular pains to ensure that every detail was just right in the publication of his songs; once he was well known, he spent extra money on expensive paper stock and decorative borders and often placed the poet's name in larger type, above his own. The first complete edition of his works was published in the 1960s.

Strauss also supervised the publication of all his songs for the general public, except for the *Four Last Songs,* which were discovered in manuscript after his death. Most current editions of his songs contain very few differences from the first editions and are in fact reprints. In 1964 a deluxe commemorative collection of his songs was published in honor of the 100th anniversary of his birth. Unfortunately, this *Gesamtausgabe der Lieder,* in four volumes, was prepared hurriedly for the centenary and contains various mistakes. Barbara Petersen, in *Ton und Wort: The Lieder of Richard Strauss,* cautions against relying on the edition's accompanying critical commentary and details its other shortcomings.[4] She also offers critical evaluation of other editions, manuscripts, and sources and considerable in-depth information about the songs. Most first editions of Strauss songs included singable English translations. Some later printings even included translations in French, Italian, and Russian.

## Transpositions

In the nineteenth century, attitudes toward transplanting and transposing individual songs evolved from the flexible approach of earlier centuries. Different composers had definite opinions about changing the order or the key of their songs. While Strauss wrote most of his songs for high voice, he was happy to have them transposed for the comfort of the general public and presented published groups for high, medium, or low voice. Rather than transposing his entire opus or a group as a block, however, Strauss recommended specific transpositions for individual songs, taking into consideration the sound of a particular key for the piano accompaniment and the comfort of the vocal tessitura.

Wolf was notoriously particular about the performance of his songs; once he even berated a singer in the middle of a performance for taking liberties he found offensive. He tried to interest several famous singers, including Lilli Lehmann, to perform his songs, but because of his reputation for being difficult, many did not want to work with him. Given his remark about his songs not being for amateurs, he probably would not have approved of his songs being transposed. The Wolf complete-works edition presents the songs in their original keys, as do the Dover scores, which are based on editions from Wolf's lifetime.

Brahms, on the other hand, was happy to change the key of a composition to suit the comfort of the singer, and while he conceived certain songs with a low voice in mind, he published many of them in a high key. He was more particular about preserving the keys of songs based on folk music sources, the *Volks-Kinderlieder* and *Deutsche Volkslieder*, even though many lie too high for the average child or folk singer.

Schumann had definite opinions about transposition and the nature of certain keys. He published his thoughts in an article entitled "Characterization of the Keys":

> It is as inadmissible to say that this or that feeling, in order to be correctly expressed in music must be translated in this or that key (anger, for example in C-sharp minor) as to agree with Zelter who declares that any feeling may be expressed in any key. . . . The process by means of which the composer selects this or that principal key for the expression of his feelings is as little explicable as the creative process of genius itself. . . . No one will deny that a composition, transposed from its original key into another produces a different effect.[5]

Schumann did not seem to be against transposing in principle, but he did indicate his strong feelings on the important contribution the choice of key makes to the composition as a whole. Since Schumann wrote many of his songs for an idealized voice rather than a particular singer, his choice of key was important in establishing the general mood and feeling of a piece. He also introduced a more important role for the piano in his songs. Transposing would change not only the vocal tessitura but also the texture and color of the piano writing. The key relationships among songs within his cycles are particularly important as well. In *Dichterliebe* and *Liederkreis,* the individual songs are fragments that cannot stand on their own but are strung together like beads on a necklace. To preserve the integrity of the harmonic construction and flow of the whole composition, the entire cycle must be transposed by the same interval.

Some of Schumann's later songs are in keys that take standard voice types into an uncomfortable range. Boosey & Hawkes published volumes of his songs edited by Clara and based on her complete works but transposed for high or low voice. Excluding the cycles, some individual songs have been transposed into more suitable keys.

Schubert composed many of his songs to suit his own voice, which was a

light high baritone. He also wrote songs for his friend Karl Freiherr von Schönstein, a gifted amateur singer, who was also a high baritone. Schönstein reports
that "Schubert had grown fond of me and enjoyed making music with me,
which he did often; he admitted to me repeatedly that from this time on [1818],
in his songs, he generally had in mind a voice of my range."[6] Schönstein also
mentions that another close friend of Schubert's, the well-known court opera
singer Johann Michael Vogl, had one of Schubert's songs transposed into a
lower, more comfortable key. Two weeks after Schubert had given him the
song, Vogl sang it for the composer. "After Vogl had sung it, without saying a
word beforehand about the song and without having made the slightest change
in it—sometimes he liked to take liberties with Schubert's songs—Schubert
cried out in his simple way, 'You know that song isn't bad! Who's it by?' After a
fortnight he no longer recognized his own creation."[7]

Schubert and Vogl had an interesting working relationship. The young composer idealized the older, famous singer and was indebted to him for promoting
his songs and offering moral and financial assistance. According to some reports, Schubert was thrilled with the way Vogl sang his songs and loved playing
for him: "the manner in which Vogl sings and the way I accompany, as though
we were one at such a moment."[8] In other accounts, Schubert was sometimes
less than happy with Vogl's operatic approach. The composer was willing, on
occasion, to compromise with Vogl regarding transposition, but he probably
would have wanted to maintain the integrity of the cycles' tonal construction.

A word about gender-specific songs: plenty of accounts exist from the nineteenth century of famous sopranos singing *An die ferne Geliebte, Winterreise,* or
the *Müllerlieder,* in which the protagonist or speaker in the poems is obviously
male. By the same token, Stockhausen sang *Frauenliebe und Leben,* in which
the voice in the poetry is decidedly female. Thus the boundaries of gender were
not considered to limit a singer's choice of songs in the days of Schubert, Schumann, or Brahms.

### German Diction and Technique

The percussive characteristics of the German language exerted a strong influence on German singers of the nineteenth century, who aimed to combine Italian vocal production with their own approach to articulation and expressivity.
Many German singing manuals throughout the century advocated the *schönen
Tone* of the Italian school, and some of the most famous German singers, including Stockhausen and Lilli Lehmann, were students of García or his disci-

ples. Yet many German singers were criticized for shrieking, yelling, shouting, whispering, and other affronts to bel canto.

Clara Schumann's father, Friedrich Wieck, advocates beautiful singing in the Italian style in his 1853 manual *Klavier und Gesang*. In the 1878 edition of his treatise, he chastises voice teachers and singers for producing tones that were "cold, ugly, tight, forced, and throaty."[9] An acquaintance of Schubert's and Vogl's recalled the singer's remarks on interpreting German lied: "in particular he emphasized the necessity for a clear enunciation of the words. If you have nothing to say to me, ran his motto, you have nothing to sing to me either."[10] Vogl was also credited with introducing Schubert's circle to the "declamatory style of singing."[11] Schubert's good friend Leopold von Sonnleithner, writing in 1857 and 1860, disapproved of the current "dramatic" style of singing Schubert: "According to this, there is as much declamation as possible, sometimes whispered, sometimes with passionate outbursts." He commented that, after having heard Schubert rehearse and perform his songs "more than a hundred times," the "singer must conceive the song *lyrically* not *dramatically. . . .* Everything that hinders the flow of the melody and disturbs the evenly flowing accompaniment is, therefore, exactly contrary to the composer's intentions and destroys the musical effect.—Consequently singers with good voices and just a natural way of singing have frequently achieved great effect with these songs. . . . Schubert, therefore, demanded above all that his songs should not be so much declaimed, as *sung* flowingly."[12]

Jenny Lind was a particularly notable exponent of this kind of lyrical approach. A student of García, Lind was famous for her Italian, French, and German operatic roles, as well as for her charming renditions of Swedish songs. Mendelssohn, who wrote songs with flowing melodies and simple accompaniments, loved her singing and often accompanied the "Swedish Nightingale" on his songs. The Schumanns greatly admired her as well, and Robert dedicated his op. 89 songs to her. Clara wrote in her diary: "Her singing is ever so sincere. There is no showmanship, no great display of emotion, yet she touches your heart. . . . No weeping, sobbing, or quavering sounds, no bad habits of any kind. . . . If we could only persuade her to sing nothing but good music and to get rid of all that rubbish by . . . Meyerbeer, Bellini, Donizetti, etc.; she is too good for that."[13]

A very different kind of singer who epitomized the dramatic style of singing was the German opera star Wilhelmine Schröder-Devrient. She too was admired by the Schumanns, and she received the dedication of Robert's op. 48

*Dichterliebe.* Mendelssohn enjoyed performing with her and persuaded her to join him, substituting at the last minute for a singer who was ill, in an 1840 performance of some Beethoven songs.[14] It was in another Beethoven work, *Fidelio,* that she first made her mark on the German opera world. Schröder-Devrient trained initially as an actress, and she never quite mastered the art of beautiful singing. Henry Chorley, an English music critic partial to bel canto, did not care for her performances of Italian opera: "Her tones were delivered without any care, save to give them due force. Her execution was bad and heavy. There was an air of strain and spasm throughout her performance."[15] Yet when she brought her mesmerizing acting ability to *Fidelio,* she used expressive declamation to heighten the intensity of her singing, deliberately sacrificing beautiful tone for dramatic effect. Her performances were a revelation, particularly to Wagner. When he heard her sing Leonore in 1829, it changed his life. She inspired him to fashion a new kind of German singing, and he went on to create several roles for her, including Senta in *Der fliegende Holländer* and Venus in *Tannhäuser.*

Writing in 1865, Wagner complained that German singers did not receive proper training, and he advocated the establishment of a national singing school. He believed that German singers were ill equipped for dramatic singing because they were trying to apply the Italian method to the German language without success: "The Italian style of vocalism, our only present model for the classic, is inappropriate to the German language. . . . A right development of Song, upon a groundwork of German Speech, is therefore the first task for us . . . that any such method should never permit euphony to be tampered with, goes without saying."[16] Ideally, Wagner wanted singers to preserve the beautiful tone of the Italian approach and infuse it with clear German diction and pronunciation so that the words and the music would have equal importance. He wanted German singers to speak in singing and above all to sing and act naturally.[17]

Clear diction and natural declamation were also extremely important to the enthusiastic Wagner disciple Hugo Wolf, as demonstrated by his reviews of singers from 1884 to 1889. Writing in the Viennese Sunday journal the *Wiener Salonblatt,* he reviewed Lilli Lehmann's first performance as Isolde and criticized her poor diction: "A shame that she enunciates so badly. Not a single word was comprehensible. A serious deficiency!"[18] Several weeks later he again mentioned his frustration with her enunciation as Donna Anna and Norma, most likely sung in German. By contrast, Lehmann, who went on to become a celebrated Wagner singer, writes in her book *How to Sing* that she sang Isolde "in a beautiful legato in the fine Italian style." She also criticizes Wagner adherents for having misguided ideas about technique and advocates a way of connecting vowels to consonants to facilitate a distinct articulation without being destructive to the voice.[19] On the other hand, Wolf did not like exaggerated diction either, and he criticized a singer portraying Alberich in Wagner's *Das Rheingold* for going too far: "Herr Horowitz seemed obviously concerned to unite the singer with the declaimer. The intention is admirable. It is only that in his over enthusiasm he went so far as to not sing at all, but only to declaim. He should try to achieve a blend of both and he will succeed."[20] Nor did he approve of a melodramatic performance of Schubert's "Erlkönig" and Mozart's "Das Veilchen" by another celebrated Wagner singer, Pauline Lucca: "This rough theatricality does not work to best advantage in the concert hall."[21]

All these accounts demonstrate that German singers in the nineteenth century were trying to define their own style and to sing expressively in their own language while still achieving a beautiful, melodic sound. Some were more successful than others at finding a workable compromise.

### Articulation and Expression Marks

Most lieder composers included relatively few articulation marks in their vocal music. They expected that singers would use the text to shape the melody appropriately. Articulation marks and performance instructions added in purely instrumental music or vocal accompaniments were meant to help the instrumentalists play expressively, as if they had diction and text. In Schubert, for instance, an accent mark can mean either a slight elongation of a stressed syllable or an added emphasis for an important word or dissonant neighbor note. For a more detailed discussion, see Clive Brown's *Classical and Romantic Performing Practice.*[22] Schubert also used varying lengths of crescendo and decrescendo marks that can sometimes be confused with accentuation marks. In the *Neue Schubert Ausgabe* volumes, the editors have tried to standardize the length of the shorter decrescendo marks into > accent marks. This approach doesn't cause a problem if you understand a > mark to mean the elongation of an expressive syllable. It can be quite confusing in the piano part, however, when trying to choose between an accent that adds more energy to a note and a slight decrescendo that would soften the energy of the gesture.[23]

For example, compare the two editions of "Suleika II" seen in example 5.1. In this song Schubert uses swelling crescendo and decrescendo marks throughout to shape the phrases. In m. 47 the NSA (ex. 5.1b) makes an accent mark out of what was a decrescendo in the old *Schuberts Werke* edition (ex. 5.1a). In this par-

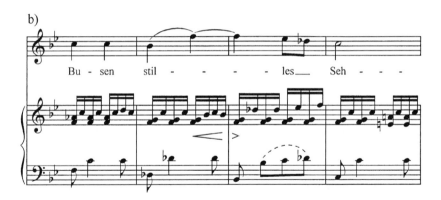

Example 5.1. Schubert: "Suleika II," mm. 45–48, in a) *Schuberts Werke* XX/vi/202; b) *Neue Schubert Ausgabe* IV/ii/99.

ticular spot, under the top of an arching melody line, an accent in the piano part on the word "stilles" would disturb the sense of awakening silent longing in the breast. The same marking in m. 57 seems equally inappropriate under the word "Hauch," since the phrase is describing a soft breath. Singers and their accompanists must be alert for these kinds of situations when using the NSA. As always, the dramatic context created by the words will suggest answers to such questions.

Brahms, too, did not include many expression marks in his vocal music. His decision to give minimal instructions to singer and pianist was apparently modeled on Schubert's approach.[24] He also had little interest in bowings or fingerings for his string writing, usually letting his good friend violinist Joseph Joachim work out these details.[25] Similarly, Brahms left most decisions about articulation and dramatic interpretation to the singer—especially a singer he admired. If he was accompanying, he would make suggestions or show his intentions by the way he played.

Strauss had much the same approach to his songs. Performance instructions such as accents, tenutos, accelerandos, ritardandos, or indications of breathing places are sparse. Most of his early songs were for his wife Pauline de Ahna, who sang while Strauss accompanied at the piano or conducted the orchestra. Strauss clearly felt they could work out such details together. In working with other singers he admired, he would often defer to their judgment and adapt his interpretations accordingly. He wrote the *Brentano Lieder,* op. 68, for Elisabeth Schumann and frequently accompanied her. Recordings of her interpretations of Strauss songs offer a glimpse into the style they created together. According to the page turner at one of their many *Liederabenden,* Strauss had a very flexible approach toward playing his own piano accompaniments. He often improvised a more orchestral rendering of the piano part, arpeggiating chords, adding octaves, and enriching the harmonies. He was even known to improvise interludes between songs, sometimes including tunes from his operas.[26]

### Embellishment

The attitude toward ornamentation and improvisation in nineteenth-century German vocal music was vastly different from the practices associated with Italian bel canto. In the early decades of the century, musicians reacted against the tasteless excesses of some singers, preferring honest, genuine expression to virtuosity and showmanship. Yet it was understood that certain small ornaments such as appoggiaturas, trills, turns, and mordents could be added at the discretion of the singer. In his 1821 article on dramatic singing, theorist Ignaz Franz von Mosel instructs the performer:

> Who on the one hand embellishes a simple melody with taste, adding a turn or two to the original form to produce a pleasing variety but who, on the other hand, does not succumb to licentious fantasy or to a desire to excel by sheer mechanical ability; instead he relies on reason, sensibility and taste, which are the prerequisites for every dramatic singer. Frequently a single suspension, a well expressed mordent, an ornament of three, four, or at most six notes, overtime new and gracious in its form, overtime pure and clear in its performance, overtime appropriate to the sense of the text, to the character of the song, the singer and the accompaniment—these may genuinely embellish the melody, intensify its expression and increase its overall effect.[27]

Vogl, who started his career in the late eighteenth-century opera houses and was the product of an earlier stylistic tradition, influenced Schubert when it came to ornamentation. Some contemporary writers report that Vogl freely altered songs and persuaded the composer to change details in published versions to reflect his interpretation.[28] Other accounts relate good-natured disagreements between the two in which Schubert's compositional decisions prevailed. According to Eduard von Bauernfeld, another of Schubert's inner circle of friends, "Small alterations and embellishments, which the skillful singer, a past master of effect, allowed himself, received the composer's consent to some extent, but not infrequently they also gave rise to friendly controversy."[29] Vogl kept notebooks of many versions of the songs with his own added ornaments. He may have had a hand in an 1829 Diabelli edition of *Die schöne Müllerin* that includes substantial alterations. Examples of Vogl's ornamented alterations can be seen in the NSA, as well as in articles by Walter Dürr and David Montgomery.[30] Vogl continued to sing Schubert's songs until shortly before his own death in 1840 at the age of seventy-two. As his vocal powers diminished, he is said to have relied increasingly on exaggerated dramatic declamation and special effects such as whispering, falsetto, and sudden outcries. Sonnleithner relates that "Michael Vogl, it is true, overstepped the permissible limits more and more as he lost his voice . . . and he merely helped himself out as well as he could, in the manner of the experienced opera singer, where his voice and strength did not suffice. And Schubert would certainly not have approved his manner of performance as it developed in his last years."[31]

As the century progressed, German composers took a firmer stand against added embellishments. Carl Maria von Weber is said to have forbade his singers any ornamentation whatsoever of his music. Mendelssohn's attitude was also conservative, but he may have allowed small additions and alterations in some cases. Chorley reports that "Mendelssohn wrote so as to allow no space or exercise of fancy for the vocal embroiderer; and thus to alter or add to his music, would be to injure it, by showing arrogant disloyalty to the master's wishes and meanings. Nevertheless, I well recollect the quiet smile of pleasure with which even Mendelssohn used to receive a shake exquisitely placed in the second verse of his delicious 'Frühlingslied' (op. 47)."[32] Chorley also relates that Mendelssohn allowed a small change of pitch in a recitative in *Elijah* that heightened the dramatic effect. Yet in some of his songs, including the op. 8 "Frühlingslied," rather than allowing the singer freedom to improvise, he wrote out his own version of an Italianate cadenza (see ex. 5.2).

Clara Schumann made her disapproval of the Italian vocal style clear in her

Example 5.2. Mendelssohn: "Frühlingslied," op. 8. no. 6, mm. 65–68, *Mendelssohn Werke* XIX/13.

remarks about Jenny Lind's choice of repertoire. She also shunned empty virtuosic display in her own restrained and pure playing. She and violinist Joseph Joachim strove to express the music simply and directly rather than to indulge in extravagant emotional outpourings. Brahms, who shared a close personal and artistic relationship with Clara, was of the same mind. Wagner, though on the opposite side of a protracted and bitter battle against Brahms and his conservative musical ideals, allowed his singers absolutely no alterations to the score. Wolf, his devoted acolyte, hated the vain displays of Italian opera and was similarly opposed to singers' making any changes to the score.

## Notated Ornaments

### APPOGGIATURAS AND GRACE NOTES

As notational practices developed over the course of the nineteenth century, composers wrote more ornaments into their scores. Increasingly they used regular-sized notation for writing out appoggiaturas and turns. By the midcentury the small ornamental note, particularly with a slash through it, came to be understood almost universally as a fast, light grace note to be performed either just before the beat or right on it (see the discussion of acciaccatura in chapter 4.) In Schubert's songs, however, the notation of appoggiaturas and grace notes is very inconsistent. The NSA offers suggested solutions to questionable situations, but they are not always the only answer. Since Schubert composed in a transitional period between late Classical practices and early Romantic ones, his music can follow the rules for graces outlined in the eighteenth-century treatises of C. P. E. Bach and others. Often a small ornamental note will add expressive dissonance in a Schubert song and should be stressed and performed on the beat. Sometimes an appoggiatura should take half the value of the note it decorates, while other times it will demand the entire value of the main note. In some situations the textual content or the notation in another part of the song may reveal the most appropriate execution. Still other situations have no clear solution.

One of the most common figures in Schubert's songs is an appoggiatura above or below two repeated notes, the second of which is unaccented. In examples 5.3a–d, the appoggiatura should take the entire value of the main note. In example 5.3b, in fact, many editions show the appoggiatura written out in large notes.

In examples 5.4a–d, the notation in another part of the song may offer clues as to how to perform a particular appoggiatura. In "Rastlose Liebe" (ex. 5.4a), Schubert writes the long kind of appoggiatura at the opening of the song, using two regular-sized quarter notes. In the E-major section at "Lieber durch Leiden" he substitutes the shorter version, with an eighth-note rhythm in large notes on "Leiden" m. 26 and on "schlagen" in m. 28. At the word "tragen" in m. 33 he writes a small ornamental note before two quarter notes. Here the performer must decide whether this ornamental figure should match the shorter execution on "schlagen" in m. 28 or the longer version on "Herzen" in m. 38. The NSA suggests the longer quarter-note execution for "tragen" as well as for "vergebens" later in the song at the return to E minor. That is what I prefer as well.

In "Frühlingstraum" (ex. 5.4b), Schubert seems to indicate that he wants the shorter sixteenth-note execution for "malte" in mm. 31 and 35 by the way he sets "an den" in m. 33 and "lacht wohl" in m. 37, and this is the solution suggested by the NSA. However, Ernest Walker, in his article "The Appoggiatura," suggests that the treatment of "Blumen" in m. 39 might instead be Schubert's intended execution for "malte."[33] It is also worth noting that the eighth-note ap-

Example 5.3. Schubert: a) "Suleika II," mm. 98–100; b) "Halt," mm. 11–13; c) "Ave Maria," m. 11; d) "Frühlingsglaube," m. 18, Peters, ed. Friedlaender.

poggiaturas on "malte" and "Blumen" are followed by sixteenth notes, whereas the written sixteenth notes on "an den" and "lacht wohl" are followed by eighths. There doesn't seem to be a conclusive solution either way.

Example 5.4c from "Lachen und Weinen" shows what could be a simple long quarter-note appoggiatura, yet on many early recordings you hear two eighth notes or a rhythmically indeterminate slide from the E-flat to the D in m. 65. I would say that this moment depends entirely on what kind of dramatic gesture you want to give the word "Lachen," be it coy, sassy, wistful, or some other choice. Example 5.4d also shows what could be a simple long appoggiatura; Vogl preferred it short, while Schubert thought about making it even longer in an earlier version by changing the meter to 6/8.

In situations involving triple time or a dotted note, eighteenth-century rules would require an appoggiatura to last two-thirds of the value of the main note. In examples 5.5a and b, both Walker and the NSA recommend that the appoggiatura be executed this way. In "Ave Maria" (ex. 5.5a), however, you rarely hear it performed that way. The length usually varies from verse to verse depending on the specific syllables. In early twentieth-century recordings you often hear a note of indeterminate length, as in "Lachen und Weinen." When combined with rubato and portamento, this treatment creates a very expressive yet imprecise rhythm. In "Frühlingsglaube" (ex. 5.5b), you could make "Herz" in m. 41 match the rhythm of "Herze" earlier in the song (m. 18: see ex. 5.3d) and use an eighth-note appoggiatura, or you could match the rhythm of "tiefste" in m. 40 and use a sixteenth-note appoggiatura. For "An die Nachtigall" (ex. 5.5c), Walker and NSA recommend a quarter-note appoggiatura for the D in m. 13. In early recordings you hear both an eighth-note appoggiatura and a gentle portamento from the D to the C that smudges the exact rhythm. The ornamental note on "guter" in m. 14 should be light, fast, and before the beat.

In *Der Hirt auf dem Felsen* (ex. 5.6), the NSA recommends a dotted half-note appoggiatura in m. 147 on the word "wich," resolving on the downbeat of the next measure. I prefer using a half-note appoggiatura and making the rhythm match the earlier phrases in this slow section: "Gram" in m. 131 and "mir" in m. 143. Again, you could use portamento and rubato to create an expressive gesture of unspecific length.

Example 5.7 shows situations in which you could treat the appoggiatura either as a slightly stressed dissonant upper neighbor note or as a fast grace note. The NSA suggests a sixteenth note on the beat for example 5.7a but a fast, before-the-beat grace note for examples 5.7b–d. In "Tränenregen" (5.7b), the tempo you choose and the way you want to inflect the different syllables in each

Example 5.4. Schubert: a) "Rastlose Liebe," mm. 25–38; b) "Frühlingstraum," mm. 29–40; c) "Lachen und Weinen," mm. 62–65, Peters, ed. Friedlaender; d) "An Emma," NSA IV/ 1a/Vorwort, p. xiii.

Example 5.5. Schubert: a) "Ave Maria," mm. 11–12; b) "Frühlingsglaube," mm. 40–42; c) "An die Nachtigall," mm. 10–17, Peters, ed. Friedlaender.

verse may affect how you choose to perform the ornament. A fast, springy gesture might not feel appropriate in a slower tempo. The more lively movement of "Halt" (5.7c), however, does invite that gesture. In "Der Einsame" (5.7d), I personally like the melodic shape that results from making two even sixteenth

Example 5.6. Schubert: *Der Hirt auf dem Felsen,* mm. 141–148, International, 1972.

notes on "stilles," and so I save the grace-note gesture for "da*her* gebracht" later on in the song.

Because Schubert composed at a time of transition, he employed both old and new ideas. Thus the suggestions for performing appoggiaturas in the NSA are a good place to start, but they are not necessarily the only solutions.

TRILLS AND TURNS

The preference for starting trills on the main note continued to grow during the nineteenth century. Noted musicians such as Johann Nepomuk Hummel and Louis Spohr recommended that if composers wanted an alternative to the main-note start, they should indicate it. Yet scholars believe that musicians most likely felt free to vary the beginnings and endings of trills to suit their taste and the particular musical situation. Composers used both ornament signs and small and large notes to indicate turns with a wide variety of patterns and speeds. Example 5.8 shows two different autographs by Spohr of his song "Nachgefühl." In the first copy from 1834, he notates the turn figure with a reg-

Example 5.7. Schubert: a) "Danksagung an den Bach," mm. 5–8; b) "Tränenregen," mm. 5–9; c) "Halt," mm. 27–30; d) "Der Einsame," mm. 17, 29, Peters, ed. Friedlaender.

ular turn sign and large notes for the D and C; this would indicate that the turn should start in the upward direction. In another handwritten copy from 1839, he uses an inverted turn sign and an appoggiatura for the D leading to the C; this might indicate starting in the downward direction, as Spohr instructed in his *Violinschule.* Yet his casual attitude toward the specific notation of the figure probably meant that he trusted the singer to execute something graceful and appropriate. Many examples of inconsistent notation of turns and controversy over their execution exist in nineteenth-century music, even in the early operas of Wagner. The same kind of controversy—one could call it freedom—exists regarding mordents. It seems there are no definitive answers.[34]

### Vibrato and Portamento

Since mid-nineteenth-century German vocal technique remained based mostly on the Italian models (except, of course, with regard to language and diction), the use of vibrato and portamento still echoed earlier Italian recommendations (see the discussion in chapter 4). Some German sources discuss vibrato in conjunction with a gesture of accentuation. In his *Violinschule,* Spohr described violin vibrato as an imitation of "the singer's voice in passionate passages, or when he forces it to its most powerful pitch. . . . Avoid however its frequent use, or in improper places. In places where the tremolo is used by the singer, it may also advantageously be applied to the Violin. This tremolo is therefore properly used in passionate passages, and in strongly marking all the *fz* or > tones."[35] The *Wiener allgemeine musikalische Zeitung* of 1813 described vibrato as "here, the notes will not be pulled out at the roots but only tickled at their tips,"[36] also indicating some kind of gentle accent. In examples 5.9a–d the > or *sf* could indicate a stress with vibrato.

Wagner occasionally went so far as to indicate vibrato with a wavy line or to include instructions for a trembling voice, steering singers to produce a special dramatic effect. While the use of instrumental vibrato gradually increased over the course of the nineteenth century, significant and continuous vocal vibrato was still considered a problem that needed to be controlled. In 1884 Wolf criticized a singer in one of his reviews: "she seldom manages to attack the upper notes securely, and this tremulous vibrato is distressing to the listener."[37] Lilli Lehmann, born in 1848, grew up listening to singers schooled in bel canto, and she developed her technical approach based on their models. In her book *How to Sing,* she states emphatically, "Even the vibrato, to which full voices are prone, should be nipped in the bud, for gradually the tremolo, and later even

(*a*)

(*b*)

Example 5.8. Spohr: "Nachgefühl," two manuscript reproductions from Clive Brown, *Classical and Romantic Performing Practice*, Oxford University Press, 1999, p. 508, used by permission of the publisher.

Example 5.9. a) Schumann: "Schneeglöckchen," mm. 7–9, Peters; b) Mendelssohn: "Bei der Wiege," mm. 17–19, *Mendelssohn Werke* XIX/87; c) Wolf: "Du denkst mit einem Fädchen," mm. 12–15, Peters, 1904, reprint Dover, 1989; d) Strauss: "Du meines Herzens Krönlein," mm. 5–12, Joseph Aibl, 1890, International, 1955.

worse, is developed from it."[38] In her late-career recordings from the early twentieth century she sings with a hardly noticeable shimmer to her voice.

Portamento was used much more freely, sometimes to great excess. Lehmann warns against its overuse, resulting in "a bad habit lacking in good taste."[39] Yet in early twentieth-century recordings, singers who had begun their careers in the nineteenth century frequently used portamento for expressive purposes. Portamento could enhance legato lines and connect small and large

Example 5.10. a) Schubert: "An die Musik," mm. 4–6, Peters, ed. Friedlaender; b) Schumann: "Ich kann's nicht fassen, nicht glauben," mm. 8–11, Peters; c) Schumann: "Ich kann's nicht fassen, nicht glauben," mm. 20–23, Peters.

leaps in either direction. It could color a specific word for dramatic reasons.[40] As mentioned in the appoggiatura section, it could help in performing small notated ornaments as in "An die Musik" (ex. 5.10a). The figures in examples 5.10b and c, common in Schumann, could be executed as springy, heroic gestures, depending upon the text, musical context, and intended dramatic inter-

Example 5.11. Strauss: "Wie sollten wir geheim sie halten," mm 1–6, Joseph Aibl, 1888, International, 1955.

pretation. In Strauss's "Wie sollten wir geheim sie halten" (ex. 5.11), the wavy lines seem to request both portamento and vibrato between the E and the low A and between the F-sharp and the high A.

Phrasing marks are used differently by individual composers, but most often in vocal music they indicate a single syllable on more than one note. One could use portamento here, but it is not necessary for simple legato singing. Sometimes, particularly in songs by Strauss, a long phrase mark may indicate the larger shape of a phrase. This could show where to breathe or merely illustrate the long-term destination of the phrase.

Portamento thus can be used in lieder for expressive, dramatic purposes both in large and small gestures, but it should be motivated by the words and the musical context. It should not be used so much that it becomes a tasteless mannerism, though what many listeners might consider tasteless today is quite different from what was accepted as the norm a century ago.

## The Piano

Between 1800 and 1880 the piano underwent a phenomenal transformation unlike that of any previous instrument. Its modifications and technical developments most certainly contributed to the blossoming of lieder. The English and Viennese approach to piano building continued to produce instruments with different sounds and technical capacities. Most German composers had access to and preferred the Viennese fortepianos. The instruments made by the Viennese piano makers Nannette and Johann Andreas Streicher and by Conrad Graf had a light touch, even tone quality from bottom to top, and a beautiful, delicate sound. Their crystalline quality inspired many of the shimmering accompaniments in Schubert's songs. The clear sound in the bass range also highlighted many of the melodic figures in the left hand of Schubert's accompaniments.

Schumann had already written a great deal of piano music before composing most of his songs, and he had worked out a pianistic language to take greater advantage of the instrument's tonal palette and expressive potential. His songs used the piano in a newly integrated way, building layers of melody shared by voice and piano and colored by rich harmonic shadings. By the middle of the century, piano makers continued to experiment with every element of the instrument. They investigated its basic shape, the thickness and number of strings, the striking action, the hammer action, the soundboard material, and the ability of the frame to withstand increased string pressure. Innovations in pedal technology contributed new kinds of tonal and dampening effects as well. Piano builders competed to satisfy the technical desires of famous virtuoso players, hoping the celebrities would play and endorse their instruments. By 1880 most of the major technical innovations were complete, and the modern concert piano, with its full, brilliant sound that could carry over an orchestra, became available. Yet even Brahms preferred his more delicate Viennese

Streicher and wrote much of his piano music with its sound and action in mind.

The spaces in which songs were performed in the nineteenth century were likely to have been more resonant than most concert halls today. The quick attack and rapid decay of the pre-1850 Viennese fortepiano provide a clear texture for such an acoustic. The total volume of this instrument is considerably less than that of a modern grand piano, which provides greater sustaining power and accumulating overtones. Singing lieder with a Viennese fortepiano thus immediately solves many balance issues between voice and keyboard. It allows the pianist to choose from a wider variety of dynamic levels without having to worry about overpowering the voice. Singer and pianist can employ more variety in accentuation and articulation as well. The fortepiano also enables a vocalist to sing more gently, with less pressure and effort. This invariably relaxes the vibrato, perhaps revealing that delicate shimmer so characteristic of early recordings.

**Tempo and Rhythm**

As discussed in chapter 4, the nineteenth century brought a more flexible approach to tempo and rhythm. This tendency became increasingly exaggerated as the century progressed. In the early 1800s, most Austrian and German composers, including Schubert and Mendelssohn, insisted, as Mozart had, that their music be played "in time." Yet they also showed a certain degree of flexibility in choosing tempos and often varied them within a work for expressive purposes. By 1833, a writer in a German musical journal complained that "ritardando and accelerando alternate all the time. This manner has already become so fixed in the minds of the musical public that they firmly believe a diminuendo must be slowed down and a crescendo speeded up; a tender phrase (e.g., in an allegro) will be performed more slowly, a powerful one faster."[41] Sonnleithner, writing in 1860, reflected midcentury practices as he described Schubert's expectations with regard to flexible tempo:

> The musical idea should be displayed in its purity. A necessary corollary to this is the *strictest observation of tempo*. Schubert always indicated exactly where he wanted or permitted a *ritardando*, an *accelerando* or any kind of freer delivery. But where he did not indicate this, he would not tolerate the slightest arbitrariness or the least deviation in tempo. . . . A trotting or galloping horse permits of no deviation of strict time; . . . —a quickly beating heart cannot suddenly stop (except from a stroke) in order to let the singer dwell on his high A at the words "Dein ist mein Herz und wird es ewig bleiben" and give rein to his excess sentimentality; . . . these wretched exam-

ples, are merely intended to serve as isolated instances, for this senseless manner of interpretation has unfortunately already become the rule. . . . This does not mean in the very least that Schubert wanted to hear his songs ground out merely mechanically. An accurate, purely musical performance in no way excludes feeling and sensitivity; but the singer should on no account give himself airs.[42]

Schubert assigned metronome markings to his first few sets of published songs but quickly gave them up in favor of descriptive tempo terms. Singers of lieder are probably all too familiar with such vague tempo qualifiers as *mäßig, ziemlich,* or *etwas* and emotional descriptions such as *zart, leise, innig,* or *ausdrucksvoll.* Sometimes these German terms impart a sense of actual speed, but more often they simply suggest the general mood or character of a song. Mendelssohn, who used Italian tempo terms in his songs, was also reluctant to assign metronome markings. It was reported of him that "though in playing he never varied the tempo once taken, he did not always take a movement at the same pace, but changed it as his mood was at the time."[43] Weber, writing in 1824, had a slightly different approach toward tempo, but it was one that represented a prevailing attitude: "The beat should not be a tyrannical restriction or the driving of a mill hammer. On the contrary, it should be to the music what the pulse beat is to the life of man. There is no slow tempo in which passages which demand a faster movement do not occur, and thereby prevent the feeling of dragging. Conversely, there is no *presto,* which does not call for the slower execution of certain passages, so that expression will not be marred by overzealousness."[44]

Brahms, too, believed that the tempos in his music should not be constant, nor was it possible to determine the "correct" tempo with a metronome mark. As he commented in a letter to the conductor George Henschel, "I am of the opinion that metronome marks go for nothing. As far as I know, all composers have as yet retracted their metronome marks in later years."[45] Most reports describe Brahms's piano playing as extremely variable with regard to tempo. Clara Schumann wrote in her journal, "It is not easy to play with Brahms; he plays too arbitrarily, and cares nothing for a beat more or less. . . . I cannot quite get used to the constant change of tempo in his works, and he plays them so according to his own fancy."[46] It is tantalizing to imagine these two close friends playing the four-hands piano accompaniment at the premiere of Brahms's *Liebeslieder* waltzes.

We are fortunate to have recordings of Strauss accompanying his own songs, none of which have assigned metronome markings. Strauss was perfectly willing to adapt the flow of a song to fit the tastes and needs of different singers, and his recordings reveal considerable flexibility and variety in tempo.[47] By the end of the century, charismatic conductors (including Strauss) demonstrated their virtuoso control of orchestras with wildly fluctuating tempos. Achieving a heightened emotional state with extremely slow tempos was also popular with certain conductors and singers, who were happy to show off their breath control.[48]

As nineteenth-century music became more complex and performers took increasing liberties with tempo, many composers decided to include more detailed performance instructions, aiming to exert more control over the performances of their works. Wolf wrote frequent tempo indications in his songs, sometimes every few measures. He and Mahler both used elaborate German descriptions as well as Italian terms to specify subtle shifts in tempo. Composers also started using time signature changes and more precise note values to control the flow of their music.

DOTTED FIGURES

The notation of dotted figures, duples, and triplets became more meticulous as the nineteenth century progressed. The songs of Schubert and Schumann, however, were still somewhat under the influence of ambiguous eighteenth-century notational practices. (See the discussion of rhythmic alteration in chapters 2 and 3.) Often a singer and accompanist must decide whether a triplet figure should agree with a dotted figure or be performed as a distinctly contrasting rhythm.[49]

There has been much debate, for instance, about the preferred approach to this issue in "Wasserflut" (ex. 5.12a) from Schubert's *Winterreise*. A 1963 performance by Peter Pears with Benjamin Britten at the keyboard provoked strong reactions when Britten made the dotted figure in the left hand agree with the triplet in the right hand. Some scholars argued that there was enough evidence to support the aligning of the rhythms in the eighteenth-century manner. Others disagreed for a variety of reasons, including their personal preference.[50] In "Des Mädchens Klage" (ex. 5.12b), the singer must decide whether to fit the duple rhythms into the steady triplets in the piano, to pull against them within the triplet, or perhaps to place the syllable after the triplet using a double dot. The text should help you weigh such choices in any song, but especially when the song is strophic. The best approach is to allow each verse to differ, depending upon the length and weight of certain syllables as well as the dramatic inflection desired. In mm. 9 and 10, it would be too complicated to simultaneously perform a duple in the voice part, a triplet in the treble of the piano, and a double dot in

Example 5.12. Schubert: a) "Wasserflut," mm. 5–8; b) "Des Mädchens Klage," mm. 9–10; c) "Frühlingsglaube," mm. 8–10, Peters, ed. Friedlaender.

the bass. Even if Schubert did want a contrasting rhythm in "Wasserflut," it is unlikely that this was his intention here. The placement of the bass note should help convey the diction, not work against it. So, for example, the second verse might lend itself to observing triplet rhythms in all parts, while the third verse might benefit from more marked dots from the voice and the bass line. Both "Frühlingsglaube" (ex. 5.12c) and "Ave Maria" (ex. 5.3c) include the same kinds of situations. Again, the text should be the deciding factor, with the understanding that a flexible approach will allow the greatest freedom for musical and dramatic expression.

A good example of this freedom and variety can be found in early recordings. Here singers frequently make duples into triplets and triplets into double dots, all to suit the text and their expressive impulses. We must remember that expectations of rhythmic exactitude were an invention of the twentieth century. In 1886 Wolf applauded a singer for his particularly good rhythm: "Especially admirable in Blauwaert's singing is its accuracy, its rhythmic precision and its lively expression."[51] He mentions this as if it were something unusual, which it probably was.

RUBATO

Another element contributing to the larger picture of rhythmic freedom was rubato. The eighteenth-century tradition of rubato, advocated by both Tosi and Mozart, allowed the melody line to become independent from the accompaniment for heightened expression. Tosi cautioned that if you stole some time you must replace it, and Mozart taught that the left hand must continue playing in time while the right hand wove around it. In the nineteenth century this concept was stretched further: the basic tempo was constantly shifting, and internal rhythms were being pushed and pulled as well. The use of an agogic accent to linger on a particular note, letting the melody go out of sync here and there, only added to the music's expressivity and fluidity. In addition to speeding up for a crescendo and slowing down for a decrescendo, it was common to rush through fast notes and stretch out longer ones. When Brahms played his own *Hungarian Dances,* the rhythm was described as "darting and halting."[52] Liszt, writing about Chopin's playing, described his use of tempo rubato as "a stolen, irregularly interrupted time-measure, desultory and languishing, then flickering like a flame in a draft . . . or like treetops leaning this way and that according to the capricious whims of the wind."[53]

Of course, different artists used all these devices to varying degrees, and composers sometimes expressed opinions about rhythm and tempo at odds with how they themselves played. Joseph Joachim's violin playing was described as conservative and noble, yet a 1903 recording reveals tempos that Robert Philip describes as quirky and volatile, with rhythms that sound almost out of control. Philip suggests that when we listen to early twentieth-century recordings we sometimes hear playing that underemphasized rhythmic detail, almost to the point of carelessness. Certainly over the course of the twentieth century we have become much more disciplined about rhythmic accuracy and precision. But Philip cautions that this lack of precision heard in the playing of the greatest soloists and virtuosos of the late nineteenth and early twentieth centuries was not a question of sloppiness but rather of style.[54]

This chapter has continued to track the changing attitudes toward ornamentation, vibrato, portamento, rubato, and tempo flexibility. In German lieder singing, elaborate added ornamentation virtually disappeared. You might feel free to add some small graces, including appoggiaturas, trills, or turns, but only to songs from early in the period. By the end of the nineteenth century, composers were notating almost all ornamentation, sometimes with small notes or signs but increasingly with regular-sized notes. The execution of notated ornaments, including appoggiaturas and turns, is still open to some interpretation, particularly in songs by Schubert, which can be influenced by eighteenth-century practices. Songs by Schubert and Schumann can also follow earlier rules for rhythmic alteration, but this remains a controversial subject.

Vibrato can be used as an expressive device in lieder and is sometimes indicated with a wavy line or a variety of accent markings. A wide, continuous vibrato, however, is still inappropriate. Portamento, on the other hand, can be used liberally in many situations for both small and large gestures. It should be employed for expressive and dramatic purposes.

Rubato and tempo flexibility can also be used to a great degree to enhance expression. By the end of the century, variation of tempo and rhythm had become so extreme that composers started trying to regulate the flow of tempo with meter and note values as well as an increased use of descriptive tempo instructions. Even though wildly fluctuating tempos, exaggerated rubato, and pervasive use of portamento were fashionable by the end of the nineteenth century for this repertoire, singers today may want to avoid going too far.

New issues presented in this chapter include approaches to editions and transposition and German diction. Scholarly Urtext editions of lieder are either available or under way, but the readily available editions based on nineteenth-century publications are generally reliable. You should be careful about transpositions, especially for song cycles and repertoire from the end of the nineteenth century. You can bring a flexible attitude to gender-specific poems, which are appropriate when sung by either male or female voices. The specific idiosyncrasies of the German language have a major impact on articulation and expression for lieder. Many prominent nineteenth-century singers strove to combine Italian vocal production with German diction, yet many German singers employed highly exaggerated dramatic declamation. You certainly need to highlight the special qualities of German without, perhaps, going to the extremes seen in the nineteenth century.

# Chapter 6 French Mélodies

This chapter surveys the French art song of the nineteenth and twentieth centuries, beginning with the romance of the mid-nineteenth century and focusing on the mélodies of Fauré, Debussy, Ravel, and Poulenc. It also includes the contributions of such prominent singers as Reynaldo Hahn, Mary Garden, Jane Bathori, Claire Croiza, Charles Panzéra, Maggie Teyte, and Pierre Bernac. Chapters 1 and 2 noted the importance of *le bon goût* (good taste) and the sanctity of the French language in music of the Baroque. Matters of taste and language continued to play a significant role in the nineteenth-century development of the mélodie, influencing the relationships between both poetry and music and composer and performer. We are fortunate to have a close link with the creators of this repertoire through recordings by singers who worked with Fauré, Debussy, and others, as well as recordings performed and supervised by Ravel and Poulenc. Some students today also still have access to teachers who studied with the major figures of this period. Many books on the French song repertoire offer advice on diction, translations of poetic texts, and interpretive suggestions (see "Chapter 6: Texts and Diction" in "For Further Reading"). This chapter does not attempt to repeat such material but rather to supplement it by considering the roots of French style as developed by the composers and singers who worked together.

The French mélodie took longer than the German lied to come into its own. This delay was due in part to the devastating effects of the French Revolution. It did not take long, however, for a new aristocracy to emerge, hungry for artistic stimulation. By the 1820s Italian opera was all the rage in Paris, where Rossini was the director of the Théâtre-Italien. Touring celebrities dazzled Parisian audiences, and the wealthy held private salons to discuss political, philosophical, and artistic ideas. Often composers, or perhaps their hostesses, sang romances, simple strophic songs with modest piano accompaniments. However, music in the salons was often merely incidental to the conversation.

Schubert's lieder were first published in French translation in the 1830s and championed in performances by the well-known tenor Adolphe Nourrit, accompanied by Liszt. Translated as "mélodies," they became wildly popular and inspired a new level of creativity in the composition of romances. Berlioz composed a set of songs to texts by Irish poet and musician Thomas Moore known as "A Selection of Irish Melodies." Published in 1830 as *Neuf mélodies imitées de l'anglais,* they helped introduce the new term *mélodie.* The French poetry available to composers at this time was also improving. Gounod, Massenet, Saint-Saëns, Delibes, and Bizet all composed songs to French texts for the delight of accomplished amateur and semiprofessional salon performers. Some songs by Berlioz, Liszt, Edouard Lalo, and Henri Duparc may have been written with professional performers in mind. Much of this Romantic song repertoire was written under the predominant influence of Italian opera stars and traveling virtuosi. Within the context of French taste, it can be approached by following the stylistic advice given in chapters 4 and 5.

The later music of Fauré, Debussy, and Ravel moved French music in a new direction and style. The Third Republic (1870–1940) witnessed a flowering of all the arts, including painting, literature, and music, transforming Paris into the artistic capital of Europe. Salons now provided a haven for a sophisticated elite and by the end of the century had become the refuge of the avant-garde. The music of Wagner had an important influence on some French composers. The International Exposition of 1889 had a profound impact on Debussy, Ravel, and many others by introducing exotic elements such as Javanese gamelans and Russian orchestral music conducted by Rimsky-Korsakov. Not long after, two other Russians, Sergei Diaghilev and Igor Stravinsky, took Paris by storm, revolutionizing the theater and involving the entire artistic community.

Composers began creating a new harmonic landscape, highlighting the sound of the music rather than the virtuosity of the performer. They sought to preserve the integrity of their music with precise notation. They also insisted on accurate performances and found performers who were willing to cooperate. The role of the performer increasingly became less about displaying skill and more about serving the needs of the composer.

Composers gravitated to performers who could fill this role, often developing close relationships such as those of Fauré and Claire Croiza or of Debussy and Jane Bathori. Some of these have been documented in fascinating memoirs that reveal the inner workings of rehearsals and performances.[1] Perhaps the most fruitful of these relationships was between Francis Poulenc and Pierre Bernac. They first met in 1926 and began a performing relationship in 1934 that lasted for twenty-five years. Poulenc composed two-thirds of his songs for Bernac, tailoring his music to the baritone's particular strengths, including his ease in singing softly in his high range and loudly in his low range. It was a truly collaborative relationship, and the singer strongly influenced the composer regarding issues of programming, tempo, dramatic presentation, and general style. As Bernac writes in his book, *Francis Poulenc: The Man and His Songs,* "we created them together."[2] We are left with many invaluable recordings of this magnificent pair, as well as with Bernac's indispensable book *The Interpretation of French Song,* which every singer of mélodies and chansons should keep close to his or her piano.[3] Yet this book, written in 1970, reflects the culmination of an evolutionary process; the advice Bernac gives is not necessarily how he sang in his early recordings. His approach also reflects the particular style he created with Poulenc, incorporating all their idiosyncrasies. It is also worth exploring the collaborative relationships of some other singers and composers to get a broader sense of French singing styles.

### Editions, Transpositions, and Voice Types

Most nineteenth-century Romantic mélodies were published for the general public, and many composers earned considerable profits from the sale of their songs, which were printed both as sheet music and in journals, newsletters, and songbooks. Often songs were transposed into a variety of keys and arranged in different combinations and orders, sometimes with new titles or even new texts. In his *French Song from Berlioz to Duparc,* Frits Noske observes that both publishers and composers treated songs with a certain casualness, considering them to be "mere trifles."[4] The variety of nineteenth-century French song editions can create confusion in determining whether composers intended songs to be presented as a distinct cycle in a certain order or whether the songs could stand alone or be recombined.

A good example of this ambiguity is Berlioz's *Les nuits d'été*, first published in 1841 as a set of six songs with piano accompaniment. Despite the awkward writing for the piano, the songs set a new standard of quality for the mélodie. In 1843 Berlioz orchestrated "Absence" for the mezzo Marie Recio, who was touring with him in Germany and whom he later married. In 1854 he orchestrated the rest of the songs, transposing them and dedicating each to a different singer. While he may have had a particular order in mind for the publication of the piano-vocal score, he never performed all the orchestrated songs together as a strict cycle. Singers today therefore can decide whether they want to perform *Les nuits d'été* with piano or with orchestra, in what order, and in what keys.[5]

As the century progressed, composers grew more careful about supervising the publication of their songs. They also became more particular about transposition. Fauré's songs appeared in three collections of twenty songs each, published by Hamelle in 1879, 1897, and 1908. The first book was clearly intended for the accomplished amateur, while the later songs demanded higher levels of technical skill and musicianship from both singer and pianist. Fauré preferred a voice of medium range and wrote most of his songs in keys that avoided operatic high notes. The "Pie Jesu" solo in his *Requiem* was written for a boy soprano only because the clergy of the Madeleine, where it was first performed, forbade women in the choir. In subsequent performances Fauré entrusted the solo to a female soprano.

Debussy wrote many of his early songs for the high, light voice of his first muse, Marie Vasnier. He met her while accompanying a singing class for society women, and she and her husband gave moral and financial support to the young composer. The *Quatre chansons de jeunesse*, written for and dedicated to her, were published posthumously in 1926. Jane Bathori, who worked with Debussy on all his later songs, believed they were issued as curiosities and that the composer had not wanted them published.[6]

Later Debussy, as well as Ravel and others, developed a preference for a lower voice type and fashioned compositions primarily for professional musicians. As their music became more subtle and harmonically complex, the choice of key was directly linked with a certain vocal tessitura and a distinct color palette for the piano or instruments. Transposing the music would disturb this delicate arrangement of sounds. Poulenc stated that he never transposed his music once he conceived it for a specific key.[7] (Pianist Dalton Baldwin, however, has said that Poulenc did transpose certain songs for Gerard Souzay.)[8] Bernac's book on

Poulenc lists all the songs with date of composition, publisher, range, and recommendations for male or female singer (some songs are only appropriate for a certain voice type). According to the baritone Martial Singher, Ravel admitted that he had originally conceived "Asie" from *Shéhérazade* and the *Chansons madécasses* for a male voice, though only female singers who were excellent musicians had been interested in performing them. Singher, who premiered Ravel's *Don Quichotte à Dulcinée* songs, did eventually perform *Chansons madécasses* and "Asie," but not until after Ravel's death.[9]

Most modern editions of French songs are reprints of nineteenth-century editions or publications supervised by the composer. The original French editions, including those by Durand, are the best places to start for this repertoire. Information on publications is available in the *New Grove* articles on individual composers as well as in an extensive appendix in Frits Noske's *French Song from Berlioz to Duparc*. The Dover editions of *French Art Songs of the Nineteenth Century* (and of the songs of Fauré, Duparc, Ernest Chausson, and Debussy) all list the original sources for the reprinted scores. The Dover edition of Ravel songs was edited by Ravel scholar Arbie Orenstein and includes introductory information, notes on each song, and further references. Much of the earlier nineteenth-century repertoire is suitable to sing in a comfortable transposition, since that was the practice of the amateur singers for whom it was intended. It is advisable, however, to sing the later repertoire in the original keys, especially works by Debussy, Ravel, and Poulenc.

The International editions of Fauré and Chausson list the original keys of transposed songs, but these don't always agree with the original keys listed in the *New Grove* or reprinted in the Dover editions. For example, both the *New Grove* and the Dover reprint of 1908 list the original key of Fauré's "Rêve d'amour" as E-flat major. The International score, however, shows the original key as F. It also prints some alternative rhythms in the vocal part. The *New Grove* Chausson article unfortunately does not list original keys for the songs. While the International edition of Debussy does not indicate transposed songs or original keys, the 1993 Hal Leonard Vocal Library edition of Debussy songs did publish all the songs in original keys, arranged in two volumes for high and medium voice. Edited by James Briscoe, it is a critical edition that includes translations, notes, and historical sources. A new scholarly edition of Debussy's complete works was begun by Durand-Costallat in 1985, but the songs have not yet been published. A new edition of the complete works of Berlioz was begun in 1969 by Bärenreiter and includes a volume with orchestral songs, but the volume of songs with piano has yet to be published. Thomas Grubb, in his diction manual *Singing in French,* warns students to be aware of the unavoidable mistakes found in most editions, particularly regarding texts and translations. He is most suspect of anthologies with unacknowledged transpositions and *ossia* interpolations.[10]

## French Taste and Aesthetics

French music of the seventeenth and eighteenth centuries had been characterized by restrained grace and beauty, especially compared with the obviously emotional and heavily ornamented style of the Italians. In his 1767 *Dictionnaire de musique,* Rousseau emphasized the need for simplicity in the composition and performance of the romance. He believed that songs should be written in a simple, moving style, according to the character of the words: "an accurate, clear voice that articulates well and sings without affectation is all that is required for singing a romance."[11] In the nineteenth century, this desire for purity and simplicity of style continued, along with a growing aversion to virtuosity. An overly demonstrative outpouring of emotion or technical skill was not considered appropriate to the intimate salon setting where romances were sung. Martin Cooper's *French Music from the Death of Berlioz to the Death of Fauré* suggests that the French composer was interested primarily in "arranging sounds in agreeable and intellectually satisfying patterns. . . . He would prefer the humbler search for perfection in all forms, however small . . . than in a work planned on a larger scale, with more obvious pretensions to greatness but less aesthetically satisfying."[12]

In 1846 Antoine Romagnesi, a well-known composer and singer of romances, published *L'art de chanter les romances, les chansonnettes et les nocturnes et généralement toute la musique de salon.* In this short treatise he presented simple suggestions that teachers and singers of French repertoire have practiced throughout the twentieth century. In distinguishing the difference between the opera singer and more delicate salon singer, "between a large and intractable voice and the more modest and manageable kind found in the larger number of non-professional musicians," he advised the salon singer to treat his or her voice with care and never to force it beyond its natural abilities; he should sing *fort bien* rather than *bien fort* (very well rather than very loudly). The singer should study the text before he sings it and convey the sense of the poem without vocal display. Breathing and facial expressions should be natural and unforced. "Good taste will warn him to search only for those means that are simple and natural; to avoid mannerism and exaggeration; finally, to model his vocal inflections on the sentiments that he is called upon to express."[13]

Fauré started performing in aristocratic salons as a young student. He was not fond of Italian opera and opera singers or "big theater bellowers" as he called them, and while he admired Liszt, he was not interested in the flashy world of the virtuoso pianist. He was an accomplished pianist himself but preferred a collaborative role to the soloist's spotlight. One of his favorite singers was Emma Bardac, the wife of a wealthy banker. She sang in an easy soprano voice and was an excellent sight-reader who preferred to perform in private. After a performance of "Soir," which Fauré had written for her, he told the poet Albert Samain, "You'll never hear it sung better." Samain recounted that "she has a feeling for nuances and especially a purity of expression which are extremely rare."[14] In a 1902 letter to a patron, Fauré wrote about his songs: "I dream of hearing them performed by perfect singers, but I don't know of any among the professionals. It's the amateurs who understand and interpret me best."[15] Since many of the singers he preferred did not possess great instruments—including the natural, untrained baritone of his friend, composer/singer Reynaldo Hahn—some assumed (much to Fauré's annoyance) that one didn't need a voice to sing his songs. He entrusted his later cycles to two young newcomers, Madeleine Grey and Charles Panzéra, whose singing was characterized by extreme refinement and purity.

Debussy's early experience also included accompanying amateurs in the salon, and in 1904 he married Emma Bardac, whose previous husband had finally lost out to her fascination and involvement with young composers. Debussy strove for a purity and simplicity of style that was governed by nuance. He included warmth and passion in his music but knew when to stop before the emotion became vulgar: "One should sing when there is something to sing about, and keep the emotional power of the voice in reserve."[16] Debussy particularly admired and worked with Mary Garden, whose intense yet simple and restrained acting made her his ideal Mélisande, and Jane Bathori, whose singing was described by Darius Milhaud as having "a pure style, clear diction and discrete interior charm."[17] Bathori, who championed the music of many early twentieth-century French composers, was also an accomplished pianist and often accompanied herself when the composers were not at the piano. The critic Georges Jean-Aubry, in an article from 1913, hailed her as "modern French song incarnate . . . her art is all of nuances . . . nevertheless it is impossible to surpass it in naturalness and in that important spontaneity which alone has importance for the listener. . . . [she possesses] vocal simplicity, the same scrupulous care of refinement, and the same absence of display even in the most ardent passion."[18]

The 1907 premiere of Ravel's *Histoires naturelles,* with the composer accompanying Bathori, incited a riotous demonstration in the concert hall and lively discussion following in the press. Even though Emmanuel Chabrier had previously set poems about animals, the public was astonished at Ravel's unusual choice of Jules Renard's text and his revolutionary treatment of it, particularly his elision of many mute "e's." In his review, Louis Laloy described Bathori as having a childlike grace: "a little girl looking at the beasts and laughing at their comical appearance or the antics they get up to, but feeling very fond of them just the same. As for the author, seated at the piano, stiff and impassive, he was the only person in the entire hall who betrayed no emotion."[19] Ravel also admired the clear voice and impeccable diction of Madeleine Grey and frequently requested that she perform his music. Their recording of *Chansons madécasses* is decidedly restrained emotionally. Poulenc, in his *Diary of My Songs,* cautions singers not to overdo the dramatic emotions of his songs. He recommends a simple seriousness, especially in some of the humorous songs where a knowing look would spoil the irony.[20] Bernac sums up the French aesthetic in writing that lyricism and passion are not absent in French music, rather that "emotions and feelings are refined, purified and controlled by reason."[21]

### Ornamentation

For the most part, added ornaments were not needed or desired in French vocal repertoire, especially by the final decades of the nineteenth century. Earlier in the century, opinion had been mixed. The critic François-Joseph Fétis, writing in 1827, disagreed with the common view that ornaments were not suited to the French language; he believed that the Italian style had a positive impact on French singing in general and particularly in ornamentation.[22] Most other French writers, however, warned singers not to go too far. Berlioz made no secret of his dislike of ornamented singing in the Italian style. Romagnesi mentioned that some types of songs—gracious, or light and courtly—may tolerate some tiny embellishments, "but they must be used sparingly so as not to stifle the basic idea under a web of parasite-like details."[23] For tender and sad romances, he cautioned to "guard against pretentious flourishes, or against clumsy appoggiaturas [*ports de voix*], which some singers take to be expression but which is only parody. He should avoid those long fermatas on the penultimate note of the phrase that poor taste on the part of several singers has made fashionable."[24] Writing about the romances of Henri Reber, Saint-Saëns mentioned that Reber "forbade in his songs neither trills nor scales nor arpeggios; gracious arabesques frequently accompany the lines of his architecture, arabesques of a very pure style, it goes without saying, and having nothing to do with those gargoyles of the old Italian school."[25]

### The Performer's New Role

As the nineteenth century progressed, composers included considerable performance instructions in their scores. Singers needed only to execute what was written accurately, without adding any embellishment of their own. Bathori advised young singers not to add any personal interpretation to Debussy's songs: only to deliver what is written in the music exactly and to have "complete musical respect."[26] When Debussy first heard Claire Croiza, another champion of contemporary French music, he said, "What a joy to hear my songs sung as I have written them!"[27] Croiza was also a favorite of Fauré's. In her master classes she said of his songs: "we must try to enter into the atmosphere he has created, and not allow our own personalities to disturb it."[28] She also insisted on scrupulous accuracy in following every detail of a composer's indications: "A singer's first duty is to sing the music as it is written and to give every note the value the composer has given it. . . . Perhaps it is because the precise composers of today mistrust the possible bad taste of some interpreters, that they note everything to the least detail. They indicate everything that should be done and the interpreter has nothing to add, nothing to modify. His magnificent role is to serve and not to collaborate."[29]

As early as 1846 Romagnesi had advised that romances should be "sung simply and following the composer's indications."[30] At the turn of the century Jean-Aubry railed against performers who used their technical gifts merely to dazzle the audience and gain applause for themselves, "whereas their sole duty is to be the humble and respectful servants of the works."[31] Ravel said, "I do not ask for my music to be interpreted, but only for it to be played."[32] Bernac, too, stressed the importance of being faithful to the work by achieving a precision of performance; he quoted Stravinsky, who required an aspiring interpreter to first be a "flawless executant." This credo, which some today mistakenly take as a given for all music, has its roots in the late nineteenth-century French reaction against the excesses of Romanticism.

### Words and Music

The French have always held the beauty and refinement of their language in high esteem. The wealth of poetry by Paul Verlaine, Charles Baudelaire, Stéphane Mallarmé, and others provided composers with rich opportunities for song settings. Curiously, the relationship between French words and mélodies was not as mutually supportive as that of German poetry and lieder. The rigorous rules required for French poetry made setting it to music problematic. This resulted in frequent prosody mistakes, even in the songs of Berlioz, Bizet, and Fauré. In an essay on the relationship between words and music in his 1885 *Harmonie et mélodie,* Saint-Saëns complained about the woeful state of text setting, which he found worse at the opera than in the salon. Since French does not have the strong rhythmic inflection of Italian or the percussive consonant clusters of English or German, syllable stress is made by duration rather than force. Because French musicians and poets believed that no syllable had an accent except either the final masculine or penultimate feminine syllable of a line, they thought that musical accents could be placed at will, often resulting in a confusing gibberish.[33]

Debussy chose to attack this problem by setting poetry in a recitative style, preserving the subtle stresses and proper syllable lengths. He was compared to Monteverdi for his natural, speechlike text setting. By contrast, Fauré often chose to stress the general mood or subtext of a poem. Claire Croiza pointed out the rhythmic differences between the settings of Verlaine's "Clair de lune" by Fauré and Debussy: In example 6.1a, Fauré sets the sung silent syllables of "paysa*ge*" in m. 14 and "mas*ques*" in mm. 16 and 17 with rhythmic placement and melodic contours that unnaturally accent those syllables. In example 6.1b, Debussy follows the traditional practice of sounding the silent syllables while deemphasizing their importance, aiming for a more natural, speechlike rhythm and contour. In learning Fauré's songs, Croiza advised singers to study the poems away from the music so as not to be led astray by the false musical rhythms. In contrast, she observed that one could declaim the poems naturally using Debussy's settings.[34] Ravel preferred to set free verse and prose so that he would not be bound by the rhythmic constraints of the text.

**Diction and Articulation**

Most French singing manuals from the late eighteenth and early nineteenth centuries stressed dramatic expression and diction without placing much emphasis on vocal technique. French singers of that period prided themselves on their precise, clear diction and dramatic presentation, but their singing often lacked line and cantabile. The proximity and popularity of Italian singers at the beginning of the nineteenth century helped to solve this problem, considerably improving the technical level of French singing. Diction never lost its primary place, however, and Romagnesi urged singers to practice speaking the text of a song before singing it, giving the words serious attention: "In singing, not only

Example 6.1. a) Fauré: "Clair de lune," mm. 12–17, Hamelle, 1897, rev. 1908, reprint Dover, 1990; b) Debussy: "Clair de lune" from *Fêtes galantes I,* mm. 5–8, E. Fromont, 1903, reprint Dover, 1981.

must one stop appropriately at points of repose, like the comma and full stop—as will have been done when declaiming the words—and not only must one lean on the long syllables and pass lightly over the short ones, but also it will be necessary to emphasize all the words much more vigorously than in speaking; one has to articulate them as if being heard by a slightly deaf person, but however, avoiding all affectation and grimacing."[35]

Reynaldo Hahn opposed singing in which virtuosity was the sole interest. For him, good singing with bad enunciation was as offensive as excellent diction with poor vocal quality. In his own singing he tried to find a balance between pure vocalism and clear, accurate, and expressive diction. His recommendations in *On Singers and Singing* include suggestions that we might find exaggerated today, including expressive breathing and sighing with the mood of the poem and enunciating double consonants for special emphasis.[36] Croiza also suggested using consonants to help convey the expression of the text: "The accent in singing is given by the attack of the consonants, but an energetic articulation of the consonants does not mean a brusque articulation. Good articulation must be searched for with suppleness. . . . In Fauré's 'Soir,' all the ex-

Example 6.2. Fauré: "Soir," mm. 34–37, Hamelle, 1908, reprint Dover, 1990.

pression of the end, 'tes yeux levés au ciel, si tristes et si doux,' depends on the way we pronounce the consonant of this word, 'doux.' French has some consonants more 'explosive' than others, and use must be made of them in interpretations. The absence of the tonic accent in French must be supplemented by the accentuation of the consonants."[37] Perhaps she meant elongating the attack of the d in "doux" by making it softer and more aspirated (instead of percussive and dentalized) to complement the rolled chord in the piano accompaniment (see ex. 6.2).

Croiza also stressed knowing how "to give more value to certain syllables that give the words their significance." While a student at Juilliard, I sang in a master class for the Swiss tenor Hugues Cuénod, who had made his debut in Paris in 1928. He encouraged me to vary the length and weight of all the sixteenth notes in Fauré's "Notre amour" to try to approximate a more natural spoken rhythm (see ex. 6.3). The underlined syllables in the first line should be slightly longer: "*Notre amour est chose légère*"; and the mute "e" syllables should receive

Example 6.3. Fauré: "Notre amour," mm. 3–5, Hamelle, 1897, rev. 1908, International, 1953.

less emphasis than the surrounding vowels, especially if they fall on a strong beat like "cho*se*" in m. 3. This is what Romagnesi meant by leaning on the long syllables and passing lightly over the short ones. This approach, of course, continues a long tradition: as mentioned in chapter 1, in 1668 Bénigne de Bacilly stressed the importance of emphasizing the differences between long and short syllables.

Ravel incorporated this approach to diction in the very fabric of his settings of Renard's *Histoires naturelles*: "The direct clear language and the profound hidden poetry of the poems in prose tempted me for a long time. My author's text demanded a particular kind of musical declamation from me, closely related to the inflections of the French language."[38] He believed that diction must lead the music, and he therefore tried to approximate the rhythms of everyday speech. Rather than set the mute "e" syllables with their own sung pitch and rhythm, he chose to elide them with the surrounding syllables and leave them silent, as in spoken French. For example, the final syllables of "arri*ve*" in example 6.4a, "appel*le*" in example 6.4b, and "regar*de*" and "nua*ges*" in example 6.4c do not get their own articulated pitches and rhythms. Rather they are silent and connected to the next syllable, as they would be in speech. In 1907 this radical approach to text setting was much more common in the music hall than on the concert platform.

These examples also show how Ravel captured the contours of the French language. A friend of his, the music critic Emile Vuillermoz, observed: "When Ravel made one of those razor-edged remarks of which he alone possessed the secret, he used to make a characteristic gesture: he put his right hand quickly behind his back, described a sort of ironical pirouette, cast down his mischievously sparkling eyes and let his voice suddenly drop a fourth or fifth. In the *Histoires naturelles* and *L'heure espagnole* one finds this characteristic intonation in all sorts of places. It is Ravel's own voice, his pronunciation, his well-known mannerisms, that have produced this *quasi parlando* melody."[39]

In contrast, Debussy cautioned against a parlando approach. His friend and biographer Louis Laloy included the following instructions to singers with the composer's approval: "A very widespread prejudice would have it that, in all modern music, it is only necessary to 'speak,' with as little voice as possible, without even observing the correctness of the intervals. This is an absurdity. . . . Even when the melody remains motionless on one note, the purpose is not to imitate the intonation of speech, which is endlessly variable. It is to paint the half-light of contemplation and silence by means of a thoroughly musical metaphor."[40] Poulenc was also opposed to a parlando approach. He loved Italian opera and beautiful singing, and admitted that he wanted some of his larger vocal works such as *Le bal masqué* and *La dame de Monte Carlo* to be sung almost in the style of *Tosca* or *Otello*. He hated what he called the "pseudo-intelligent singer, usually without voice. . . . I like to hear some *singing* with a good

Example 6.4. Ravel: *Histoires naturelles,* a) "Le paon," m. 26; b) "Le paon," m. 33; c) "Le cygne," mm. 15–18, Durand, 1907, reprint Dover, 1990.

sauce of pedal (the butter!), without which my music is destroyed."[41] In addition to insisting on impeccable precision and accuracy in diction, Bernac also promoted the legato, non parlando style favored by Poulenc in most situations.

Most French diction manuals today stress an even, legato approach with fast, clear consonants and consistent long vowels. For American singers, the emphasis on the International Phonetic Alphabet and the lack of tonic accent in French often omits the issue of long and short syllables altogether. In *The Singer's Debussy* Marie-Claire Rohinsky comments that classical French singers today favor a diction close to normal speech, not as informal and casual as that used for cabaret or musical theater, but not as affected with mannerism as that of nineteenth-century poetic readings. Her observation implies that French diction at the turn of the twentieth century was more exaggerated than what we commonly hear today, including more variety in the articulation of consonants and in the length and weight of vowels. Many early recordings of French singers such as Croiza, Garden, Bathori, Panzéra, and others are available on CD and provide fascinating demonstrations of this approach to diction.

### Portamento and Vibrato

Early twentieth-century recordings also show French singers using portamento as a gentle slide or stretch to enhance legato and connect small and large leaps. As with everything else in the French style, portamento was used with refinement and subtle expression. Hahn distinguishes between the technical and expressive use of portamento: "Singers cannot totally avoid *portamento,* for without it, their singing would be too dry. Unconsciously, most singers make frequent use of this sliding from note to note, barely audible sliding which in fact contributes smoothness and connection to singing, which makes *legato* passages possible. But this subtle sliding should not really be called *portamento.* The real thing is much more obvious, more conscious. It is a means very often abused in singing to add expression; but the quality of expression thus produced very easily becomes whimpering, silly and odiously vulgar."[42] In some situations he even advises attacking a note gently from below to achieve a certain expressive effect. In a discussion of Fauré's "Le parfum impérissable" (ex. 6.5), for instance, he suggests inflecting the last note of m. 16, "par*fu*mée," from below.[43] In this particular harmonic context, the F-sharp at the end of m. 16 helps to turn the harmony back toward the tonic E major after a brief excursion into more distant flat keys; Hahn probably believed that shading the pitch from below would clarify the harmony in addition to being expressive. I might give a special inflection to the F-sharp at the beginning of m. 17 on "par*fu*mée," but

Example 6.5. Fauré: "Le parfum impérissable," mm. 15–17, Hamelle, 1908, reprint Dover, 1990.

probably not on the previous note and syllable. Hahn does caution that "of course these little tricks must be used with extreme discretion and tact."[44] This particular trick of gently sliding into a pitch from below, which singers today rarely employ, is heard frequently in early recordings.

Jane Bathori gives specific recommendations for discreet, expressive portamenti in Debussy songs. In "Fantoches" she encourages a slight portamento from the low G to high A on "sous la charmille" (ex. 6.6a). She also allows some very gentle portamenti in "Placet futile" (*Trois poèmes de Mallarmé*) on "Princesse!" (ex. 6.6b) and the final word "sourires" (ex. 6.6c). For "La mort des amants" she cautions, "beware of effects which the tessitura of certain descending phrases could permit: I speak of too-obvious *portamenti* which would be in bad taste."[45]

Example 6.6. a) Debussy: "Fantoches" from *Fêtes galantes I,* mm. 37–39, E. Fromont, 1903, reprint Dover, 1981; b) Debussy: "Placet futile" from *Trois poèmes de Mallarmé,* m. 3, Durand, 1913, reprint Rolland Père et Fils, 1971; c) Debussy: "Placet futile" from *Trois poèmes de Mallarmé,* mm. 32–33, Durand, 1913, reprint Rolland Père et Fils, 1971; d) Ravel: "Placet futile" from *Trois poèmes de Stéphane Mallarmé,* m. 17, Durand, 1914, reprint Dover, 1990.

Ravel occasionally used portamento as a special effect, marking it into his setting of Mallarmé's "Placet futile" on "coiffeurs," (ex. 6.6d) and "Princesse!" (see ex. 6.10, m. 6). Poulenc, in keeping with his fondness for Italian operatic style, allowed portamento as long as it was used with discernment and taste. He always cautioned against exaggerating any effect that would become vulgar.[46] Thomas Grubb explains the difference between the types of portamento appropriate for French versus Italian singing: [in French] "the syllable upon which the *portamento* takes place must give way to the following one as soon as this syllable's note is reached at the end of the *portamento,* unlike the *portamento* in Italian where the old syllable is extended indefinitely into the note of the new syllable."[47]

Vibrato in the French style is not discussed by most writers and teachers. Romagnesi mentions that some singers employed a light trembling of the voice to heighten the expression of grief. But he warns that, if used too much, "their incessant little tremolos become the most unbearable thing that one can hear. Therefore this effect must only be employed relatively rarely where it can be used in a rational way."[48] Early recordings of French singers reveal the typical small fast vibrato mentioned in previous chapters. Though still mostly a delicate shimmer, it is slightly more pronounced than in recordings of Italian and German singers.

### Rhythm and Tempo

Chapter 5 discussed how a free approach to tempo and rhythm gained force throughout the nineteenth century. This resulted in performances that were sometimes described as sloppy and careless, in which the singer may have sounded unconcerned about coordinating with the accompaniment. Performances of the early romances and mélodies most likely enjoyed this same kind of freedom within the tighter bounds of conservative French taste. Songs by Bizet, Massenet, César Franck, Delibes, Chausson, Chabrier, and Duparc can be approached within the context of this Romantic style. Bernac, writing in 1970, even allows certain purely vocal effects and rubato for the songs of Gounod, though he cautions that "we should not go so far as the interpreters of the period, whose style would undoubtedly be unacceptable to us now."[49] Fauré, with his dislike of flamboyance, wished for a simpler, more accurate approach to rhythm and tempo in his songs. As he became more famous and respected, his attitude influenced the younger generation of composers and performers. They in turn began to insist on a precise and accurate execution of the rhythms and tempos specified in the music. Yet we must remember that what they considered to be precise and accurate is quite different from what we are used to hearing today. They were reacting against the excesses of the Romantic style while still somewhat under its influence.

RHYTHM AND RUBATO

Fauré's son described his father's musical values as follows: "He had a horror of virtuosity, of rubato and effects aimed at making the audience swoon. He followed the printed notes meticulously, keeping strict time."[50] Croiza called him a "metronome incarnate" and advised students working on his "Clair de lune" to practice with a metronome.[51] Marguerite Long, a noted concert pianist who worked closely with Fauré from 1902 to 1912, believed that she played his solo piano music as it should be played and—much to his chagrin—designated herself his disciple and champion. Fauré did not necessarily approve of her virtuoso approach, but she left many fascinating observations in her book *Au piano avec Gabriel Fauré*. "This music requires that one 'play it straight' without camouflage or trickery," she writes. She also mentions that rubato in Fauré is for pacing the long line and rounding the phrase, cautioning that "Fauré thought that the search for effect was the worst sin of all . . . with Fauré it is the line that counts."[52]

Long also worked with Debussy and describes his playing: "Debussy was an incomparable pianist. How could one forget his suppleness, the caress of his touch? While floating over the keys with a curious penetrating gentleness, he could achieve an extraordinary power of expression." She relates how he played his preludes with an almost metronomic precision and became annoyed at pianists who took any liberties with his music. She tells of a pianist who came to play some of the composer's music for him. At a certain passage the pianist stopped and said, "Master, according to me this should be 'free.'" Debussy responded by looking at the carpet and vowing that the offending pianist would never tread on it again. Rubato in Debussy, Long explains, "adds up to a series of nuances that are not to be defined unless they are felt. . . . it is confined by a rigorous precision, in almost the same way as a stream is the captive of its banks. *Rubato* does not mean alteration of line or measure, but of nuance or *élan*."[53]

Bathori, Croiza and Hahn all complain in their writings about singers' rhythmic imprecision. They frequently admonish their students to study the rhythm and to respect the note values. Croiza even begs singers to listen to the accompaniment and try to sing with it. Hahn argues that "good singing is sustained by steady, firm rhythm, allowing the diction to remain flexible . . . within the limits set by the rhythm."[54] In recordings in which Bathori accom-

Example 6.7. Debussy: a) "Les ingénus" from *Fêtes galantes II,* mm. 1–8, Durand, 1904, reprint Dover, 1981; b) "La flûte de Pan" from *Trois chansons de Bilitis,* mm. 3–5, E. Fromont, 1899, reprint Dover, 1981.

panies herself at the piano, her rhythm ranges from absolutely metronomic in Debussy's "Les ingénus" (see ex. 6.7a) to subtly flexible in "La flûte de Pan" (see ex. 6.7b).[55] She advises studying the latter song "WITH RIGOROUS ATTENTION TO RHYTHMIC VALUES," making sure to give the duplets and triplets their proper length. She cautions that Debussy's marking, *Lent et sans rigueur de rythme,* "does not mean that one's fancy can be the basis of interpretation, but that the sounds must succeed one another without stiffness, with a flow so natural that the phrase seems to be improvised." In a later recording of this song by Maggie Teyte, the rhythm is precise throughout most of the song, yet she takes greater liberties with exaggerated ritardandos.

Teyte succeeded Mary Garden in the role of Mélisande, but she caused Debussy to complain bitterly about her. In a recording of "La chevelure" from *Chansons de Bilitis,* she holds the high note on "bouche," forcing the pianist to stretch the last four beats of m. 12 considerably (see ex. 6.8a). She also elongates "tendre" in m. 24, almost putting a fermata on the C-flat. She follows this with an indulgent portamento down to the A-flat and an expressive double "s" on "frisson" in m. 25 (see ex. 6.8b). Croiza cites this song when admonishing singers to follow the rhythms indicated in the score: "if the composer had wanted a pause on the word 'tendre,' he would certainly have indicated it; most singers, however, make one."[56] Bathori discusses the same moment in the song: "The last phrase is full of gentle and subtle emotion: *et il me regarda d'un regard si tendre, que je baissai les yeux,* separating this with a tiny break from the following words *avec un frisson,* as simply as possible. 'And above all, no shiver,' Claude Debussy said before the last phrase, so painful was it to him to hear the word *frisson* sung in this way."[57]

Bathori describes rubato in Debussy as we have encountered it before: "in an expressive passage one steals a fragment of time from one measure by hurrying a bit and, in the following measure, one gives it back by slowing down . . . one must have good taste and sensitivity." Interestingly, the tempo marking in Debussy's "Le faune" is *Andantino (Tempo rubato),* yet Bathori plays only the opening three measures with rubato and adopts a metronomically even tempo from m. 4 on. In contrast, in her recording of Chabrier's "L'île heureuse" (see ex. 6.9) she uses a great deal of rhythmic flexibility and rubato, as the tempo marking *Animato, molto rubato ed appassionato* indicates. Croiza, too, mentions "L'île heureuse," observing that Chabrier demands special treatment: "there is a rubato which is not in the French character. There is a kind of supple right hand, whilst the left hand 'va son train' [goes on its way], unlike the exactness of a Ravel or a Debussy. . . . For the liberty allowed to the interpreter is not a

Example 6.8. Debussy: "La chevelure" from *Trois chansons de Bilitis*, a) m. 12; b) mm. 24–25, E. Fromont, 1899, reprint Dover, 1981.

Example 6.9. Chabrier: "L'île heureuse," mm. 1–9, Enoch & Costallat, 1890, reprint Belwin-Mills, [197?].

modern characteristic."[58] Bernac notes that the lyricism in this song approaches caricature, and he writes that the dynamics, nuances, and rubatos "should be made without fear of exaggeration."[59]

Poulenc demanded strict observance of note values, and his playing on recordings reveals steady and accurate rhythm. He said he was against rubato of any kind, but Bernac acknowledged that "because of his love for the voice, he was a little less strict at times (which was in fact true) in order to allow the singer to 'sing,' to prepare certain effects, and to breathe."[60]

### TEMPO AND METRONOME MARKS

Berlioz—known for his rhythmic precision as a conductor—used metronome markings on his orchestral songs. Given the importance he assigned to rhythmic accuracy, his markings probably reflect the tempos he wanted. Fauré complained that his songs were usually sung too slowly. Croiza acknowledges that "I am certainly among the interpreters of Fauré who adopt the fastest tempi, and yet the composer himself often found I did not go fast enough." She asked him what tempo he wanted for "Après un rêve," and he replied "sans ralentir!" Fauré deplored the common practice of slowing down at a diminuendo or at the end of a song, and he rarely specified a rallentando unless he really wanted it. The Dover score of all sixty Fauré songs includes many metronome markings, mostly in the second and third collections. These may have been added with Fauré's consultation or by the original editors. Duparc also lamented that singers generally took his songs too slowly. He confided to Croiza that "If I had known what some singers do with them I would never have put any rallentandi in my songs."[61] The tradition of greatly speeding up for crescendos or for high, loud passages and drastically slowing down for diminuendos, rallentandos, and softer moments was so ingrained in most performers that composers had to insist, demand, plead, and beg for their music to be performed at a consistent tempo. Even in a recording by Charles Panzéra, the baritone who sang the *Requiem* solo at Fauré's memorial service and for whom Fauré wrote *L'horizon chimérique,* singer and pianist make a significant ritardando during the last five measures of "Après un rêve."

Debussy wrote many tempo indications into his scores to try to control the flow of the rhythm and the tempo. Bathori advises following all these tempo markings precisely. She relates an interesting story about the tempo and metronome marking of "Mandoline": "I remember having sung 'Mandoline' for Debussy in the tempo indicated in the first edition: *allegretto,* without a metronome marking. After the first measures Debussy exclaimed, 'It's twice as fast as that.' When I told him no one would understand the tempo with *allegretto* as only the indication, he had later editions emended to include the metronome marking."[62] In 1904 recordings of Debussy accompanying Mary Garden, the tempos for "Green" and "Il pleure dans mon coeur" are surprisingly fast yet not hectic.[63] They both achieve a simplicity and calmness dominated by a long flowing line.

Ravel wanted exactitude of rhythm, but as pianist Vlado Perlemuter explains, "Ravel's strict approach doesn't scorn subtlety."[64] Perlemuter, who studied all Ravel's solo piano music with the composer, cautions pianists not to rush in fast passages or to slow down where it is not marked. Ravel does ask for rubato and a flexible flow of tempo, but only where he specifies it in the score. His tempo indications often require merely a subtle nuance without a significant change of speed. In "Placet futile" (see ex. 6.10), Ravel gives a metronome marking but also controls the flow of rhythm and tempo with meter changes and several different tempo indications, including rubato, in each of the first eight measures. The rhythm thus must be precise yet infinitely flexible within a subtle range of tempos.

Poulenc demanded a steady tempo and disliked slowing down at the end of a song. In 1960 he declared that "all my metronomic speeds, worked out with Bernac, are exact." Yet in writing about *Tel jour, telle nuit* he cautioned that "the tempo, which no metronome can indicate exactly, must be felt instinctively."[65] Bernac observed from countless performances and recordings made at different times that Poulenc's tempos varied over the course of their long association: "He played more quickly (too quickly, in my opinion) in his youth than in his maturity." Bernac also allowed that "Poulenc knew better than anyone how to take a breath to prepare an unexpected modulation, or to hesitate for a sudden change of dynamics, but this without ever altering the basic tempo."[66] Poulenc and Bernac provided an important link between the new attitudes of the turn of the twentieth century and our present modern style. They helped transmit to the next generation of singers the French ideals of tasteful reserve and scrupulous attention to details in the score.

The most important new ideas presented in this chapter have had to do with the turn away from virtuosity toward a strict observance of the notated score. Performers were expected to serve the composer, following the details of the music with scrupulous accuracy. This was the genesis of an approach that is sometimes mistakenly applied to music of all earlier periods. French composers of the late nineteenth century reacted against the earlier excesses of Romanti-

Example 6.10. Ravel: "Placet futile" from *Trois poèmes de Stéphane Mallarmé*, mm. 1–8, Durand, 1914, reprint Dover, 1990.

cism and demanded accurate rhythms and steady tempos. Portamento and rubato were governed by French "good taste" and used only with subtlety and restraint. As they had since the seventeenth century, French composers and performers shunned empty display in favor of a refined purity of expression and a simple, natural approach. The performers' job by the beginning of the twentieth century was to enter into the world of the composer and to leave their own showmanship—including ornamentation and even expressive interpretation—behind. For this repertoire, subtlety and simplicity are crucial. Following exactly what is written in the score will probably feel familiar and comfortable.

Attitudes toward French diction were quite different through the nineteenth and early twentieth centuries than they are today. In contrast with the even vowels and fast, light consonants taught today, singers at the turn of the century used vowels with a variety of weights and lengths, as well as expressive double consonants. You might consider observing some of Bénigne de Bacilly's seventeenth-century rules for long and short syllables when you approach French mélodies of the late nineteenth and early twentieth centuries.

# Chapter 7 Second
# Viennese School

This chapter discusses works by Arnold Schoenberg and his students Alban Berg and Anton Webern. These three composers, commonly known as the Second Viennese School, ventured beyond the increasing chromaticism of late nineteenth-century music to explore a new realm of atonal and twelve-tone composition. In addition to demanding new techniques for singing and for solo instrumental and orchestral playing, Schoenberg and Berg refined the use of melodrama, or speaking over music, into the more exacting art of *Sprechstimme,* also known as *Sprechgesang,* fully exploited in one of the most important early twentieth-century works, Schoenberg's *Pierrot lunaire.*

All three composers wrote much vocal music, from songs and chamber music to choral and stage works. Yet their relationships with performers, and particularly with singers, were quite different from those of their predecessors. Their motivation for writing vocal music was primarily either the text or the composition itself, rather than a potential performance or a relationship with a singer. Like their French predecessors and contemporaries, all three reacted against the excesses of nineteenth-century Romanticism, developed an aversion to virtuosity for its own sake, and stressed the need to respect the score. Because of World War I and the resulting political antagonism between Austria and France, however, these ideas emerged in Vienna largely independent of direct French influence. The main goal of the Second Viennese School composers, through performance or intellectual contemplation, was to communicate the meaning of the music with a clarity and precision that would reveal its inner workings and construction.

At the turn of the twentieth century, the general Viennese public was particularly conservative in its musical tastes, and waltzes and operetta reigned supreme. Simultaneously, however, the city was a magnet for avant-garde experimentation in all the arts, including art, architecture, poetry, literature, philosophy, and music. Schoenberg's circle of friends included painters Oskar Kokoschka, architect Adolf Loos, and writer Karl Kraus. Kraus, in his magazine *Die Fackel* (The Torch), sought to preserve his beloved German language from deterioration, choosing his words precisely in order to achieve exact meanings. Architect Loos eliminated ornament from his designs in order to reveal and clarify the formal structure of a building. Kokoschka chose to portray the inner reality of his subjects rather than a literal exterior view. All these ideas had an important impact on Schoenberg as he embarked on the intellectual journey that Webern would later describe in his book *The Path to the New Music*.[1]

Schoenberg had an overwhelming effect on the lives and work of Berg and Webern. He was a demanding teacher and imprinted both his ideals and his difficult personality on his friends and students. They called him "the master" and said he was as possessive as an octopus.[2] He and his inner circle often felt unappreciated and misunderstood. On the one hand, artists in Vienna in the first decades of the twentieth century deliberately created work that would shock and provoke the city's complacent, philistine audiences. On the other hand, the hostility and isolation they felt drove them into their own creative worlds. The composers, particularly Schoenberg and Webern, had an ambivalent attitude toward performers and audiences: they wanted their works presented in public, but, anticipating a lack of understanding on everyone's part, felt contempt for the very people who could bring their music to life. They therefore wrote music primarily for themselves and for their art, and in some cases—such as Berg's *Wozzeck* and Schoenberg's *Moses und Aron*—didn't know if their work was even performable.

Yet these composers also believed they were continuing the long tradition of German/Austrian masters such as Bach, Beethoven, and Brahms. The young Schoenberg, Berg, and Webern, along with everyone else at the time, were greatly affected by Wagner's music and philosophy. Mahler's towering presence in Vienna at the turn of the century also had a powerful impact on them. After taking tonality and free chromaticism as far as it could go, all three, following Schoenberg's lead, turned to the twelve-tone method of composition, which they believed was the inevitable destination of German Romanticism. It is ironic that later their own country, under the Nazi regime, rejected their work as "degenerate."[3]

## Publications and Editions

Most editions of vocal music by Berg, Webern, and Schoenberg are extremely reliable because they were scrupulously prepared by the composers. Universal Edition in Vienna published most of their music, and now Belmont Music in Los Angeles handles all of Schoenberg's works. Some scores were published in the composers' lifetimes, and some were not commercially available until after their deaths. The *New Grove* articles on Schoenberg, Webern, and Berg list publication dates in the works lists. A critical edition of Schoenberg's complete works, published by Universal, was begun in 1966 and is still under way: the first three volumes include the songs, and series 6, vol. 24, issued in 1996, includes *Pierrot lunaire* and other vocal chamber music. The Dover collection of Schoenberg songs, based on publications in his lifetime, includes sources and translations. *Pierrot* was first published by Universal in 1914 and reprinted several times in Schoenberg's lifetime. In 1990 Belmont issued a new edition in a larger, easier-to-read format with some earlier mistakes corrected. Universal has published several critical editions of vocal music by Berg, including *Der Wein,* the *Altenberg Lieder,* and *Sieben früher Lieder.*

Unlike nineteenth-century German lieder and French mélodies, vocal music by the Second Viennese School composers was not published for the general public. It was composed out of necessity and inspiration, and published when possible. Sometimes works would appear in journals or magazines to be considered and appreciated intellectually, in the same spirit as Schumann's early nineteenth-century journal. Sometimes the composer would publish a score himself. After quarreling with Berlin publishers over their version of his opera *Von heute auf morgen,* Schoenberg published the piano-vocal score at his own expense. Berg paid to publish a piano-vocal score of *Wozzeck* to show to prospective producers and conductors. Georg Büchner's play, upon which the opera was based, was well known in literary and theatergoing circles; as the score circulated and was evaluated, Berg was transformed from an unknown young composer into the notorious creator of an unperformable atonal spectacle. The conductor Hermann Scherchen was intrigued, however, and performed three excerpts with a singer at a well-received concert in 1924. The 1925 premiere of the full opera changed Berg's life overnight: after the public and critics enthusiastically hailed the performance, Berg was catapulted into international recognition and success.

This was not the case for Schoenberg, who was always searching for supplemental income that would enable him to compose. In the first years of the century he worked as a conductor at the Überbrettl, a literary cabaret in Berlin. Although he appreciated good performances of Viennese operetta, he believed the gulf between serious and popular entertainment was too wide, and he tried to fill the gap with his early *Brettl-Lieder* (cabaret songs). Only "Nachtwandler" was ever performed, and it was poorly received because of an unsuitable trumpet player. The rest of the *Brettl-Lieder* were not published until 1970. He also spent some of his early years working for the new Vienna-based publisher Universal Edition, preparing orchestrations, arrangements, and piano reductions of light music and operetta. Later Universal agreed to publish Schoenberg's own scores under his supervision.

Webern was also constantly seeking sources of income to support not only himself but also his mentor, Schoenberg. He found his way into and out of numerous conducting positions: semiprofessional orchestras and choruses seemed to suit him better than jobs in the theater, which he disliked and never stayed with for long. He programmed mostly standard German repertoire, as well as new music of his own and by Schoenberg, Berg, and others. In his diary entries about his various performances, even in works with voice, he restricts his comments to how the orchestra played or how he felt about the overall concert; he makes very few remarks about how the chorus or soloists sang.[4] Despite this distant attitude, Webern composed many groups of songs, some with piano accompaniment, others with instrumental ensembles. Some of these collections were published by Universal in the 1920s under his supervision, others posthumously in the 1950s and '60s. But since Webern prepared all his manuscripts with meticulous care, it was easy for editors to produce final scores that reflected his wishes.

Berg had composed songs long before he started studying with Schoenberg. His self-taught style of song writing was modeled after the works of Schubert, Schumann, Wolf, Wagner, and Mahler. He was more interested in French composers than his colleagues, and he was influenced by the music of both Debussy and Milhaud. According to Berg's wife, Helene, Berg believed that his youthful compositions, aside from the *Sieben früher Lieder,* were not of a high enough quality to be published.[5] Nevertheless, after her death in 1976, much previously guarded material, including the early songs, became available. This shed an entirely new light on Berg scholarship. In 1985 Universal published the unknown songs in two volumes, and Dietrich Fischer-Dieskau recorded them.[6] In 1904, when the nineteen-year-old Berg first came to study with Schoenberg, the master remarked that his new protégé was "an extraordinarily gifted composer. But the state he was in when he came to me was such that his imagination apparently could not work on anything but Lieder. . . . He was absolutely incapable of writing an instrumental movement or inventing an instrumental theme. You can hardly imagine the lengths I went to in order to remove this defect in his talent. . . . [I] am convinced that in time Berg will actually become very good at instrumentation."[7] The *Sieben früher Lieder,* composed from 1905 to 1908, were orchestrated and performed in Vienna in 1928. A revised piano-vocal score, which some think is a reduction of the orchestration, was published at that time by Universal. The orchestrated version was not issued until 1969.[8]

A powerful and unfortunate incident had a decidedly negative impact on Berg the song composer. In 1911, while he was preparing a piano reduction of Schoenberg's cantata *Gurrelieder,* he was inspired by the premiere of Mahler's orchestral song cycle *Das Lied von der Erde* and set out to compose his own orchestral songs. In 1913 he sent his *Five Orchestral Songs on Picture-Postcard Texts of Peter Altenberg* (*Fünf Orchesterlieder nach Ansichtskartentexten von Peter Altenberg*) to Schoenberg, who performed two of the songs on a famously scandalous concert in Vienna.[9] The audience's hostile and violent reaction, along with some critical remarks from the father figure Schoenberg, devastated the young Berg, who subsequently turned away from song writing. These *Altenberg Lieder,* op. 4, were not performed in their entirety or published until 1953. In 1929 Berg was commissioned by the singer Ruzena Herlinger to compose a concert aria with orchestra. Herlinger performed *Der Wein* in June 1930, at which point Universal published a piano-vocal score. The orchestral score did not appear until 1966.

Given the importance of the inner workings of these compositions, as well as the delicate relationships among pitches and lines of counterpoint, all of Schoenberg's, Berg's, and Webern's vocal works should be performed only in their original forms and keys. Transpositions are unacceptable.

## Performance and Analysis

All three composers were performers of a sort and enjoyed getting together to play chamber music with a close circle of friends. Schoenberg, self-taught on the cello, learned basic skills for the violin and viola as well. Webern played the cello and (less frequently) the viola, and Berg could play the piano and harmonium. Schoenberg presided over famous Sunday chamber music marathons at which both professionals and amateurs played and discussed the classics. The object was not to deliver a polished performance, but rather to discover the inner workings and meaning of the music and to experiment with interpretive choices that might convey and clarify these ideas. Schoenberg was more of a coach than a collaborator, discussing his philosophy of music during the breaks in the playing and helping his colleagues to penetrate the harmonic and rhythmic mysteries of musical form and structure. As a conductor he also had limited technical facility but great insight and understanding, and he applied a similar coaching style to his rehearsals. Webern adopted this detailed, investigative coaching style in his teaching and conducting as well. The violinist Louis Krasner remembers that when Webern gave some lectures on the Beethoven piano sonatas, his passionate analysis of the music was a performance in itself: "His voice was quiet and sometimes hesitant, but always enormously expressive and emotionally captivating."[10]

As a teacher, Schoenberg was famous for his fascinating analyses of the standard German repertoire, and he believed that a thorough understanding and appreciation of a work could result from merely studying the score. As his idol Brahms had declared when invited to see *Don Giovanni* at the Vienna Opera, he heard the best performance in his head when he read the score.[11] Unfortunately, after years of bitter disappointment and rejection, Schoenberg's attitude toward performers became even more sour. Dika Newlin, one of his students at the University of California at Los Angeles in 1940, recalls him railing against conductors: "The interpretation, good or bad, is much less important than the music! Music need not be performed any more than books need be read aloud, for its logic is perfectly represented on the printed page; and the performer, for all his intolerable arrogance, is totally unnecessary except as his interpretations make the music understandable to an audience unfortunate enough not to be able to read it in print. 'Now do not tell anyone I said this!' he added; 'for there are those who would stone me for it!'"[12] Sadly, he passed this attitude onto many of his disciples, and it still pervaded the atmosphere in the music department at Princeton when I was an undergraduate in the late 1970s. (Happily, this is no longer the case today.) Yet Schoenberg's brilliance in applying analysis to performance also inspired many performers, including Rudolf Kolisch and the Kolisch Quartet, Felix Galimir and the Galimir Quartet, pianists Edward Steuermann and Rudolf Serkin, and conductor Otto Klemperer, who would carry on his ideals in their performing and teaching.

### The Society for Private Musical Performance

A professional organization that did fulfill Schoenberg's performance ideals was his Society for Private Musical Performance (Verein für Musikalische Privataufführungen). It was founded in Vienna in the summer of 1918 specifically for the performance of new music. Schoenberg was the president, with Berg and Webern handling much of the logistics and organization and other close friends filling out the board. The society presented weekly Sunday concerts of chamber music, including songs and vocal chamber music as well as reductions of orchestral works for piano or chamber ensemble. Critics were banned, and only an invited audience of members could attend. Virtuosity was shunned, and rather than engaging established artists, Schoenberg favored excellent young professional musicians who were less well known. Each work had one rehearsal leader or coach, usually Schoenberg, Berg, or Webern; pianist Edward Steuermann, who studied composition with Schoenberg and performed most of the piano works of the Second Viennese School, and Erwin Stein, another Schoenberg student, also served as *Vortragsmeister*. They scheduled plenty of rehearsals, and only performed a work when it was thoroughly ready. New works were repeated on subsequent concerts so that the audience could become familiar with them, and the programs were not announced in advance (so that attendees would arrive without preconceived expectations). Audience response, either positive or negative—including the clapping, hissing, whistling, or shouting then typical at public concerts of new music—was strictly forbidden. In the three years (1918–21) during which the society operated, it gained 320 members and presented over 100 concerts.[13] Rudolf Serkin, who participated in many society performances, later transferred most of these practices, not including the ban on applause, to his Marlboro Music Festival in Vermont.

In a statement of the aims of the society, Berg described its performance ideals as "the attainment of the greatest possible clarity and the fulfillment of all the composer's intentions as revealed in his work."[14] Schoenberg's basic idea, taken up by the Kolisch Quartet and other performers in his circle, was vividly described by another society pianist, Lona Truding: "[let] the music speak without any interference of personal emotions."[15] The fundamental goal was to analyze the music, understand what the composer had in mind, and transmit this without letting personal interpretations, idiosyncratic mannerisms, or technical display get in the way. While this approach resembled what French composers and performers were also striving for at the time (see chapter 6), Schoenberg claimed to be the source of these new ideas. (The society did, however, program French and Russian works, and in 1920 Ravel visited Vienna and performed some of his own music at a society concert.)

Singers who participated in the society's concerts included Marie Gutheil-Schoder, a well-known soprano at the Vienna Opera, who sang the premieres of Schoenberg's Second String Quartet, op. 10, with the Rosé Quartet in 1908, and of *Erwartung* in 1924. Another favorite was Felicie Hüni-Mihacsek, a Mozart soprano at the Vienna Opera, who sang music of Debussy, Berg, and Webern. Other singers included Marya Freund and Erika Stiedry-Wagner, major players in the story of *Pierrot,* as well as Emmy Heim, Stella Eisner, Stefanie Bruck-Zimmer, and Arthur Fleischer.

### Music and Text

Of the three composers, Berg had the most Romantic approach to text and music. As mentioned above, his earliest compositions were songs that were strongly influenced by the nineteenth-century lieder tradition. Even in *Wozzeck* he preserved the Wagnerian principle of music serving drama.[16] He was also somewhat willing to consider the needs of a singer. In writing *Der Wein,* because he was uncertain about the capabilities of the soprano who commissioned the work, he composed a vocal line with a more moderate range than in his other works. He also included some optional lower notes in the vocal part and instrumental lines to double and support the voice (see ex. 7.1). He hoped that the work would also be performed by tenors, but it never was in his lifetime.

Webern came to songwriting from an early interest in lieder concerts and opera. He developed a strong interest in poetry, and it is hard to say whether his love of poems led him to compose songs, or that working on songs inspired his exploration of poetry. He was also passionate about nature, wildflowers, and mountain hikes, and therefore chose poems that expressed a devout and sincere love of nature. In 1926 Webern met poet Hildegard Jone, and they developed a close relationship; from then on, he set only her poems. He often turned to songwriting in times of compositional uncertainty, using the text to give the new atonal and twelve-tone music a form.

Webern's songs are subtle and intimate, never grandiose or vulgar. The rhythms and contours of the music fit the text well, achieving expressive settings of the poems. Yet the vocal lines often contain large leaps and challenging rhythms (see exs. 7.9 and 7.10). Steuermann relates an anecdote revealing Webern's attitude toward singers: "I expressed a doubt to Webern once about the possibility of singing some melodic patterns. He said 'Don't worry; we feel and

Example 7.1. Berg: *Der Wein*, mm. 32–34. Copyright 1931 by Universal Edition, A.G.,
Wien. Copyright renewed. All Rights Reserved. Used by permission of European
American Music Distributors LLC, US and Canadian agents for Universal Edition, A.G.,
Wien.

write, they will find a way.'"[17] In 1938, when a performance of his choral work
*Das Augenlicht* was being prepared in London, only the BBC Singers, a select
group of sixteen exceptional musicians, could handle the challenge, because
"no normal choir can do it."[18] Webern was more concerned with the poetry,
the expression, and the form than with the singability of his music.

Schoenberg's attitude toward the relationship between text and music most
decidedly favored the music. In a 1912 article, "The Relationship to the Text,"
he explains:

A few years ago I was deeply ashamed when I discovered in several Schubert songs, well known to me, that I had absolutely no idea what was going on in the poems on which they were based . . . since the poems did not make it necessary for me to change my conception of the musical interpretation in the slightest degree. . . . it appeared that, without knowing the poem, I had grasped the content, the real content, perhaps even more profoundly than if I had clung to the surface of the mere thoughts expressed in words. For me, even more decisive than this experience was the fact that, inspired by the sound of the first words of the text, I had composed many of my songs straight through to the end without troubling myself in the slightest about the continuation of the poetic events . . . I divined everything that obviously had to follow this first sound with inevitability.[19]

In fact, in his *Das Buch der hängenden Gärten*, op. 15, settings of fifteen poems by Stefan George, he achieved exactly this effect: "for the first time [I was] successful in coming near an ideal of expression and form which I had had in mind for years. But up to that point I had lacked the strength and certainty to realize it. Now that I have finally embarked upon this path I am conscious that I have broken all barriers to past aesthetic."[20] The George songs are completely free from any sense of key or tonality, creating what Schoenberg described as a world of "sound and mood."[21] Martha Winternitz-Dorda, who had absolute pitch, sang the premiere at a Berlin concert in February 1912. Schoenberg thought she was very musical and that her voice was beautiful, but he found her interpretation of the songs "much too dramatic, taking everything from the words instead of from the music." He admonished another singer in 1913: "not too accented pronunciation of the text but a musical working out of the melodic lines!—So don't emphasize a word which is not emphasized in my melody, and no 'intelligent' caesuras which arise from the text. Where a 'comma' is necessary, I have already composed it."[22]

In the instructions at the beginning of the *Pierrot lunaire* score, Schoenberg cautions the singer/speaker: "It is never the task of performers to recreate the mood and character of the individual pieces on the basis of the meaning of the words, but rather solely on the basis of the music. To the extent that the tone-painting-like rendering of the events and feelings given in the text was important to the author, it is found in the music anyway. Where the performer finds it is lacking, he should abstain from presenting something that was not intended by the author. Otherwise he would be detracting rather than adding."[23] In the 1926 foreword to his texts for *Die glückliche Hand* and other works, he continues to explain his approach to text setting, as well as his deep mistrust of singers: "These are texts: that means they only yield something complete together with the music. . . . The musician is in the position of being relatively untouched by his text. He needs it mainly in order to arrange the succession of vowels and consonants according to principles which would also be decisive without the text. . . . singers are most satisfactory when they perform it as euphoniously as a well understood do-re-mi."[24]

In a 1932 radio lecture about his *Orchestral Songs* (*Vier Orchesterlieder,* op. 22), we see him softening somewhat in his campaign against dramatic presentations of his texts. He still does not set evocative words such as "Wilder See" (wild sea) or "Finster Sturm" (dark storm) literally, "reflected by some musical symbol," but rather treats them on the same level as abstract words in the way they relate to the meaning of the whole text (see ex. 7.2, mm. 22–23). Yet he allows that "if a performer speaks of a passionate sea in a different tone of voice than he might use for a calm sea, my music does nothing else than to provide him with an opportunity to do so, and to support him."[25]

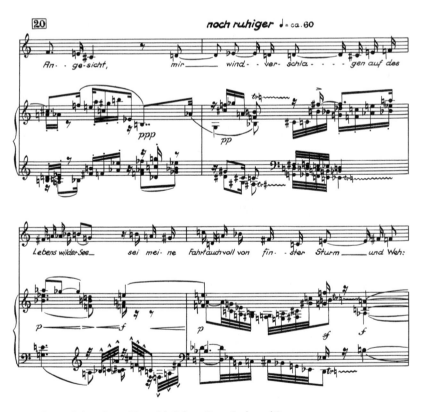

Example 7.2. Schoenberg: "Seraphita" from *Four Orchestral Songs,* op. 22, mm. 20–23, piano reduction, Belmont, 1968. Used by permission of Belmont Music Publishers.

By 1949 Schoenberg felt the need to address a situation that had gotten out of hand. In an article entitled "This Is My Fault," he amended the stern warnings in the preface to *Pierrot*, acknowledging that music must both heighten the expression of the text and express something provoked by that text.[26] Performers and composers had taken his ideas too literally. After World War II, many composers were writing songs that had nothing whatsoever to do with their chosen texts. The pendulum had swung too far in the direction of executing music without any expression of the text or any glimmer of personal interpretation. Performances of serial and twelve-tone music had become cold, stiff, and detached, which was not what the Second Viennese School composers had originally intended.

### *Pierrot lunaire*

Stravinsky called *Pierrot* "the solar plexus of Twentieth Century music."[27] It was revolutionary in many ways, including its treatment of the voice, its construction as a song cycle, and its use of an instrumental grouping that became the twentieth-century chamber ensemble of choice. The last work in Schoenberg's atonal period (1908–21) before he unveiled the twelve-tone method in 1923, it has probably been performed and recorded more than any other vocal work by Second Viennese School composers. Schoenberg included detailed instructions for the vocal performer, yet the exact meaning of these remarks has proved elusive and controversial. Learning how to deliver the vocal style and *Sprechstimme* needed for this work is almost as difficult as learning the music itself. Both require a familiarity with its performance history.

BACKGROUND

In early 1912 Schoenberg received a commission from a well-known actress, Albertine Zehme, to compose some melodramas for the poems from *Pierrot lunaire* by Albert Giraud, in the German translation by Otto Erich Hartleben. Zehme had already been touring Germany reciting these poems to other music that she felt was unsuitable. She originally requested piano accompaniment, but as Schoenberg worked on the project he asked whether he could add a clarinet, then a violin, a flute, and finally a cello, reaching the full instrumental complement. (There are also passages for piccolo, bass clarinet, and viola that are played by the flutist, clarinetist, and violinist.)

Melodrama, or speaking text over music, was not an uncommon dramatic form in the late nineteenth century. As mentioned in chapter 5, some German singers were even criticized for overly declaiming music that should be sung.

Schoenberg's friend Karl Kraus was famous for recitation performances of everything from his own work to plays by Goethe and Shakespeare and to the operettas of Offenbach, in which he sang/declaimed all the different parts. His singing style reportedly was similar to Schoenberg's *Sprechstimme*.[28]

*Pierrot,* however, made musical demands of the speaker far beyond any melodrama before it. Steuermann was assigned the daunting task of teaching Albertine Zehme her part. He remembers that "she was an intelligent and artistic woman, but by profession an actress and only as musical as the well-bred German ladies of that time. I still remember that sometimes, in despair of ever making her feel the exact difference between three-part and two-part rhythm, I would ask her to dance a few bars of a waltz, then a polka, alternating in ever shorter intervals to try finally the first bars of the 'Dandy.'" (see ex. 7.3).[29]

Steuermann also recalls that though the instrumentalists were all excellent players from Berlin, they needed twenty-five composer-conducted rehearsals before the first performance: "Schoenberg's magnetic personality always provided enough thrill and inspiration. . . . I well remember his trying to get the speaker away from the tragic-heroine expression she was inclined to assume."[30]

### EARLY PERFORMANCES

At the Berlin premiere on October 16, 1912, Zehme appeared in the costume of Pierrot, the commedia dell'arte clown. She insisted that she be alone onstage, with the instrumentalists and conductor behind a screen in such an arrangement that they were visible to her but hidden from the audience. The performance caused a scandal of sorts, but it also received a huge ovation. The audience hissed and applauded after the individual pieces, and some poems were repeated. The reviews of Zehme's performance were mixed, but on the whole the event was considered a tremendous success. A tour of eleven German and Austrian cities followed, Hermann Scherchen conducting, with enthusiastic receptions everywhere.

Albertine Zehme felt she had exclusive performing rights to *Pierrot* for a number of years after the premiere, but in 1920 Schoenberg started looking for other reciters. Some reports suggest that he maintained a friendly relationship with Zehme, while others claim that he was frustrated and unsatisfied with her. Steuermann tried to teach the part to his sister Rosa, an actress: "he laid special emphasis on rhythmic precision and avoidance of singing tone."[31] Schoenberg wanted Marie Gutheil-Schoder to learn the part for a performance with the Society for Private Musical Performance. She started coaching it with Erwin Stein, but she said it hurt her voice. Stein replaced her with actress and singer

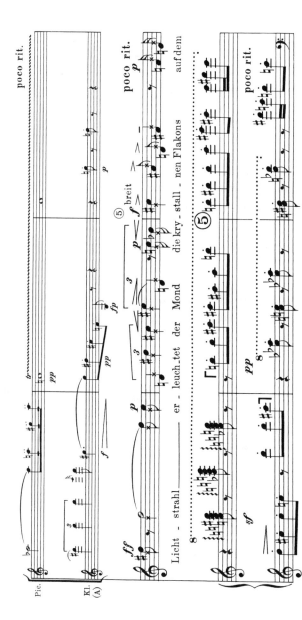

Example 7.3. Schoenberg: *Pierrot lunaire*, "Der Dandy," mm. 3–5. Used by permission of Belmont Music Publishers.

Erika Stiedry-Wagner, who ultimately performed *Pierrot* in Vienna in 1921, on tour, and in a 1940 recording with Schoenberg conducting. Stiedry-Wagner later related that, since she was not a trained musician, she had to work extremely hard to learn the part. She had to feel it in her body. After she worked on it alone with Stein, she had thirty rehearsals with Schoenberg and the musicians, who already knew it well. Schoenberg told her "it is absolutely wrong if you sing the notes. It is not meant this way. He always said that to me. And he was satisfied because I was—I mean I am not a musician, but I was quite musical and I could speak and I could give expression. . . . Nobody laughed at me— nobody. . . . You have to make it very strong and very suggestive and then nobody laughs. You have to have the expression for it."[32]

The 1921 performances in Vienna were a great success and inspired a French performance in Paris, conducted by Darius Milhaud. The Paris speaker was Marya Freund, who had sung the Wood Dove in performances of Schoenberg's *Gurrelieder* in 1913 and 1914. She prepared a French translation of the German text after finding the original French poems by Giraud unsuitable. She and Milhaud had twenty-five rehearsals with the Parisian ensemble. When Milhaud, Poulenc, and Ravel visited Vienna later that year, a special evening was arranged at Alma Mahler's house, where *Pierrot* was performed twice: once by Erika Stiedry-Wagner in German, with Erwin Stein (some reports indicate it was Schoenberg) conducting the instrumentalists from the society performance, then by Marya Freund in French with Milhaud conducting the same ensemble. Milhaud left the following impressions of the evening:

> It was a most exciting experience; Schoenberg's conducting brought out the dramatic qualities of his work, making it harsher, wilder, more intense; my reading on the other hand emphasized the music's sensuous qualities, all the sweetness, subtlety and translucency of it. Erika Wagner spoke the German words in a strident tone and with less respect for the notes written than Marya Freund, who if anything erred on the side of observing them too carefully. I realized on that occasion that the problem of recitation was probably insoluable.[33] . . . It was interesting to note the differences in atmosphere that were produced. Perhaps the French and German languages used by the singers determined the "colors" that were imposed upon the instruments. . . . The French language being the softer, made all the delicate passages appear the more subtle; but in the German interpretation the dramatic passages seemed more powerful, while the delicate ones assumed more weight.[34]

Alma Mahler left this account:

> It was first spoken [*gesprochen*] by Erika Wagner, coached by Schoenberg himself— then sung [*gesungen*] by Marya Freund coached by Milhaud. Schoenberg scarcely

recognized his work—but the majority of those present were for Milhaud's interpretation. Doubtless it was more original in Schoenberg's more rhythmical style of accented speaking than in the song, where one noticed rather the similarity with Debussy. The authentic interpretation was naturally the one by Schoenberg-Stein.[35]

It is interesting to note, in light of the performance ideals discussed in chapter 6, that the French performance was more accurate than the German, even to a fault. Yet Schoenberg criticized Marya Freund's performance for being too sung throughout.

In 1940 Schoenberg performed and then recorded *Pierrot* in New York with Erika Stiedry-Wagner. In arranging the rehearsals he wrote to her: "We must freshen up the speaking part fundamentally—at least I am going to try this time to see if I can bring out perfectly the light, ironic and satirical tone in which the piece was really conceived. . . . It is difficult to immortalize the authentic performance on records in two weeks."[36] The recording, aside from a dry acoustic and muffled balance, is fascinating as a document of Schoenberg's intentions: Stiedry-Wagner's recitation is quite reserved dramatically overall, compared with more recent recordings and performances. Her basic expression, while not exactly light and satirical, is not overly tragic either. The contours and pitches of her vocal line are only approximations of those notated, while the few sung pitches are quite accurate. She uses a large palette of vocal colors, including glissandi with both wide vibrato and straight tone. She makes interesting transitions in and out of chest voice and head voice, sometimes even going against the written contours of the vocal line. Her diction is virtuosic, with a wide variety of consonants, both fast and percussive and slow and sustained. Milton Babbitt, who attended one of the recording sessions, told me that while Schoenberg was extremely demanding about details in the instrumental parts, he didn't have many comments for Stiedry-Wagner.[37]

At the time of the New York performance and recording, Schoenberg wished that *Pierrot* could be performed in English for an English-speaking audience. It eventually was, to Schoenberg's delight, and a number of translations, including one by his student Dika Newlin, have been made. On a 1974 RCA recording, jazz singer Cleo Laine recites the piece in English.

MORE RECENT PERFORMANCES

As singers and instrumentalists became more familiar with *Pierrot* particularly, and atonal music in general, it became much easier to learn the work. Steuermann, who taught at Juilliard from 1948 to 1964, remarked that "young people today [1963] perform the work sometimes after five rehearsals, but one should not forget what an unknown language this was at the time and also that works become easier when already performed."[38] Problems of rhythm and ensemble became less daunting. Singers also came closer to Schoenberg's instructions for the *Sprechstimme*: "to transform it into a speech-melody, taking into account the given pitch. . . . speaking tone gives the pitch but immediately leaves it again by falling or rising."[39]

In her 1971 recording for Nonesuch, Jan DeGaetani achieved a new kind of vocalism, coming much closer than previous reciters to many of Schoenberg's notated pitches while avoiding a sustained singing tone. In 1992, when I was performing at the Marlboro Music Festival, one of Jan's former students was rehearsing *Pierrot* with violinist Felix Galimir, who had worked with Schoenberg in Vienna. Mezzo Mary Nessinger, an extraordinary musician and compelling performer, had performed *Pierrot* before, sounding many of the notated pitches in a rising or falling spoken tone that moved immediately from one note to the next. Galimir insisted that this was not the correct Viennese style, encouraging her not to speak on the pitches because no one in Schoenberg's circle ever did.

Yet Schoenberg did notate specific pitches that, if vocalized, do contribute to the overall sound and architecture of the composition. And he did specify that the speech-melody should take into account the given pitch. Should today's singers, who have the musicianship to achieve this accuracy, choose a less precise approach because that is what Stiedry-Wagner did? If Schoenberg had heard Jan DeGaetani's performance, would he have liked it, or would he have criticized her, as he did Marya Freund, for singing too much? Since what Schoenberg said he wanted regarding the *Sprechstimme* in *Pierrot* and what he got in his lifetime were quite different, we can never determine what the "correct" style really is.

I personally favor using both approaches depending on the situation, which can change from measure to measure. In busy, noisy passages, where there are balance issues and thick counterpoint, I often choose a pitch level higher or lower than notated to produce the most volume and projection without strain. I also give more energy to the consonants and less definable pitch to the vowels, while still trying to maintain the relative contours and distance between notes. Such passages can be found in "Rote Messe," "Galgenlied," and "Enthauptung" (see ex. 7.4). Soprano Bethany Beardslee, celebrated for her many performances and recordings of Second Viennese School works, told me that she favors a lower placement to create atmosphere in "Eine blasse Wäscherin" and "Nacht," and finds that certain pieces, such as "Der kranke Mond" and "Paro-

Example 7.4. Schoenberg: *Pierrot lunaire*, "Enthauptung," mm. 12–15. Used by permission of Belmont Music Publishers.

Example 7.5. Schoenberg: *Pierrot lunaire,* a) "Der kranke Mond," mm. 1–5; b) "Heimweh," mm. 25–27. Used by permission of Belmont Music Publishers.

die," have more pitch content than others. Where the texture is more transparent, as in "Madonna," "Der kranke Mond," "Heimweh," or "Heimfahrt," I find speaking on the notated pitches enhances the harmony (see ex. 7.5). In "Parodie" (ex. 7.6a) the viola is in canon with the vocal line through much of the piece, and in "O alter Duft" (ex. 7.6b) the piano doubles the vocal line. Reciting (without singing!) close to the written pitches helps clarify the instrumental lines.

If you want your *Sprechstimme* to be close to the notated pitches, there are two approaches. You can learn to sing the pitches first and then move toward a speaking tone. Alternatively, you can speak the text in rhythm in an approximate contour and then get closer to the pitches as you learn the music better. I prefer the first method. For a more detailed discussion of *Sprechstimme* technique, see Sharon Mabry's *Exploring Twentieth-Century Vocal Music.*[40]

### *Sprechstimme* in Other Works

Schoenberg used *Sprechstimme* in other works, including *Gurrelieder, A Survivor from Warsaw, Moses und Aron, Ode to Napoleon,* and *Kol nidre.* His notation and instructions for the speaking voice vary. In *Gurrelieder,* the *Sprechstimme* is notated with empty square noteheads on a five-line staff (see ex. 7.7a).

Example 7.6. Schoenberg: *Pierrot lunaire,* a) "Parodie," mm. 10–15; b) "O alter Duft," mm. 1–5. Used by permission of Belmont Music Publishers.

Yet in a letter to Erika Stiedry-Wagner, who was preparing for a performance of the speaking part, Schoenberg explained what he desired: "As against *Pierrot,* there are no pitches here. The only reason why I wrote notes was because I thought that I could make my phrasing, accentuation and declamation clearer. So no speech melodies. The only likeness with *Pierrot* is in the necessity of remaining in time with the orchestra."[41] In complaining about the Stokowski recording of *Gurrelieder*, Schoenberg chastised both the speaker for singing his part too much and one of the singers for speaking too much: "Finally I found out the best thing is to give [the speaker role] to a singer who no longer has the necessary beauty of voice to sing great parts. It should if possible, be a higher voice, about Tenor range or high Baritone. For the first performance, which I conducted myself in 1914, I had the part of the speaker carried out by Mrs. Albertine Zehme. She was very, very good and it was quite possible to make this piece also with a woman's voice, because it is orchestrated in this manner."[42]

In *Moses und Aron* (ex. 7.7b), the *Sprechstimme* is notated with ✕'ed noteheads on a five-line staff, while in *Die Jakobsleiter*, *Die glückliche Hand*, and *Pierrot* it is notated with regular noteheads with ✕'s on their stems. In *A Survivor from Warsaw* and the *Ode to Napoleon* (ex. 7.7c), Schoenberg used a one-line staff with regular notes distributed above and below it.

Berg used *Sprechstimme* for a few isolated moments in songs and more extensively in his operas *Wozzeck* and *Lulu*. In his 1929 article "The Preparation and Staging of *Wozzeck*," which was written to accompany the performance materials, Berg discussed the different kinds of vocal writing in the score indicated by "recitative," "parlando," and "cantabile":

> It is important to differentiate between these directions, which indicate where a *cantabile*, that is a *bel canto* treatment of the voice is clearly required and feasible, and where it is not. . . . The following remarks amplify the instructions for the execution of the *Sprechstimme* as given in both the full score and the vocal score. No singing, under any circumstances! Still, the pitches are to be stated and held exactly as indicated by the notes, but held with the tone quality of the speaking voice. To be sure, such a speaking voice need not be restricted to chest tones throughout. Head tones are also possible, even necessary, since the normal speaking voice is often too low and of too limited a compass. For this reason these spoken pitches are placed where they will cause the singer no more difficulty or harm than the sung tones suitable to the different registers and to various changes in expression.
>
> Only in those cases where, in spite of these directions, an unnatural and mannered timbre is unavoidable, is it permitted to execute the spoken melody in a narrower compass, within which, however, "the relationship of the individual pitches to one another" must be absolutely maintained.[43]

Berg's instructions thus differ from Schoenberg's in that he wants the singer to sustain the notated pitch with a speaking tone, rather than move continuously toward and away from it. Berg was just as demanding and exacting in rehearsals as Schoenberg and Webern, but he was warmer and more appreciative of per-

a) Gurrelieder

b) Moses und Aron

c) Ode to Napoleon

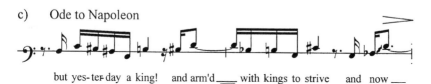

Example 7.7. Schoenberg *Sprechstimme* notation: a) *Gurrelieder*; b) *Moses und Aron*; c) *Ode to Napoleon*. Used by permission of Belmont Music Publishers.

formers' efforts. Webern did not include *Sprechstimme* in his vocal compositions.

### Dynamics and Articulation

In a 1929 letter about the preparations for his opera *Von heute auf morgen,* Schoenberg revealed his thoughts on dynamics and articulation:

> Above all: my music calls for singers who are able to sing 9/10 of their parts between **pp** and **mf**, in order to achieve appropriate climaxes with an occasional *forte* and with

very few *fortissimos*. In other words, they should not just scream the text all evening (as is too customary in Berlin and elsewhere in Germany). . . . The singers must be able to sing *piano* and *mezza voce,* and *legato* when that is called for; even in *détaché* passages, their style must remain *cantabile.* They must cut their tones short only where *staccato* is indicated; but this is for purposes of special musical characterization, not because of the text. . . . The singing must always remain dignified. The singers must never *characterize* at the expense of vocal beauty, must never exaggerate. Better colorless than crude—it is not necessary to "help out" my music; in itself it is so characteristic that, when it is performed correctly, all the characterization is automatically present. This has proven to be the case with all my works up till now.[44]

Schoenberg also disapproved of too much portamento and vibrato, exaggerated *sforzandi,* and the familiar Romantic tradition of speeding up with a crescendo and slowing down with a decrescendo.[45] He did indicate where he wanted portamenti with a wavy line connecting two notes (see ex. 7.8).

Webern, another perfectionist about detail, wanted every note to be clear and just right. His most important musical goals were clarity, comprehensibility, emotion, and expression; unfortunately, most audiences in his lifetime found his works incomprehensible. He often preferred soft dynamics in his music (see ex. 7.9), and many of his songs are sparse and transparent miniatures. As a conductor, Webern sometimes spent so much time perfecting the opening measures of a work that he didn't have enough time to rehearse the rest of the program. Yet his conducting was described as emotional and sensitive, achieving an intensely intimate expressiveness. He believed that "every note has its own life"[46] and deserved to be heard completely. In his recording of the Berg Violin Concerto with Louis Krasner and the BBC Orchestra, he never hurries,

Example 7.8. Schoenberg: *Das Buch der hängenden Gärten,* op. 15, "V," mm. 13–15, Universal, 1914, reprint Dover, 1995.

Example 7.9. Webern: "Die Sonne" from *Sechs Lieder*, op. 14, mm. 4–6, Universal, 1924.

lingering lovingly over every harmony and caressing every turn of phrase. His friends thought he was the greatest conductor since Mahler.

### Tempo and Rubato

To counteract the excessive abuses of rhythm and tempo common in the late nineteenth century, the Second Viennese School composers wrote many more tempo indications into their scores. They also controlled the flow of tempo with notated rhythms, which became dauntingly intricate and complex. In "Des Herzens Purpurvogel" from *Drei Lieder,* op. 25 (ex. 7.10), for instance, Webern constantly adjusts the pacing with ritardandos and *A tempos* while barring groups of notes across the bar lines.

Yet all three composers remained still under the influence of the Romantic tradition, and a subtle flexibility was part of all their music making. In an interview with Joan Allen Smith, Felix Galimir discussed rhythm and flexibility in rehearsing with Schoenberg and Webern:

> They were terribly meticulous about rhythms, and you know, that these sixteenths or the triplet comes after the second sixteenth, and you played and you finally could

Example 7.10. Webern: "Des Herzens Purpurvogel" from *Drei Lieder,* op. 25, mm. 25–32. Copyright 1956 by Universal Edition A.G., Wien. Copyright renewed. All Rights Reserved. Used by permission of European American Music Distributors LLC, US and Canadian agents for Universal Edition, A.G., Wien.

make it just right, and that was it. And when you finally got it and he says, "Yes, but it sounds stiff and . . . it has to be free," and that was really very important that one does play the music although very correct but with a certain freedom and not in a straitjacket because of the complications or the expression. I think the paramount thing was that one should not, especially because of the row and the intonation and dissonances, overlook the expressional aspect of the piece. And you know that Schoenberg's or Webern's music is so terribly expressive.[47]

Edward Steuermann remembers that when Webern played a new score for him at the piano, "Webern himself was the freest interpreter of his own music that could be imagined . . . he played so freely that I hardly could follow the music, but it was extraordinary."[48] Otto Klemperer was similarly struck when Webern played some of his symphony for him on the piano: "He came and played every note with enormous intensity and fanaticism, not coolly, passionately!"[49]

Finding the correct tempo was essential to Schoenberg, but much of what he wrote over the years about it is extremely contradictory. He complained about conductors who were too free with violent changes of tempo in his music, but then he confessed that some of his tempo markings were too exaggerated. In 1926 he wrote that performers should follow composers' metronome markings, but then in 1950 he cautioned that we shouldn't take them too literally.[50] Some of these discrepancies resulted from the large body of writing that Schoenberg produced over an extended period of changing performance styles. Many reports say that Schoenberg took very slow tempos when he conducted his music. This could be simply because orchestras in the early part of his career found his music hard to understand and difficult to play. In his 1940 *Pierrot* recording, Schoenberg's tempos are generally close to or a little faster than his metronome markings. Erika Stiedry-Wagner tends to be a bit slower when the vocal line and diction dominate the instrumental lines. Rubato and changes of tempo within a given poem are flexible, but not overdone.

Edward Steuermann, in discussing Schoenberg's *Six Little Piano Pieces,* op. 19, gives the following advice: "In the case of Schoenberg you must try to keep the balance between unity of tempo and the expressive demands. . . . My advice is: play always so that the expression and the characters are established absolutely and in the way you feel it. Then try to give the piece the unity of movement which comes out of your feeling. . . . The deviations from the general tempo should be as slight as possible. The more you are able to give the impression of a constant tempo, the better."[51] Although Schoenberg mistrusted most performers and counseled them not to add emotion or characterization to his music, Steuermann was one of his most faithful interpreters. We can rely on his advice when it comes to style.

### Learning This Music

In his 1929 letter about *Von heute auf morgen,* Schoenberg states, "I think that only singers who can sight-read these parts and who have absolute pitch can really learn them reliably."[52] Certainly this does not have to be the case today. After having had atonal music in our ears for almost a century, we are much more accustomed to learning works with difficult pitches and rhythms. Singers with absolute pitch do have an advantage, but even those without perfect pitch can master this language.

Here are some tips to make the learning process a little easier: learn a work in layers; deal separately with the rhythms, the pitches, the language, the expression, and the coordination with the accompaniment. Don't attempt to put it all together until you feel comfortable with each individual task. In a work with large intervals, try thinking of them as their smaller inversions; for example, jumping up a minor ninth is the same as going down a half step and then up an octave. Calculating intervals like this resembles solving a puzzle, and the more you do it the better you get at it. Work on tough rhythms and pitches only for short periods of time. When you reach the point of mental fatigue, stop and then do more the next day.

I find that if I chip away at difficult pitches over a number of days, eventually they begin to make sense and to sound familiar. At this point, muscle memory starts to work as well, and, as a friend of mine who sang *Moses und Aron* at the New York City Opera remarked, "once it's in there, it's in there." He also cautioned that it can be impractical to "mark" this music, either by singing down an octave or singing half voice, because of the large intervals and wide range combined with subtle gradations of dynamics. When you need to find your note from the accompaniment and remember it over other distracting pitches, a very soft, breathy whistle on the necessary pitch will help keep it in your ear without anyone else hearing.

But merely executing the correct pitches is not the end of our job. We must sing our notes in relation to each other and to the accompaniment, just as we did within the bounds of tonality. In the realm of atonal or twelve-tone music, it feels a bit different. In twelve-tone music it is possible to learn the row and to recognize repeated contours and groupings either by hearing them or feeling them in your voice. In atonal music that is not twelve-tone, most composers establish some kind of context that determines a hierarchy among the notes.

Pitches are no longer merely consonant or dissonant, but they do seem to have more or less tension or to belong with what's going on to a greater or lesser degree. In example 7.8., for instance, on the first beat of m. 13, the F-sharp in the vocal line feels almost like a G-flat in a B-flat-minor chord against the B-flat/E-flat in the piano. The top A seems like the dissonant note. On the second beat, however, when the chord in the piano changes, the F-sharp in the vocal line feels like part of an E-major seventh chord. Then the C on "ich" feels like a more dissonant passing note. The D and E on "meine" have slightly less tension because of the unisons with notes in the accompanying piano chords. The F-natural on the downbeat of the next measure, however, seems to have slightly more tension, but only until the piano chord changes on the second beat, creating even more dissonance as the F squeezes between F-sharp in the bass and E and G in the treble. When the voice slips down to E on "Wan*ge*," some of that tension seems relieved, but then a new kind of tension builds toward the suspension on the downbeat of m. 15. Once you get used to hearing and feeling this music in a new kind of harmonic context, you can shape and inflect it just as you would Brahms, Wolf, or Strauss.

Schoenberg, Berg, and Webern had an unusually ambivalent attitude toward both performers and audiences. They felt unappreciated and frequently distrustful of singers in particular. Their vocal music was often written without specific singers or performance situations in mind.

Like their French colleagues, the Second Viennese School composers wanted their works presented with clarity and precision. They wanted performers to transmit the meaning of their music without added personal interpretation. They used increasingly detailed notation to control every aspect of the music, including dynamics, articulation, rhythm, and tempo. They expected singers to execute all these elements accurately while negotiating increasingly difficult atonal pitches. Yet these composers did not want dry, unemotional performances of their vocal music. This repertoire still reflects the influence of nineteenth-century Romantic traditions, even though tempo fluctuations, rubato, and expression were now specifically written into the music. Singers today should not be intimidated by the challenging pitches and rhythms, but instead approach this rich music as an extension of nineteenth-century German lieder.

The new issue introduced in this chapter is *Sprechstimme*. This technique involves a variety of notations and a wealth of confusing, contradictory advice about exactly how to do it. The crucial points concern how accurately the pitches, if indicated, should be sounded, and with what kind of tone. Different composers had different kinds of sounds in mind for specific pieces. Despite all his demands for precision and accuracy, it is particularly interesting that Schoenberg found a French performance of *Pierrot lunaire* too precise and accurate, and too tastefully sung. It is possible that singers today can come closer than many of the original performers to what these composers actually asked for. But whether the composers would ultimately approve of this approach remains unanswerable.

# Chapter 8 Early Twentieth-
# Century Nationalism

This chapter considers nationalistic trends in the first half of the twentieth century in Russia, Spain, England, and the United States, focusing on vocal music by Musorgsky, Rachmaninov, Prokofiev, Shostakovich, Falla, Rodrigo, Britten, Ives, Copland, and Barber. It investigates cultural and political issues as well as the folk heritage that contributed to the distinctive musical flavor of each country. It also examines what motivated these composers to write vocal music as well as some of the singers who inspired and championed them; Fyodor Chaliapin, Maria Olenina-d'Alheim, Galina Vishnevskaya, Victoria de los Angeles, Peter Pears, Eleanor Steber, and Leontyne Price. It is much easier to get a sense of these singers' individual styles because of their many recordings, which include premieres of works written for them. We can also hear composers playing and conducting their own works. We can use the recordings to learn these composers' intentions and to glimpse their working relationships with singers.

In the early twentieth century, greater ease of travel allowed for more extensive exchange of ideas between different national cultures. Performances of Russian music in Paris had a tremendous effect on

French composers. Spaniards and Americans studying in Paris absorbed the influence of French composers and included French ideals in their own music. Spanish-flavored music by Russian composers also influenced the development of Spanish nationalism. Russian composers performing in the United States adapted to the demands of American audiences. Friendships between Copland and Britten, Britten and Shostakovich, and Barber and Poulenc yielded inspiration for composition and performance. Despite this cross-pollination of ideology and tradition, composers still established distinctive national styles, incorporating their folk heritage and adapting to the circumstances of their homelands.

The format of this chapter differs slightly from previous chapters. It considers questions of text, tempo, rhythm, rubato, metronome markings, and editions within the context of particular composers and singers.

## RUSSIA

The discussion here of Russian national style focuses primarily on vocal chamber music from the "realist" period. I will not address songs by Tchaikovsky, Glinka, or Rimsky-Korsakov from the salon romance tradition because their style follows closely that of nineteenth-century European Romanticism (see chapter 5). As in chapter 4, opera will be considered only as an aid to discovering the vocal styles created by singers and composers.

Industrialism did not reach Russia until near the end of the nineteenth century. Before the 1917 revolution, much of the country remained agrarian, with peasants working on country estates owned by landed gentry. The peasants' life and culture had changed little over the nineteenth century. Singing accompanied many aspects of peasant life, including work in the fields and religious and social rituals. Peasant songs that were often not much more than sung speech captured a wide range of emotions, including lamentation and celebration. The vocalism was throaty and guttural, with glottal ornamentation.[1]

The aristocracy, particularly in the cities, was more interested in the latest operas by Verdi and touring European virtuosos than in new Russian music. In the 1860s a group of composers began gathering to perform and discuss their own new compositions as well as to study works by European masters. These five—Mily Alexeyevich Balakirev, Alexander Borodin, Modest Musorgsky, César Cui, and Nikolay Rimsky-Korsakov—became known as the Mighty Handful (*moguchaya kuchka*) or the New Russian Musical School. They believed in promoting "musical truth," which, in terms of vocal music, required words and music to work together to present a realistic flow of action and drama. Their text settings highlighted natural inflection and phrasing, favoring the rough, spoken quality of peasant songs. Songs, particularly those by Musorgsky, presented everyday, commonplace themes with comic or vulgar texts about children, fishwives, and beggars, in sharp contrast with the lofty love poetry found in most European chansons or lieder.

By the start of the twentieth century, Russian artists of all types were collaborating, both embracing and rejecting realism. This richly creative environment spawned such personalities as the impresario Sergei Diaghilev and the director Konstantin Stanislavsky, and endeavors such as the Moscow Art Theater and the Evenings of Contemporary Music in St. Petersburg.

The 1917 revolution and succeeding civil war of 1918–20 brought terrible suffering to Russia. Some artists who came from bourgeois backgrounds fled the country, and their property was confiscated. Conservatories and theaters stayed open, but only the most dedicated music lovers attended concerts, because finding heat and food became all-consuming needs. Conservatory students were ordered to perform at Red Army headquarters, factories, and worker communes in an attempt to lift people's spirits.[2] Once the Communist Party was in power, it encouraged music with a social message and wide public appeal. Gone were the elegant salons of the wealthy and educated, which had featured solo songs expressing personal emotions. The cultural revolution of 1928 and the state-sponsored Russian Association of Proletarian Musicians increasingly required that music glorify Soviet ideals. Artists who believed otherwise had to change their views or suffer official criticism and banishment. Some, despite great personal hardship, still managed to find a way to get their musical messages across.

### Musorgsky and Olenina

Although Modest Musorgsky died well before the revolution, he had been a radical in his own time and was both misunderstood and underappreciated. His music challenged the prevailing boundaries of rhythm and harmony and was considered by many to be coarse, crude, and ugly. Tchaikovsky grudgingly acknowledged Musorgsky's remarkable originality and believed that he had introduced a new musical language despite his lack of formal training. This fresh language came from a desire to capture the natural rhythms and dramatic inflections of Russian speech. In Musorgsky's words, "my music must be an artistic reproduction of human speech in all its finest shades, that is the *sounds of human speech* . . . must become music that is truthful, accurate, *but* artistic, highly

Example 8.1. Musorgsky: "With Nanny" from *The Nursery*, mm. 1–10, ed. Rimsky-Korsakov, 1882, International, 1955.

artistic."[3] Musorgsky based his song cycle *The Nursery* on his own transcriptions of typical children's conversations. The changing meters and declamatory rhythms of the first song, "With Nanny" (see ex. 8.1), were unlike anything that had come before it in Russian song.

A gifted mimic and pianist, Musorgsky delighted his young cousins as he sang and accompanied himself in his "enactment" of songs. In his operatic setting of Gogol's play *The Marriage,* he tried to reproduce the inflection and phrasing of the actors onstage. He sang through this opera for his friends, who were perplexed by both the harmonic progressions and his antilyrical approach to ordinary conversations of the play. Musorgsky abandoned *The Marriage* after completing the first act, but he triumphed in 1874 with his next operatic attempt, *Boris Godunov.*

Despite the successes of *Boris, The Nursery,* and other works, Musorgsky succumbed to alcoholism and poverty in the last years of his life. He often accompanied singers as a means of income, only rarely performing his own songs. He was grateful for any bit of work or public recognition and became dependent on his friends for moral and financial support. Penniless and miserable, he died in 1881 at the age of forty-two. Many of his compositions were left unfinished and were completed and published posthumously by his friends. Rimsky-Korsakov, who first edited most of his works, smoothed over what he considered to be coarse harmonies and offensive part-writing. As avant-garde composers in the early twentieth century came to know Musorgsky's works, they objected to Rimsky-Korsakov's corrections and tried to uncover the original rough and innovative music. Musorgsky's music profoundly influenced many later composers.

The singer Maria Olenina-d'Alheim was one of Musorgsky's most important posthumous champions, and she helped introduce his vocal music to the rest of the world. Olenina became a link between centuries: the nineteenth century of her childhood and the twentieth century in which she performed and taught. In 1963, at the age of ninety-five, she coached two young professional Russian vocalists in songs by Musorgsky. In these master classes she transmitted her firsthand experience with Musorgsky's world and style.[4]

Olenina, born to a noble family, had grown up on a country estate. In 1887 her family moved to St. Petersburg, where she sang in prominent salons and came to the attention of the Mighty Handful. At first she studied voice with Yulia Platonova, a famous opera singer who had championed music by the New Russian Music School and worked with Musorgsky in the first staging of *Boris.* Through Platonova, Olenina heard stories of Musorgsky and worked on his music. Platonova encouraged Maria to pursue an opera career, but Olenina had other plans. At the suggestion of the Mighty Handful, she began studying with Rimsky-Korsakov's sister-in-law, Alexandra Purgold-Molas. Purgold-Molas, an exquisite lieder singer, was not a professional, but she had performed at many of the Mighty Handful's musical evenings. Attracted to Musorgsky, she had hoped, in vain, that the great composer would return her affections. Though disappointed in love, she had remained one of his most gifted and faithful interpreters. Musorgsky's friends were delighted that she would pass her knowledge and dedication on to the talented young Olenina.

In 1893 Olenina moved to Paris and became involved with her cousin, writer and historian Pyotr d'Alheim, whom she eventually married. Together they created unusual performance experiences, introducing Paris's musical elite to the works of Musorgsky. Their lecture recitals, known as *conférences*, featured commentaries by Pyotr followed by Maria's recitals. Begun in 1896, these events were a tremendous success, attracting the attention of both the French and Russian press. In 1901 Debussy reviewed a performance of *The Nursery*, hailing it as a masterpiece: "Mme Marie Olénine sang these songs at a recent concert of the Société Nationale, so well that Mussorgsky himself would have been pleased—if I may dare speak on his behalf."[5] Ravel heard these performances as well, and his 1907 work *Histoires naturelles* was clearly inspired by *The Nursery* in both text choice and declamation style.[6]

In the midst of this rich Parisian cultural life, Olenina developed a personal artistic philosophy based on the idea that a performer should renounce one's self in the service of the composer and artistic truth. Some of this credo may have been inspired by Musorgsky's ideals, but many performers in Paris at the turn of the century were pursuing a similar path. Perhaps she absorbed the prevailing wisdom; perhaps she contributed to it as well.

In the first decades of the new century, Maria concertized in Paris, London, Moscow, and St. Petersburg. She established a new standard for recital programming, constructing groups of songs by a single poet or composer, organized to highlight the music, rather than presenting audience favorites. Her concerts, without the use of assisting artists or guest virtuosos, were seen as a new genre of musical performance, and she was hailed as the first Russian chamber singer. A review by César Cui declared her a revelation: "Mme. Olenina is an artist of conviction. She does not follow the public, she does not chase after success and does not toady to public taste. . . . [She] has a medium-strength mezzo-soprano voice, beautiful, high and even in all its registers. Her technique is superb and consists in splendid diction, phrasing, rich, varied and subtle nuances, and a rare ability to impart various timbre to her voice—now metallic, now gentle and caressing. Every nuance of human feeling is equally accessible to her—both a childlike, touchingly naïve lisp that evokes smiles of sympathy (Musorgsky's *Nursery*), and profound, fateful and soul-shaking tragedy (Schubert's 'Der Doppelgänger')."[7] Other reviewers, while sometimes finding fault with her voice, praised her declamatory expression and captivating dramatic presentation.

From 1908 to 1918 she and her husband directed the Dom pesni (House of Song), based in Moscow, which sought to promote the music of Musorgsky and other nineteenth-century Russian composers. The organization produced concerts, lectures, and publications and by 1913 had 900 members. It also sponsored a competition for translating song texts and harmonizing folk songs; Ravel won in 1911. After the revolution, Maria and Pyotr fled to Paris, where they continued their activities in the transplanted Maison du Lied, involving singers such as Marya Freund, Madeleine Grey, Claire Croiza, and Jane Bathori. After her husband died in 1922, Olenina occasionally participated in concerts of new music by French composers, but mostly she continued to promote and teach the Russian style of Musorgsky. Tragically, she descended into poverty and eventually returned to Russia, alone and forgotten.

Olenina's artistic goals set an example for all Russian chamber singers who followed. We can follow her advice today when approaching this repertoire: she believed that a singer must give special attention to the text, dedicate all vocal gestures to the needs of the composer, and lose oneself completely in the dramatic world of the song.[8] In her master classes in the 1960s, she told singers that they would find everything they needed in the text and the music.[9] They must perform simply and naturally and not invent or exaggerate. The presentation of the characters in the songs should, however, be genuine and realistic.[10] As she discussed "The Hobby Horse" from *The Nursery,* she warned soprano Galina Pisarenko not to force the melody and sing too sentimentally when the mother comes to comfort the child: "You made the mother too fancy sounding . . . the mother speaks in a much more simple fashion. You don't have to make her sing." Pisarenko then explained that she imagined the mother as an aristocratic lady, all in lace. Olenina responded with a laugh, "And my mother was also an aristocratic lady, but she never spoke with me that way."[11]

In discussing "Evening Prayer," Olenina reminisced about how her own nanny had taught her to recite her prayers before bed, revealing that she not only absorbed Musorgsky's desired style of performance but also that she had grown up in the very world of his *Nursery.* In the first song from the cycle, she demonstrated that the dramatic expression and motivation of the text must determine the changing tempo: the little girl is fascinated by various frightening and funny fairy tales, and the music's rhythm and pacing must respond to her changing thoughts as she describes different scenes and characters. On the tape of these master classes, Olenina's voice is somewhat ragged from her advanced age, yet it still conveys a childlike wonder and excitement and a vibrant flexibility of rhythm and tempo as she half speaks, half sings through the opening of "With Nanny." Musorgsky writes a series of quarter-note rhythms in changing meters (see ex. 8.1). It is crucial for the singer to be familiar with the spoken inflection of the Russian text, so each quarter note, rather than having equal length and weight, can be shaded and shaped like natural speech. The singer must also fully envision each changing character, from the bogeyman to the queen who sneezes, so that the characterizations can be genuine.

### Rimsky-Korsakov, Rachmaninov, and Chaliapin

Rimsky-Korsakov is commonly considered to have been both the first architect of the Russian national style and its first ambassador to western Europe. In the 1870s he collected and arranged a groundbreaking volume of Russian folk songs. As he did in editing Musorgsky's music, however, he corrected and smoothed over rhythms and harmonies that he found questionable or problematic, compromising the music's authenticity. His *Capriccio espagnole* of 1888 captured a Spanish flavor that would later inspire Spanish composers. His orchestral concerts at the Paris Exposition of 1889 sparked a western European fascination with Russian music that would continue into the new century. Most of his songs were in the traditional Romantic style, melodious and singable, and by his own admission "conforming to the tastes of singers and of the public at large."[12] In his later operas he perfected the kind of declamatory recitative heard in Musorgsky's vocal music, composing several leading roles for Fyodor Chaliapin, a master of this style of singing. According to Rimsky-Korsakov's son, Andrey, the composer "demanded from his interpreters accurate intonation, tempo and rhythm; he did not tolerate arbitrary cuts, fermatas, hums or shouts, and so on. But my father never accused Chaliapin of any of these things."[13]

Chaliapin was probably the most celebrated singer in Russian history. He created a sensation with his 1895 debut at age twenty-one with the Imperial Mariinsky Theater as Mephistopheles in Gounod's *Faust,* and he soon became famous throughout Russia and the world. In addition to his magnificent voice, he was renowned for his intense acting and overwhelming stage presence. Although he left many recordings, a British critic wrote in 1926 that "he is among all singers the one most in need of being seen in order to be properly heard. Those who could only know his art from gramophone records can have but a faint idea of his power of swaying and subduing the audience."[14] Stanislavsky often credited the bass for inspiring his system of method acting and said that his opera workshop was really a Chaliapin school.[15] Chaliapin favored Musorgsky's music, performing some of the songs and offering the first of his many unforgettable renditions of *Boris Godunov* in 1898. The Russian public, however, continued to prefer Italian opera, much to his frustration.

Around the turn of the century Chaliapin became friendly with Sergei Rachmaninov, then a conductor at Savva Mamontov's Private Russian Opera in Moscow. The two enjoyed giving concerts together, both in public and at private gatherings of friends. These occasions have been described in superlatives: "two giants stimulated each other and literally produced miracles. This was no longer singing or music in the generally accepted sense of the words. This was inspiration breaking out in two great artists."[16] Rachmaninov said of Chaliapin, "I cannot name a single artist who has given me such deep and pure artistic pleasure. To accompany him was the greatest joy of my life."[17] In turn, Chaliapin said of Rachmaninov, "When he is at the piano, I am not singing alone—we are both singing. He interprets the very soul of the composition with the utmost delicacy, and if a pause or a suspended note is required, the singer may be sure that he will indicate them perfectly."[18]

The relationship proved mutually beneficial. Rachmaninov composed songs for Chaliapin, one of which they performed for Leo Tolstoy on a particularly memorable occasion. Rachmaninov also helped the bass learn the part of Salieri in Rimsky-Korsakov's new chamber opera *Mozart and Salieri*, demanding the utmost attention in accurately following the score. Rimsky-Korsakov was sensitive to criticism and reluctant to make changes to suit the singer. Rimsky-Korsakov may have worried that Chaliapin's charisma would overshadow his music, yet he and the singer maintained a close relationship and traveled to Paris in 1907 for concerts with Diaghilev.

Because of his peasant background, Chaliapin had no need to leave Russia after the revolution. Ironically, unfounded accusations of involvement with the Bolsheviks tarnished his reputation in the West. Rachmaninov, in contrast, was from an aristocratic family and left Russia forever in 1917. He became famous as a concert pianist, performing his own music and other works in Europe and the United States. He was one of the first virtuoso pianists of the modern era who took surprisingly few liberties and accurately followed the text of the score. He left many recordings that display both dazzling technique and rich, warm musicality. His thrilling virtuosity was not just for show. While he did employ rhythmic flexibility and gentle rubato, it was always used to shape the musical phrase and highlight the structure of the piece. Rachmaninov believed that every composition had a culminating moment, "the Point" as he called it. He and Chaliapin always tried to construct their performances to reveal that moment.[19]

Chaliapin's principal voice teacher, Dmitri Usatov, had been trained according to the Italian school of García and Francesco Lamperti and had been the first Lensky in Tchaikovsky's *Eugene Onegin*. He passed on a firm grounding in bel canto technique as well as a knowledge and love for Russian music. He also introduced his student to the idea of dramatic intonation or coloration of the voice. In his book *Man and Mask,* Chaliapin asks "how must breathing be controlled so as to express a musical situation, the mental state of a character, with the appropriate intonation? I am speaking here not of musical intonation, of the production of such and such a note, but of the colour of the voice which, even in ordinary conversation, assumes various shades."[20] In fact, this quality of his singing, along with its precise diction, gave the impression of human speech: "The realism of his declamation was amazing," wrote critic Nikolay Fyodorovich Findeyzen. "I sometimes found it positively unbelievable that I was listening to a phrase which had been learnt from written-down music. It was live, free speech, adapting itself to convey all the shades of emotion."[21]

In his recordings Chaliapin used a wide variety of sounds—light and broad, round and dark—but always easy and never forced, even when the full richness of his voice poured forth. He was not afraid to make an ugly sound to enhance the drama, and his articulation could be quite conversational or extremely legato. He allowed for flexible tempos, which complemented his dramatic inflection, and his suspenseful pauses were legendary.

Chaliapin's biographer brings up an interesting point about the title of his book, *Maska i dusha,* translated into English as *Man and Mask.* The Russian word *dusha* can be translated as "soul," but it really has a much more subtle association that includes a sense of "innermost feelings."[22] Chaliapin's commitment to revealing his innermost feelings with colorful declamation and honest dramatic interpretation epitomized the soul of the Russian style.

### Prokofiev

Just as Rachmaninov had studied piano, conducting, and composition at the Moscow Conservatory, Sergei Prokofiev studied all three subjects at the St. Petersburg Conservatory. In 1907 he began to participate in the Evenings of Contemporary Music concerts as a pianist, revealing himself as a controversial and innovative young composer. In 1913 he visited Paris, where he heard Ravel and

Stravinsky. He met Diaghilev, which paved the way for future collaborative theater projects. He also met Anna Zherebtsova-Andreyeva, a voice professor from the St. Petersburg Conservatory. Her husband, a tenor, was performing opposite Chaliapin in a sensational Diaghilev production of *Boris Godunov* in London. Zherebtsova-Andreyeva appeared often at the Evenings of Contemporary Music and performed several of Prokofiev's songs, including the first version of *The Ugly Duckling,* op. 18. This extended through-composed song demonstrates Prokofiev's reverence for Musorgsky and the particular influence of *The Nursery.* The text is Prokofiev's own version of the Hans Christian Andersen tale. The music highlights the changing narrative and different characters of the story with sections of declamatory recitative interspersed with lyrical passages (see ex 8.2). As with *The Nursery,* the singer must "enact" the story using expressive, dramatic diction and a large palette of vocal colors.

Prokofiev left Russia in 1918, committed to return someday despite his mixed to negative feelings about the Bolshevik regime. He spent several years in the United States but became frustrated with the conservative taste of American audiences. He felt overshadowed by Rachmaninov, who had wider public appeal as a pianist and composer. While he tried to simplify his compositional language, he didn't want to compromise his artistic standards. He returned in 1923 to Paris, where he married the Spanish-born singer Lina Llubera, who often performed his songs with him on concert tours. In 1932 Prokofiev revised and orchestrated *The Ugly Duckling* so that they could perform it together when he conducted orchestral concerts.

Llubera also helped prepare French translations of his vocal works for publication. Prokofiev wanted his vocal works to be accessible to as wide a public as possible and often participated in or sanctioned performances of his songs and operas in French or English. Yet because they were most often conceived with a Russian text for a Russian-speaking audience, he preferred them in the original language.

European audiences appreciated his music and he had many successes, but the dominating presence of Stravinsky kept him in second place. In the spring of 1936 he returned to Soviet Russia, where he adapted his musical language to suit the demands of the Communist Party. Russian singers Nina Dorliak and Zara Dolukhanova performed some of his songs. As the years went on, he wrote fewer songs and more large-scale works for public occasions and for the theater. Ironically, while his music enjoyed increasingly positive receptions in Europe and the United States, it met with more criticism and restriction in the Soviet Union. By 1948 many of his works were withdrawn from public perfor-

Example 8.2. Prokofiev: *The Ugly Duckling*, op. 18 (first version), mm. 116–25, Breitkopf & Härtel, 1922, reprint Belwin-Mills, 1970.

mances, his concert tours abroad were canceled, and his wife was arrested and later sent to a labor camp.

Prokofiev left a legacy of solo piano recordings that reveal his personal style. Soviet recordings from midcentury also document state-authorized performances of his larger works from that period. Poulenc observed that Prokofiev played "quite straightforwardly . . . without any sham 'effects' and with impeccable technique." Another reviewer evaluated his playing as "brilliant, rather dry, but extremely polished, pure and finished . . . perfectly balancing spontaneity with rigorous precision."[23] In his book *The Great Pianists,* Harold Schonberg writes that "as a pianist Prokofiev was the New Man of the century. He had little in common with the past, and his playing was completely original."[24] In a recording of some small piano studies entitled *Visions fugitives,* Op. 22, the composer uses a subtle and flexible rubato to shape the line, often adding slight ritardandos at the ends of phrases. Fast, brilliant passages almost sound rushed, yet everything he does enhances the musical gesture. Nothing is heavy or overdone; slow, introspective passages are touching and a bit sad without being overly serious. His playing of these miniatures might suggest how he accompanied his songs.

### Shostakovich

Dmitri Shostakovich, fifteen years younger than Prokofiev, entered the St. Petersburg Conservatory just after the revolution. He was a brilliant pianist and earned money in the difficult war years improvising accompaniments for the cinema. As a composer, he achieved early fame with his First Symphony. In a sense he led a double life, keeping his public persona and ideology separate from his private thoughts and feelings. He produced some symphonic works that appealed to the masses and supported Soviet doctrine, while writing "serious music for 'the desk drawer'"[25] that had no chance of public performance but expressed his true creative ideals. During his career he both enjoyed tremendous success and suffered terrible criticism and humiliation, depending on the whims of the Communist Party. His music has been criticized as Soviet propaganda, yet much of it contains a bitter, ironic condemnation of the very institutions it was meant to celebrate.

As a pianist, he was known for incredibly fast tempos. He had natural facility and technique and rarely practiced. Nathan Perlman, a fellow pianist in Leningrad (St. Petersburg), describes Shostakovich's playing: "It was an altogether idiosyncratic way of playing. . . . Shostakovich emphasized the linear aspect of music and was precise in all the details of performance. He used little rubato in his playing, and it lacked extreme dynamic contrasts. It was an 'antisentimental' approach to playing which showed incredible clarity of thought. . . . His Chopin playing didn't resemble anything I have heard before or since. It reminded me of his performances of his own music, very direct and without much plasticity, and very laconic in expression."[26] By the 1930s he performed only his own music. Cellist Arnold Ferkelman enjoyed collaborating with him on his cello sonata: "In general he was very modest, and it was very easy to play with him. He had no sense of ambition or pride, and wasn't offended if one made a suggestion. Most of his comments in regard to his sonata related to the tempi. Dmitri Dmitriyevich was a brilliant pianist and had incredible technique . . . he liked playing quickly and loudly, and he took incredibly fast tempi. His playing was on the dry side, but on the other hand he played very loudly, no doubt because of his great force of temperament."[27]

As a composer, Shostakovich heard all the details of a work in his head and notated them with clarity and precision. His scores are flawless and include both exactly what he wanted and everything the performer needs. At rehearsals he would listen quietly and answer questions politely but rarely allow any changes to be made in the score. Occasionally he would make comments about the tempo and acknowledge that the indicated metronome markings were not quite right. In general, he trusted and respected the performers he asked to play his music and allowed them their own interpretations. Yet soprano Galina Vishnevskaya admits that Shostakovich's musical authority was unshakable, and she always followed his scores to the letter: "Before Shostakovich everyone was intimidated. Even Slava [her husband, cellist and conductor Mstislav Rostropovich] became nervous in front of him as with no one else. When we performed Shostakovich's Blok cycle for him, the hands of that great artist David Oistrakh shook from nerves."[28]

In the 1940s Shostakovich, like Prokofiev, found performances of his works banned. In 1948 he showed a newly composed cycle of songs, *From Jewish Folk Poetry*, op. 79, to the soprano Nina Dorliak and asked her to find a mezzo and tenor to fill out the ensemble. Small, private performances of the cycle for groups of friends were well received, and the work gained a large underground following despite a public campaign against it. Even though Dorliak was married to the eminent pianist Sviatoslav Richter, Shostakovich always insisted on accompanying these performances. He believed that the piano lid should always be fully open, even when accompanying, because the piano sounded its best that way. In 1955 the songs were finally performed publicly and subsequently recorded with soprano Dorliak, mezzo Zara Dolukhanova, tenor Alexei Maslenikov, and the composer at the piano. The singing is expressive, with wonderfully inflected Russian text. Shostakovich's playing is simple and straightforward, with tempos slightly different than indicated by the score's metronome markings.[29]

In the last years of his life, Shostakovich wrote works primarily for a small circle of trusted friends and colleagues. These included song cycles for mezzo and bass as well as a number of works for Vishnevskaya and Rostropovich. The original artists have recorded some of these.[30] In her 1984 autobiography, Vishnevskaya relates horrifying details of the political entanglements surrounding many performances and recordings of Shostakovich's music. She also shares her views on the "Soviet style" of singing: The average audience that came to the opera was made up of uncultured workers. While they were thrilled to sit in the great Bolshoi Theater, they were also frequently exhausted from a day battling the frustrations of Soviet life:

> Something had to be done to rouse that impassive crowd and involve them in the performance. Unless everything was greatly overemphasized, the audience wouldn't understand. And to communicate the meaning of the operas, the words had to be given precedence over the music. Hence the excessive emotions, the exaggeration of words and gestures, the forced voices that have come to characterize Soviet opera. When Soviet singers perform abroad, they are often criticized for their overacting, the shrillness of their voices, and a lack of vocal blending and musical phrasing in their singing. But that is our style, the style of Soviet theater.[31]

It is a fascinating journey from Chaliapin's first experiments with method acting and declamatory recitative to the overexaggeration of these elements described by Vishnevskaya. Perhaps few other examples could illustrate so starkly how the cultural and political environment can influence the development of singing and acting styles.

## Editions and Language

Both Rimsky-Korsakov and Rachmaninov prepared editions of their songs for the general public, and both Russian and European editions are available. The Dover collection of Musorgsky songs is a reprint of the 1960 edition prepared by the Soviet State Music Publishing House. It includes new translations and transliterations. Other Russian and European editions of Musorgsky songs contain significant discrepancies. A critical edition of Musorgsky is under way as a collaborative effort of Muzyka in Moscow and Schott Musik International in Mainz, Germany. It includes all the various versions of his works edited by Rimsky-Korsakov, as well as orchestrations by Ravel and Shostakovich and original reconstructions; unfortunately, the volumes containing the songs have not yet been completed. Prokofiev prepared scores of his vocal music for Boosey & Hawkes before he returned to the Soviet Union; these are quite reliable. The complete works of Shostakovich, published by the Moscow State Publishing House, includes all the vocal music and is the most dependable, though a new complete edition is under way. Many editions of Russian vocal music print only the Russian text in Cyrillic. Some editions include translations in English, German, or French. However, it is best to preserve the integrity of the Russian language with its idiomatic stresses and accents.

The Russian vocal music discussed in this chapter is highly emotional and dramatic, yet genuine and realistic, capturing the natural rhythms of the language in a declamatory style. Acting is an integral part of the performance tradition. For these reasons it is especially important for singers approaching this repertoire to learn the Russian language and to understand both the correct pronunciation and the meaning of each word. Russian language and diction classes are not always offered in conservatory vocal programs, and good diction books are few. Private coaching with a native speaker is the best way to get the sounds and rhythms of this language in your ear and mouth.

One other cautionary note: the names of Russian musicians have received a variety of transliterated spellings over the years. For example, the current *New Grove Dictionary of Music and Musicians* spells Musorgsky with one "s," while his name may appear as Mussorgsky on many scores, books, or recordings. Most recordings or books about Chaliapin spell his name with a "ch" while the *New Grove* offers both that spelling and Shalyapin, which is a more accurate transliteration. Titles of individual songs and larger vocal works are known by a variety of English translations as well. When searching for Russian composers and repertoire in library catalogues or other databases, be prepared to try several different spellings or translations.

## SPAIN

For most of the nineteenth century, Spain remained culturally and politically isolated from the rest of Europe. Its musical traditions included zarzuela (a popular operetta-style of entertainment) and flamenco or *cante jondo*. The folk songs of flamenco, originally associated with a style of singing as opposed to dancing, expressed the desperate existence of gypsy life, with such turbulent emotions as jealousy, rage, anguish, recklessness, boisterousness, and generosity revealing an intensity of spirit similar to that of Russian peasant music. They often accompanied social rituals such as weddings and funerals; at the latter, professional mourners were hired to sing songs of grief. The microtonal ornamentation and modal cadences in *cante jondo* have roots in Moorish, Arabian,

Indian, and Oriental chants. Some songs feature a flexible recitative style with much rubato and an improvised guitar accompaniment between the verses. Often in these types of songs the singer will "tune" his or her voice with an exclamation on the syllable "ay" before proceeding with the first line of the sung text. Other songs are based on traditional dances such as the caña, toná, polo, seguidilla, and fandango—each with its own rhythmic patterns. Complex polymeters between vocal line and accompaniment allow for the characteristic hand-clapping/foot-stomping cross rhythms of flamenco dance.

By the beginning of the twentieth century, many Spanish composers and performers were studying in Paris. Ironically, they often found inspiration in the "Spanish" music of Debussy, Ravel, Glinka, and Rimsky-Korsakov. The Russian composers took the rough, raw flamenco material and gave it an exotic eastern sheen, while the French composers objectified it with their cool, detached sensibility. Spanish composers absorbed the stimulating Paris atmosphere and included all these elements in their own national music. Oddly, the prevailing musical taste in Spain at the turn of the twentieth century rejected Debussy and Ravel in favor of a fascination with Wagner and Strauss. Spanish music by Spanish composers remained largely unappreciated until much later in the century.

### Falla

Manuel de Falla was a gifted pianist, although he never became as famous as his compatriots Isaac Albéniz, Enrique Granados, or Ricardo Viñes. He had a passion for composing. In order to support himself and raise money to study in Paris, he wrote several zarzuelas. The genre frustrated him because he felt it lacked national flavor and depended on Italian opera style. Nevertheless, the zarzuelas gave him valuable experience in orchestral writing and managed to finance his travels.

In Paris he studied with Debussy and Paul Dukas, who taught him the importance of precisely notated scores and the expectation that performers should play exactly what was written. Ricardo Viñes, well established in Paris as a virtuoso, played some of Falla's piano works. In a 1910 performance at the Société Musicale Indépendante, Falla accompanied a French singer in his *Three Songs on Poems of Théophile Gautier.* In 1914 he composed the *Seven Popular Spanish Songs,* hoping to perform them while he was still in Paris. However, the premiere actually took place in Madrid the following year at a concert honoring his return from France. Falla accompanied soprano Luisa Vela and was very pleased with her voice and her sense of style. These songs, now the most widely performed in the Spanish repertoire, were greeted at that occasion by complete indifference.[32]

In 1922 Falla organized a competition for singers of *cante jondo* (literally, "deep song"). His goal was to restore the original purity of traditional flamenco singing, which he believed had become overly commercial in the twentieth century. In the eighteenth century *cante jondo* existed in peasant villages as a tough, gritty, macho style of singing in marked contrast with that used for the languid and ornate vocal music of France and Italy. In the nineteenth century it became fashionable in city cafés and cabarets, developing a broad popular appeal, particularly in Andalusia. Here it embraced a brilliant virtuosity, not at all in the Italian opera style, delivered in a distinctively hoarse, nasal vocal tone. It also came to be associated with the alcohol and prostitution found in café life.[33] In the twentieth century, charismatic stars including Pepe Manchena indulged in elaborate, operatic ornamentation and developed their own schools of flamenco singing. Flamenco culture was increasingly lifted from its poor gypsy roots toward professionalism and commercialization.

Falla excluded all professional singers from his competition and forbade showy, theatrical ornamentation. He wanted to purge *cante jondo* of its more seedy, grimy, and depraved elements. Ironically, these very elements gave the tradition its distinctive flavor.

*EL AMOR BRUJO*

Falla's most valuable working relationship was not with a particular singer, but with Gregorio Martínez Sierra, the librettist for many of his stage works. Not long after Falla's return to Madrid, the two were asked to create a song and dance for the famous Andalusian gypsy dancer, Pastora Imperio. This commission resulted in *El amor brujo* (*Love the Magician*). At the time, Imperio was the most important performer of authentic Spanish dance. Sierra wrote that she "was truly the empress of all the Spanish dancers who have shaken the floor boards with the drumming of their heels during the twentieth century." Falla reported that "I have never worked with more enthusiasm or satisfaction than during the months it took me to write *Love the Magician*. The work is an eminently gypsy piece. To write it I employed only ideas of a popular character, some of them borrowed from Pastora Imperio herself, who has the custom of singing them, and whose 'authenticity' cannot be denied. . . . Her ear for music is such that at first one takes her to be a trained musician, when she knows not a single note."[34]

The three songs in the work feature typical elements of *cante jondo*, including an introductory and decorated "Ay!" in the first song (see ex. 8.3). This gesture can also be seen in "Polo" from *Seven Popular Spanish Songs* (see ex. 8.4). These melismas should not be executed like Italian coloratura. Rather they are an attempt to notate the microtonal kind of embellishment found in flamenco song. Falla explains: "They have to be considered, therefore, as extensive vocal inflections rather than as ornamental turns, although they sound like the latter when they are 'translated' into the geometric intervals of the temperate scale."[35]

*El amor brujo* premiered in Madrid in 1915 and was repeated some thirty times in twenty days. The pianist Arthur Rubinstein left a wonderful description of one of these first performances:

Example 8.3. Falla: "Canción del amor dolido" from *El amor brujo,* mm. 1–6, Chester, 1924.

Example 8.4. Falla: "Polo" from *Siete canciones populares españolas,* mm. 1–9, Max Eschig Editions, 1922.

The performance took place very late at a theater after the work they were showing finished. The music was played by six or seven musicians—the type of group that tends to play in night clubs—and the pianist had an upright piano. But that music fascinated me—in particular the dance called "The Fire Dance" which Pastora executed so marvelously. "Could you lend me the score of the music of that dance?" I asked Falla, "I'd like to do an arrangement for piano to play at a concert." He replied smiling: "Of course I'll give it to you. Though I strongly doubt that the music will have the least effect." I did the arrangement basing myself solely on the original. And when I played it as an encore, the audience literally went mad. I had to repeat it three times.[36]

*El amor brujo* thus started out much like *Pierrot lunaire*: a chamber work of music theater written as a showcase for a nonprofessional musician. Falla revised and expanded it into both an orchestral version and a fully staged ballet. The orchestral version premiered in Paris in 1924 on a concert conducted by

Serge Koussevitzky, during which Prokofiev played the premiere of his Second Piano Concerto as well as the extensive piano part in the Falla work. In this arrangement, a concert singer performs the songs from the original cabaret entertainment. The ballet version, without the songs, was produced in many theaters in Paris, Buenos Aires, and Madrid, where the 1934 production featured Pastora Imperio.

Falla clearly had in mind a "folk" singer or traditional *cantaora* for these songs. The intimacy of the original chamber version makes it easier to achieve the intended flamenco flavor of the work. Projecting over the full orchestration demands the abilities of a trained concert singer, even though the range of the songs is low and often requires the use of chest voice. The classically trained singer must find a way to include a taste of that raw, hoarse quality of *cante jondo* while upholding Falla's prescription to follow the score with accuracy and precision.

### Rodrigo

Like Falla, Joaquín Turina, and Granados, Joaquín Rodrigo was another Spanish composer whose studied in Paris. He worked with Dukas from 1927 until 1935, and while in Paris he married the Turkish pianist Victoria Kamhi. Although he had become blind from diphtheria at the age of three, he composed and performed as a pianist well into his old age. His wife was an invaluable help to him, transcribing the music that he composed in Braille. Rodrigo loved composing songs for the soprano voice and accompanying such singers as Victoria de los Angeles, Montserrat Caballé, Teresa Berganza, and Pilar Lorengar. While many of his songs were written for particular well-known artists, he also wanted his songs to be accessible to all: "I do not object to transposition if this brings them into the reach of a greater number of singers. However, most of my songs have been composed for a specific soprano voice, keeping in mind the particular range and qualities or characteristics of that voice."[37] He and his wife heard the debut of the twenty-year-old de los Angeles and were captivated: "She sang two of Joaquín's songs with a purity of style and diction, and a sensitivity that left us enthralled. And what a voice she had! That twenty-year-old girl was already a diva!"[38] This was the beginning of many years of collaboration.

His *Cuatro madrigales amatorios* are the most well known and frequently performed of his songs. However, he composed nearly one hundred songs, many of which are not known or not available in the United States. It has been said that Rodrigo is not "merely another musician dealing in Andalusian scales and dance rhythms inspired by flamenco singers, dancers and guitarists."[39] His songs employ a variety of texts and styles. Suzanne Draayer's *A Singer's Guide to the Songs of Joaquín Rodrigo* lists invaluable information on how to obtain his music. She also includes a selected discography with recordings by de los Angeles, Caballé, Plácido Domingo, and others. These Spanish performers certainly sing with a modern technique and sound, but they also provide an inside look at their own national style.

### Editions

Manuel de Falla had a publishing contract with Max Eschig in Paris, and he supervised the publication of his music. As yet there is no critical edition of his works. Nico Castel's *A Singer's Manual of Spanish Lyric Diction* includes a reference list of Spanish repertoire and publications.[40] Draayer also includes publication and ordering information for music of Rodrigo, and she recommends the Schott edition of *Joaquín Rodrigo: Thirty-five Songs for Voice and Piano*.[41] Cockburn and Stokes's *The Spanish Song Companion* is mostly a collection of song texts, but it includes a useful discography in an appendix.[42]

### ENGLAND

In the first decades of the twentieth century, London was a magnet for international performances, attracting favorite Italian and German opera stars, Russian artists such as Chaliapin, Olenina, Prokofiev, and Rachmaninov, and Diaghilev's touring productions of Russian, Spanish, and French ballets. There was also a marked countervailing taste for local singers and homegrown entertainments, including music hall shows and drawing-room ballads performed by amateurs in private settings. Songs by Vaughan Williams, Holst, Delius, Peter Warlock, John Ireland, and Gerald Finzi were written in a Romantic style for nonprofessionals to sing and enjoy. Even conservatory training stressed the amateur ideal, catering to the "English gentleman" who had no interest in "superficial and insincere technical brilliance."[43] Opera had never been as popular or influential in England as church, oratorio, or concert music. "As a result," writes Sydney Northcote, "the English style of singing is at its best in religious music, and reveals a sympathetic aptitude for the more intimate kind of vocal music which is exemplified in solo song."[44] British audiences did not favor much contemporary music either, and most English composers were not interested in pursuing avant-garde ideas. As late as the 1930s the Royal College of Music had no score of Schoenberg's *Pierrot lunaire* in its library.[45]

An English singing manual from 1912 by Harry Plunkett Greene complains about singers' poor rhythm and diction and reveals a performance environment more reminiscent of nineteenth-century Germany than of contemporary France or Russia:

> During no period of our musical history have technique and invention made such strides as in the last generation. The Wagner score of thirty years ago, the terror of the orchestral player and the wonder of the composer, have become commonplace of the one and textbook of the other. Each has risen to the level of his responsibilities and played a man's part. The singer alone has stood still. The reasons need not be discussed here. The fact remains that our platforms are overrun with voices half-developed and quarter-trained, singers without technique, without charm and without style, to whom rhythm is of no account and language but the dead vehicle of sound, whose ambitions soar no higher than the three-verse song with organ obbligato, and to whom the high-note at the end and the clapping of hands spell the sublimity of achievement.[46]

In his *Interpretation in Song,* Greene also instructed English singers in the most basic issues of musicianship: don't break the flow of rhythm or add extra beats when taking a breath; don't chop up the phrase by taking too many breaths; don't distort the rhythm by holding a note (complete with arms spread wide) just for effect. He warned accompanists not to wait for singers or to follow them should they tastelessly distort the rhythm. He did allow singers to add an indulgent ritardando if they had a particularly long phrase. He bemoaned Italianate diction that made the text from *The Messiah* all but unintelligible: "arnd crorse tar-r-rknaiss-a the peopurlla." He urged singers to create atmosphere and mood in a song, without artificiality. He also suggested that they disregard expression markings in scores (though perhaps he is referring to the editorial additions of nineteenth-century publications) because they might not suit the individual singer and his or her interpretation. Altogether, Greene painted a fairly dismal picture of British singing at the time.

### Britten and Pears

Composer Benjamin Britten and tenor Peter Pears were key figures in revitalizing this stale and old-fashioned English vocal scene. As in several other famous composer-singer working relationships (Schubert and Vogl, Poulenc and Bernac), each had an immeasurable impact on the other in creating a body of work and a performance style. In addition to their musical collaboration, their devoted life partnership colored everything they did. Britten told Imogen Holst that "if it hadn't been for me, he'd never have been a singer, and although *he* might have been happier, lots of people wouldn't have been."[47] Pears inspired Britten to write opera roles, concert works, and song cycles that they could perform together. Pears also contributed advice about vocal, textural, and theatrical matters. Britten wrote music that suited Pears's particular gifts but also challenged him to greater vocal accomplishments, as well as providing performance exposure that enhanced his career. As a friend of theirs put it, "Ben wanted, and found, imagination and sensitivity in Peter's singing and approach, and from this he conjured what he wanted for his music."[48] Pears, in return, provided the motivation for Britten to become one of the most important twentieth-century composers of opera and vocal music. Aside from Gilbert and Sullivan's operettas, the 1945 premiere of Britten's *Peter Grimes* marked the first enduringly successful English opera since Purcell's *Dido and Aeneas.*

Britten was fortunate to enjoy both recognition and financial success. Unlike his Russian colleagues, he had the freedom to produce his own projects and to choose his texts and forms. From the English Opera Group to the Aldeburgh Festival, he was involved in all aspects of planning and performance. He wrote for churches and theaters, schoolchildren and adults, amateurs and professionals, and always had specific performers and situations in mind for the works he created. As he explained, "almost every piece I have ever written has been composed with a certain occasion in mind, and usually for definite performers. . . . When I am asked to compose a work for an occasion, great or small, I want to know in some detail the conditions of the place where it will be performed, the size and acoustics, what instruments or singers will be available and suitable. . . . I prefer to study the conditions of performance and shape my music to them."[49] Although he was internationally known, Britten preferred writing for people and places that were close to home. He lived and worked in Aldeburgh, which provided occasions for specific compositions and models for characters and situations in his operas, coloring the moods of his works. People who visit Aldeburgh receive a new appreciation for Britten's music when they see the gray sky, feel the penetrating cold, and hear the sea pounding into the East Anglican shore.

Britten was not fond of the "pastoral school" of British composers represented by Vaughan Williams and Elgar. He didn't like overexaggerated sentimentality in compositions or performances, nor did he approve of deliberately obscure modern music. He was interested in Berg, not sure about Schoenberg, and didn't feel the need to be original just for the sake of originality. He wanted to find his own way, but he also freely borrowed from the great masters and felt a particular connection to the music of John Dowland and Purcell. As he put it, "it doesn't matter what style a composer chooses to write in, as long as he has something definite to say and says it clearly."[50]

Britten's scores are clearly and precisely marked. "To achieve perfect clarity of expression, that is my aim," he once remarked.[51] Steuart Bedford, a conductor Britten favored because he tried to understand composers' intentions, points out that there "is hardly a vocal line that does not have some meticulous instruction as to how it should be performed, or how it should sound. Even if he was doing a quick rewrite, Britten would automatically add those kinds of marks. Such precision can be a terrifying prospect for a singer coming to the music afresh."[52]

Britten played the piano with a natural and precise technical ability, though he was a nervous performer and disliked practicing. Fellow pianists speak with awe and reverence about his playing and say "it went straight from his musical brain to his fingers without hindrance."[53] Rather than compose solo piano music, he preferred to write challenging and virtuosic song accompaniments for himself to play with Pears. He was not comfortable in the role of conductor, but musicians loved playing and singing for him.

Britten's complex and contradictory personality made him extremely demanding of musicians, but he was also supportive. According to his longtime assistant Imogen Holst, "The professional singers and players who work with him are not just 'good' musicians: they have to be superlatively good, and they have to be prepared to go on getting better and better all the time. There can never be any possibility of a compromise, because the music always comes first."[54] Director Basil Coleman observed of Britten's rapport with singers that "if he saw that they were committed wholeheartedly to him, there was nothing he would not do to encourage them, and they felt they could give their best with the composer there to support them."[55] The composer wanted his singers to be completely meticulous yet flexible. According to tenor Robert Tear, "he managed to give an artist great space in which to work, and yet maintain total control over the piece as a whole."[56] Dame Janet Baker recounts that "he gave artists the framework in which to work out their vocal problems. Whatever the music, one knew with him that the tempo would be ideal."[57]

Though sensitive and patient, Britten could also be relentless in his pursuit of what he wanted, offering singers breathing and phrasing advice to get the performances he desired. He was frustrated working with musicians he felt were not up to his standards, and he loathed bad performances. As he wrote to Imogen Holst, "How essential good performances are! I have recently heard several performances of my own pieces and I felt so depressed that I considered chucking it all up! Wrong tempi, stupid phrasing and poor technique—in fact nonsense."[58]

In some situations he preferred working with amateurs and children who may not have been technically polished but had the right spirit: "There is something very fresh and unrestrained in the quality of the music produced by amateurs. What annoys me more is the ineptitude of some professionals who don't know their stuff. I have no patience with that."[59] He composed a good deal of music for young boys and had definite opinions about their singing style. Early sketches for *A Ceremony of Carols* indicate sopranos and altos, but he changed his mind and published the score for treble (boys') voices. According to his assistant Rosamund Strode, he found the traditional "pure" English cathedral boys' choir sound "insipid and inadequate."[60] He preferred a rougher and more raucous sound that he felt represented boys' natural robust energy.

A big, beautiful, creamy voice was not as important to Britten as the character in the voice. He once told friend and recording producer John Culshaw, "Frankly, I'm not interested in beautiful voices as such. I'm interested in the person behind the voice."[61] Most important was the singer's ability to communicate character and drama: "The singers must, of course, have good voices, but these should be used to interpret the music, not for self-glorification."[62] The singers he wrote for, including Baker, Dietrich Fischer-Dieskau, Kathleen Ferrier, and Galina Vishnevskaya, all possessed a depth of soul in their singing as well as the impeccable musicianship that Britten required. They were also people he admired. Britten and Pears traveled to Russia and were warmly hosted by Rostropovich and Vishnevskaya, who in turn visited Britten and performed at the Aldeburgh Festival. Britten wrote cello works for Rostropovich and a song cycle in Russian for Vishnevskaya. His *War Requiem* was conceived for Pears, Fischer-Dieskau, and Vishnevskaya; in a gesture of peace and reconciliation, he wanted to have an Englishman, a German, and a Russian all performing on the same stage together. Though the Soviet government contrived to make Vishnevskaya unavailable for the premiere, she ultimately performed and recorded it with Britten conducting.[63]

In order to facilitate characterization, diction was of supreme importance to Britten: "I have always been interested in the setting of words. . . . My interest in the human voice has grown, especially in the relation of sound to sense and colour . . . to the English voice in particular, singing our subtle and beautifully inflected language. Also I believe passionately in the intelligibility of the words."[64] He particularly admired Pears's ability to color words dramatically and to infuse them with character. This set a high standard for others (and particularly tenors) who sing Britten's works, and in fact the composer often didn't like other tenors singing music he'd written for Pears. In general, he felt that the first production of a work was definitive; as a result, subsequent performances with other singers would be considered inferior.

Robert Tear, who worked with Britten and developed professionally in Pears's shadow, partly modeled his style and technique on Pears. He believed that if the music written for Pears were "not sung in the Pears fashion, it will sound wrong-headed." He also believed, however, that Pears's style and technique were difficult to use in other repertoire. He noted that since the *Les illuminations* songs were not originally conceived for Pears's voice (this cycle was written for Sophie Wyss, who was Britten's favorite singer until he met Pears) they are easier to sing.[65]

Tenors today can listen to the many recordings of Peter Pears singing the music written for him and appreciate his unique vocal and dramatic gifts. Trying to copy his highly individual sound, technique, and style, however, would be a mistake. Instead, singers should strive to emulate the underlying qualities of musicianship and dramatic coloration that made his performances so compelling.

THE PURCELL REALIZATIONS

Britten and Pears gave countless recitals together, performing a wide variety of repertoire in addition to Britten's works. They were particularly famous for their Schubert cycles. After hearing one of their performances, Poulenc declared to Bernac that he would never play Schubert again.[66] Britten and Pears always included a group of Purcell songs. In the late 1930s and early 1940s the music of Purcell was surprisingly unknown and unavailable in England. Few songs were obtainable in print, and those that were had old-fashioned realizations of the bass line. Britten wrote his own realizations, some of which were published. He believed that "since the accompaniments were originally intended to be improvised, they must be personal and immediate."[67] He also thought that since tastes change over time, the accompaniments should be modified to suit the times. Thus he rewrote his realizations every few years. He hoped to reintroduce Purcell's songs to a wider public, and he encouraged more people to prepare their own arrangements "with plenty of boldness and imagination."[68]

Singers who encounter Britten's realizations of Purcell must understand that they were intended for piano and a modern style of performance. Purcell performance-practice authority and opera director Michael Burden observes that "the Britten realizations actually are rather good; but only when played by Britten! I think the point to emphasize is that they are designed for a very particular performance approach, and one that is piano based. It also, I think, relies on a style of singing which we would not today accept. Pears simply sang the songs the way he wanted to sing them. (Not actually a bad policy, of course!)"[69] Pears's particular sound and technique featured a use of legato, phrasing, and vibrato representative of a mid-twentieth-century style of singing; it reflected an approach toward early music that was prevalent more than fifty years ago. Burden points out that the quest for an appropriate or "authentic" Purcell performance style is different today than it was twenty or even ten years ago, much less fifty. He recommends, like Britten, that performers tailor their own realizations to be flexible, personal, and not too elaborate. The Britten realizations, while preserving this spirit of improvisation and flexibility, should definitely be considered and credited as music by Britten. Singers may even choose to program them as twentieth-century music rather than music of the Baroque.

### Editions

Britten was extremely meticulous about preparing his scores for publication, and strove to complete any revisions or corrections before sending a work out into the world. Usually a score was not published until after the first performance. In order to make his wishes absolutely clear to the performer, he was particular about the visual layout of a score. His assistant Rosamund Strode had the daunting task of checking for discrepancies between various prepublication sources, including manuscript, conducting score, and piano-vocal score, in order to ensure the most accurate presentation of the performance instructions. In 1964 Britten founded Faber Music Ltd. in order to publish his music; most of his earlier works were published by Boosey & Hawkes.

### THE UNITED STATES

In the early twentieth century, the United States attracted touring virtuosos from Europe and Russia. American audiences flocked to hear famous artists play and sing well-known Romantic repertoire. With their conservative tastes, these listeners tended not to be interested in new or avant-garde music. Rachmaninov was a sensation playing his own music because of its traditional Romantic language. Prokofiev and other more innovative composers did not receive the same warm welcome. Yet as the century progressed, American composers found encouragement and opportunity in the form of fellowships, grants, competitions, and prizes. University music departments and conservatories flourished and produced large numbers of hopeful young composers who had growing opportunities to have their music performed. Some composers included elements of American folk and popular music in their works, giving them a nationalistic flavor. Other young composers followed in the footsteps of famous Europeans such as Stravinsky, Hindemith, Schoenberg, and Milhaud, who were all living and teaching in the United States by the late 1940s. Yet mainstream audiences remained wary of music that was strange or unusual, preferring the familiar and accessible. Most well-known performers and concert series were reluctant to embrace new American music, which thrived primarily in small, specialized communities of performers and appreciative audiences. Samuel Barber was one of the few composers of vocal music who managed to bridge this gap, writing music that large audiences enjoyed and famous artists wanted to perform.

### Ives

Charles Ives, who made his living as an insurance executive, stopped composing in 1927. It wasn't until years later that his music became well known and widely performed. He grew up in Danbury, Connecticut, singing hymns at church camp meetings and listening to town bands. His father encouraged independent thinking and musical experimentation, helping him develop his ear by having him sing a song in one key while playing the accompaniment in another. "This was to stretch our ears and strengthen our musical minds," according to Ives.[70] Trained as an organist, he began playing in churches while still in his teens. By the turn of the century he was attending Yale and composing marches and other music for the glee club and popular shows. He was also writing organ and other church works based on Romantic models.

Ives's early vocal music was in the style of French and German parlor songs. However, he also composed music for himself that was more adventurous. When he showed the song "At Parting" to his composition teacher at Yale, he was chastised for leaving unresolved dissonances. His supportive father replied that "every dissonance doesn't have to resolve, if it doesn't happen to feel like it, any more than every horse should have to have its tail bobbed just because it is the prevailing fashion."[71]

Although Ives tempered his imagination for his church singers, they often found his songs extremely difficult to learn. After his father died, Ives had only a few friends who encouraged his compositions. One was Dr. John C. Griggs, the choirmaster and baritone soloist at the Center Church in New Haven. In 1914, when Ives showed him the song "General William Booth Enters into

Heaven," Griggs commented, "it's not difficult vocally, it's difficult mentally. Unless the mind grasps and senses a tone from the ear, the voice can't sing it." Ives replied, "If you can't sing it, nobody can."[72] In fact Ives was quite frustrated by the limited ability and interest he found in most singers, and sometimes he composed songs with instrumental parts doubling or substituting for the vocal lines: "The principal reason for this was because singers made such a fuss about the intervals, time etc. . . . My experience has been, not always but most always:—the more voice a man has, the less music he has. Apparently in a singer's education the muscles of the throat get the training, and not the muscles of the ear and brain."[73] Most Ives-supervised performances took place between 1902 and 1924. The majority of these were in the Connecticut churches where he played the organ. It is impossible to know the level of musicianship among the church performers, or how his music might have been received by more skilled musicians. It may well be that he took a certain pride in his music being difficult to play, sing, and understand.

In the early 1920s he published some works himself, including *114 Songs*. He sent them to friends and prominent musicians, hoping to stimulate wider interest in his music. The publications met with little initial success, and only a few isolated professional singers included the songs in their recitals. It was not until 1932, when Aaron Copland and Hubert Linscott presented seven of his songs at the Yaddo new-music festival in Saratoga Springs, New York, that a wider public became aware of Ives's songs. Copland admitted that he had "only an inkling of the existence of the music of Charles Ives in the twenties."[74]

More performances followed throughout the 1930s and '40s, and many of his works were revised, published, and finally performed. By the midcentury, professional singers interested in new music had more experience with challenging pitches and rhythms, and they had a much easier time with Ives's songs and could appreciate his quirky combination of band music, hymn tunes, and early Americana. These were the performances that established a successful stylistic approach to Ives and that singers today can use as models. Unlike other composers discussed in this chapter, the early performances involving Ives himself didn't really launch a definitive tradition; rather, they reflected the conservative attitude of American performers in the early decades of the century.

### Copland

Aaron Copland was more than a composer who captured a uniquely American sound; he was also a writer and critic, a concert organizer, a faithful supporter of other composers, and an invaluable promoter of American new music in general. In the 1920s in Paris he studied piano with Ricardo Viñes and composition with Nadia Boulanger. Stravinsky was his hero, and he also admired Fauré, Milhaud, and Mahler. In 1923 he met conductor Serge Koussevitzky, with whom he began a long and rewarding collaborative relationship. Koussevitzky, who had shown a devotion to new works and composers throughout his career (Scriabin, Stravinsky, and Prokofiev in Russia; Ravel, Arthur Honegger, and others in Paris), brought this enthusiasm with him when he moved to the United States in 1924. As the new conductor of the Boston Symphony Orchestra, he frequently programmed the music of many American composers, including Copland, Barber, Howard Hanson, Roy Harris, Walter Piston, and William Schuman.

In 1928 Copland joined the New York–based League of Composers. With Roger Sessions, he produced a series of new music concerts in New York that presented works by a range of young American composers. He also helped found the Cos Cob Press to publish new music. In 1932 he visited Mexico and in the 1940s he traveled to South America, absorbing sounds and colors that would find their way into his own music. In 1938 he visited England, showing Britten his opera for schoolchildren, *The Second Hurricane.* This example may well have inspired Britten to write dramatic works for young performers. Copland was also especially interested in composing for choreographers and dancers.

Copland wrote only a few songs, including two sets of American folk songs, but these are beloved and frequently performed. The 1964 recording of the *Twelve Poems of Emily Dickinson,* with the composer accompanying Adele Addison, offers an exquisite presentation of the work.[75] The clear singing and simple playing are models that still inform the way the songs are usually performed today. Copland rejected the idea of a definitive performance of his works, but he did demonstrate "how my music should go"[76] through conducting and playing his own works on recordings. He criticized the emotional excesses of some Romantic composers but didn't approve of the overly intellectual approach of many modern composers. Copland wanted performances of his works to be expressive yet not overly sentimental, and he preferred simple, straightforward playing without excessive vibrato.

### Barber

Samuel Barber had a charmed career: virtually every door he came to opened for him. He started to compose vocal works at the age of seven, and entered the Curtis Institute of Music in Philadelphia at fourteen, studying piano, voice, and composition. His aunt and uncle Louise and Sidney Homer, a well-known contralto and composer respectively, had a great influence on him. In 1934 he went to Vienna to study voice and became interested in early music. He searched the archival manuscript collections in the Vienna libraries and learned works by Monteverdi, Purcell, Francesco Cavalli, Emilio de' Cavalieri, Giovanni Gabrieli, and other seventeenth-century composers. When he returned to the United States the following year, he performed some of this repertoire, accompanying himself on a little spinet he had brought back from Munich. A review of one of these concerts praised Barber as "an artist in every sense, for he combines a beautiful voice with remarkable ease of style, and a musicality which never fails to 'cross the t's and dot the i's.' Mr. Barber has learned the invaluable art of voice modulation, and wisely believes that an ounce of singing is worth a ton of shouting."[77] Certainly his understanding of early music style was different from ours today, but he apparently found a gentle, easy musicality and vocalism that made this unfamiliar music appealing.

In 1935 Barber got a job singing on the radio for the NBC Music Guild series. On the February 4 broadcast he played some of his solo piano works, accompanied himself singing some of his own songs, and sang his *Dover Beach* cycle with the Curtis String Quartet. Barber had written *Dover Beach* in 1931 for his own baritone voice range, but he occasionally asked a Curtis friend, mezzo-soprano Rose Bampton, to perform it. Critics declared of Barber's radio debut that his music had "singular charm and beauty . . . intelligent music intelligently sung—and with a naturally beautiful voice." They also agreed that he had won for himself "instant recognition as a triple-fold musician—composer, singer and pianist."[78] Poulenc was so impressed with Barber's singing on a 1936 recording of *Dover Beach* that he offered to compose some songs for the young American. In 1935 Barber also won the prestigious Rome Prize, which secured his rising reputation as a composer. From then on, all his works were commissioned by well-known artists or ensembles and were premiered in prominent venues.

In many instances, a text inspired Barber to compose a song setting. In 1947 he came across James Agee's prose poem "Knoxville: Summer of 1915" and was powerfully moved. It was around this time that Koussevitzky requested a piece for voice and orchestra and that soprano Eleanor Steber also approached Barber about writing a vocal work for her. No American singer had previously commissioned a work for voice and orchestra, and Steber's manager believed that using new American music would be an innovative way to help promote her career. As he composed *Knoxville,* Barber had some reservations about both Steber and the orchestral setting, since his original conception had been for an intimate piece. As negotiations developed and he realized that she would probably sing the premiere he modified his plans: "I suspect that what she really wanted was a big, whooping thing to do with Koussevitzky and the Boston Symphony, but of course, *Knoxville* is not that kind of piece. I also knew that Koussevitzky preferred the full orchestra, so I continued with the original scoring, and it was premiered that way."[79] During the rehearsals he raised parts of the vocal line so that Steber's voice could be heard over the orchestra. Later he considered the possibility of a chamber orchestra version, and he ultimately reduced the full orchestration for the 1949 Schirmer score.

In 1950 Eileen Farrell and twenty players premiered a chamber version in Washington, conducted by William Strickland. The score for this version was published in 1952. For the same concert, Strickland asked Barber to compose a song cycle for Farrell. Since the majority of his music was vocal, Barber spent a great deal of time reading poetry, looking for suitable texts. He had come across several unusual French poems by Rilke and was happy for an opportunity to set them. When he asked his friend Poulenc to look at the songs and check his French prosody, Poulenc immediately wanted to give the premiere with Bernac. They did eventually perform *Mélodies passagères*, op. 27, but not until after Barber accompanied Farrell at the Washington concert.

Many of Barber's stage works were performed and recorded in the 1950s, which kept the composer busy. Between large projects he often worked on songs. Having come across some medieval Gaelic poetry from various sources, translated into English by several different people, he began composing the *Hermit Songs*. A year later he received a commission from the Elizabeth Sprague Coolidge Foundation for a song cycle for a specific event. It was not until then that he started searching for the ideal singer to premiere the work. Leontyne Price was already known for her performances in *Porgy and Bess,* but she was still a relative newcomer and had not yet made a recital debut. After her voice teacher introduced her to Barber, she learned the songs and sang them for him, thus beginning a long collaborative relationship. She premiered the songs at the Library of Congress in 1953 with Barber accompanying, and they recorded them the next year.

This recording, like Copland's and Addison's *Twelve Poems of Emily Dickinson,* shows a wonderful presentation of the composer's wishes. Most performances today of the *Hermit Songs* are modeled after it.[80] Barber's playing is warm and richly expressive. Price's singing is young and fresh, not quite the opera diva we associate with her later recordings. After Barber got to know and love her singing, he wrote other works specifically tailored to her abilities. He also composed *Andromache's Farewell,* op. 39, expressly for Martina Arroyo and her particular strengths. For the most part, however, Barber conceived of his music first and then searched for appropriate performers after: "It seems to me that the most practical thing is to simply write your music the way you want to write it. Then you go out and find the interpreters who will give it voice."[81]

Barber's music continued the traditions of nineteenth-century Romanticism and appealed to a broad audience. We don't really need to find a new style in order to sing it. In fact the approach we use could be called the prevailing "modern" style of singing: it is based on nineteenth-century traditions, but with more faithful adherence to the details in the score and with fewer wild tempo fluctuations, rubato, and portamento. This approach is, however, still rich, flexible, and expressive.

### Editions

In the majority of cases, the available editions of twentieth-century American music offer reliable presentations of the composers' wishes. Ives prepared the early editions of his songs and supervised the later corrected and revised editions of various works. Copland facilitated the publication of many new works and helped set a high standard of care and precision that composers and publishers subsequently followed as a matter of course.

This chapter has surveyed how a complex sharing of different national traditions resulted in the flourishing of distinctive national styles of vocal performance in the early twentieth century. Two central artistic goals were common to all: the importance of communicating the text with a more realistic acting style, and a growing demand for accuracy and precision in performance. Because Paris was the most vibrant center of cultural life at the time, many musicians from Russia, Spain, and the United States performed and studied there, absorbing the French ideal of serving the score with precision and clarity. Performances that offered a more accurate presentation of the composers' wishes replaced Romantic offerings of virtuosic showmanship and heightened expressivity.

A straightforward projection of texts and a more restrained, realistic style of acting became preferable to the overly showy and sentimental displays often associated with nineteenth-century Romanticism. Chaliapin and Olenina established new standards of vocal acting that would have far-reaching influence on singers in Russia and elsewhere. Britten chose his singers not for the beauty of their voices, but for their ability to color their characterizations and to convey the drama.

The particular qualities of the Russian, Spanish, and English languages contributed the most important element to each national vocal style. The folk song tradition in each culture also conveyed a distinctive emotional and rhythmic flavor to its concert vocal music. When learning Russian or Spanish repertoire, the more comfortable you are with the language, the more subtle understandings you will be able to bring to your pronunciation and acting. If you have an understanding of the folk music heritage of these cultures, it will help you infuse the concert music of Musorgsky, Rachmaninov, Prokofiev, and Shostakovich or of Falla and Rodrigo with an appropriate sense of style. For repertoire in English, we naturally have an easier time dealing with our native language. Remember, however, that the inflections and idiomatic expressions of British English are a bit different from those of American English; the folk music roots are different as well.

This chapter has also described the gradual emergence of what could be called the "modern" vocal style. Singing with modern piano and orchestral instruments in larger concert halls encouraged a fuller, more projecting style of voice production. We can hear on recordings from the middle of the twentieth century onward a use of vibrato, portamento, legato, and articulation that sound familiar and resemble the ways in which we are trained to sing today.

# Chapter 9 Working with Living Composers

This chapter explores the working relationships between American singers and composers over the last thirty years. It draws from conversations with several well-known singers, including sopranos Phyllis Bryn-Julson and Benita Valente and tenor Paul Sperry, who have worked with composers such as Pierre Boulez, György Ligeti, David Del Tredici, George Crumb, Daron Hagen, and William Bolcom.[1] It also includes anecdotes from Cheryl Bensman's years as a member of the Steve Reich ensemble,[2] as well as my own experiences from twenty years of working with composers at Princeton University and various new-music groups.

Most of these stories have parallels in earlier chapters. Composers write for specific singers, but they frequently make changes for subsequent performances, recordings, publication, and other general purposes. Singers collaborate in the compositional process, grapple with the meaning of notation, and add their own idiosyncratic styles to a work. Recordings are now a much more important part of the picture; when performed or supervised by the composer, they can define a work. Recordings can also differ from both the published score and live performances. They often present several interpretations of a particular piece or show the development of a composer's thought on a work years after it was composed.

Over the course of the twentieth century, especially from the second half of the century to the present, the scope of serious vocal concert music has expanded to include a wider variety of compositional and singing styles than ever before. "New music" (and some of what is still considered contemporary is hardly new anymore) can range from one end of the vocal spectrum to the other. Some works may feature an untrained or pop singing style, while traditional, tonal art songs require classically trained vocalism and other songs call for a jazzy or cabaret approach. More experimental works often include challenging rhythms, difficult pitches, microtones, nontraditional use of text or phonemes, electronics or amplification, as well as extended vocal techniques including a variety of spoken vocalization, whispering, shouting, laughing, humming, trilling, singing with a straight tone or a breathy tone, and so on. Singers are also sometimes asked to improvise, to play percussion instruments or to use props and movement.

This chapter does not delve into the vast realm of innovative vocal techniques. For that, I recommend Sharon Mabry's *Exploring Twentieth-Century Vocal Music*.[3] It also will not attempt to cite the ever-growing list of new repertoire for the voice. (For that, see the books by Jane Manning and Patricia Lust under "Chapter 9: Repertoire" in "For Further Reading.") Instead, the chapter examines how composers and singers jointly develop new ideas and styles, how performers work to realize composers' intentions, and how singers can contribute their gifts and experience to the final outcome. The stories are the same as those discussed throughout this book, but now *we* are the singers in the stories. When you work with a composer on a new work, you are participating in the creation of a new performance-practice tradition that may in turn give you invaluable insights into performance-practice traditions of the past.

## Voice Types

Contemporary composers write vocal music both for general voice types and for specific singers with unusual abilities. In some situations a particular voice inspires a composition. In others a number of factors may come into play, including the politics of commissions, performers' availability, and venue possibilities. Luciano Berio wrote much of his vocal music for his wife, Cathy Berberian, who was well known for the wide variety of dramatic effects and special sounds in her vocal palette. She inspired several other composers, including

John Cage, to write music for her, and she also composed for herself. Steven Mackey wrote his chamber opera *Ravenshead* for Rinde Eckert, who possesses a huge range and unique sound, as well as a large assortment of uninhibited special effects. In some cases it may be difficult or unlikely to find another singer who could perform such works in the future. In other cases, new singers will rise to the challenge.

Many composers have written music for soprano Phyllis Bryn-Julson. She speaks of her special connection to David Del Tredici, whom she met when she was a student at Tanglewood in the mid-1960s. His numerous *Alice* works were conceived with her voice and personality in mind. "He blames me and I blame him," she says of the wild and very high music of the complete *An Alice Symphony*, which she performed a number of times and recorded in 1991. But it was Barbara Hendricks who premiered and recorded his *Final Alice* with the Chicago Symphony in 1975. Benita Valente also had a working relationship with Del Tredici, whom she met at Marlboro in the mid-'60s. She recorded a number of his works and performed the premiere of "All in the Golden Afternoon" (*Child Alice*, part 2, movement 3) with the Philadelphia Orchestra in 1981.

Sometimes composers write with opera singers in mind, but other times they want another kind of singer altogether. In his *La Pasión según San Marcos*, Osvaldo Golijov requires classically trained concert singers for some of the solo parts and Latin American pop or jazz singers for others. He composed the work for a nonprofessional choir, the Schola Cantorum de Caracas, and requests that they take part in any performances. The choir understands and vocalizes the Latin American sound and style that is central to the work. "Hopefully," Golijov told critic Paul Griffiths, "in 10 or 20 years, singers will think it's as essential to sing like this as it is to sing in the Italian or German style, because this is a world of emotion that is as big as those other European traditions."[4]

Some composers have a folksinger sound in mind. When Cheryl Bensman auditioned for Steve Reich after training as a classical lieder singer, he asked whether she could sound like Joni Mitchell. "I can do that," she said, and she was hired. Reich wrote parts with scat syllables for a jazzy kind of sound. He also wrote very high parts for a particular singer he knew could easily sing soft and straight-toned high Cs. In his notes for the recording of *Tehillim*, he writes that "the non-vibrato, non-operatic vocal production will also remind listeners of Western music prior to 1750."[5] Other composers such as Arvo Pärt write vocal music with a Renaissance choral sound in mind. I had a fascinating time working on Princeton faculty member J. K. Randall's "Cleophila," an *a cap-*

*pella* setting of a Christina Rossetti poem. On the page the music looked straightforward and modest in range. But by working closely with me, Jim explained the sound and approach to articulation he wanted, which was not really something he could notate. This newly created style felt like a unique combination of singing an American folk song and an early seventeenth-century lute song.

Some composers write for a cabaret or musical theater singer. William Bolcom has written many volumes of cabaret songs, both to perform with his wife, Joan Morris, and for use by the general singer population. I recently talked with composer Jon Magnussen about his latest vocal project, which was inspired by a play and his collaboration with a librettist. When asked what kind of singers he had in mind, he said he wanted natural voices that could convey the words easily: "probably a musical theater sound, not beefed-up or overwrought like opera singers."[6] George Crumb, now in his seventies, has started writing music for his daughter, Ann, who is an experienced Broadway singer and television actress. Yet these same composers have also written music for classically trained voices: Golijov for Dawn Upshaw, Bolcom for Benita Valente, Crumb for Jan DeGaetani, and many others.

The most satisfying new-music experience is when a composer writes a piece that fits your voice, as Mozart put it, like a custom-tailored suit. A few years ago Philadelphia's Network for New Music commissioned David Rakowski to write a piece for small chamber group and soprano. Not knowing that David and I had been students together at Princeton, they had asked me to sing the premiere. I hadn't seen David for many years, and we had a happy reunion at the first rehearsal. He told me that he had known I was to sing *The Gardener* when he wrote it. Even though David hadn't heard me sing in a long time, and I now had many more technical tricks up my sleeve, his work sat in the most comfortable part of my voice and fit my musical personality perfectly. It was a complete delight to sing.

Sometimes it takes a little work to arrive at a perfect fit. When Bolcom wrote *Let Evening Come* for Valente, she asked him to make some changes so that climactic phrases would lie in the most beautiful parts of her voice. "Dead Calm" by Earl Kim had already been conceived and composed when Valente first sang it in 1966. She liked it so much, however, that she asked the composer to write more for her voice. He complied by expanding the work into *Exercises en Route,* which was fitted to her strengths. Kim and Valente worked closely together toward the 1971 premiere, and she also asked him to be involved, either through coaching or conducting, whenever she performed the work in the following years.

When another person sings a work written for a specific singer, it can bring out different qualities in the composition. Aaron Jay Kernis heard me sing songs he had composed for one particular soprano, which had also been performed by a number of other singers. He commented on what our different voices had brought to his music: one singer had more powerful high notes but less voice in the lower middle, another had a stronger middle but less comfortable top, I had a good middle and easy high notes but a lighter quality overall. A new singer can also influence a composer, making a work more accessible. Paul Sperry heard a tape of *The Seven Deadly Sins,* a song cycle by Robert Beaser, and wanted to sing it. The cycle had originally been written for and premiered by a baritone; Paul believed that the cycle as a whole sat too high in places for most baritones yet was also too low for most tenors. He approached the composer and suggested that more singers would be able to sing his work if he offered some alternatives to the extremes of range. In response to Paul's suggestions, Beaser prepared a score for publication with a piano part and two slightly different vocal lines, one for tenor and one for baritone. Paul went on to record the cycle and perform it often.

### Manuscripts, Revisions, and Published Scores

When you work on new music, you can come in contact with a variety of scores: handwritten manuscripts, computer-generated manuscripts, and published, printed scores. These come quite literally in all shapes and sizes. Handwritten manuscripts can be difficult to read. They may include mistakes and corrections, irregularly spaced rhythms, or imprecise vertical alignment, not to mention messy or illegible penmanship. Yet they can also transmit an indefinable aspect of the composer's personality as well as his or her feeling for the music. Phyllis Bryn-Julson much prefers handwritten scores, especially when the composer's penmanship is neat and clear like Boulez's. The autograph score for his *Pli selon pli,* she says, looks like lace, and the texture of the music also resembles lace. The work must be performed with the delicacy and transparency that is reflected in the appearance of the handwritten score. Some autograph scores can be visual works of art. I recently performed some settings for voice and vibraphone of ninth- and tenth-century Japanese poetry about the moon. The composer, Brooke Joyce, carefully hand-copied the music onto special translucent vellum, set over small pieces of dark blue paper with a hand-tied binding. The title and notes were written in silver ink, and the singer was instructed not to use a music stand in performance, but rather to hold the small pamphlet "as if reading from a book of poetry." The score was as beautiful as the songs.

Computer-generated scores are certainly the most practical to create and edit, though they lack somewhat in charm or personality. Composers can make parts from a score, add changes or corrections, reformat the layout, and print as many versions as necessary. One wonders what musicologists of the future might make of the remains of different computer-based versions of a work in progress.

Published scores may present music in a typeset format or simply reproduce a computer-generated score or a handwritten manuscript. Some published scores of Crumb or Cage are as interesting visually as they are aurally. Published scores are not necessarily the last word on a work, however; they might contain mistakes. A composer may also change various details post-publication. When rehearsing Aaron Jay Kernis's *Songs of Innocents,* the pianist and I felt that one of the songs should move more quickly than the indicated metronome marking. Perhaps it was for dramatic reasons or for vocal comfort, but the song just seemed to flow better faster. In the end, not having a chance to coach the songs with the composer, we decided to try to make the song work at his indicated slower tempo. After the performance Kernis told us that we could move that song a bit more than the written metronome marking if we wanted to, confirming our gut reaction.

Sometimes the published score is very different from what was performed at the premiere. A few years ago I was asked to sing John Corigliano's song cycle *Mr. Tambourine Man: Seven Poems of Bob Dylan* at a concert in his honor in Philadelphia. I found the thirty-five-minute work challenging, not because of difficult pitches or rhythms but for reasons of dramatic and vocal pacing. The three songs before the postlude were angry and emotionally intense, with lots of loud, sustained high notes. The final song began as a floating unaccompanied hymn tune with large leaps from very low notes to luminously high ones—sheer terror for me. I wasn't able to coach the songs with the composer before the concert, but he sent me a tape of Hila Plitman, a colleague of mine, with whom he had worked extensively. He said she sang the songs exactly as he wanted them. At the performance, after the sixth song, my heart pounding in my chest and my head reeling from sustained triple *fortes,* I did the best I could to calm down for the last song. Mr. Corigliano, whom I had not yet met, sat in the front row, listening with his eyes closed. Composers are usually warm and complimentary after you perform their music, and Mr. Corigliano seemed pleased with the performance. He told me that he had not really enjoyed a live performance of the cycle before. Surprised, I asked him about Sylvia McNair's premiere in Carnegie Hall. He said that she had asked him to significantly shorten the fifth and sixth songs and to recompose some of the large leaps in the final postlude. Astonished, I asked him about Hila Plitman's tape. He responded that she had not yet performed the songs live and had made the recording in a studio!

When a composer is involved in the performance of his or her own work, the score may be intelligible only to the performers. Cheryl Bensman said she sang Reich's hour-long *Music for 18 Musicians* from a one-page cue sheet. All the performers knew what the repetitions were and how to give visual cues to move on to the next section, but the work could only be performed by that ensemble. As Reich explains, "I wrote the piece in a kind of musical shorthand directly into my music notebook. From there I wrote out individual parts for the musicians in my ensemble without making a full score. The parts themselves were also in shorthand that was only fully intelligible with considerable oral explanation—spoken, then finally jotted down, i.e. 'look at Russ,' etc. The result was that from 1976 until 1997 *Music for 18 Musicians* was, with a few unusual exceptions, only performed by my own ensemble."[7] In 1995 a graduate student at Cornell wanted to write a doctoral dissertation on the work and ended up creating a full score and new set of parts. These were ultimately published, with Steve Reich's supervision, by Boosey & Hawkes. The first score he created for general use was in 1981 for *Tehillim.* This work was intended for his group of four singers and chamber ensemble, but he also created an orchestral version, and therefore the performing materials had to be made accessible to a larger group of musicians.

Meredith Monk is another composer (as well as singer and choreographer) who creates pieces directly on performers. She rarely writes any of her work down, instead developing and teaching the music and the movement as part of the rehearsal process. If a group other than her own wants to perform one of her existing works, she collaborates with them to teach them the piece and the style. When she was commissioned by Michael Tilson Thomas to create *Possible Sky* for the New World Symphony in 2003, she grappled for the first time with the task of notating her work. She is currently working with Boosey & Hawkes to prepare her other works in written form so that future generations of performers will be able to re-create them.[8]

**Notation**

In the past half century musical notation has undergone a revolution. Experimentation in the 1950s and '60s resulted in two innovative and divergent paths: one attempted to notate every element of performance with more precision and control, and the other rejected precision by seeking more freedom in improvisation and indeterminacy. Composers developed new systems and symbols for notating tempo, pitch, duration, intensity, articulation, and color, using them alone or in combination with traditional notation.

Unfortunately, these new systems and symbols are not used consistently from composer to composer. Sharon Mabry devotes considerable space in her book to a discussion of new kinds of notation. She also recommends a number of specialized books on notation, including Howard Risatti's *New Music Vocabulary,* Kurt Stone's *Music Notation in the Twentieth Century,* David Cope's *New Music Notation,* and Erhard Karkoschka's *Notation in New Music* (see "Chapter 9: Notation" in "For Further Reading"). The lists of symbols and explanations in these books are extensive and complex. In some ways they are reminiscent of the seventeenth- and eighteenth-century treatises on ornamentation discussed in chapters 1 and 2.

Many composers, including Boulez, György Kurtág, Ligeti, and Crumb, try to incorporate as much information as possible in their scores. Some even include pages of instructions. In his scores to *Aventures* and *Nouvelles aventures,* Ligeti writes descriptive words over almost every vocal or instrumental gesture, as well as paragraphs of explanation in the margins. The Peters study score comes with two supplements: one a translation of all the handwritten German annotations in the score, and the other an explanation of all the special notational symbols. Deciphering such instructions can be as challenging as singing the works. But, as Bryn-Julson cautions, even if you know what the instructions mean, can you do them? Or if you can do them all, is that really what the composer wants?

In preparing Milton Babbitt's *Phonemena,* which was written for Bethany Beardslee, I worked diligently to execute the serial dynamics indicated over almost every note. When I coached the work with the composer, however, he told me to use the dynamics to make shapes with the lines instead of isolated events. He may not have given this comment to another singer, but it was obviously a suggestion I needed at that point in my work. In any case, I was pleasantly surprised that I could use a little more flexibility in my approach.

Conversely, some composers don't put enough information into their scores.

Then you have to discover if they really want the music plain and uninflected, or if they expect you to add your own coloring, articulation, and dynamics. If you work with the composers, you can ask them what they want. If they are not available, then you must decide on your own, in collaboration with your fellow musicians.

Even a familiar notation like a grace note can take on a completely unique meaning and require a special type of execution, depending upon the composer and context. For example, the atmosphere and text by García Lorca in Crumb's *Ancient Voices of Children* invite a certain execution of the notated grace notes. The Chinese poetry of the Song Dynasty and the music of Chen Yi's *As in a Dream* inspire a completely different approach. Barry Shiffman, the second violinist in the St. Lawrence String Quartet, describes how Osvaldo Golijov demonstrated the grace notes in his *Yiddishbbuk*:

> If you played literally what Ozzie had on the page, it sounded pretty empty. How were we to know that his strange little crushed grace notes that preceded a difficult, dissonant and ugly chord were echoes of the vocal inflections of screams? We tried to make his music sound "good" before meeting him, and we got more and more frustrated. When we met Ozzie, he listened and heard our frustration. He began to describe what he was after. When we asked him to sing it, well, everything changed. He was not "singing." It was more like crying, screaming, praying, all mixed up together. We got it.[9]

Tania León wrote many grace notes into the vocal part of *Singin' Sepia,* composed for the New York new-music group Continuum. Some were within a half or whole step of the following main note, but some were over an octave away. Some were to be sung on vowels, some on consonants, and others hummed. She indicated in the score that the vocal style she wanted should have elements of jazz and gospel, while imitating the inflections of southern black speech. Yet the tessitura was consistently above the staff. When I first started learning the work I was unsure how to combine all those elements. When I finally met Tania and she demonstrated what she wanted, it sounded natural and colorful, evoking exactly the elements she described. I still had a difficult time transferring those gestures to my voice, but hearing her do it made all the difference.

### Special Vocal Effects

Special vocal effects, also known as extended techniques, are often seen in new vocal music. Jane Manning regards them as "a variety of everyday sounds, which would all be familiar in a different context."[10] Yet they are even more problematic to notate than traditional singing gestures. Speaking or recitation can be unpitched or intoned, in rhythm or freely declaimed. Composers can use a number of now-standard notations to describe spoken rhythms and contours, but it is still impossible to notate all the subtleties of speech. When speaking or whispering, singers become actors with an infinite variety of nuances at their disposal. We are also asked to shout, whoop, whistle, and laugh— sometimes on pitch and in rhythm. We are asked to use our lips and tongues to make trilling or percussive sounds, or to distort a sung sound. We can also be asked to modify sung sounds by placing a hand over the mouth, or opening and closing our mouths to different degrees. Growling, grunting, and heavy breathing can be required in a variety of situations as well.

It is best when the composer can be there to demonstrate these effects or to help you experiment until you arrive at the sound he or she wants. Bryn-Julson says that there was nothing she had to do in *Aventures* that Ligeti couldn't demonstrate himself. Continuum performs a number of fanciful theater pieces by Francis Schwartz that require unusual and uninhibited effects, including talking, improvisation, and expressive breathing. The directors of the group have worked with Schwartz over many years and can explain the techniques to new players and singers. It is a special treat, however, when Schwartz himself is there to coach an existing piece or to unveil a new creation along the same lines.

If the composer is not available for the rehearsals of a new work, you have to be creative and make educated guesses. If you are working on an existing piece, you may be able to get advice from someone who has sung or played it with the composer's supervision. If a recording exists by the players or singers for whom it was written, it may well offer answers to questions about special vocal effects.

It can be liberating to be adventurous and daring with vocalization. However, if a composer asks you to do something that feels uncomfortable or that you think might be harmful vocally, you must be polite but honest about your reservations. In choosing repertoire with extended techniques, you must make sensible decisions in the interest of vocal health. Bryn-Julson was once asked to crack her voice in the middle of a swoop from high to low range; of the wide variety of vocal effects she has performed and recorded, that was one thing she was not comfortable doing. Sometimes composers ask us to re-create vocalizations heard in native or indigenous music from exotic cultures. Some singers will have less trouble using their instruments and imaginations to achieve these effects. Remember that many seemingly outrageous and bizarre vocal gestures were written for singers who could do them easily.

### Other Special Instructions or Requirements

Some new works include instructions for special stage setups or movement and choreography. Francis Schwartz's scores often indicate hand gestures, foot stomps, and facial expressions to be performed by both singers and instrumentalists. Sometimes the instrumentalists are required to make vocal sounds. (Percussionists are usually game, but other instrumentalists often feel uncomfortable doing this.) Sometimes singers must use props, as in Crumb's *Ancient Voices of Children,* where the singer is instructed to speak through a cardboard tube. Performers may be placed offstage or at different locations in a hall. Many new works call for special instruments such as a prepared piano or exotic percussion equipment, or they require unusual uses of standard instruments. You may be asked to sing into the piano to create sympathetic vibrations or to play a small percussion instrument. It is advisable to learn whatever techniques are required for playing that instrument and to practice it as you would the singing. I have always wanted to play the triangle, but when Cynthia Folio wrote a work for me in which I had to sing complex rhythms and play the triangle at the same time, I had to practice more than doubly hard to master the coordination. It was a challenge, but ultimately the experience was rewarding.

Some new vocal works use amplification or electronics. Others use prepared tape with synthesized or computer-generated sounds. Babbitt's *Philomel,* for soprano and synthesized tape, was written for Bethany Beardslee and includes her voice on the tape. Anyone who performs the work now and rents the tape from the publisher sings with Bethany's voice. When I was still a student, I was asked to record some bits of singing and talking that were then processed and combined with special effects to produce a seven-part chorus for Martin Butler's opera *The Sirens' Song.* The premiere took place in an outdoor amphitheater on the island of Crete. Unfortunately I was not there, but my voice was.

In some works with electronics, the special effects can be created during the performance. My cousin, a cellist, once played a new piece originally written as a cello solo. When the composer asked her to perform it again ten years later, he decided to add a recording engineer who manipulated her sound electronically as she played. This process created an entirely new work that could be different each time it was performed. In some pieces with prepared tape, the electronics are not meant to be synchronized with the live performer. In those works where the voice and tape are meant to be coordinated, the score indicates cues that are more or less accurate, depending on the nature of the taped sounds.

Working with a tape can be comforting because it is always exactly the same, whether in practice or performance. Babbitt uses the synthesizer to create electronic works because it enables him to retain precise control over the flow of events, "particularly temporal events. As I don't have to tell you, much of the problem of having unusual, intricate rhythms performed has nothing to do with the incapacity of the performer or the incapacity of the ear. It's the damn notation."[11] His *Phonemena,* which exists with both a synthesized tape and a notated piano accompaniment, was fascinating for me to perform in both versions. They felt in many ways like completely different works, both from the ways they sounded and the ways the rhythms worked when collaborating with the pianist or the tape.

It is undeniably exciting to participate in creating new and unusual effects or a tape or video portion of a work. As with special vocal effects, however, you must be honest with the composer about what you are able and willing to do. When I was a still relatively inexperienced performer, I was rehearsing a new work in which the composer asked me to walk all over the stage, face different directions, and even lie on the floor face down. I was still struggling with the rhythms and pitches and really needed to keep my eyes glued on the conductor. I told the composer I was sorry, but I wouldn't be able to manage the choreography. (Hopefully he was able to have the piece performed later with a singer who could include all the movement.)

### Learning Difficult Rhythms and Pitches

The first task in approaching any new piece should be to learn the correct rhythms and pitches. Singers can have a bad reputation for not taking notation seriously, especially when it comes to rhythm. In music from past periods and styles, the rhythm can be subtly flexible to support and highlight the text. This can also be the case in new music written in a traditional, tonal style. But the more complex and abstract the music, the more exacting and precise the rhythm must be. Bryn-Julson has never heard a composer tell her not to worry about the rhythm; she remembers Boulez saying, "I took the time to write it, you should sing it that way." If Crumb writes a series of thirteen repeated sixteenth notes accelerating over three seconds, or a two-note trill repeated three times (for a total of six notes), she believes one must do exactly that number of repetitions; otherwise it doesn't sound right. When the vocal line forms a delicate counterpoint to a piano accompaniment or instrumental lines, I have been grateful to my instrumental colleagues for insisting that we figure out the alignments exactly. Often this extra effort makes the difference between a piece's sounding muddy and vague or magically transparent and clear.

Mastering complex rhythms is like doing a crossword puzzle or a math problem. Often if you find the smallest common note value (the lowest common denominator), you can line up each tiny pulse and put your notes exactly where they belong. Then you can gradually increase the speed until you reach the correct tempo. Arthur Weisberg's *Performing Twentieth-Century Music* includes a detailed discussion about figuring out complex rhythms. My ear-training teacher at Juilliard made us perform difficult rhythms by conducting and speaking on "ta." This practice has served me well over the years. I remember learning *Phonemena* during a Christmas season when my daughter was involved in a production of *The Nutcracker*. During the long hours of rehearsal that parents had to stay in the theater, I sat in the lobby using the swing of whichever Tchaikovsky dance happened to be playing in the background as my sixteenth-note or eighth-note pulse. I then conducted the measures and spoke the complex rhythms until I knew where all the groups of five or seven went. (The other parents couldn't imagine what I was doing.) If you practice enough, tough rhythms will start to make sense. Cheryl Bensman says that the Reich ensemble was lucky to be able to rehearse many hours until the group rhythm "locked in." She also reports that sometimes she would rebar the rhythms for herself so the stresses made sense to her. This can be helpful in a lot of music, as long as you don't rewrite the rhythm itself.

Learning difficult pitches in nontonal music can be a real challenge for singers without perfect pitch. But plenty of well-known new-music singers (Jan DeGaetani, Bethany Beardslee, Lucy Shelton, Benita Valente) have achieved great things with hard work in place of perfect pitch. I spend a lot of time working with intervals. Sometimes it helps to transpose large leaps to smaller intervals within an octave, enabling you to really get the pitches in your ear. For example, a major seventh would become a half step down, or a minor tenth would be a minor third. If the spelling of the pitches is confusing, I often write the generic interval above the notes. I also check my pitch against pitches in the accompaniment to make sure I'm in the right place. I always try to understand my note in some harmonic or dissonant context (see the discussion regarding learning twelve-tone music at the end of chapter 7). One of my voice teachers used to say that singers need "infinite patience, infinite faith," and this is certainly true when learning tough pitches. With enough gentle and patient practice, you will find that eventually the pitches start to make sense in your head and feel comfortable in your throat.

Singing microtones is a special challenge for the brain and ear, involving an additional level of calculation to the procedure: sing a major third up plus a quarter tone down, or sing a perfect fourth a little bit sharp. Even Bryn-Julson, who with her perfect pitch impressed Del Tredici by sight-reading his *I Hear an Army*, has been stumped by some difficult microtonal music with large leaps. She asked Boulez if she could trade parts with the flute player in one particularly challenging piece; he agreed, but the flute part proved to be even harder. If Bryn-Julson couldn't sing the part, it would be difficult to find another singer who could. Yet composers continue to write very difficult pitches and rhythms, expecting or hoping to find singers who can manage. Throughout the centuries we have seen composers challenging singers to extend their boundaries of skill and musicianship. Singers today must continue to rise to the challenge and learn to execute difficult pitches and rhythms accurately. We have an advantage with today's technology—it is possible to generate a computer realization of a new work as an aid in learning a difficult part.

### Vibrato

This book has traced the changing attitudes toward the use of vibrato in vocal music. By the middle of the twentieth century, most singers' vibratos were bigger and more consistently employed than ever before. Today many composers ask singers to remove their vibrato as a color contrast in an isolated moment, or even for an entire work. Bensman says she often thought of a child's voice instead of a woman's to achieve the straight-toned sound required in Reich's music. She always sang softly to keep her throat from getting tight. This was easy for her to do, since Reich's singers were amplified. Bryn-Julson recommends not singing loud or high for straight tones and keeping the breath and throat relaxed. She says she always adds some vibrato to notes above the staff. Sometimes, however, composers specifically ask singers to sing straight tones high and/or loud; whether this can work depends on the ability and comfort of the singer. If you are rehearsing with a composer, you may be able to negotiate such issues. A wonderful interaction for me came when I was working with Brooke Joyce on a new work and asked him whether he wanted a particular note or section sung straight-toned or not. He said, "What do *you* think?"

Vibrato can be varied and straight tones added in places not specifically marked in a score. You might use a straight tone to create an exotic or native style of singing, or to make the intonation of microtones clear. You can also adjust vibrato to match or blend with different accompanying instruments. I use different kinds of vibrato to color harmonies and inflect dissonances. Bryn-Julson says she varies her vibrato to inflect the text and suit the dramatic situation. Paul Sperry lets the text help him make vibrato choices to create anything from a cold, stark sound to a jazzy or cabaret style. Your choice of vibrato should complement the harmony, instrumental textures, and the text in music of all periods and styles.

### Text and Music

Composers today treat the relationship between text and music in a wide variety of ways. In some traditional approaches, the meaning of the text can be clearly and directly related to the musical setting. In others it can seem completely independent or irrelevant. A composer can set an expressive text in an abstract way and instruct the singer not to add emotion or inflection to the poetry. Composers can use the voice instrumentally, with vowels and consonants merely providing texture. I find that when I am asked to sing without expression, I have to be careful not to sing without energy and commitment as well. The composer may want the text to be neutral, but I don't want my performance to be lifeless. This can be a tricky balance to achieve.

Composers can also use a nonsense text, phonetic symbols, or phonemes to create singable sounds. These can be used in an abstract and unexpressive context, or they can take on an inner meaning all their own. Bryn-Julson says that Ligeti's *Aventures* contains the largest number of phonetic symbols she has ever seen. Its list of over 100 requested sounds creates a nonsense language that, when combined with the music, communicates a compelling drama. The combination of phonemes and music in Babbitt's *Phonemena* suggests a vivid subtext to me. This was most likely not part of Babbitt's conception of the work, but it helps me shape the phrases, as he suggested, and makes the performance livelier and more interesting.

Many contemporary composers set text in a traditional way with appropriate prosody and rhythm. For *Tehillim,* Reich modeled the vocal lines on the natural spoken inflections of the Hebrew text. According to Bensman, Reich preferred a non legato, speechlike approach to the singing, reminiscent of Monteverdi. Combined with the music's intricate counterpoint and the required nonvibrato production, this creates a unique sound world that is at once both abstract and expressive. Benita Valente reports that all the vocal rhythms in *Exercises en Route* are derived from the ways Earl Kim spoke the text. His setting combines spoken and sung declamation, with the instrumental parts following and complementing the singer's flexible approach to declaiming the text.

Some composers expect singers to communicate the emotional and dramatic meaning of a text by using the full range of colors available to us. The subject matter of texts chosen by contemporary composers ranges much farther afield than nineteenth-century poems about love and nature. Singers today thus must be able to express a wide variety of poetic and dramatic situations. Sperry says that he doesn't think about colors specifically, instead concentrating on the poem and the music. He first tries to find a speaking voice that would work for the text, whether it is serious, humorous, or theatrical: "Out of my speaking voice and what I hear in the music comes what the singing voice ought to be for the song." From a wealth of possibilities he picks what seems appropriate and hopes that it works. Daron Hagen heard Sperry sing a song in which he used a white, hollow tone to create a particular dramatic atmosphere. The composer then wrote a work for him, choosing a text that would require that very color. Some composers try to control and notate every aspect of the expression of the text, using articulation marks, dynamics, and color suggestions. This can feel restrictive, but it can also assure us that we really know what the composer wants.

If you are involved in the compositional process, you may be able to have input regarding the text setting's prosody, vocal comfort, and expression. Some composers are happy to make changes to suit the singer. Others are less approachable or less flexible. Peter Westergaard, a Princeton professor with whom I have often worked, offers a glimpse of a composer's approach to text and music. As he finished work on a concert setting of scenes from Melville's *Moby Dick,* he sent the score to a singer he thought might be good for the role of Ahab. Baritone William Parcher had sung the role of Prospero in Westergaard's operatic setting of Shakespeare's *The Tempest.* Peter liked working with him and admired his singing. Yet the role of Ahab was not conceived for Bill or for any particular singer, but rather for a standard high dramatic baritone. When Parcher looked at the score, he considered the role both vocally and dramatically, and then phoned Peter with some concerns about how the high tessitura might affect his characterization of Ahab. Peter responded, trying to combine the needs of the singer with the requirements of his compositional structure:

31 October 2003

Dear Bill:

I can't tell you how exciting it was for me to get your read on Ahab. To say I learned a lot is the understatement of the week. It was particularly important for me to understand that it was not a question of whether you could or could not sing the high-lying lines, but what staying that high that much and that early on would mean for our perception of Ahab's mental state. I wholeheartedly agree that the last thing we'd want would be an Ahab verging on hysteria from the moment we meet him. Flashes of something the crew might find spellbinding and we in retrospect might understand as madness, yes, but he must be resolute, articulate, not frantic.

Unfortunately, the way the piece is put together does not allow easy fixes at the local level. One reason for this is the way the vocal lines, at least Ahab's and Ishmael's, are conceived of as central to the long-range pitch trajectories. (I really hate the kind of opera where the orchestra plays a symphony and the singers do a kind of recitative, using whatever pitches are flowing by. I want the vocal line to be at the core of what we hear.) What this usually comes down to in *Moby Dick* is that Ahab's and Ishmael's lines create their own four-part harmony which is supported by the instruments. The top line of that four-part texture is of course audibly the most obvious, but its motion is supported by the others. Furthermore, the others are often supported by the instruments. In short, this makes it difficult to make changes to a couple of measures of the vocal line without changing the surrounding measures as well, and it is usually impossible to change the vocal line without also changing the instruments.

So what I am sending you here represents a set of minimal fixes, changes that I can make without upsetting the whole apple cart. The question is, are they sufficient— I'm sure from what you've said they'll make things better, but are they sufficient to make Ahab the character I think we both envision?[12]

Westergaard's music includes challenging pitches and rhythms, but it always reflects the way he wants the line of text read. Large leaps magnify the contours of spoken inflection, and complex rhythms attempt to notate the natural subtle patterns of speech. The changes he offered, which Bill Parcher gladly accepted, included moving pitches and resetting rhythms to emphasize different words and syllables. This kind of close collaboration is truly rewarding.

### Composers as Performers

Composers have been performing their own vocal works throughout music history. They have sung, accompanied from the keyboard, or directed from the podium. This still happens today. Steve Reich leads rehearsals of his group from a percussion instrument or the piano in works that don't require a conductor and usually participates in performances, either playing percussion or adjusting the electronics. Pierre Boulez remains one of the great conductors of our time in his own music or any repertoire. Leonard Bernstein was the twentieth century's answer to Brahms or Liszt, achieving multiple renown as a composer, conductor, and pianist; Paul Sperry remembers Bernstein's overwhelming generosity of spirit as he conducted his *Dybbuk Suite No. 1* or coached singers for his *Songfest*. Many other contemporary composers who do not have full-time careers as professional conductors conduct their own works.

Composers who are pianists often accompany their songs. Louise Talma, a prodigious pianist, asked Sperry to perform many of her songs (though they were not written specifically for him). Sperry recalls that she played her music exactly the way she wanted it to go, performing her prescribed metronome markings perfectly. George Walker, an accomplished pianist, gave many more comments to the pianist than to me when he coached us for a performance of his songs.

When a composer rehearses and performs music with you, the communication becomes immediate and intimate. You can achieve exactly the right kind of articulation or phrasing, precisely the right tempo. Of course the experience can also be problematic if what the composer wants in performance is contrary to what you want or need to do in the work, or what may seem to be indicated in the score. Delicate negotiations must be worked out in any kind of chamber music or collaborative situation, whether between singer and accompanist, singer and conductor, among instrumental colleagues, or between the composer and the other players.

Composers who are also singers can write for their own instruments and sing the music exactly the way they want. Joan La Barbara has composed works for her own unique vocabulary of extended techniques. She has also premiered works written for her by many experimental composers, including Reich, Cage, and Morton Feldman. Some of her own works are meant to be performed live, usually with the aid of amplification or electronics. Others were created in the studio, with multiple vocal tracks and various kinds of electronic and digital manipulation, for radio or recordings. Meredith Monk started by experimenting with her own solo voice and then added other voices to her compositions:

> What happened to me was that I started working alone, and I didn't really have any references except that I wanted to make my voice as flexible as my hand could be. And I wanted to find a vocabulary that was built on my own instrument. . . . There are universal vocal sounds that you just come upon as you're working on expanding your own vocal palette. At the same time, each person's vocal apparatus is totally unique, so there are certain things, for example, that members of the ensemble do that I can't quite figure out, and there are certain things that I can do that they can't quite get exactly. . . . We all share a common, cross-cultural huge palette of archetypal sounds that people in the world that sing have in common. And that's a wonderful combination of things, and it's kept me captivated all these years.[13]

Susan Botti also writes and performs music conceived for her own soprano instrument: "I try to create a satisfying singing experience so that it's not simply sounds but also lyricism and enjoyment of what the voice can do."[14] Unlike Monk, her music is notated and intended for other singers as well. Her style combines elements of classical, jazz, and world-music vocalism, reflecting her eclectic background.

### Using Recordings

Recordings of new music can be an invaluable help in discovering composers' intentions. They reveal the choices made by particular performers and can inspire us to imagine our voices making new sounds. They can also be misleading. A recording made by the performers for whom a work was written, with the composer's supervision or participation, can be the definitive version of that piece. If the work was written for special forces or particularly distinctive performers, the recording may be the last word on the work and even its last performance for many years. But a performance captured in a recording studio can be very different from what the performers could achieve in a live concert. Composers also often make changes for a recording. Discrepancies between the score and a recording can result from a number of factors, including mistakes in the score, mistakes made by performers, or changes agreed on by all involved. A recording of a new work may also be made by performers other than those who performed the premiere, in a different location or years later. Popular works may be recorded numerous times by different performers, resulting in a range of different interpretations, even with the composer's involvement. Later generations of players may be able to approach a difficult work with more technical facility than the original players on the recording. All these variables suggest that, as with recordings of earlier music, we should use a recording only as a starting place from which to craft our own rendition of a work.

When I was preparing for a performance of Lucas Foss's *Thirteen Ways of Looking at a Blackbird*, I listened to a number of different recordings of this now well-known cycle. Some things about the various recordings were similar, while others were strikingly different. Some recordings were made with Foss's involvement, others not. The work contains many innovative notational devices, instructions for using unusual percussion instruments inside the piano, and a variety of special vocal effects. Unfortunately, Foss was unable to come to our rehearsals or performance, but when one member of our group called him to inquire about several issues, he actually couldn't remember definitive decisions he had made about those items. We seemed to have his permission to do, within a certain range of possibilities, what would work well for us in that performance situation. Ultimately, that is what musicians must do in every new rehearsal or performance situation. A recording can be a helpful place to start, but we must make the piece work for the given players and circumstances.

When I was working on *As in a Dream* by Chen Yi, I wasn't able to work with the composer but I was able to hear a recording by the Chinese soprano Rao Lan, who had inspired the composition. Listening to the recording was helpful, but it didn't answer all my questions. The work is sung in Chinese and includes elements of traditional Chinese opera. Two versions exist: one for violin and cello, and the other (used for the recording) for traditional Chinese instruments. I was working with a cellist and a Chinese violinist, who luckily could help me with pronunciation and word-for-word translation of the text. But there were many differences between what we saw in our scores for modern instruments and what we heard on the recording. Rao Lan's instrument and vocal production were also quite different from mine. I had difficulties deciphering which gestures were indicative of Chinese opera and which were her personal idiosyncrasies, either technical or interpretive. I knew I could not just copy what I heard but instead would have to discover how to make the piece work for me both vocally and dramatically. Inspiration eventually came when I was singing the work on tour with Continuum in Mongolia. Just before we were to perform, a group of Mongolian folk musicians presented some songs with traditional instruments. The microtonal sliding grace notes I heard from the Mongolian woman created a sound model that suddenly made sense for my voice, and I decided to use some of those stylistic elements in *As in a Dream*. I don't know whether the composer would have approved, but it helped me make the piece work in that situation.

## Conclusions: Finding the Composers' Intentions

If a composer is present when we are working on his or her piece, we will make our best effort to do what the composer wants. Yet the nature of composer-performer interactions can vary widely. Some composers defer easily to the needs of performers. Others are unapproachable and unyielding in their conception of how their music should go. Younger composers can be quite picky about what they want from performers, yet they often gain flexibility with experience. Sometimes—because the experience of performing and listening to a work can be completely different—a piece may make absolutely no sense to the performers who are playing it. With some new pieces I have been so busy counting or trying to find my notes that I have initially had no real idea what the work sounds like as a whole. Only much later, after I heard a recording of the performance, would I realize what an interesting composition it was. This is not an uncommon experience. In these kinds of situations, you must trust the composer. You could be working with a genius and not realize it. At least if you do what they ask and it doesn't work, they will learn.

In other situations, however, it is important to make changes in order to achieve the composers' goals and assure that the work is successful. Some of the most accomplished new-music players and singers I have asked agree that they certainly adjust details in a score in order to make a piece work well. Serving the new-music composer does not necessarily mean a slavish devotion to the details of notation. Most composers want performers to feel comfortable performing their music, so that it will sound good. If they are working with excellent players and singers whom they admire and trust, they will welcome suggestions that would help transmit their ideas more effectively. If you try an adjustment that works well and you ask the composer for a reaction, he or she will most likely be pleased. Of course it all depends on the particular chemistry between composer and performer. There can be a large gray area between serving the score and serving the composer, between doing what the composer asks and making a work effective. Performers of new music face these kinds of choices all the time and must find workable solutions for each situation.

Singing new music is both challenging and liberating. In creating a new vocal work you get to explore your own instrument and discover uncharted realms of vocalism and expression. Working with a composer enables you to experience a fluid and dynamic relationship, out of which new vocal styles may emerge. You also get to contribute to the continuation of vocal art by adding to the body of literature for the voice. Not every work will be a masterpiece, but you will help create an environment in which masterpieces can come into being. In the process you will gain a much more personal understanding of the working relationships between singers and composers in history. You will also gain an appreciation for all the elements that go into creating a style of singing from any period. In the interest of serving the composers of the present, we can bring our gifts, our experience, and our hearts to the collaborative process. The insights we gain from these interactions can also help us as we try to serve the composers of the past.

# Notes

## CHAPTER 1. THE EARLY BAROQUE

1. Bénigne de Bacilly, *Remarques curieuses sur l'art de bien chanter* (Paris, 1668), trans. Austin B. Caswell as *A Commentary upon the Art of Proper Singing* (New York: Institute of Mediæval Music, 1968), 16.

2. Robert Donington, *Baroque Music: Style and Performance* (London: Faber Music, 1982), 12.

3. Giulio Caccini, *Le nuove musiche* (Florence, 1602), trans. and ed. H. Wiley Hitchcock, *Recent Researches in the Music of the Baroque Era* 9 (Madison, Wis.: A-R Editions, 1970), 56.

4. Giovanni Piccioni, in the preface to his *Concerti ecclesiastici à 1–8 voci con il suo Basso seguito* (Venice: Vincenti, 1610), quoted in Franck Thomas Arnold, *The Art of Accompaniment from a Thorough-Bass as Practiced in the Seventeenth and Eighteenth Centuries* (New York: Dover, 1965), 66, n. 10.)

5. Howard Mayer Brown, "Editing," *The New Grove Dictionary of Music and Musicians,* ed. Stanley Sadie (London: Macmillan, 1980), vol. 5, 846–48.

6. John Wilson, ed., *Roger North on Music* (London: Novello, 1959), 26.

7. Ibid., 238.

8. Lodovico Zacconi, *Prattica di musica utile et necessaria si al compositore . . . si anco al cantore* (Venice, 1596), quoted in Carol MacClintock, *Readings in the History of Music in Performance* (Bloomington: Indiana University Press, 1979), 73.

9. Michael Praetorius, *Syntagma musicum,* quoted in MacClintock, *Readings,* 164.

10. Christoph Bernhard, *Von der Singe-Kunst, oder Manier* (ca. 1649), trans. in Walter Hilse, "The Treatises of Christoph Bernhard," *Music Forum* 3 (1973): 14.

11. Bacilly, *Remarques,* 83.

12. Wilson, *Roger North on Music,* 18.

13. Pier Francesco Tosi, *Opinioni de' cantori antichi e moderni* (Bologna, 1723), trans. and ed. John Ernst Galliard as *Observations on the Florid Song* (London, 1742), ed. with additional notes by Michael Pilkington (London: Stainer and Bell, 1987), 8.

14. Hermann Finck, *Practica musica* (Wittenberg, 1556), quoted in MacClintock, *Readings,* 62.

15. Gioseffo Zarlino, *Le istitutioni harmoniche* (Venice, 1558), iii, chap. 46, 253; quoted in Richard Wistreich, "'La voce e grata assai, ma . . . ' Monteverdi on Singing," *Early Music* 22 (1994): 9.

16. *The Letters of Claudio Monteverdi,* ed. Denis Stevens (Oxford: Clarendon Press, 1995), 66–67.

17. Tosi, *Opinioni,* 4.

18. Caccini, *Le nuove musiche,* 44.

19. John Dowland, *Andreas Ornithoparcus His Micrologus, or Introduction: Containing the Art of Singing* (London, 1609), quoted in MacClintock, Readings, 162.

20. Claudio Monteverdi, letter of December 9, 1616, quoted in MacClintock, *Readings,* 179; see also Monteverdi, *Letters,* 111.

21. Marin Mersenne, *Harmonie universelle, contenant la théorie et la pratique de la musique* (Paris, 1636), quoted in MacClintock, Readings, 173.

22. See also Bacilly, *Remarques,* parts 2 and 3; Sally Sanford, "Solo Singing 1," in *A Performer's Guide to Seventeenth-Century Music,* ed. Stewart Carter (New York: Schirmer, 1997), 5; and Sanford, "A Comparison of French and Italian Singing in the Seventeenth Century," *Journal of the Society for Seventeenth-Century Music* 1 (1995), http://sscm-jscm.press.uiuc.edu/jscm/vi/noi/sanford.html.

23. Caccini, *Le nuove musiche,* 56.

24. Tosi, *Opinioni,* 6; see also Julianne Baird, "Solo Singing 2" in A *Performer's Guide to Seventeenth Century Music,* ed. Stewart Carter (New York: Schirmer, 1997).

25. Rodolfo Celletti, *A History of Bel Canto,* trans. Frederick Fuller (Oxford: Clarendon Press, 1991), 15, n. 2.

26. Tosi, *Opinioni,* 26.

27. Wistreich, "'La voce e grata,'" 7–15.

28. Giovanni Camillo Maffei, *Libri due: Discorso . . . i cantar di garganta senza maestro* (Naples, 1562), quoted in MacClintock, *Readings,* 53.

29. Ibid., 52.

30. Zacconi, *Prattica di musica,* 70.

31. Adrian Petit Coclico, from *Compendium musices,* 1552, quoted in MacClintock, *Readings,* 33.

32. Minter also recommends the following sources for examples of diminutions: Diego Ortiz, *Tratado de glosas sobre clausulas y otros generos de puntos en la musica de violones* (Rome, 1553), ed. Max Schneider (New York: Bärenreiter, 1967); *Italienische Diminutionen—*

*Italian Diminutions: The Pieces with More than One Diminution from 1553 to 1638,* ed. Richard Erig (Zürich: Amadeus, 1979).

33. Caccini, *Le nuove musiche,* 51.

34. See H. Wiley Hitchcock, "Vocal Ornamentation in Caccini's *Nuove musiche,*" *Musical Quarterly* 56 (1970): 391, and Edward Huws Jones, *The Performance of English Song, 1610–1670* (New York: Garland Press, 1989), 70.

35. Tosi, *Opinioni,* 4.

36. Caccini, *Le nuove musiche,* 48–49.

37. Giovanni Battista Bovicelli, *Regole, passaggi di musica* (Venice, 1954), 11, as quoted in Hitchcock, "Vocal Ornamentation," 392, n. 10.

38. Caccini, *Le nuove musiche,* 48.

39. Ibid., 49.

40. Robert Toft, *Tune Thy Musicke to Thy Hart: The Art of Eloquent Singing in England, 1597– 1622* (Toronto: University of Toronto Press, 1993), 15–56, 108–26.

41. See Olive Baldwin and Thelma Wilson, "Purcell's Stage Singers," and Timothy Morris, "Voice Ranges, Voice Types, and Pitch in Concerted Works," in *Performing the Music of Henry Purcell,* ed. Michael Burden (Oxford: Clarendon Press, 1966), 105–29, 130–42.

42. See Andrew Parrott, "Performing Purcell," in *The Purcell Companion,* ed. Michael Burden (London: Faber and Faber, 1995), 387–444.

43. Olive Baldwin and Thelma Wilson, "Purcell's Sopranos," *Musical Times* 123 (1982): 602.

44. Jones, *Performance of English Song,* 56.

45. Wilson, *Roger North on Music,* 149.

46. Baldwin and Wilson, "Purcell's Stage Singers," in Burden, *Performing the Music of Henry Purcell,* 124.

47. Michael Burden, e-mail message to author, January 14, 2004.

48. Wilson, *Roger North on Music,* 150.

49. Baldwin and Wilson, "Purcell's Stage Singers," 119.

50. Jones, *Performance of English Song,* 233–43.

51. Bacilly, *Remarques,* 42.

52. Mersenne, *Harmonie universelle,* 173.

53. Bacilly, *Remarques,* 42–43, 32–33.

54. Bacilly, *Remarques,* 23; see also Peter Giles, *The History and Technique of the Counter-Tenor* (Aldershot, U.K.: Scolar Press, 1994), 37–38.

55. Neal Zaslaw, "The Enigma of the Haute-Contre," *Musical Times* 115, no. 11 (1974): 939–41.

56. Bacilly, *Remarques,* 23.

57. Ibid., 22.

58. James Anthony, *French Baroque Music: From Beaujoyeulx to Rameau,* rev. ed. (Portland, Ore.: Amadeus Press, 1997), 134–39.

59. David Fuller, "Notes inégales," *The New Grove Dictionary of Music and Musicians,* ed. Stanley Sadie (London: Macmillan, 1980), vol. 13, 420–27.

60. Bacilly, *Remarques,* 118.

61. Ibid., 24.

62. Ibid., 49.

63. Ibid., 64.

64. Ibid., 95.

65. Hellmuth Christian Wolff, ed. *Original Vocal Improvisations from the 16th–18th Centuries,* Anthology of Music 41 (Cologne: A. Volk, 1972): 95–100.

## CHAPTER 2. THE LATE BAROQUE

1. Johann Friedrich Agricola, *Anleitung zur Singkunst* (Berlin, 1757), trans. Julianne Baird as *Introduction to the Art of Singing* (Cambridge: Cambridge University Press, 1995), 34.

2. Nikolaus Harnoncourt, *Baroque Music Today: Music as Speech* (Portland, Ore.: Amadeus Press, 1982), 29.

3. Paul Steinitz, *Performing Bach's Vocal Music* (Croydon, U.K.: Addington Press, 1980), 26.

4. Carl Philipp Emanuel Bach, *Versuch über die wahre Art das Clavier zu spielen* (Berlin, 1753; part 2, 1762), trans. W. J. Mitchell as *Essay on the True Art of Playing Keyboard Instruments* (New York: Norton, 1949), sec. III.10, 151.

5. Leopold Mozart, *Versuch einer gründlichen Violinschule* (Augsburg, 1756), trans. Editha Knocker as *A Treatise on the Fundamental Principles of Violin Playing,* 2nd ed. (Oxford: Oxford University Press, 1985), sec. I.ii.7, 33.

6. Harnoncourt, *Music as Speech,* 39–40.

7. Johann Quantz, *Versuch einer Anweisung die Flöte traversiere zu spielen* (Berlin, 1752), trans. Edward Reilly as *On Playing the Flute,* 2nd ed. (New York: Schirmer, 1985), sec. XI.10, 122–23.

8. Agricola, *Anleitung,* 102.

9. Ibid., 152–53.

10. John Butt, *Bach Interpretation: Articulation Marks in Primary Sources of J. S. Bach* (Cambridge: Cambridge University Press, 1990), 2–3.

11. Harnoncourt, *Music as Speech,* 44.

12. Quantz, *Versuch,* sec. XI.19, 127.

13. C. P. E. Bach, *Versuch,* sec. V.14, 101; sec. III.12, 151–52.

14. Agricola, *Anleitung,* 86.

15. Jean-Baptiste Bérard, *L'art du chant* (1755), trans. and commentary by Sydney Murray (New York: Pro Musica Press, 1969), 27, 103–4.

16. Butt, *Bach Interpretation,* 15.

17. L. Mozart, *Versuch,* sec. V.4, 97.

18. Michel Pignolet de Montéclair, *Principes de musique* (Paris, 1736), trans. in *Cantatas for One and Two Voices,* ed. James R. Anthony and Diran Akmajian (Madison, Wis.: A-R Editions, 1978), xiii.

19. L. Mozart, *Versuch,* sec. XI.1.3, 203.

20. Agricola, *Anleitung,* 149.

21. Bérard, *L'art du chant,* 71–73.

22. Arthur Mendel, "On the Pitches in Use in Bach's Time," *Musical Quarterly* 41 (1955): 332–54, 466–80.

23. Agricola, *Anleitung,* 83.

24. Ibid., 173.

25. See Laurence Dreyfus, *Bach's Continuo Group: Players and Practices in His Vocal Works* (Cambridge, Mass.: Harvard University Press, 1987), 106.

26. See Henry Pleasants, *The Great Singers* (New York: Simon and Schuster, 1966); John Rosselli, *Singers of Italian Opera* (Cambridge: Cambridge University Press, 1992); C. Steven Larue, *Handel and His Singers: The Creation of the Royal Academy Operas, 1720–1728* (Oxford: Clarendon Press, 1995).

27. Charles Burney, *A General History of Music* (London, 1789), 814.

28. Agricola, *Anleitung*, 91.

29. See Agricola, chap. 2; Quantz, chap. VIII; C. P. E. Bach, chaps. 1 and 2; and L. Mozart, chap. IX.

30. Frederick Neumann, *Ornamentation in Baroque and Post-Baroque Music, with Special Emphasis on J. S. Bach* (Princeton, N.J.: Princeton University Press, 1978), part V, 29.

31. Winton Dean, *G. F. Handel: Three Ornamented Arias* (Oxford: Oxford University Press, 1976), 3–4. See also Hellmuth Christian Wolff, *Original Vocal Improvisations from the 16th–18th Centuries,* Anthology of Music 41 (Cologne: A. Volk, 1972), 109–17.

32. Agricola, *Anleitung*, 205.

33. Ibid., 192–93.

34. See also Howard M. Brown, "Embellishing Eighteenth-Century Arias: On Cadenzas," in *Opera and Vivaldi,* ed. Michael Collins and Elise K. Kirk (Austin: University of Texas Press, 1984), 268–76.

35. See Jens Peter Larsen, *Handel's Messiah: Origins, Composition, Sources* (Westport, Conn.: Greenwood Press, 1990); Donald Burrows, *Handel: Messiah* (Cambridge: Cambridge University Press, 1991); and Watkins Shaw, *A Textual and Historical Companion to Handel's 'Messiah'* (London: Novello, 1965).

36. James R. Oestreich, "Rejoicing in a 'Messiah' of Good Taste (No Mad Scenes, Please)," *New York Times,* sec. E, December 23, 1999.

37. Christoph Bernhard, *Von der Singe-Kunst, oder Manier* (ca. 1649), trans. in Walter Hilse, "The Treatises of Christoph Bernhard," *Music Forum* 3 (1973): 13–29.

38. See Wolff, *Original Vocal Improvisations,* 143–68.

39. Agricola, *Anleitung*, 92.

40. Ibid., 97, 101, 107, 109, 110.

41. Neumann, *Ornamentation in Baroque,* 145–46.

42. Ibid., 219.

43. John Butt, "Ornamentation," in *The Sacred Choral Music of J. S. Bach: A Handbook* (Brewster, Mass.: Paraclete Press, 1997), 52.

44. Agricola, *Anleitung*, 129, 139.

45. Quantz, *Versuch,* 101.

46. See Joshua Rifkin, "Bach's Chorus: A Preliminary Report," *Musical Times* 123 (1982): 747–51; Robert Marshall, "Bach's Chorus: A Reply to Rifkin," *Musical Times* 124 (1983): 19–22; Rifkin, "Bach's Chorus: A Response to Marshall," *Musical Times* 124 (1983): 161–62; Rifkin, "Bach's Choruses: The Record Cleared," *High Fidelity* (October 1982): 58–59; Marshall, "Bach's Choruses Reconstituted," *High Fidelity* (October 1982): 64–66; and Andrew Parrott, "Bach's Chorus: A 'Brief yet Highly Necessary' Reappraisal," *Early Music* 24 (1996): 551–80.

47. Andrew Parrott, *The Essential Bach Choir* (Woodbridge, Suffolk: Boydell Press, 2000).

48. Quantz, *Versuch,* 328–29.

49. David Tunley, *The Eighteenth-Century French Cantata* (Oxford: Clarendon Press, 1997), viii.

50. Bérard, *L'art du chant,* part II, chap. 3.

51. Montéclair, *Principes,* xiii.

### CHAPTER 3. THE CLASSICAL ERA

1. Charles Rosen, *The Classical Style: Haydn, Mozart, Beethoven* (New York: Norton, 1972), 20–23.

2. Sandra P. Rosenblum, *Performance Practices in Classic Piano Music: Their Principles and Applications* (Bloomington: Indiana University Press, 1988), 2.

3. Emily Anderson, trans. and ed., *The Letters of Mozart and His Family,* 3rd. ed. (London: Macmillan, 1985), 259.

4. Elliot Forbes, ed., *Thayer's Life of Beethoven* (Princeton, N.J.: Princeton University Press, 1967), 405, 554, and 716.

5. A. Peter Brown, *Performing Haydn's "The Creation"* (Bloomington: Indiana University Press, 1986), 74.

6. Rosenblum, *Classic Piano Music,* 24.

7. Jaap Schröder, "A Performer's Thoughts on Mozart's Violin Style," in *Perspectives on Mozart Performance,* ed. R. Larry Todd and Peter Williams, 121 (Cambridge: Cambridge University Press, 1991). See also Robin Stowell, *Violin Technique and Performance Practice in the Late Eighteenth and Early Nineteenth Centuries* (Cambridge: Cambridge University Press, 1985).

8. Malcolm Bilson, "Restoring Ingredients: Malcolm Bilson on the Fortepiano," in *Inside Early Music: Conversations with Performers,* ed. Bernard D. Sherman (New York: Oxford University Press, 1997), 299.

9. Domenico Corri, *The Singer's Preceptor* (London, 1810), reprinted in Edward Foreman, ed., *The Porpora Tradition* (New York: Pro Musica Press, 1968), 52.

10. Daniel Gottlob Türk, *Klavierschule,* trans. and ed. Raymond H. Haggh as *School of Clavier Playing* (Lincoln: University of Nebraska Press, 1982), 345–48.

11. Clementi quoted in Rosenblum, *Classic Piano Music,* 154.

12. Leopold Mozart quoted in Rosenblum, *Classic Piano Music,* 154.

13. Neal Zaslaw, "Introduction to Part II, The Classical Era," in *Performance Practice: Music after 1600,* ed. Howard Mayer Brown and Stanley Sadie (New York: Norton, 1990), 213.

14. Wye Jamison Allanbrook, *Rhythmic Gesture in Mozart* (Chicago: University of Chicago Press, 1983), 27–28.

15. See Jean-Pierre Marty, "Mozart's Tempo Indications and the Problems of Interpretation," in *Perspectives on Mozart Performance,* ed. R. Larry Todd and Peter Williams, 55–73 (Cambridge: Cambridge University Press, 1991).

16. See Rosenblum, *Classic Piano Music,* 306–11.

17. Richard Kramer, "Notes to Beethoven Education," *Journal of the American Musicological Society* 28, no. 1 (Spring 1975): 75.

18. Rosenblum, *Classic Piano Music,* 312.

19. Forbes, *Thayer's Life of Beethoven,* 555.

20. For a more complete discussion of the periodic phrase, see Rosen, *Classical Style,* chap. 3; Roger Norrington, "Taking Music Off the Pedestal: Roger Norrington on Beethoven," in *Inside Early Music: Conversations with Performers,* ed. Bernard D. Sherman, 341 (New York: Oxford University Press, 1997); and Charles Rosen, *The Romantic Generation* (Cambridge, Mass.: Harvard University Press, 1995), 261.

21. Anderson, *Letters of Mozart,* 340.

22. Türk, *Klavierschule,* 363–64.

23. Corri, *Singer's Preceptor,* 6.

24. Ibid., 35.

25. Paul and Eva Badura-Skoda, *Interpreting Mozart on the Keyboard,* trans. Leo Black (New York: St. Martin's Press, 1962), 31.

26. Forbes, *Thayer's Life of Beethoven,* 688.

27. See Clive Brown, "Historical Performance, Metronome Marks, and Tempo in Beethoven's Symphonies," *Early Music* 19 (May 1991): 247–58; Willy Hess, "The Right Tempo: Beethoven and the Metronome," *The Beethoven Newsletter* 3 (1988): 16–17; Peter Stadlen, "Beethoven and the Metronome," *Soundings* 9 (1982): 38–73; and Rosenblum, *Classic Piano Music,* 323–48.

28. See William Malloch, "Carl Czerny's Metronome Marks for Haydn and Mozart Symphonies," *Early Music* 16 (February 1988): 72–82.

29. Nicholas Temperly, "Haydn's Tempos in *The Creation,*" *Early Music* 19 (1991): 235–45.

30. Corri, *Singer's Preceptor,* 69.

31. Brown, *Performing Haydn's "The Creation,"* 23.

32. Anderson, *Letters of Mozart,* 121–22.

33. Corri, *Singer's Preceptor,* 67.

34. Anderson, *Letters of Mozart,* 171.

35. Ibid., 486.

36. Ibid., 581.

37. Ibid., 769.

38. See also Thomas Bauman, "Mozart's Belmonte," *Early Music* 19 (1991): 557–64; Patricia Lewy Gidwitz, "'Ich bin die erste Sängerin': Vocal Profiles of Two Mozart Sopranos," *Early Music* 19 (1991): 565–79; and Alessandra Campana, "Mozart's Italian Buffo Singers," *Early Music* 19 (1991): 580–84.

39. Anderson, *Letters of Mozart,* 552.

40. Corri, *Singer's Preceptor,* 3–4.

41. Charles Burney, *The Present State of Music in France and Italy* (London, 1773; facs. New York: Broude Brothers, 1969), vii, 19.

42. Corri, *Singer's Preceptor,* 70.

43. Anderson, *Letters of Mozart,* 631.

44. Laurence Dreyfus, *Bach's Continuo Group: Players and Practices in His Vocal Works* (Cambridge, Mass.: Harvard University Press, 1987), 87–88.

45. See Will Crutchfield, "The Prosodic Appoggiatura in the Music of Mozart and His Contemporaries," *Journal of the American Musicological Society* 42 (1989): 229–74, and

Crutchfield, "Voices," in *Performance Practice: Music after 1600,* ed. Howard Mayer Brown and Stanley Sadie, 298–99 (New York: Norton, 1990).

46. Frederick Neumann, *Ornamentation and Improvisation in Mozart* (Princeton, N.J.: Princeton University Press, 1986), 184–215. See also Neumann, "A New Look at Mozart's Prosodic Appoggiatura," in *Perspectives on Mozart Performance,* ed. R. Larry Todd and Peter Williams, 92–116 (Cambridge: Cambridge University Press, 1991).

47. Badura-Skoda, *Interpreting Mozart,* 76.

48. Neumann, *Ornamentation in Mozart,* 16.

49. Badura-Skoda, *Interpreting Mozart,* 70.

50. See the discussions of this particular problem in Neumann, *Ornamentation in Mozart,* 22–23, and Badura-Skoda, *Interpreting Mozart,* 87.

51. Paul Badura-Skoda, "Mozart's Trills," in *Perspectives on Mozart Performance,* ed. R. Larry Todd and Peter Williams, 8–12 (Cambridge: Cambridge University Press, 1991). See also Rosenblum, *Classic Piano Music,* 246–47.

52. Neumann, *Ornamentation in Mozart,* 114.

53. See also Crutchfield, "Voices," 301, and John Spitzer, "Improvised Ornamentation in a Handel Aria with Obbligato Wind Accompaniment," *Early Music* 16 (1988): 515–16.

54. For the complete aria, see "Luigi Marchesi Embellishing a Cherubini Rondo" as reproduced from a Vienna manuscript in Robert Haas, *Aufführungspraxis der Musik: Handbuch der Musikwissenschaft* (Wildpark-Potsdam: Akademische Verlagsgesellschaft Athenaion, 1931), 225–30.

55. Burney, *Present State of Music,* 377.

56. For the complete aria, see *Joseph Haydn Werke* (Munich: G. Henle), XXVIII/1:180–201. For an excerpt from the aria, see Eva Badura-Skoda, "Improvisation: I. 3. The Classical Period," *The New Grove Dictionary of Music and Musicians,* ed. Stanley Sadie (London: Macmillan, 1980), vol. 9, 43–48.

57. Neumann's general attitude is one of cautious conservatism, while pianist Robert Levin advocates a more adventurous approach: see his review of Neumann's book in *Journal of the American Musicological Society* 41 (1988): 355–68. See also Levin, "Improvised Embellishments in Mozart's Keyboard Music," *Early Music* 20 (1992): 221–33; "Robert Levin on Mozart and Improvisation," in *Inside Early Music: Conversations with Performers,* ed. Bernard D. Sherman, 341 (New York: Oxford University Press, 1997), 315–38; and Christoph Wolff, "Cadenzas and Styles of Improvisation in Mozart's Piano Concertos," in *Perspectives on Mozart Performance,* ed. R. Larry Todd and Peter Williams, 228–38 (Cambridge: Cambridge University Press, 1991).

### CHAPTER 4. ITALIAN BEL CANTO

1. Philip Duey, *Bel Canto in Its Golden Age* (New York: King's Crown Press, 1951), 5.

2. Owen Jander and Ellen T. Harris, "Bel canto," *The New Grove Dictionary of Music and Musicians,* ed. Stanley Sadie (New York: Grove's Dictionaries, 2001), vol. 3, 161.

3. Ibid.

4. For a more detailed discussion, see Clive Brown, *Classical and Romantic Performing Practice, 1750–1900* (New York: Oxford University Press, 1999), chapters 2–6.

5. Charles de Bériot, *Méthode de violon* (Mainz, 1858), iii, 219–20, quoted in Brown, *Classical and Romantic*, 55–57.

6. Gesualdo Lanza, *The Elements of Singing* (London, 1809); Domenico Corri, *The Singer's Preceptor* (London, 1810); Giacomo Gotifredo Ferrari, *A Concise Treatise on Italian Singing* (London, 1818); and Isaac Nathan, *An Essay on the History and Theory of Music, and on the Qualities, Capabilities, and Management of the Human Voice* (London, 1823; rev. as *Musurgia Vocalis*, 1836). For a more detailed discussion of all these sources, see Robert Toft, *Heart to Heart: Expressive Singing in England, 1780–1830* (New York: Oxford University Press, 2000).

7. Manuel García, *Traité complet de l'art du chant* (Paris, 1874; facs. Geneva, 1985), trans. Donald V. Paschke as *A Complete Treatise on the Art of Singing: Part Two* (New York: Da Capo Press, 1975) and *A Complete Treatise on the Art of Singing: Part One* (New York: Da Capo Press, 1984); García, *Hints on Singing* (New York: Edward Schuberth, 1894).

8. Charles Santly, *Student and Singer: Reminiscences of Charles Santly* (London, 1892), 79–80.

9. García, *Complete Treatise: Part Two*, 26–31.

10. Brown, *Classical and Romantic*, 344, 321; for a more detailed discussion of tempo terms, see chaps. 10 and 11.

11. García, *Hints on Singing*, 62.

12. Charles Rosen, *The Romantic Generation* (Cambridge, Mass.: Harvard University Press, 1995), 611.

13. García, *Traité complet*, 22.

14. Howard Bushnell, *Maria Malibran: A Biography of the Singer* (University Park: Pennsylvania State University Press, 1979), 11.

15. Henry Pleasants, *The Great Singers* (New York: Simon and Schuster, 1966), 167; see his entire entry on Nourrit and Duprez, 161–70.

16. Duey, *Bel Canto*, 153.

17. Isaac Nathan, *Musurgia Vocalis: An Essay on the History and Theory of Music, and on the Qualities, Capabilities and Management of the Human Voice* (London, 1836), reprinted in *The Porpora Tradition*, ed. E. Foreman (New York: Pro Musica Press, 1968), 145.

18. Bushnell, *Maria Malibran*, 9, quoted from an 1828 musical magazine.

19. Ibid., 4.

20. García, *Complete Treatise, Part One*, 66.

21. Gioacchino Rossini, *Vocalises and Solfèges* (Bloomington, Ind.: Frangipani Press, 1986), 3.

22. Nathan, *Musurgia Vocalis*, 145.

23. Thomas Busby, *A Musical Manual or Technical Directory* (London, 1828; facs. New York: Da Capo Press, 1976), 182.

24. García, *Complete Treatise: Part Two*, 150.

25. García, *Complete Treatise: Part One*, 137.

26. See *The Era of Adelina Patti*, Nimbus Records (NI 7840/41). See also Robert Philip, *Early Recordings and Musical Style: Changing Tastes in Instrumental Performance, 1900–1950* (Cambridge: Cambridge University Press, 1992), and Will Crutchfield, "Vocal Ornamentation in Verdi: The Phonographic Evidence," *19th-Century Music* 7 (1983–4): 3–54.

27. See Toft, *Heart to Heart*, 58–64, and Brown, *Classical and Romantic*, chap. 15.

28. Nicola Vaccai, *Practical Method of Italian Singing* (New York: Schirmer, 1975), 18.

29. García, *Complete Treatise, Part Two*, 82–83.

30. See Brown, *Classical and Romantic*, 429–38 and chap. 15.

31. Vaccai, *Practical Method*, 3.

32. Pleasants, *Great Singers*, 91–93.

33. Richard Osborne, "*Il Barbiere di Siviglia* (ii)," *Grove Music Online*, ed. Laura Macy, http://www.grovemusic.com (accessed June 2, 2004).

34. Bushnell, *Maria Malibran*, 88.

35. Laure-Cinthie Damoreau, *Classic Bel Canto Technique*, trans. and introduction by Victor Rangel-Ribeiro (New York: Dover, 1997).

36. Vaccai, *Practical Method*, 16.

37. Ibid., 18.

38. Malcolm Sterling Mackinlay, *Garcia the Centenarian and His Times* (Edinburgh, 1908), 34, quoted in Brown, *Classical and Romantic*, 419.

39. Will Crutchfield, "Improvisation—II, 5, ii. Nineteenth-Century Vocal Music," *The New Grove Dictionary of Music and Musicians*, ed. Stanley Sadie (New York: Grove's Dictionaries, 2001), vol. 12, 121.

40. See Austin Caswell, ed., "Embellished Opera Arias," *Recent Researches in the Music of the 19th and Early 20th Centuries*, vols. 7 and 8 (Madison, Wis.: A-R Editions, 1989), no. 13.

41. Crutchfield, "Improvisation," 122.

### CHAPTER 5. GERMAN LIEDER

1. Eric Sams and Susan Youens, "Hugo Wolf," *Grove Music Online*, ed. Laura Macy, http://www.grovemusic.com (accessed January 8, 2002).

2. Edward F. Kravitt, "The Lied in 19th-Century Concert Life," *Journal of the American Musicological Society* 18 (1965): 210. See also Lorraine Gorrell, *The Nineteenth-Century German Lied* (Portland, Ore.: Amadeus Press, 1993), 89.

3. Otto Erich Deutsch, *Schubert: Memoirs by His Friends* (New York: Macmillan, 1958), 49.

4. Barbara A. Petersen, *Ton und Wort: The Lieder of Richard Strauss* (Ann Arbor, Mich.: UMI Research Press, 1980), 104.

5. Robert Schumann, *On Music and Musicians* (Berkeley: University of California Press, 1983), 59–60.

6. Deutsch, *Memoirs*, 101.

7. Ibid.

8. Robert Winter, "Franz Schubert," *Grove Music Online*, ed. Laura Macy, http://www.grovemusic.com (accessed August 30, 2001). See also Walter Dürr, "Schubert and Johann Michael Vogl: A Reappraisal," *19th-Century Music* 3 (1979/80): 128.

9. Philip Duey, *Bel Canto in Its Golden Age* (New York: King's Crown Press, 1951), 8–9.

10. Deutsch, *Memoirs*, 216.

11. Ibid., 273.

12. Ibid., 116, 336.

13. Quoted in Dietrich Fischer-Dieskau, *Robert Schumann: Words and Music, the Vocal Compositions,* trans. Reinhard G. Pauly (Portland, Ore.: Amadeus Press, 1981), 135, 176.

14. Gorrell, *German Lied,* 83.

15. Henry Pleasants, *The Great Singers* (New York: Simon and Schuster, 1966), 155–56.

16. William Ashton Ellis, ed. and trans., *Richard Wagner's Prose Works,* vol. 4, *Art and Politics* (1895; repr., New York: Broude Brothers, 1966), 182.

17. Ellis, Wagner's *Prose Works,* vol. 5, *Actors and Singers,* 204.

18. Henry Pleasants, trans. and ed., *The Music Criticism of Hugo Wolf* (New York: Holmes and Meier, 1979), 108.

19. Lilli Lehmann, *How to Sing,* trans. Richard Aldrich (New York: Macmillan, 1955), 281, 239.

20. Pleasants, *Music Criticism of Wolf,* 95.

21. Ibid., 259.

22. Clive Brown, *Classical and Romantic Performing Practice, 1750–1900* (Oxford: Oxford University Press, 1999), 114–27.

23. See David Schroeder, "Schubert the Singer," *Music Review* 49 (1988), 259.

24. Gorrell, *German Lied,* 110.

25. Jan Swafford, *Johannes Brahms: A Biography* (New York: Knopf, 1997), 448.

26. Petersen, *Ton und Wort,* 156.

27. Quoted in Dürr, "Schubert and Vogl," 136.

28. Ibid., 126.

29. Deutsch, *Memoirs,* 226.

30. David Montgomery, "Modern Schubert Interpretation in the Light of Pedagogical Sources of His Day," *Early Music* 25 (1997): 101–18; Montgomery, "Franz Schubert's Music in Performance: A Brief History of People, Events, and Issues," in *The Cambridge Companion to Schubert,* ed. Christopher Gibbs, 270–83 (Cambridge: Cambridge University Press, 1997).

31. Deutsch, *Memoirs,* 116–17.

32. Quoted in Brown, *Classical and Romantic,* 426.

33. Ernest Walker, "The Appoggiatura," *Music and Letters* 5 (1924): 140.

34. For a more complete discussion of turns and mordents, see Brown, *Classical and Romantic,* 493–516.

35. Quoted in Robert Philip, *Early Recordings and Musical Style* (Cambridge: Cambridge University Press, 1992), 208.

36. Quoted in Brown, *Classical and Romantic,* 519.

37. Pleasants, *Music Criticism of Wolf,* 22.

38. Lehmann, *How to Sing,* 143.

39. Ibid., 254.

40. See Philip, *Early Recordings,* 172–76, 216.

41. Quoted in Brown, *Classical and Romantic,* 384.

42. Deutsch, *Memoirs,* 337–38.

43. Quoted in R. Larry Todd, "Felix Mendelssohn-Bartholdy," *Grove Music Online,* ed. Laura Macy, http://www.grovemusic.com (accessed October 13, 2001).

44. Quoted in Philip, *Early Recordings*, 219.
45. Ibid., 218.
46. Quoted in Swafford, *Brahms*, 110.
47. Petersen, *Ton und Wort*, 156.
48. Edward F. Kravitt, "Tempo as an Expressive Element in the Late Romantic Lied," *Musical Quarterly* 59 (1973): 516.
49. See Gwilym Beechey, "Rhythmic Interpretation: Mozart, Beethoven, Schubert, and Schumann," *Music Review* 33 (1972): 233–48.
50. Desmond Shawe-Taylor, "Schubert as Written and Performed," *Musical Times* 104 (1963): 626–28.
51. Pleasants, *Music Criticism of Wolf*, 203.
52. Swafford, *Brahms*, 343.
53. Quoted in Pleasants, *Music Criticism of Wolf*, 174.
54. Philip, *Early Recordings*, 6.

### CHAPTER 6. FRENCH MÉLODIES

1. See especially Betty Bannerman, ed. and trans., *The Singer as Interpreter: Claire Croiza's Master Classes* (London: Victor Gollancz, 1989); Jane Bathori, *On the Interpretation of the Mélodies of Claude Debussy*, trans. Linda Laurent (Stuyvesant, N.Y.: Pendragon Press, 1998); and Pierre Bernac, *Francis Poulenc: The Man and His Songs* (London: Victor Gollancz, 1977).
2. Bernac, *Poulenc*, 13.
3. Pierre Bernac, *The Interpretation of French Song*, 2nd ed. (New York: Norton, 1976).
4. Frits Noske, *French Song from Berlioz to Duparc*, trans. Rita Benton (New York: Dover, 1970), 328.
5. See Graham Johnson, *French Song Companion* (Oxford: Oxford University Press, 2000), 17. See also *Songs for Solo Voice and Orchestra*, ed. Ian Kemp, vol. 13 of *Hector Berlioz: New Edition of the Complete Works* (Kassel: Bärenreiter, 1967).
6. Bathori, *Debussy*, 69.
7. Francis Poulenc, *Diary of My Songs*, trans. Winifred Radford (London: Victor Gollancz, 1985), 77.
8. Paul Sperry, telephone conversation with author, December 8, 2003.
9. Arbie Orenstein, ed., *A Ravel Reader* (New York: Columbia University Press, 1990), 507.
10. Thomas Grubb, *Singing in French: A Manual of French Diction and French Vocal Repertoire* (New York: Schirmer, 1979), 18.
11. Quoted in Noske, *French Song*, 2.
12. Martin Cooper, *French Music from the Death of Berlioz to the Death of Fauré* (New York: Oxford, 1951), 1–2.
13. Romagnesi's treatise is excerpted and translated in David Tunley, *Salons, Singers, and Songs: A Background to Romantic French Song, 1830–1870* (Burlington, Vt.: Ashgate, 2002); for these passages, see pp. 258, 265, and 262.
14. Jean-Michel Nectoux, *Gabriel Fauré: A Musical Life*, trans. Roger Nichols (Cambridge: Cambridge University Press, 1991), 27, 51, 189.

15. Quoted in Nectoux, *Musical Life*, 471–72. See also *Gabriel Fauré: His Life through His Letters*, ed. Jean-Michel Nectoux, trans. J. A. Underwood (New York: Marion Boyars, 1984), 252.

16. Quoted in Cooper, *French Music*, 114.

17. Bathori, *Debussy*, 25.

18. Georges Jean-Aubry, *French Music of Today*, trans. Edwin Evans (Plainview, N.Y.: Books for Libraries Press, 1976), 222–23.

19. Louis Laloy, *Louis Laloy (1874–1944) on Debussy, Ravel, and Stravinsky*, trans. Deborah Priest (Burlington, Vt.: Ashgate, 1999), 248–49.

20. Poulenc, *Diary*, 21, 51, 63, 71, 79.

21. Bernac, *Interpretation of French Song*, 33.

22. Tunley, *Salons*, 43.

23. Ibid., 259.

24. Ibid., 263.

25. Ibid., 103.

26. Bathori, *Debussy*, 29.

27. Bannerman, *Singer as Interpreter*, 13.

28. Ibid., 81.

29. Ibid., 36–37.

30. Tunley, *Salons*, 259.

31. Jean-Aubry, *French Music*, 212.

32. Marguerite Long, *At the Piano with Ravel*, trans. Olive Senior-Ellis (London: J. M. Dent and Sons, 1973), 16.

33. See Noske, *French Song*, 163.

34. Bannerman, *Singer as Interpreter*, 51.

35. Tunley, *Salons*, 260.

36. Reynaldo Hahn, *On Singers and Singing*, trans. Léopold Simoneau (Portland, Ore.: Amadeus Press, 1990), 29, 60–65.

37. Bannerman, *Singer as Interpreter*, 44.

38. Orenstein, *Ravel Reader*, 30–31.

39. Arbie Orenstein, *Ravel: Man and Musician* (New York: Columbia University Press, 1975), 163.

40. Laloy, *Louis Laloy*, 108.

41. Poulenc, *Diary*, 79, 113, 41, 69.

42. Hahn, *Singers*, 114–15.

43. Ibid., 63.

44. Ibid., 62.

45. Bathori, *Debussy*, 41, 85, 81.

46. Bernac, *Poulenc*, 45, 48.

47. Grubb, *Singing in French*, 104.

48. Tunley, *Salons*, 265.

49. Bernac, *Interpretation of French Song*, 42.

50. Nectoux, *Musical Life*, 43, 294.

51. Bannerman, *Singer as Interpreter*, 86.

52. Marguerite Long, *At the Piano with Fauré*, trans. Olive Senior-Ellis (New York: Taplinger, 1981), 68.

53. Marguerite Long, *At the Piano with Debussy*, trans. Olive Senior-Ellis (London: J. M. Dent and Sons, 1972), 19, 63, 71, 13, 25.

54. Hahn, *Singers*, 115.

55. Bathori's singing is now available on a CD, *Jane Bathori: Complete Solo Recordings* (Marston 51009).

56. Bannerman, *Singer as Interpreter*, 42.

57. Bathori, *Debussy*, 33.

58. Bannerman, *Singer as Interpreter*, 79.

59. Bernac, *Interpretation of French Song*, 82.

60. Bernac, *Poulenc*, 44.

61. Bannerman, *Singer as Interpreter*, 92, 82, 95.

62. Bathori, *Debussy*, 65.

63. These recordings are available on a CD, *Claude Debussy: The Composer as Pianist* (Pierian Recording Society, Pierian 0001).

64. Vlado Perlemuter and Hélène Jourdan-Morhange, *Ravel according to Ravel*, trans. Frances Tanner (London: Kahn and Averill, 1988), 13.

65. Poulenc, *Diary*, III, 33.

66. Bernac, *Poulenc*, 45.

### CHAPTER 7. SECOND VIENNESE SCHOOL

1. Anton Webern, *The Path to New Music*, ed. Willi Reich, trans. Leo Black (Bryn Mawr, Pa.: Theodore Presser, 1963). The essays in this publication were taken from lectures given by Webern in a private home in Vienna in 1932 and 1933.

2. Quoted by Steuermann's sister, Salka Viertel, in Joan Allan Smith, *Schoenberg and His Circle: A Viennese Portrait* (New York: Schirmer, 1986), 97.

3. Kathryn Bailey, *The Life of Webern* (Cambridge: Cambridge University Press, 1998), 50.

4. See Bailey, *Webern*, 54–58, 116, 140–47.

5. Nicholas Chadwick, *A Survey of the Early Songs of Alban Berg* (Oxford: Bodleian Library, 1972), 81.

6. Alban Berg, *Jugenlieder*, ed. Christopher Hailey, 2 vols. (Vienna: Universal Edition, 1985); *Alban Berg: Jugenlieder*, Dietrich Fischer-Dieskau, baritone; Aribert Reimann, piano (Angel/EMI 27 0195 1).

7. Quoted in Mark DeVoto, "Berg the Composer of Songs," in *The Berg Companion*, ed. Douglas Jarman (London: Macmillan, 1989), 37.

8. See George Perle, *The Operas of Alban Berg* (Berkeley: University of California Press, 1980), 1:3. See also Chadwick, *Survey*, 49.

9. See DeVoto, "Composer of Songs," 47–52.

10. Louis Krasner and D. C. Seibert, "Some Memories of Anton Webern, the Berg Violin Concerto, and Vienna in the 1930s," *Fanfare* 11, no. 2 (1987): 335.

11. H. H. Stuckenschmidt, *Arnold Schoenberg*, trans. Edith Temple Roberts and Humphrey Searle (New York: Grove Press, 1959), 147.

12. Dika Newlin, *Schoenberg Remembered: Diaries and Recollections (1935–76)* (New York: Pendragon Press, 1980), 164.

13. See Smith, *Schoenberg and His Circle,* app. 3, 255–68, for all of the Society for Private Musical Performance programs and performers.

14. Ibid., 246.

15. Ibid., 96.

16. See Berg's article "The 'Problem of Opera'" in Willi Reich, *Alban Berg,* trans. Cornelius Cardew (New York: Harcourt, Brace and World, 1963), 63–64.

17. Edward Steuermann, *The Not Quite Innocent Bystander: Writings of Edward Steuermann,* ed. Clara Steuermann, David Porter, and Gunther Schuller (Lincoln: University of Nebraska Press, 1989), 83.

18. Lewis Foreman, "Webern and the BBC and the Berg Violin Concerto," *Tempo,* no. 178 (September 1991): 10.

19. Arnold Schoenberg, *Style and Idea: Selected Writings of Arnold Schoenberg,* ed. Leonard Stein, trans. Leo Black (Berkeley: University of California Press, 1984), 144.

20. Stuckenschmidt, *Arnold Schoenberg,* 45.

21. H. H. Stuckenschmidt, *Schoenberg: His Life, World, and Work,* trans. Humphrey Searle (London: John Calder, 1977), 117.

22. Ibid., 158, 188.

23. Arnold Schoenberg, *Arnold Schoenberg Self-Portrait: A Collection of Articles, Program Notes, and Letters by the Composer about His Own Works,* ed. Nuria Schoenberg Nono (Pacific Palisades, Calif.: Belmont Music, 1988), 14.

24. Schoenberg, *Self-Portrait,* 27.

25. Ibid., 62.

26. Schoenberg, *Style and Idea,* 146.

27. From Pierrot to Marteau: An International Conference and Concert Celebrating the Tenth Anniversary of the Arnold Schoenberg Institute (University of Southern California School of Music, 1987), 4.

28. Smith, *Schoenberg and His Circle,* 52–53.

29. Steuermann, *Innocent Bystander,* 36.

30. Ibid., 37.

31. Stuckenschmidt, *Life, World, and Work,* 214.

32. Smith, *Schoenberg and His Circle,* 100.

33. Stuckenschmidt, *Life, World, and Work,* 279.

34. Smith, *Schoenberg and His Circle,* 88.

35. Ibid.

36. Stuckenschmidt, *Life, World, and Work,* 441.

37. Milton Babbitt, conversation with author, October 13, 2002.

38. Steuermann, *Innocent Bystander,* 36–37.

39. From the preface to the *Pierrot Lunaire* score (Pacific Palisades, Calif.: Belmont Music, 1990).

40. Sharon Mabry, *Exploring Twentieth-Century Vocal Music: A Practical Guide to Innovations in Performance and Repertoire* (New York: Oxford University Press, 2002).

41. Stuckenschmidt, *Life, World, and Work,* 515.

42. Schoenberg, *Self-Portrait*, 117.

43. Perle, *Operas of Berg*, vol. 1, 203–5.

44. Schoenberg, *Self-Portrait*, 36.

45. See Schoenberg, *Style and Idea*, 346, 300.

46. Krasner and Seibert, "Memories of Webern," 340.

47. Smith, *Schoenberg and His Circle*, 112.

48. Steuermann, *Innocent Bystander*, 176.

49. Peter Heyworth, ed., *Conversations with Klemperer* (London: Victor Gollancz, 1973), 76.

50. Schoenberg, *Self-Portrait*, 117–18; see also Schoenberg, *Style and Idea*, 342.

51. Steuermann, *Innocent Bystander*, 104.

52. Schoenberg, *Self-Portrait*, 36.

## CHAPTER 8. EARLY TWENTIETH-CENTURY NATIONALISM

1. See Caryl Emerson, *The Life of Musorgsky* (Cambridge: Cambridge University Press, 1999), 15.

2. See Elizabeth Wilson, *Shostakovich: A Life Remembered* (London: Faber and Faber, 1994), 20–23.

3. Richard Taruskin, "Musorgsky" (opera entry), *Grove Music Online*, ed. Laura Macy, http://www.grovemusic.com (accessed June 20, 2003).

4. See Alexander Tumanov, *The Life and Artistry of Maria Olenina-d'Alheim*, trans. Christopher Barnes (Edmonton: University of Alberta Press, 2000).

5. Claude Debussy, *Debussy on Music*, ed. Richard Langham Smith, trans. François Lesure (Ithaca, N.Y.: Cornell University Press, 1977), 21.

6. Arbie Orenstein, *Ravel: Man and Musician* (New York: Columbia University Press, 1975), 53.

7. Tumanov, *Olenina-d'Alheim*, 94.

8. Ibid., 142.

9. I am especially grateful to Caryl Emerson for providing a recording of Olenina's 1963 master classes and to Ivan Eubanks for translating the transcript of the recording.

10. Tumanov, *Olenina-d'Alheim*, 280.

11. Eubanks, translation of master class transcript, 15.

12. Robert Kenneth Evans, "The Early Songs of Sergei Prokofiev" (Ph.D. diss., Ohio State University, 1971), 74.

13. Victor Borovsky, *Chaliapin: A Critical Biography* (London: Hamish Hamilton, 1988), 221.

14. Ibid., 10.

15. Ibid., 4.

16. Ibid., 206, n. 140.

17. Ibid., 206.

18. Feodor Chaliapin, *Man and Mask: Forty Years in the Life of a Singer*, trans. Phyllis Mégroz (London: Victor Gollancz, 1932), 184.

19. Harold C. Schonberg, *The Great Pianists* (New York: Simon and Schuster, 1987), 391.

20. Chaliapin, *Man and Mask*, 60.

21. Borovsky, *Chaliapin,* 196.

22. Ibid., 13.

23. Prokofiev, *Piano Concerto No. 3 and Other Works,* Great Recordings of the Century, Angel Records COLH 34 (33 rpm), liner notes, pp. 2, 11.

24. Schonberg, *Great Pianists,* 417.

25. Wilson, *Shostakovich,* 200.

26. Ibid., 58–59.

27. Ibid., 104–5.

28. Galina Vishnevskaya, *Galina: A Russian Story,* trans. Guy Daniels (New York: Harcourt Brace, 1984), 356.

29. This recording was first issued in the West as an LP on Monitor MC 2020.

30. The *Suite on Poems by Michelangelo,* op. 145, was written for bass Evgeny Nesterenko and issued on LP as Melodiya C10-06161-62. The Blok cycle, *Seven Songs,* op. 127, was written for Vishnevskaya, Rostropovich, Oistrakh, and pianist Moisei Vainberg; Vishnevskaya and Rostropovich later recorded it with Ulf Hoelscher and Vasso Devetzi for EMI, issued on LP as SLS 5055. Symphony No. 14, also written for Vishnevskaya and Rostropovich, was issued on LP as Melodiya M34507.

31. Vishnevskaya, *Galina,* 179.

32. Gonzalo Armero and Jorge de Persia, eds., *Manuel de Falla: His Life and Works,* trans. Tom Skipp (Madrid: Ministerio de Cultura, Ediciones Opponax, 1996), 69.

33. See Timothy Mitchell, *Flamenco Deep Song* (New Haven, Conn.: Yale University Press, 1994).

34. Armero and de Persia, *Falla,* 108.

35. Manuel de Falla, *On Music and Musicians,* trans. David Urman and J. M. Thomson (London: Marion Boyars, 1979), 105.

36. Armero and de Persia, *Falla,* 109.

37. Suzanne Rhodes Draayer, *A Singer's Guide to the Songs of Joaquín Rodrigo* (London: Scarecrow Press, 1999), 8.

38. Ibid., 23.

39. Ibid., ix.

40. Nico Castel, *A Singer's Manual of Spanish Lyric Diction* (New York: Excalibur Publishing, 1994), 137–41.

41. Draayer, *Songs of Rodrigo,* 8–11.

42. Jacqueline Cockburn and Richard Stokes, trans. and eds., *The Spanish Song Companion* (London: Victor Gollancz, 1992), 249–52.

43. See Humphrey Carpenter, *Benjamin Britten: A Biography* (London: Faber and Faber, 1992), 35.

44. Sydney Northcote, *Byrd to Britten: A Survey of English Song* (London: John Baker, 1966), 22.

45. Imogen Holst, *The Great Composers: Britten* (London: Faber and Faber, 1966), 26.

46. Harry Plunket Greene, *Interpretation in Song* (New York: Macmillan, 1912), x.

47. Carpenter, *Britten,* 101.

48. Ibid., 112.

49. Benjamin Britten, *On Receiving the First Aspen Award* (London: Faber and Faber, 1964), 11–13.

50. Holst, *Britten,* 35.
51. Alan Blyth, *Remembering Britten* (London: Hutchinson, 1981), 66.
52. Ibid., 94.
53. Ibid., 40.
54. Holst, *Britten,* 64.
55. Blyth, *Remembering Britten,* 116.
56. Ibid., 154.
57. Ibid., 138.
58. Ibid., 56.
59. Carpenter, *Britten,* 265.
60. Rosamond Strode, "Working for Benjamin Britten (II)," in *The Britten Companion,* ed. Christopher Palmer (Cambridge: Cambridge University Press, 1984), 53.
61. John Culshaw, "'Ben'–A Tribute to Benjamin Britten," in *The Britten Companion,* ed. Christopher Palmer (Cambridge: Cambridge University Press, 1984), 65.
62. Blyth, *Remembering Britten,* 13.
63. Britten, *War Requiem,* Decca OSA 1255, 33 rpm. Reissued on CD as Decca 414383.
64. Benjamin Britten, "On Writing English Opera," *Opera* 12, no. 1 (1961): 7.
65. Blyth, *Remembering Britten,* 155.
66. Anthony Gishford, ed., *Tribute to Benjamin Britten on His Fiftieth Birthday* (London: Faber and Faber, 1963), 13.
67. Benjamin Britten, "On Realizing the Continuo in Purcell's Songs," in *Henry Purcell, 1659–1695: Essays on His Music,* ed. Imogen Holst (London: Oxford University Press, 1959), 8.
68. Ibid., 13.
69. Michael Burden, e-mail message to author, September 1, 2003.
70. Charles E. Ives, *Memos,* ed. John Kirkpatrick (New York: Norton, 1972), 115.
71. Ibid., 116.
72. Ibid., 116–17.
73. Ibid., 127, 117.
74. Aaron Copland, *Copland on Music* (New York: Doubleday, 1960), 166.
75. This recording was first issued as an LP on CBS Masterworks 3211 0017. It has been reissued on CD as part of vol. 3 of *A Copland Celebration* (Sony 89329).
76. Howard Pollack, "Aaron Copland," section I, *Grove Music Online,* ed. Laura Macy, http://www.grovemusic.com (accessed July 23, 2003).
77. Barbara B. Heyman, *Samuel Barber: The Composer and His Music* (New York: Oxford University Press, 1992), 104.
78. Heyman, *Barber,* 107, 122.
79. Ibid., 287.
80. The Price/Barber studio recording of the *Hermit Songs* was reissued on LP as Odyssey 32 16 0230, also including Steber singing *Knoxville;* both of these performances have been reissued on CD as part of Sony Masterworks Heritage MHK 60899.
81. Heyman, *Barber,* 326.

## CHAPTER 9. WORKING WITH LIVING COMPOSERS

1. Phyllis Bryn-Julson, conversation with author, Ocean Grove, N.J., November 15, 2003; Benita Valente, telephone conversations with author, January 13, 28, 2004; and Paul Sperry, conversation with author, Princeton, N.J., December 8, 2003, and by telephone, January 17, 2004.
2. Cheryl Bensman, telephone conversation with author, January 3, 2004.
3. Sharon Mabry, *Exploring Twentieth-Century Vocal Music: A Practical Guide to Innovations in Performance and Repertoire* (New York: Oxford University Press, 2002).
4. Quoted in Paul Griffiths, "Writing Music That Sings, Cries, Screams and Prays," *New York Times,* October 27, 2002.
5. Steve Reich, *Tehillim* LP recording (ECM Records 1-1215), liner notes.
6. Jon Magnussen, conversation with author, Princeton, N.J., January 6, 2004.
7. Steve Reich, "About This Edition," in *Music for 18 Musicians* (London: Boosey & Hawkes, 2000).
8. Meredith Monk, remarks made at a Composers Colloquium at Princeton University, March 13, 2003.
9. Griffiths, "Writing Music."
10. Jane Manning, *New Vocal Repertory,* vol. 2 (London: Oxford University Press, 1998), 1.
11. William Duckworth, *Talking Music: Conversations with John Cage, Philip Glass, Laurie Anderson, and Five Generations of American Experimental Composers* (New York: Schirmer, 1995), 91.
12. Peter Westergaard to William Parcher, October 31, 2003. Used by permission.
13. Duckworth, *Talking Music,* 357.
14. Cori Ellison, "Downtown Divas Expand Their Horizons," *New York Times,* sec. 2, October 28, 2001.

# For Further Reading

CHAPTER 1. THE EARLY BAROQUE

## Primary Sources

Bacilly, Bénigne de. *Remarques curieuses sur l'art de bien chanter.* Paris, 1668. Translated by Austin B. Caswell as *A Commentary upon the Art of Proper Singing.* New York: Institute of Mediæval Music, 1968.

Bardi, Pietro de'. Letter to G. B. Doni. Florence, 1634. In *Source Readings in Music History: The Baroque Era,* edited by Oliver Strunk. New York: Norton, 1965.

Bernhard, Christoph. *Von der Singe-Kunst, oder Manier.* Ms., ca. 1649. In *Die Kompositionslehre Heinrich Schützens in der Fassung seines Schulers Christoph Bernhard,* edited by Joseph Maria Müller-Blattau. Kassel: Bärenreiter, 1963. Translated by Walter Hilse as "On the Art of Singing: or, Manier." *Music Forum* 3 (1973): 13–29.

Caccini, Giulio. "*Euridice*—Dedication." Florence, 1600. In *Source Readings in Music History: The Baroque Era,* edited by Oliver Strunk. New York: Norton, 1965.

———. *Le nuove musiche.* Florence, 1601. Reprint, New York: Broude Brothers, 1987. Modern edition edited by H. Wiley Hitchcock in *Recent Researches in the Music of the Baroque Era,* vol. 9. Madison, Wis.: A-R Editions, 1970. Preface translated into English in John Playford, *An Introduction to the Skill of Musick.* London, 1654. (Preface also in *Source Readings in Music History: The Baroque Era,* edited by Oliver Strunk. New York: Norton, 1965.)

Cofone, Charles J. F., ed. *Elizabeth Rogers, Hir Virginall Booke*. 1656. Reprint, New York: Dover, 1975.

Dowland, John. *Andreas Ornithoparcus His Micrologus, or Introduction: Containing the Art of Singing*. London, 1609. Excerpted in *Readings in the History of Music in Performance,* edited by Carol MacClintock. Bloomington: Indiana University Press, 1979.

Finck, Hermann. *Practica musica,* book V. Wittenberg, 1556. In *Readings in the History of Music in Performance,* edited by Carol MacClintock. Bloomington: Indiana University Press, 1979.

Maffei, Giovanni Camillo. Letter on singing. Naples, 1562. In *Readings in the History of Music in Performance,* edited by Carol MacClintock. Bloomington: Indiana University Press, 1979.

Mersenne, Marin. *Harmonie universelle, contenant la théorie et la pratique de la musique.* Paris, 1636. Excerpted in *Readings in the History of Music in Performance,* edited by Carol MacClintock. Bloomington: Indiana University Press, 1979.

Monteverdi, Claudio. *The Letters of Claudio Monteverdi.* Edited by Denis Stevens. Oxford: Clarendon Press, 1995.

Ortiz, Diego. *Tratado de glosas sobre clausulas y otros generos de puntos en la musica de violones.* Rome, 1553. Edited by Max Schneider. New York: Bärenreiter, 1967.

Peri, Jacopo. "*Euridice*–Foreword." Florence, 1601. In *Source Readings in Music History: The Baroque Era,* edited by Oliver Strunk. New York: Norton, 1965.

Playford, John. *An Introduction to the Skill of Musick.* London, 1694. 12th ed. corrected and amended by Henry Purcell. Edited by Franklin B. Zimmerman. Reprint, New York: Da Capo Press, 1972.

Praetorius, Michael. *Syntagma musicum.* Wolfenbüttel, 1619. Excerpted in *Readings in the History of Music in Performance,* edited by Carol MacClintock. Bloomington: Indiana University Press, 1979.

Simpson, Christopher. *The Division Violist.* London, 1659. Reprint, New York: Schirmer, 1955.

Tosi, Pier Francesco. *Opinioni de' cantori antichi e moderni.* Bologna, 1723. Reprint, Bologna: Forni, 1968. Translated by [John Ernst] Galliard as *Observations on the Florid Song.* 2nd ed., London, 1743. Reprint edited by Michael Pilkington. London: Stainer and Bell, 1987.

Vicentino, Nicola. *L'antica musica.* Rome, 1555. Excerpted in *Readings in the History of Music in Performance,* edited by Carol MacClintock. Bloomington: Indiana University Press, 1979.

Wilson, John, ed. *Roger North on Music.* London: Novello, 1959.

Zacconi, Lodovico. *Prattica di musica utile et necessaria si al compositore. . . si anco al cantore.* Venice, 1596. Excerpted in *Readings in the History of Music in Performance,* edited by Carol MacClintock. Bloomington: Indiana University Press, 1979.

## General

Brown, Howard Mayer. "Editing." *The New Grove Dictionary of Music and Musicians,* edited by Stanley Sadie, vol. 5, 846–48. London: Macmillan, 1980.

———. "Performing Practice." *The New Grove Dictionary of Music and Musicians,* edited by Stanley Sadie, vol. 14, 370–93. London: Macmillan, 1980.

Brown, Howard Mayer, and Stanley Sadie, eds. *Performance Practice: Music after 1600.* New York: Norton, 1989.

Carter, Stewart, ed. *A Performer's Guide to Seventeenth-Century Music.* New York: Schirmer, 1997.

Charles, Sydney Robinson. "Editions, Historical." *The New Grove Dictionary of Music and Musicians,* edited by Stanley Sadie, vol. 5, 848–69. London: Macmillan, 1980.

Cyr, Mary. *Performing Baroque Music.* Portland, Ore.: Amadeus Press, 1992.

Donington, Robert. *Baroque Music: Style and Performance.* London: Faber Music, 1982.

———. *The Interpretation of Early Music.* New version. London: Faber, 1974.

———. "Ornaments." *The New Grove Dictionary of Music and Musicians,* edited by Stanley Sadie, vol. 13, 827–67. London: Macmillan, 1980.

———. *A Performer's Guide to Baroque Music.* New York: Scribner, 1973.

Fuller, David. "Performer as Composer." In *Performance Practice: Music after 1600,* edited by Howard Mayer Brown and Stanley Sadie. New York: Norton, 1989.

Harnoncourt, Nikolaus. *Der musikalische Dialog: Gedanken zu Monteverdi, Bach und Mozart.* Salzburg: Residenz, 1984. Translated by Mary O'Neill as *The Musical Dialogue: Thoughts on Monteverdi, Bach and Mozart.* Portland, Ore.: Amadeus Press, 1989.

Harris, Ellen T. "Voices." In *Performance Practice: Music after 1600,* edited by Howard Mayer Brown and Stanley Sadie. New York: Norton, 1989.

MacClintock, Carol, ed. *Readings in the History of Music in Performance.* Bloomington: Indiana University Press, 1979.

Neumann, Frederick. *Essays on Performance Practice.* Ann Arbor, Mich.: UMI Press, 1982.

Rangel-Ribeiro, Victor. *Baroque Music: A Practical Guide for the Performer.* New York: Schirmer, 1981.

Rogers, Nigel. "Voices." In *Companion to Baroque Music,* edited by Julie Anne Sadie. London: J. M. Dent and Sons, 1990.

Sadie, Julie Anne, ed. *Companion to Baroque Music.* London: J. M. Dent and Sons, 1990.

Sanford, Sally. "Solo Singing 1." In *A Performer's Guide to Seventeenth-Century Music,* edited by Stewart Carter. New York: Schirmer, 1997.

Sherman, Bernard D., ed. *Inside Early Music: Conversations with Performers.* New York: Oxford University Press, 1997.

Stevens, Denis. "Performance Practice in Baroque Vocal Music." *College Music Symposium* 18 (1978): 9–19.

Strunk, Oliver, ed. *Source Readings in Music History.* Vol. 3, *The Baroque Era.* New York: Norton, 1965.

Wolff, Hellmuth Christian, ed. *Original Vocal Improvisations from the 16th–18th Centuries.* Anthology of Music 41 (Cologne: A. Volk, 1972), 95–100.

## Accompaniment Instruments

Buetens, Stanley. "Theorbo Accompaniments of Early Seventeenth-Century Italian Monody." *Journal of the Lute Society of America* 6 (1973): 37–45.

Dart, Thurston, and John Morehen. "Tablature." *The New Grove Dictionary of Music and Musicians,* edited by Stanley Sadie, vol. 18, 506–15. London: Macmillan, 1980.

Lindley, Mark. *Lutes, Viols and Temperaments.* Cambridge: Cambridge University Press, 1984.

North, Nigel. *Continuo Playing on the Lute, Archlute and Theorbo.* Bloomington: Indiana University Press, 1987.

Poulton, Diana. "Lute." *The New Grove Dictionary of Music and Musicians,* edited by Stanley Sadie, vol. 11, 342–65. London: Macmillan, 1980.

Spencer, Robert. "Chitarrone, Theorbo and Archlute." *Early Music* 4 (1976): 409–22.

### Figured Bass

Arnold, Franck Thomas. *The Art of Accompaniment from a Thorough-Bass as Practiced in the Seventeenth and Eighteenth Centuries.* London: Oxford University Press, 1931. Reprint, New York: Dover, 1965.

Borgir, Tharald. *The Performance of the Basso Continuo in Italian Baroque Music.* Studies in Musicology 90. Ann Arbor, Mich.: UMI Research Press, 1987.

Buelow, George J. *Thorough-Bass Accompaniment According to Johann David Heinichen.* Rev. ed. Studies in Musicology 86, 219–36. Ann Arbor, Mich.: UMI Research Press, ca. 1986.

Hill, John Walter. "Realized Continuo Accompaniments from Florence c. 1600." *Early Music* 11, no. 2 (April 1983): 194–208.

Holman, Peter. "Continuo Realization in a Playford Songbook." *Early Music* 6 (1978): 268–69.

Mangsen, Sandra. "The Unfigured Bass and the Continuo Player: More Evidence from France." *Early Keyboard Journal* 3 (1984–85): 5–12.

O'Dette, Paul, and Jack Ashworth. "Basso Continuo." In *A Performer's Guide to Seventeenth-Century Music,* edited by Stewart Carter. New York: Schirmer, 1997.

Williams, Peter. *Figured Bass Accompaniment.* Edinburgh: Edinburgh University Press, 1970.

### Pitch

Ellis, Alexander John. "On the History of Musical Pitch." *Journal of the [Royal] Society of the Arts* 28 (1880): 293–336, 400–403; 29 (1881): 109–12.

Haynes, Bruce. *A History of Performing Pitch: The Story of "A."* Oxford: Scarecrow Press, 2002.

Karp, Cary. "Pitch." In *Performance Practice: Music after 1600,* edited by Howard Mayer Brown and Stanley Sadie. New York: Norton, 1989.

Lindley, Mark. "Tuning and Intonation." In *Performance Practice: Music after 1600,* edited by Howard Mayer Brown and Stanley Sadie. New York: Norton, 1989.

Mendel, Arthur. "Pitch in the Sixteenth and Early Seventeenth Centuries." *Musical Quarterly* 34 (1948): 28–45, 199–221, 336–57, 575–93.

———. "Pitch in Western Music since 1500: A Re-Examination." *Acta Musicologica* 50 (1978): 1–93, 328.

Meyers, Herbert W. "Praetorius's Pitch." *Early Music* 12, no. 3 (August 1984): 369–71.

———. "Pitch and Transposition." In *A Performer's Guide to Seventeenth-Century Music,* edited by Stewart Carter. New York: Schirmer, 1997.

Pirrotta, Antonino. "Temperaments and Tendencies in the Florentine Camerata." Translated by Nigel Fortune. *Musical Quarterly* 40, no. 2 (1954): 169–89.

Rhodes, J. J. K., and W. R. Thomas. "Pitch." *The New Grove Dictionary of Music and Musicians,* edited by Stanley Sadie, vol. 14, 779–86. London: Macmillan, 1980.

## Vibrato

Donington, Robert. "Vibrato." *The New Grove Dictionary of Music and Musicians,* edited by Stanley Sadie, vol. 19, 679–98. London: Macmillan, 1980.

Gable, Frederick K. "Some Observations concerning Baroque and Modern Vibrato." *Performance Practice Review* 5 (1992): 90–102.

Moens-Haenen, Greta. *Das Vibrato in der Musik des Barock: Ein Handbuch zur Aufführungspraxis für Vokalisten und Instrumentalisten.* Graz: Akademische Druck- und Verlagsanstalt, 1988.

———. "Vibrato." *The New Grove Dictionary of Opera,* edited by Stanley Sadie, 982–83. London: Macmillan, 1992.

Neumann, Frederick. "Authenticity and the Vocal Vibrato." In *New Essays on Performance Practice.* London: Research Press, 1989.

## Historical Pronunciation

Copeman, Harold. *Singing in Latin.* Oxford: by the author, 1990.

Dobson, Eric J. *English Pronunciation, 1500–1700.* 2 vols. Oxford: Clarendon Press, 1968.

McGee, Timothy J., ed. *Singing Early Music: The Pronunciation of European Languages in the Late Middle Ages and Renaissance.* Bloomington: Indiana University Press, 1996.

Termini, Olga. "The Role of Diction and Gesture in Italian Baroque Opera." *Performance Practice Review* 6 (1993): 146–57.

## Italian: *Dispositione* and Ornamentation

Carter, Stewart. "Francesco Rognoni's *Selva de varii passaggi* (1620): Fresh Details concerning Early Baroque Ornamentation." *Performance Practice Review* 2 (1989): 5–33.

Dickey, Bruce. "Ornamentation in Early-Seventeenth-Century Italian Music." In *A Performer's Guide to Seventeenth-Century Music,* edited by Stewart Carter. New York: Schirmer, 1997.

Erig, Richard, ed. *Italienische Diminutionen–Italian Diminutions: The Pieces with More than One Diminution from 1553 to 1638.* Zürich: Amadeus, 1979.

Galliver, David. "'*Cantare con la gorga*': Coloratura Technique of the Renaissance Singer." *Studies in Music* 7 (1973): 10–18.

Greenlee, Robert. "*Dispositione di voce:* Passage to Florid Singing." *Early Music* 15 (1987): 47–55.

Hitchcock, H. Wiley. "Caccini's 'Other' *Nuove musiche.*" *Journal of the American Musicological Society* 27 (1974): 438–60.

———. "Vocal Ornamentation in Caccini's *Nuove musiche.*" *Musical Quarterly* 56 (1970): 389–404.

MacClintock, Carol. "Caccini's Trillo: A Re-examination." *National Association of the Teachers of Singing Bulletin,* October 1976, 38–41.

Sanders, Donald C. "Vocal Ornaments in Durante's *Arie devote* (1609)." *Performance Practice Review* 6 (1993): 60–76.

Sherman, Joy, and Lawrence R. Brown. "Singing Passaggi: Modern Application of a Centuries-Old Technique." *Choral Journal* (1995): 27–36.

Uberti, Mauro. "Vocal Technique in Italy in the Second Half of the Sixteenth Century." Translated by Mark Lindley. *Early Music* 9 (1981): 486–95.

### Italian: General

Aldrich, Putnam. *Rhythm in Seventeenth-Century Italian Monody, with an Anthology of Songs and Dances.* London: J. M. Dent and Sons, 1966.

Baird, Julianne. "Solo Singing 2: The Bel Canto Style." In *A Performer's Guide to Seventeenth-Century Music,* edited by Stewart Carter. New York: Schirmer, 1997.

Celletti, Rodolfo. *A History of Bel Canto.* Translated by Frederick Fuller. Oxford: Clarendon Press, 1991.

Palisca, Claude V. *The Florentine Camerata.* New Haven, Conn.: Yale University Press, 1989.

Rosselli, John. *Singers of Italian Opera.* Cambridge: Cambridge University Press, 1992.

Sawkins, Lionel. "For and Against the Order of Nature: Who Sang the Soprano?" *Early Music* 15 (1987): 315–24.

Wistreich, Richard. "'La voce e grata assai, ma. . .' Monteverdi on Singing." *Early Music* 22 (1994): 9–15.

### English

Baldwin, Olive, and Thelma Wilson. "Purcell's Sopranos." *Musical Times* 123 (1982): 602–9.

Burden, Michael, ed. *Performing the Music of Henry Purcell.* Oxford: Clarendon Press, 1996.

———, ed. *The Purcell Companion.* London: Faber and Faber, 1995.

Butler, Gregory. "Music and Rhetoric in Early Seventeenth-Century English Sources." *Musical Quarterly* 66, no. 1 (1980): 53–64.

Duckles, Vincent. "English Song and the Challenge of Italian Monody." In *Words to Music: Papers on English Seventeenth-Century Song.* Los Angeles: William Andrews Clark Memorial Library, University of California, 1967.

———. "Florid Embellishment in English Song of the Late Sixteenth and Early Seventeenth Centuries." *Annales Musicologiques* 5 (1957): 332–45.

Giles, Peter. *The Counter Tenor.* London: Frederick Muller, 1982.

———. *The History and Technique of the Counter-Tenor.* Aldershot, U.K.: Scolar Press, 1994.

Jones, Edward Huws. *The Performance of English Song, 1610–1670.* New York: Garland Press, 1989.

Parrott, Andrew. "Performing Purcell." In *The Purcell Companion,* edited by Michael Burden. London: Faber and Faber, 1995.

Rose, Gloria. "A New Purcell Source." *Journal of the American Musicological Society* 25 (1972): 230–34.

Spink, Ian. *English Song: Dowland to Purcell.* New York: Scribner, 1974.

———. "Playford's Directions for Singing after the Italian Manner." *Monthly Musical Record* 89 (1959):130–35.

Toft, Robert. *Tune Thy Musicke to Thy Hart: The Art of Eloquent Singing in England, 1597–1622.* Toronto: University of Toronto Press, 1993.

Wells, Robin H. "The Ladder of Love: Verbal and Musical Rhetoric in the Elizabethan Lute-Song." *Early Music* 12 (1984): 173–89.

### French

Anthony, James R. *French Baroque Music: From Beaujoyeulx to Rameau.* Rev. and expanded ed. Portland, Ore.: Amadeus Press, 1997.

Fuller, David. "Notes inégales." *The New Grove Dictionary of Music and Musicians,* edited by Stanley Sadie, vol. 13, 420–27. London: Macmillan, 1980.

Gérold, Théodore. *L'art du chant en France au XVIIe siècle.* Strasbourg: Commission des publications de la Faculté des lettres, 1921.

Hefling, Stephen E. *Rhythmic Alteration in Seventeenth- and Eighteenth-Century Music: Notes Inégales and Overdotting.* New York: Schirmer, 1993.

Mather, Betty Bang, with Dean M. Karns. *Dance Rhythms of the French Baroque: A Handbook for Performance.* Bloomington: Indiana University Press, 1988.

Rosow, Lois. "French Baroque Recitative as an Expression of Tragic Declamation." *Early Music* 11 (1983): 468–79.

Sanford, Sally. "A Comparison of French and Italian Singing in the Seventeenth Century." *Journal of the Society for Seventeenth-Century Music* 1 (1995), http://sscm-jscm.press.uiuc.edu/jscm/v1/no1/sanford.html.

Seares, Margaret. "Mersenne on Vocal Diminutions." *Performance Practice Review* 6 (1993): 141–45.

Zaslaw, Neal. "The Enigma of the Haute-Contre." *Musical Times* 115, no. 11 (1974): 939–41.

#### CHAPTER 2. THE LATE BAROQUE

### Primary Sources

Agricola, Johann Friedrich. *Anleitung zur Singkunst.* A translation [with additions] of Pier Francesco Tosi's *Opinioni de' cantori antichi e moderni.* Berlin, 1757. Translated by Julianne Baird as *Introduction to the Art of Singing.* Cambridge: Cambridge University Press, 1995.

Bach, Carl Philipp Emanuel. *Versuch über die wahre Art das Clavier zu spielen.* Berlin, 1753; part 2, 1762. Translated by W. J. Mitchell as *Essay on the True Art of Playing Keyboard Instruments.* New York: Norton, 1949.

Bérard, Jean-Baptiste. *L'art du chant.* Paris, 1755. 2nd ed., 1756. Translated with commentary by Sydney Murray. Milwaukee: Pro Musica Press, 1969.

Montéclair, Michel Pignolet de. *Principes de musique.* Translated in *Cantatas for One and Two Voices,* edited by James R Anthony and Diran Akmajian. Madison, Wis.: A-R Editions, 1978.

Mozart, Leopold. *Versuch einer gründlichen Violinschule.* Augsburg, 1756. Translated by Editha Knocker as *A Treatise on the Fundamental Principles of Violin Playing.* 2nd ed. Oxford: Oxford University Press, 1985.

Quantz, Johann. *Versuch einer Anweisung die Flöte traversiere zu spielen.* Berlin, 1752. Translated by Edward R. Reilly as *On Playing the Flute.* 2nd ed. New York: Schirmer, 1985.

## General

Glover, Cedric Howard. *Dr. Charles Burney's Continental Travels.* London: Blackie and Sons, 1927.

Harnoncourt, Nikolaus. *Baroque Music Today: Music as Speech.* Translated by Mary O'Neill. Portland, Ore.: Amadeus Press, 1988.

Hefling, Stephen E. *Rhythmic Alteration in Seventeenth- and Eighteenth-Century Music: Notes Inégales and Overdotting.* New York: Schirmer, 1993.

Pleasants, Henry. *The Great Singers.* New York: Simon and Schuster, 1966.

Yorke-Long, Alan. *Music at Court: Four Eighteenth-Century Studies.* London: Weidenfeld and Nicolson, 1954.

## Ornamentation

Baird, Julianne. "An 18th-Century Controversy about the Trill." *Early Music* 15 (1987): 36–44.

Brown, Howard Mayer. "Embellishing Eighteenth-Century Arias: On Cadenzas." In *Opera and Vivaldi,* edited by Michael Collins and Elise K. Kirk. Austin: University of Texas Press, 1984.

Buelow, George J. "A Lesson in Operatic Performance Practice by Madame Faustina Bordoni." In *A Musical Offering: Essays in Honor of Martin Bernstein,* edited by Edward H. Clinkscale and Claire Brook. New York: Pendragon Press, 1977.

Dean, Winton. "Vocal Embellishment in a Handel Aria." In *Essays on Opera.* Oxford: Clarendon Press, 1990.

———, ed. *G. F. Handel: Three Ornamented Arias.* Oxford: Oxford University Press, 1976.

Haböck, Franz. *Die Gesangskunst der Kastraten.* Vienna: Universal, 1923.

———. *Die Kastraten und ihre Gesangskunst.* Stuttgart: Deutsche Verlags-Anstalt, 1927.

Hall, James S., and Martin V. Hall. "Handel's Graces." *Handel Jahrbuch* 3 (1957): 25–43.

Neumann, Frederick. *Ornamentation in Baroque and Post-Baroque Music, with Special Emphasis on J. S. Bach.* Princeton, N.J.: Princeton University Press, 1978.

## Handel

Burrows, Donald. *Handel: Messiah.* Cambridge Music Handbooks. Cambridge: Cambridge University Press, 1991.

Larsen, Jens Peter. *Handel's Messiah: Origins, Composition, Sources.* Westport, Conn.: Greenwood Press, 1990.

Larue, C. Steven. *Handel and His Singers: The Creation of the Royal Academy Operas, 1720–1728.* Oxford: Clarendon Press, 1995.

Rogers, Patrick. *Continuo Realization in Handel's Vocal Music.* Ann Arbor, Mich.: UMI Research Press, 1989.

## Bach

Butt, John. *Bach: Mass in B Minor*. Cambridge Music Handbooks. Cambridge: Cambridge University Press, 1991.

————. *Bach Interpretation: Articulation Marks in Primary Sources of J. S. Bach*. Cambridge: Cambridge University Press, 1990.

————. *Music Education and the Art of Performance in the German Baroque*. Cambridge: Cambridge University Press, 1994.

————, ed. *The Sacred Choral Music of J. S. Bach: A Handbook*. Brewster, Mass.: Paraclete Press, 1997.

Dreyfus, Laurence. *Bach's Continuo Group: Players and Practices in His Vocal Works*. Cambridge, Mass.: Harvard University Press, 1987.

Little, Meredith, and Natalie Jenne. *Dance and the Music of J. S. Bach*. Bloomington: Indiana University Press, 1991.

Marshall, Robert L. *The Music of Johann Sebastian Bach*. New York: Schirmer, 1989.

Mendel, Arthur. "On the Pitches in Use in Bach's Time." *Musical Quarterly* 41 (1953): 332–54; 466–80.

Parrott, Andrew. *The Essential Bach Choir*. Woodbridge, Suffolk: Boydell Press, 2000.

Sherman, Bernard D., ed. "Triple Counterpoint: Jeffrey Thomas, Philippe Herreweghe, and John Butt on Singing Bach." In *Inside Early Music*. New York: Oxford University Press, 1997.

Steinitz, Paul. *Performing Bach's Vocal Music*. Croydon, U.K.: Addington Press, 1980.

## French

Cyr, Mary. "Declamation and Expressive Singing in Recitative." In *Opera and Vivaldi*, edited by Michael Collins and Elise K. Kirk. Austin: University of Texas Press, 1984.

————. "On Performing Eighteenth-Century Haute-Contre Roles." *Musical Times* 118 (1977): 291–95.

————. "Performing Rameau's Cantatas." *Early Music* 11 (1983): 480–88.

Rosow, Lois. "French Baroque Recitative as an Expression of Tragic Declamation." *Early Music* 11 (1983): 468–79.

Sawkins, Lionel. "*Doucement* and *légèrement:* Tempo in French Baroque Music." *Early Music* 21 (1993): 365–74.

Tunley, David. *The Eighteenth-Century French Cantata*. Oxford: Clarendon Press, 1997.

### CHAPTER 3. THE CLASSICAL ERA

## Primary Sources

Anderson, Emily, ed. *The Letters of Mozart and His Family*. London: Macmillan, 1985.

Burney, Charles. *The Present State of Music in France and Italy*. Facsimile of the 1773 London ed. New York: Broude Brothers, 1969.

Corri, Domenico. *The Singer's Preceptor*. London, 1810. In *The Porpora Tradition*, edited by Edward Foreman. New York: Pro Musica Press, 1968.

Hiller, Johann Adam. *Anweisung zum musikalisch-zierlichen Gesange.* Leipzig, 1780. Translated and edited by Suzanne J. Beicken as *Treatise on Vocal Performance and Ornamentation.* Cambridge: Cambridge University Press, 2001.

Mancini, Giambattista. *Riflessioni pratiche sul canto figurato.* Vienna, 1774, 1777. Translated by Edward Foreman as *Practical Reflections of Figured Singing.* Champaign, Ill.: Pro Musica Press, 1967.

Türk, Daniel Gottlob. *Klavierschule.* Leipzig, 1798. Translated and edited by Raymond H. Haggh as *School of Clavier Playing.* Lincoln: University of Nebraska Press, 1982.

## General

Bilson, Malcolm. "The Viennese Fortepiano of the Late Eighteenth Century." *Early Music* 8 (1980): 158–62.

Brown, Howard Mayer, and Stanley Sadie, eds. *Performance Practice: Music after 1600.* [See Part Two: The Classical Era.] New York: Norton, 1989.

Heyer, Anna Harriet. *Historical Sets, Collected Editions, and Monuments of Music: A Guide to Their Contents.* 3rd ed. Chicago: American Library Association, 1980.

Hill, George R., and Norris L. Stephens. *Collected Editions, Historical Series and Sets, and Monuments of Music: A Bibliography.* Berkeley, Calif.: Fallen Leaf Press, 1997.

Krummel, D. W., and Stanley Sadie, eds. *Music Printing and Publishing.* New York: Norton, 1990.

Rosen, Charles. *The Classical Style: Haydn, Mozart, Beethoven.* New York: Norton, 1972.

Rosenblum, Sandra P. *Performance Practices in Classic Piano Music: Their Principles and Applications.* Bloomington: Indiana University Press, 1988.

Sherman, Bernard D., ed. *Inside Early Music.* New York: Oxford University Press, 1997.

Stowell, Robin. *Violin Technique and Performance Practice in the Late Eighteenth and Early Nineteenth Centuries.* Cambridge: Cambridge University Press, 1985.

## Tempo and Rhythm

Allanbrook, Wye Jamison. *Rhythmic Gesture in Mozart.* Chicago: University of Chicago Press, 1983.

Brown, Clive. "Historical Performance, Metronome Marks and Tempo in Beethoven's Symphonies." *Early Music* 19 (1991): 247–58.

Malloch, William. "Carl Czerny's Metronome Marks for Haydn and Mozart Symphonies." *Early Music* 16 (1988): 72–82.

## Ornamentation

Badura-Skoda, Eva. "Improvisation: Western Classical." *The New Grove Dictionary of Music and Musicians,* edited by Stanley Sadie, vol. 9, 43–48. London: Macmillan, 1980.

Crutchfield, Will. "The Prosodic Appoggiatura in the Music of Mozart and His Contemporaries." *Journal of the American Musicological Society* 42 (1989): 229–74.

Haas, Robert. *Aufführungspraxis der Musik: Handbuch der Musikwissenschaft.* Wildpark-Potsdam: Akademische Verlagsgesellschaft Athenaion, 1931.

Levin, Robert. "Improvised Embellishments in Mozart's Keyboard Music." *Early Music* 20 (1992): 221–33.

———. Review of Frederick Neumann's *Ornamentation and Improvisation in Mozart* in *Journal of the American Musicological Society* 41 (1988): 355–68.

Neumann, Frederick. *Ornamentation and Improvisation in Mozart*. Princeton, N.J.: Princeton University Press, 1986.

Smiles, Joan E. "Directions for Improvised Ornamentation in Italian Method Books of the Late Eighteenth Century." *Journal of the American Musicological Society* 31 (1978): 495–509.

———. "Improvised Ornamentation in Late Eighteenth-Century Music: An Examination of Contemporary Evidence." Ph.D. diss., Stanford University, 1975.

Spitzer, John. "Improvised Ornamentation in a Handel Aria with Obbligato Wind Accompaniment." *Early Music* 16 (1988): 514–22.

## Haydn

Brown, A. Peter. *Performing Haydn's "The Creation."* Bloomington: Indiana University Press, 1986.

Landon, H. C. Robbins. *Haydn: Chronicle and Works.* 5 vols. Bloomington: Indiana University Press, 1976–80.

Temperley, Nicholas. *Haydn: The Creation.* Cambridge Music Handbooks. Cambridge: Cambridge University Press, 1991.

## Mozart

Badura-Skoda, Paul and Eva. *Interpreting Mozart on the Keyboard.* Translated by Leo Black. New York: St. Martin's Press, 1962.

Bauman, Thomas. "Mozart's Belmonte." *Early Music* 19 (1991): 557–64.

Bilson, Malcolm. "Interpreting Mozart." *Early Music* 12 (1984): 519–22.

Campana, Alessandra. "Mozart's Italian Buffo Singers." *Early Music* 19 (1991): 580–84.

Eisen, Cliff. "The Old and New Mozart Editions." *Early Music* 19 (1991): 513–32.

Gidwitz, Patricia Lewy. "'Ich bin die erste Sängerin': Vocal Profiles of Two Mozart Sopranos." *Early Music* 19 (1991): 565–79.

Söderström, Elisabeth. "A Life of Mozart Singing." *Early Music* 20 (1992): 139–41.

Todd, R. Larry, and Peter Williams, eds. *Perspectives on Mozart Performance.* Cambridge: Cambridge University Press, 1991.

## Beethoven

Cooper, Barry. *Beethoven's Folksong Settings: Chronology, Sources, Style.* Oxford: Clarendon Press, 1994.

———, ed. *The Beethoven Compendium: A Guide to Beethoven's Life and Music.* London: Thames and Hudson, 1991.

Forbes, Elliot, ed. *Thayer's Life of Beethoven.* Princeton, N.J.: Princeton University Press, 1967.

Stowell, Robin, ed. *Performing Beethoven.* Cambridge: Cambridge University Press, 1994.

CHAPTER 4. ITALIAN BEL CANTO

## Primary Sources

Damoreau, Laure-Cinthie. *Classic Bel Canto Technique.* Translated and introduced by Victor Rangel-Ribeiro. New York: Dover, 1997.

García, Manuel. *Hints on Singing.* New York: Edward Schuberth, 1894.

————. *Traité complet de l'art du chant.* Paris, 1847, facs. Geneva, 1985. Translated by Donald V. Paschke as *A Complete Treatise on the Art of Singing: Part Two,* New York: Da Capo Press, 1975, and *A Complete Treatise on the Art of Singing: Part One,* New York: Da Capo Press, 1984.

Nathan, Isaac. *Musurgia Vocalis: An Essay on the History and Theory of Music, and on the Qualities, Capabilities, and Management of the Human Voice.* London, 1836. In *The Porpora Tradition,* edited by Edward Foreman. New York: Pro Musica Press, 1968.

Vaccai, Nicola. *Practical Method of Italian Singing.* London, 1834. Reprint, New York: Schirmer, 1975.

## Performance Practice

Brown, Clive. *Classical and Romantic Performing Practice, 1750–1900.* Oxford: Oxford University Press, 1999.

Crutchfield, Will. "Voices." In *Performance Practice: Music after 1600,* edited by Howard Mayer Brown and Stanley Sadie, 424–58. New York: Norton, 1989.

Toft, Robert. "The Expressive Pause: Punctuation, Rests and Breathing in England, 1770–1850." *Performance Practice Review* 7 (1994): 199–232.

————. *Heart to Heart: Expressive Singing in England, 1780–1830.* Oxford: Oxford University Press, 2000.

## General

Bushnell, Howard. *Maria Malibran: A Biography of the Singer.* University Park: Pennsylvania State University Press, 1979.

Celletti, Rodolfo. *A History of Bel Canto.* Translated by Frederick Fuller. Oxford: Clarendon Press, 1991.

Duey, Philip A. *Bel Canto in Its Golden Age: A Study of Its Teaching Concepts.* New York: Kings Crown Press, 1951.

Franca, Ida. *Manual of Bel Canto.* New York: Coward-McCann, 1959.

Manén, Lucie. *Bel Canto: The Teaching of the Classical Italian Song-Schools, Its Decline and Restoration.* Oxford: Oxford University Press, 1987.

Pleasants, Henry. *The Great Singers.* New York: Simon and Schuster, 1966.

Rosen, Charles. *The Romantic Generation.* Cambridge, Mass.: Harvard University Press, 1995.

Rosselli, John. *The Life of Bellini.* Cambridge: Cambridge University Press, 1996.

————. *The Opera Industry in Italy from Cimarosa to Verdi.* Cambridge: Cambridge University Press, 1984.

————. *Singers of Italian Opera.* Cambridge: Cambridge University Press, 1992.

## Ornamentation

Caswell, Austin. "Mme Cinti-Damoreau and the Embellishment of Italian Opera in Paris, 1820–1845." *Journal of the American Musicological Society* 28 (1975): 459–92.

———. "Vocal Embellishment in Rossini's Paris Operas: French Style or Italian?" *Bollettino del Centro Rossiniano di Studi* 1–2 (1975): 5–21.

———, ed., "Embellished Opera Arias." *Recent Researches in the Music of the Nineteenth and Early Twentieth Centuries.* Vols. 7 and 8. Madison, Wis.: A-R Editions, 1989.

Crutchfield, Will. "Vocal Ornamentation in Verdi: The Phonographic Evidence." *19th-Century Music* 7 (1983–84): 3–54.

### CHAPTER 5. GERMAN LIEDER

## Primary Sources

Deutsch, Otto Erich, ed. *Schubert: Memoirs by His Friends.* London: Adam and Charles Black, 1958.

Ellis, William Ashton, ed. and trans. *Richard Wagner's Prose Works.* London, 1895. Reprint, New York: Broude Brothers, 1966.

Holland, Henry Scott, and W. S. Rockstro. *Jenny Lind the Artist, 1820–1851: A Memoir of Madame Jenny Lind Goldschmidt, Her Art-Life and Dramatic Career.* New York: Charles Scribner, 1893.

Lehmann, Lilli. *How to Sing.* Translated by Richard Aldrich. New York: Macmillan, 1902.

Nauhaus, Gerd, ed. *The Marriage Diaries of Robert and Clara Schumann.* Translated by Peter Ostwald. Boston: Northeastern University Press, 1993.

Pleasants, Henry, ed. *The Music Criticism of Hugo Wolf.* New York: Holmes and Meyer, 1979.

Schumann, Robert. *On Music and Musicians.* Edited by Konrad Wolf. Translated by Paul Rosenfeld. New York: Pantheon, 1946.

## Performance Practice

Beechey, Gwilym. "Rhythmic Interpretation: Mozart, Beethoven, Schubert and Schumann." *Music Review* 33 (1972): 233–48.

Brown, Clive. *Classical and Romantic Performing Practice: 1750–1900.* Oxford: Oxford University Press, 1999.

Dürr, Walter. "Schubert and Johann Michael Vogl: A Reappraisal." *19th-Century Music* 3 (1979–80): 126–40.

Kravitt, Edward F. "Tempo as an Expressive Element in the Late Romantic Lied." *Musical Quarterly* (1973): 497–518.

Montgomery, David. "Franz Schubert's Music in Performance: A Brief History of People, Events and Issues." In *The Cambridge Companion to Schubert,* edited by Christopher Gibbs. Cambridge: Cambridge University Press, 1997.

———. *Franz Schubert's Music in Performance: Compositional Ideals, Notational Intent, Historical Realities, Pedagogical Foundations.* Hillsdale, N.Y.: Pendragon Press, 2003.

———. *Historical Information for Musicians: Sourcebooks for the Style of Performance Prac-*

*tices in European Classical Music.* Vol. 1, *Musical Tutors, Methods and Related Sources: c. 1650–1995.* Huntingdon, U.K.: Kings Music, 1997.

———. "Modern Schubert Interpretation in the Light of the Pedagogical Sources of His Day." *Early Music* 25 (1997): 101–18.

Philip, Robert. *Early Recordings and Musical Style: Changing Taste in Instrumental Performance, 1900–1950.* Cambridge: Cambridge University Press, 1992.

Schenkman, Walter. "Beyond the Limits of Urtext Authority: A Contemporary Record of Early Nineteenth-Century Performance Practice." *College Music Symposium* 23 (1983): 145–63.

Schroeder, David. "Schubert the Singer." *Music Review* 49 (1988): 254–66.

Shawe-Taylor, Desmond. "Schubert as Written and Performed." *Musical Times* 104 (1963): 626–28.

Van Tassel, Eric. "'Something Utterly New': Listening to Schubert Lieder—1. Vogl and the Declamatory Style." *Early Music* 25 (1997): 703–14.

Walker, Ernest. "The Appoggiatura." *Music and Letters* 5 (1924): 121–44.

Winter, Robert. "Keyboards." In *Performance Practice: Music after 1600,* edited by Howard Mayer Brown and Stanley Sadie. New York: Norton, 1989.

## General

Bell, Craig. *The Songs of Schubert.* Lowestoft, U.K.: Alston Books, 1964.

Daverio, John. *Crossing Paths: Schubert, Schumann, and Brahms.* New York: Oxford University Press, 2002.

———. *Robert Schumann: Herald of a "New Poetic Age."* New York: Oxford University Press, 1997.

Ferris, David. *Schumann's Eichendorff "Liederkreis" and the Genre of the Romantic Cycle.* New York: Oxford University Press, 2000.

Fischer-Dieskau, Dietrich. *Robert Schumann: Words and Music–The Vocal Compositions.* Translated by Reinhard G. Pauly. Portland, Ore.: Amadeus Press, 1981.

———. *Schubert's Songs: A Biographical Study.* New York: Limelight Editions, 1984.

Gorrell, Lorraine. *The Nineteenth-Century Lied.* Portland, Ore.: Amadeus Press, 1993.

Kravitt, Edward F. *The Lied: Mirror of Late Romanticism.* New Haven, Conn.: Yale University Press, 1996.

———. "The Lied in 19th-Century Concert Life." *Journal of the American Musicological Society* 18 (1965): 207–18.

Miller, Richard. *Singing Schumann: An Interpretive Guide for Performers.* New York: Oxford University Press, 1999.

Petersen, Barbara. *Ton und Wort: The Lieder of Richard Strauss.* Ann Arbor, Mich.: UMI Research Press, 1980.

Porter, Ernest Graham. *Schubert's Song Technique.* London: D. Dobson, 1961.

Rosen, Charles. *The Romantic Generation.* Cambridge, Mass.: Harvard University Press, 1995.

Sams, Eric. *The Songs of Hugo Wolf.* Oxford: Oxford University Press, 1962.

———. *The Songs of Johannes Brahms.* New Haven, Conn.: Yale University Press, 2000.

Stein, Deborah, and Robert Spillmann. *Poetry into Song: Performance and Analysis of Lieder.* Oxford: Oxford University Press, 1996.

Swafford, Jan. *Johannes Brahms: A Biography.* New York: Knopf, 1997.

Youens, Susan. *Hugo Wolf: The Vocal Music.* Princeton, N.J.: Princeton University Press, 1992.

———. *Hugo Wolf and His Mörike Songs.* Cambridge: Cambridge University Press, 2000.

———. *Retracing a Winter's Journey: Schubert's "Winterreise."* Ithaca, N.Y.: Cornell University Press, 1991.

———. *Schubert: Die schöne Müllerin.* Cambridge Music Handbooks. Cambridge: Cambridge University Press, 1992.

———. *Schubert's Late Lieder: Beyond the Song-Cycles.* Cambridge: Cambridge University Press, 2002.

## CHAPTER 6. FRENCH MÉLODIES

### Primary Sources

Bannerman, Betty, ed. and trans. *The Singer as Interpreter: Claire Croiza's Master Classes.* London: Victor Gollancz, 1989.

Bathori, Jane. *On the Interpretation of the Mélodies of Claude Debussy.* Translated by Linda Laurent. Stuyvesant, N.Y.: Pendragon Press, 1998.

Bernac, Pierre. *Francis Poulenc: The Man and His Songs.* Translated by Winifred Radford. London: Victor Gollancz, 1977.

———. *The Interpretation of French Song.* New York: Norton, 1970.

Garden, Mary, and Louis Biancolli. *Mary Garden's Story.* New York: Simon and Schuster, 1951.

Hahn, Reynaldo. *On Singers and Singing.* Translated by Léopold Simoneau. Portland, Ore.: Amadeus Press, 1990.

Jean-Aubry, Georges. *French Music of Today.* Translated by Edwin Evans. London, 1919. Reprint, Plainview, N.Y.: Books for Libraries Press, 1976.

Laloy, Louis. *Louis Laloy (1874–1944) on Debussy, Ravel, and Stravinsky.* Translated by Deborah Priest. Burlington, Vt.: Ashgate, 1999.

Long, Marguerite. *At the Piano with Debussy.* Translated by Olive Senior-Ellis. London: J. M. Dent and Sons, 1972.

———. *At the Piano with Fauré.* Translated by Olive Senior-Ellis. New York: Taplinger, 1963.

———. *At the Piano with Ravel.* Translated by Olive Senior-Ellis. London: J. M. Dent and Sons, 1973.

Perlemuter, Vlado, and Hélène Jourdan-Morhange. *Ravel according to Ravel.* Translated by Frances Tanner. London: Kahn and Averill, 1988.

Poulenc, Francis. *Diary of My Songs.* Translated by Winifred Radford. London: Victor Gollancz, 1985.

Stravinsky, Igor. *An Autobiography.* New York, 1936. Reprint, New York: Norton, 1962.

## Texts and Diction

Grubb, Thomas. *Singing in French: A Manual of French Diction and French Vocal Repertoire.* New York: Schirmer, 1979.

Johnson, Graham, and Richard Stokes. *A French Song Companion.* New York: Oxford University Press, 2000.

Meister, Barbara. *Nineteenth Century French Song: Fauré, Chausson, Duparc, and Debussy.* Bloomington: Indiana University Press, 1980.

Rohinsky, Marie-Claire. *The Singer's Debussy.* New York: Pelion Press, 1987.

## General

Briscoe, James R., ed. *Debussy in Performance.* New Haven, Conn.: Yale University Press, 1999.

Cooper, Martin. *French Music from the Death of Berlioz to the Death of Fauré.* London: Oxford University Press, 1951.

Nectoux, Jean-Michel. *Gabriel Fauré: A Musical Life.* Translated by Roger Nichols. Cambridge: Cambridge University Press, 1991.

————, ed. *Gabriel Fauré: His Life through His Letters.* Translated by J. A. Underwood. London: Marion Boyars, 1984.

Noske, Frits. *French Song from Berlioz to Duparc.* Translated by Rita Benton. 2nd ed. New York: Dover, 1988.

Orenstein, Arbie. *Ravel: Man and Musician.* New York: Columbia University Press, 1975.

————, ed. *A Ravel Reader: Correspondence, Articles, Interviews.* New York: Columbia University Press, 1990.

### CHAPTER 7. SECOND VIENNESE SCHOOL

## Primary Sources

Foreman, Lewis. "Webern, the BBC and the Berg Violin Concerto." *Tempo* no. 178 (September 1991): 2–10.

Heyworth, Peter, ed. *Conversations with Klemperer.* London: Victor Gollancz, 1973.

Krasner, Louis, and D. C. Siebert. "Some Memories of Anton Webern, the Berg Violin Concerto, and Vienna in the 1930s." *Fanfare* 11, no. 2 (1987): 335–47.

Milhaud, Darius. "To Arnold Schoenberg on His Seventieth Birthday: Personal Recollections." *Musical Quarterly* 30 (October 1944): 379–84.

Newlin, Dika. *Schoenberg Remembered: Diaries and Recollections (1938–76).* New York: Pendragon Press, 1980.

Schoenberg, Arnold. *Arnold Schoenberg Self-Portrait: A Collection of Articles, Program Notes, and Letters by the Composer about His Own Works.* Edited by Nuria Schoenberg Nono. Pacific Palisades, Calif.: Belmont Music, 1988.

————. *Style and Idea: Selected Writings of Arnold Schoenberg.* Edited by Leonard Stein. Translated by Leo Black. Berkeley: University of California Press, 1975.

Searle, Humphrey. "Conversations with Webern." *Musical Times* 81 (1940): 405–6.

Smith, Joan Allen. *Schoenberg and His Circle: A Viennese Portrait.* New York: Schirmer, 1986.

Steuermann, Edward. *The Not Quite Innocent Bystander: Writings of Edward Steuermann.* Edited by Clara Steuermann, David Porter, and Gunther Schuller. Translated by Richard Cantwell and Charles Messner. Lincoln: University of Nebraska Press, 1989.

———. "*Pierrot lunaire* in Retrospect." *Journal of the Arnold Schoenberg Institute* 2, no. 1 (1977): 49–51.

Webern, Anton. *The Path to the New Music.* Edited by Willi Reich. Translated by Leo Black. London: Universal, 1963.

## Schoenberg

Brinkmann, Reinhold. "On Pierrot's Trail." *Journal of the Arnold Schoenberg Institute* 2, no. 2 (1978): 42–48.

Dunsby, Jonathan. *Schoenberg: Pierrot lunaire.* Cambridge Music Handbooks. Cambridge: Cambridge University Press, 1992.

Frisch, Walter, ed. *Schoenberg and His World.* Princeton, N.J.: Princeton University Press, 1999.

Stein, Leonard. "A Note on the Genesis of the Ode to Napoleon." *Journal of the Arnold Schoenberg Institute* 2, no. 1 (1977): 52–54.

Stuckenschmidt, H. H. *Arnold Schoenberg.* Translated by Edith Temple Roberts and Humphrey Searle. New York: Grove Press, 1959.

———. *Schoenberg: His Life, World, and Work.* Translated by Humphrey Searle. London: John Calder, 1977.

## Berg

Chadwick, Nicholas. "Berg's Unpublished Songs in the Österreichische Nationalbibliotek." *Music and Letters* 52, no. 2 (1971): 123–40.

———. "A Survey of the Early Songs of Alban Berg." Bodleian Library thesis, 1972.

Defotis, William. "Berg's Op. 5: Rehearsal Instructions." *Perspectives of New Music* 17, no. 1 (1986): 131–37.

DeVoto, Mark. "Some Notes on the Unknown Altenberg Lieder." *Perspectives of New Music* 5, no. 1 (1966): 37–74.

Jarman, Douglas, ed. *The Berg Companion.* London: Macmillan Press, 1989.

Perle, George. *The Operas of Alban Berg.* 2 vols. Berkeley: University of California Press, 1980, 1985.

Reich, Willi. *Alban Berg.* Translated by Cornelius Cardew. New York: Harcourt, Brace and World, 1963.

## Webern

Bailey, Kathryn. *The Life of Webern.* Cambridge: Cambridge University Press, 1998.

Moldenhauer, Hans and Rosaleen. *Anton von Webern: A Chronicle of His Life and Work.* London: Victor Gollancz, 1978.

## General

Austin, William. *Music in the Twentieth Century: From Debussy through Stravinsky.* New York: Norton, 1966.

Heyworth, Peter. *Otto Klemperer: His Life and Times.* Vol. 1. Cambridge: Cambridge University Press, 1983.

Mabry, Sharon. *Exploring Twentieth-Century Vocal Music: A Practical Guide to Innovations in Performance and Repertoire.* New York: Oxford University Press, 2002.

Simms, Bryan R. "The Society for Private Musical Performance: Resources and Documents." *Journal of the Arnold Schoenberg Institute* 3, no. 2 (1979): 127–49.

Slonimsky, Nicolas. *Music since 1900.* New York: Norton, 1938.

Weisberg, Arthur. *Performing Twentieth-Century Music: A Handbook for Conductors and Instrumentalists.* New Haven, Conn.: Yale University Press, 1993.


### CHAPTER 8. EARLY TWENTIETH-CENTURY NATIONALISM

## Russia

Borovsky, Victor. *Chaliapin: A Critical Biography.* London: Hamish Hamilton, 1988.

Chaliapin, Feodor. *Man and Mask: Forty Years in the Life of a Singer.* Translated by Phyllis Mégroz. London, 1932. Reprint, St. Clair Shores, Mich.: Scholarly Press, 1973.

Emerson, Caryl. *The Life of Musorgsky.* Cambridge: Cambridge University Press, 1999.

Evans, Robert Kenneth. "The Early Songs of Sergei Prokofiev and Their Relation to the Synthesis of the Arts in Russia, 1890–1922." Ph.D. diss., Ohio State University, 1971.

Nice, David. *Prokofiev: From Russia to the West, 1891–1935.* New Haven, Conn.: Yale University Press, 2003.

Redepenning, Dorothea. "Sergei Prokofiev." *Grove Music Online,* edited by Laura Macy, http://www.grovemusic.com, 2003.

Schonberg, Harold C. *The Great Pianists.* New York: Simon and Schuster, 1987.

Semeonoff, Boris. "Chaliapin's Repertoire and Recordings." *Record Collector* 20 (1971–72): 171–230.

Taruskin, Richard. "Musorgsky" (opera entry). *Grove Music Online,* edited by Laura Macy, http://www.grovemusic.com, 2003.

———. "Prokofiev" (opera entry). *Grove Music Online,* edited by Laura Macy, http://www.grovemusic.com, 2003.

Tumanov, Alexander. *The Life and Artistry of Maria Olenina-d'Alheim.* Translated by Christopher Barnes. Edmonton: University of Alberta Press, 2000.

Vishnevskaya, Galina. *Galina: A Russian Story.* Translated by Guy Daniels. New York: Harcourt Brace Jovanovich, 1984.

Wilson, Elizabeth. *Shostakovich: A Life Remembered.* London: Faber and Faber, 1994.


## Spain

Armero, Gonzalo, and Jorge de Persia, eds. *Manuel de Falla: His Life and Works.* Translated by Tom Skipp. Madrid: Ediciones Opponax, 1996.

Cockburn, Jacqueline, and Richard Stokes, eds. and trans. *The Spanish Song Companion.* London: Victor Gollancz, 1992.

Draayer, Suzanne Rhodes. *A Singer's Guide to the Songs of Joaquín Rodrigo.* London: Scarecrow Press, 1999.

Falla, Manuel de. *On Music and Musicians.* Translated by David Urman and J. M. Thompson. London: Marion Boyars, 1979.

Hess, Carol A. "Manuel de Falla." *Grove Music Online,* edited by Laura Macy, http://www.grovemusic.com, 2003.

Katz, Israel J. "Flamenco." *Grove Music Online,* edited by Laura Macy, http://www.grovemusic.com, 2003.

Mitchell, Timothy. *Flamenco Deep Song.* New Haven, Conn.: Yale University Press, 1994.

## England

Blyth, Alan, ed. *Remembering Britten.* London: Hutchinson, 1981.

Brett, Philip. "Benjamin Britten." *Grove Music Online,* edited by Laura Macy, http://www.grovemusic.com, 2003.

Britten, Benjamin. "On Realizing the Continuo in Purcell's Songs." In *Henry Purcell, 1659–1695: Essays on His Music,* edited by Imogen Holst. London: Oxford University Press, 1959.

———. *On Receiving the First Aspen Award.* London: Faber and Faber, 1964.

———. "On Writing English Opera." *Opera* 12, no. 1 (1961): 7–8.

Carpenter, Humphrey. *Benjamin Britten: A Biography.* London: Faber and Faber, 1992.

Duncan, Ronald. *Working with Britten: A Personal Memoir.* Bideford, U.K.: Rebel Press, 1981.

Gishford, Anthony, ed. *Tribute to Benjamin Britten on His Fiftieth Birthday.* London: Faber and Faber, 1963.

Greene, Harry Plunket. *Interpretation in Song.* New York: Macmillan, 1912.

Holst, Imogen. *Britten.* London: Faber and Faber, 1966.

Johnson, Graham. *Britten, Voice and Piano: Lectures on the Vocal Music of Benjamin Britten.* London: Guildhall School of Music and Drama, 2003.

Northcote, Sydney. *Byrd to Britten: A Survey of English Song.* London: John Baker, 1966.

Palmer, Christopher, ed. *The Britten Companion.* Cambridge: Cambridge University Press, 1984.

Reed, Philip, ed. *The Travel Diaries of Peter Pears, 1936–1978.* Woodbridge, U.K.: Boydell Press, 1995.

## United States

Burkholder, Peter. "Charles Ives." *Grove Music Online,* edited by Laura Macy, http://www.grovemusic.com, 2003.

Copland, Aaron. *Copland on Music.* New York: Doubleday, 1960.

Heyman, Barbara B. *Samuel Barber: The Composer and His Music.* New York: Oxford University Press, 1992.

Ives, Charles E. *Memos.* Edited by John Kirkpatrick. New York: Norton, 1972.

Pollack, Howard. "Aaron Copland." *Grove Music Online,* edited by Laura Macy, http://www.grovemusic.com, 2003.

## Diction

Castel, Nico. *A Singer's Manual of Spanish Lyric Diction.* New York: Excalibur Publishing, 1994.

Cheek, Timothy. *Singing in Czech: A Guide to Czech Lyric Diction and Vocal Repertoire.* London: Scarecrow Press, 2001.

Piatak, Jean, and Regina Avrashov. *Russian Songs and Arias: Phonetic Readings, Word-by-Word Translations, and a Concise Guide to Russian Diction.* Dallas: Pst. Inc., 1991.

### CHAPTER 9. WORKING WITH LIVING COMPOSERS

## General

Duckworth, William. *Talking Music: Conversations with John Cage, Philip Glass, Laurie Anderson, and Five Generations of American Experimental Composers.* New York: Schirmer, 1995.

Mabry, Sharon. *Exploring Twentieth-Century Vocal Music: A Practical Guide to Innovations in Performance and Repertoire.* New York: Oxford University Press, 2002.

Rockwell, John. *All American Music: Composition in the Late Twentieth Century.* New York: Da Capo Press, 1997.

Weisberg, Arthur. *Performing Twentieth-Century Music: A Handbook for Conductors and Instrumentalists.* New Haven, Conn.: Yale University Press, 1993.

## Repertoire

Lust, Patricia. *American Vocal Chamber Music, 1945–1980: An Annotated Bibliography.* London: Greenwood Press, 1985.

Manning, Jane. *New Vocal Repertory: An Introduction.* London: Macmillan Press, 1986.

————. *New Vocal Repertory 2.* Oxford: Clarendon Press, 1998.

## Notation

Cope, David. *New Music Notation.* Dubuque, Iowa: Kendall/Hunt, 1976.

Karkoschka, Erhard. *Notation in New Music.* New York: Praeger, 1972.

Read, Gardner. *Music Notation: A Manual of Modern Practice.* New York: Taplinger, 1979.

Risatti, Howard. *New Music Vocabulary: A Guide to Notational Signs for Contemporary Music.* Urbana: University of Illinois Press, 1975.

Stone, Kurt. *Music Notation in the Twentieth Century: A Practical Guidebook.* New York: Norton, 1980.

# Index